DUNGEONS & DRAGONS®

PLAYERS HANDBOOK II

David Noonan

CREDITS

DESIGN
David Noonan

ADDITIONAL DESIGN
Frank Brunner, Luke Johnson,
Christopher Lindsay, Robert J. Schwalb

DEVELOPMENT TEAM
Andy Collins, Jesse Decker, Mike Mearls,
Stephen Schubert

EDITORS
Michele Carter, John D. Rateliff,
M. Alexander Jurkat, Penny Williams

EDITING MANAGER
Kim Mohan

DESIGN MANAGER
Christopher Perkins

DEVELOPMENT MANAGER
Jesse Decker

DIRECTOR OF RPG R&D
Bill Slavicsek

PRODUCTION MANAGERS
Josh Fischer, Randall Crews

SENIOR ART DIRECTOR D&D
Stacy Longstreet

ART DIRECTOR D&D
Karin Jaques

COVER ARTIST
Dan Scott

INTERIOR ARTISTS
Steve Belledin, Steve Ellis,
Emily Fiegenschuh, Carl Frank,
Ralph Horsley, David Hudnut,
Michael Komarck, Howard Lyon,
Mike May, Jim Nelson, Lucio Parillo,
Eric Polak, Steve Prescott, Mike Schley,
Ron Spencer, Franz Vohwinkel,
Eva Widermann

CARTOGRAPHER
Mike Schley

GRAPHIC DESIGNERS
Dee Barnett, Karin Jaques

GRAPHIC PRODUCTION SPECIALIST
Erin Dorries

IMAGE TECHNICIAN
Christina Wiley

Some information in this book is taken from or derived from these sources: *Complete Adventurer* by Jesse Decker; *Complete Arcane* by Richard Baker; *Complete Divine* by David Noonan; *Complete Warrior* by Andy Collins, David Noonan, and Ed Stark; and *Defenders of the Faith* by Rich Redman and James Wyatt.

Based on the original Dungeons & Dragons® rules created by E. Gary Gygax and Dave Arneson, and the new Dungeons & Dragons game designed by Jonathan Tweet, Monte Cook, Skip Williams, Richard Baker, and Peter Adkison.

This product uses updated material from the v.3.5 revision.

U.S., CANADA, ASIA, PACIFIC,
& LATIN AMERICA
Wizards of the Coast, Inc.
P.O. Box 707
Renton WA 98057-0707
+1-800-324-6496

ISBN-10: 0-7869-3918-4

620–95374720–001–EN
9 8 7 6 5 4 3 2 1
First Printing: May 2006

EUROPEAN HEADQUARTERS
Hasbro UK Ltd
Caswell Way
Newport, Gwent NP9 0YH
GREAT BRITAIN
Please keep this address for your records

ISBN-13: 978-0-7869-3918-3

Visit our website at **www.wizards.com/dnd**

Contents

Introduction

When you play a character in a DUNGEONS & DRAGONS® game, it's all about the choices you make. Every facet of your character that makes him or her unique is the product of a conscious decision on your part.

Player's Handbook II is all about expanding your choices—sometimes in ways you might expect (new classes, new feats) and other times in ways you might find surprising, such as a set of rules for re-engineering your character (about which we have more to say below).

Chapter 1: New Classes expands the roster of standard classes by four, with the addition of the beguiler, the dragon shaman, the duskblade, and the knight. Any of these classes would be a fine choice if you want to play a character that doesn't fit any of the archetypes that are represented by the other classes we have published.

Chapter 2: Alternate Class Options revisits eighteen of those other classes—the eleven from the *Player's Handbook* as well as seven others (such as the scout and the favored soul) that made their debuts in supplements. We look at these classes with a fresh set of eyes, providing for each one an alternate class feature, three new starting packages, and a discussion of character themes that are appropriate for the class in question. If you're intrigued by the idea of playing a cleric who spontaneously casts domain spells instead of *cure* spells, check out page 37 for the particulars.

Player's Handbook II would not be a book worthy of its title if it didn't present new feats and spells. **Chapter 3: New Feats** contains more than 100 additions to the vast selection of feats in the D&D® game, and **Chapter 4: New Spells** presents a similar number of new choices for spellcasters of all sorts.

This book starts to blaze its own trail in **Chapter 5: Building Your Identity,** which contains dozens of brief discussions on how to add more depth and realism to your character's background and personality, plus some advice on how best to fulfill your role as a player at the gaming table.

Chapter 6: The Adventuring Group takes a step back in perspective, focusing on the characters who collectively make up a particular kind of party. How did these would-be heroes come together in the first place, and what part does each one of them play in a well-rounded group of adventurers? The chapter also includes a few new teamwork benefits, expanding on a concept that was introduced in *Dungeon Master's Guide II*.

Characters are defined not only by who they are as individuals and by the other PCs they travel with, but also by the relationships they form with likeminded individuals whose heritage or interests compel them to follow a common cause. **Chapter 7: Affiliations** describes a new kind of group that characters can belong to—they rise or fall in status within their affiliations according to their deeds and their qualifications, and the most motivated and successful of them all can even advance to a leadership position. In addition to a number of fully fleshed-out example affiliations, this chapter provides guidelines for players and DMs who want to create affiliations that are unique to their campaign.

Perhaps the most intriguing new concept in this book is presented in **Chapter 8: Rebuilding Your Character.** While many DMs and players have created house rules for handling situations involving the reselection of feats, reallocation of skill ranks, altering ability scores, and so forth, the D&D game has never before had official rules on the topic of revising your entire character. So whether your dwarf fighter just regrets a single bad feat choice or wishes he were actually a half-orc barbarian or an elf sorcerer, Chapter 8 offers rules and advice that covers the subject of character rebuilding from start to finish.

Finally, an extensive **Appendix** sets forth an efficient method for quick generation of new player characters or NPCs, which (among other things) streamlines the process of selecting skills and feats. The next time you need a character in a hurry—or even if you don't—check out this system.

WHAT YOU NEED TO PLAY

Player's Handbook II makes use of the information in the three D&D core rulebooks: *Player's Handbook* (PH), *Dungeon Master's Guide* (DMG), and *Monster Manual* (MM). It also includes material that expands upon some of the content of several supplements, including *Complete Warrior*, *Complete Divine*, *Complete Arcane*, *Complete Adventurer*, and *Miniatures Handbook*. Although possession of any or all of these supplements will enhance your enjoyment of this book, they are not strictly necessary for you to make use of the vast majority of this book.

SWIFT AND IMMEDIATE ACTIONS

The *Miniatures Handbook* introduced the concept of a new action type: the swift action. Likewise, *Expanded Psionics Handbook* introduced another new action type: the immediate action. Some of the class features, feats, spells, and items in *Player's Handbook II* use these concepts. A description of how they work follows.

Swift Action: A swift action consumes a very small amount of time, but represents a larger expenditure of effort and energy than a free action. You can perform one swift action per turn without affecting your ability to perform other actions. In that regard, a swift action is like a free action. However, you can perform only a single swift action per turn, regardless of what other actions you take.

Casting a quickened spell a swift action. In addition, casting any spell with a casting time of 1 swift action (such as *blade of blood*; see page 103) is a swift action. Casting a spell with a casting time of 1 swift action does not provoke attacks of opportunity.

Immediate Action: Much like a swift action, an immediate action consumes a very small amount of time, but represents a larger expenditure of effort and energy than a free action. Unlike a swift action, an immediate action can be performed at any time—even if it's not your turn.

Using an immediate action on your turn is the same as using a swift action, and counts as your swift action for that turn. You cannot use another immediate action or a swift action until after your next turn if you have used an immediate action when it is not currently your turn (effectively, using an immediate action before your turn is equivalent to using your swift action for the coming turn). You also cannot use an immediate action if you are currently flat-footed.

Illus. by R. Horsley

This chapter introduces four new standard classes, each designed to fill a specific niche in the game. Like any new classes, they provide players with more options when it's time to make characters and provide DMs with new potential foes to pit against the PCs.

Beguiler: The warmage (described in *Complete Arcane*) is an arcane spellcaster who focuses on a tightly themed group of spells. The beguiler takes that idea and does for enchantment and illusion spells what the warmage did for evocation. With a dash of transmutation thrown in, the beguiler is the ultimate versatile spellcaster, with a trick or solution for every encounter.

Dragon Shaman: Drawing on the ancient power of dragons, the dragon shaman provides powerful boosts to every character in the party. The defensive and augmentation abilities of this class allow a group with a dragon shaman to adventure without a cleric.

Duskblade: This class provides melee combat abilities and arcane spellcasting in equal measure. Although other ways to achieve this mix of powers exist, including multiclass characters and prestige classes, the duskblade offers this combination from 1st level and throughout all levels of play.

Knight: Skilled with armor and shield, a knight controls the battlefield in ways that no fighter or paladin ever could and can ensure that foes center their attacks on the knight rather than on more vulnerable allies. No other melee-oriented class has so much defensive prowess or ability to influence what foes do in combat, aspects of the game that are usually the province of spellcasters. While an able melee combatant, the knight is different in play from all previous melee combat classes because of his control-oriented abilities.

NEW STARTING PACKAGES

One of the features of *Player's Handbook II* is a new treatment for starting packages, expanding on the concept behind the starting packages previously presented in the *Player's Handbook* and other publications. The new classes described in this chapter and the eighteen other classes discussed in Chapter 2 have three starting packages for you to choose from. Each package has an evocative title that describes the character's role in the party (such as "Defender" or "Controller") to give you an idea of the concept behind it. Some descriptions appear more than once—for example, both the fighter and the ranger have a starting package called "The Archer." Some of these titles match those in Table A–3: Feat Progressions by Party Role (starting on page 209), but such similarities do not necessarily extend to the feats recommended. A race is specified for each package, but you can adjust the details to fit any race without too much trouble.

Each package specifies a race, ability scores (which include racial modifiers), skills, feats, gear, and if appropriate, spells and class features. The skills all have maximum ranks—4 ranks in each class skill and 2 ranks in each cross-class skill. (Cross-class skills are designated by the letters "cc.") Spells in parentheses are available only if your character's key ability score for spellcasting is high enough to grant a bonus 1st-level spell (or, if the character is a wizard, her Intelligence bonus is high enough to grant bonus spells in her spellbook). The class features section appears only for characters who have optional class features available at 1st level, such as clerics (domains), druids (animal companions), and sorcerers and wizards (familiars).

You can use these starting packages in any way you like. You are welcome to swap one skill for another, one feat for another (provided that your character meets the prerequisites), one spell for another, or one piece of gear for another of roughly equivalent value (within 5 gp). With a couple of exceptions, the starting packages in this book use only information available in the *Player's Handbook*. Thus, if you have access to other rulebooks, you might want to swap out a few feats or weapons for options provided in those publications. The class features are likewise customizable.

Most packages include the standard adventurer's kit—backpack, belt pouch, bedroll, flint and steel, two sunrods, ten days worth of trail rations, 50 feet of hempen rope, and waterskin. (Monks don't get the sunrods because they have too few gp at 1st level.)

BEGUILER

"You know me. I'm as good as my word, and my life is an open book."
—said with a straight face by Anastria Nailo,
half-elf beguiler

Some hold truth to be the greatest virtue, but it can do more damage than fiction. Everyone lives in a constant state of deception. White lies, false smiles, and secret thoughts keep society running smoothly. Honesty is a virtue only up to a certain point. Beguilers understand these ideas better than anyone, and they use deception, misunderstanding, and secrets as skillfully as a soldier employs weapons of war.

Beguilers see lying and manipulation as tools. Just as a hammer can be used to build a house or crack a skull, deceit and the ability to control others can be used for good or ill. A lie whispered in the right ear can ruin lives, but a dishonest smile and honeyed words can open doors, turn foes into friends, and even end wars. Beguilers have reputations as rakes, thieves, spies, and puppet masters, but they can also be diplomats, peacemakers, or heroic leaders who give hope in desperate situations.

If you delight in manipulating others, either to their disadvantage or for their own good, then the beguiler is the class for you. More than any other kind of character, you rely on Charisma-based skills to change the reactions of others, while your other class abilities enable you to catch others off guard with devastating spell-based attacks.

MAKING A BEGUILER

As a beguiler, you possess many useful skills and spells. If your adventuring group lacks a rogue, you make a great substitute for all but the rogue's melee combat strengths. If the group lacks a wizard or other arcane caster, you can also fill that role with your command of illusions and enchantments, although you lack a wizard's array of spells that deal damage and you possess less spellcasting versatility. Your main strategy should be to control enemies, bolster your allies, and take command of the battlefield.

Abilities: Beguilers have quick wits, deft hands, and compelling personalities. You need a high Intelligence to get the most from your spells and skills. A high Charisma helps you be more convincing in your deceptions, while a high Dexterity helps you with the sneaky tasks you are likely to pursue. Don't neglect Constitution; although you have the same Hit Die as a rogue, your Constitution score influences your ability to cast defensively and thus how well you can use your surprise casting class feature.

Races: Beguilers can be found among any race, but gnomes and half-elves seem to most appreciate the beguilers' flexible philosophy about truth. Being tricksters and inquisitive by nature, gnomes gravitate to the beguiler class due to the interesting deeds it allows them to accomplish. Half-elves, trapped as they are between the worlds of elves and humans, find that a beguiler's abilities help them better exist in both. Humans, elves, and halflings also foster beguilers in their midst, but dwarves and half-orcs rarely become members of the class. Dwarves tend to dislike dissembling, and half-orcs typically lack the mental discipline and likable personality required to make a good beguiler.

Alignment: The beguilers' outlook about truth is neither good nor evil, and beguilers of all alignments walk the world. Nevertheless, those well practiced in the arts of deception and manipulation rarely put much stock in others' laws, and they often display a self-centered attitude. Lawful good beguilers are like lawful good necromancers—rare and foreign even to their fellows.

Starting Gold: 6d4×10 gp (150 gp).
Starting Age: As wizard (PH 109).

CLASS FEATURES

Your spells and skills make you well suited to espionage and dungeon delving. In addition to being able to find and disarm traps your group might encounter, you can charm and confound guards, turning what could be dangerous encounters into simple steps toward your goal. In combat, you can use your spells to trick and outmaneuver foes.

Weapon and Armor Proficiency: Beguilers are proficient with all simple weapons plus the hand crossbow, rapier, shortbow, and short sword. Beguilers are proficient with light armor, but not with shields.

Spells: A beguiler casts arcane spells, which are drawn from the beguiler spell list on page 11. When you gain access to a new level of spells, you automatically know all the spells for that level on the beguiler's spell list. You can cast any spell you know without preparing it ahead of time. Essentially, your spell list is the same as your spells known

TABLE 1–1: THE BEGUILER   **HIT DIE: d6**

Level	Base Attack Bonus	Fort Save	Ref Save	Will Save	Special	0	1st	2nd	3rd	4th	5th	6th	7th	8th	9th
										— Spells per Day —					
1st	+0	+0	+0	+2	Armored mage, trapfinding	5	3	—	—	—	—	—	—	—	—
2nd	+1	+0	+0	+3	Cloaked casting (+1 DC), surprise casting	6	4	—	—	—	—	—	—	—	—
3rd	+1	+1	+1	+3	Advanced learning	6	5	—	—	—	—	—	—	—	—
4th	+2	+1	+1	+4	—	6	6	3	—	—	—	—	—	—	—
5th	+2	+1	+1	+4	Silent Spell	6	6	4	—	—	—	—	—	—	—
6th	+3	+2	+2	+5	Surprise casting (move action)	6	6	5	3	—	—	—	—	—	—
7th	+3	+2	+2	+5	Advanced learning	6	6	6	4	—	—	—	—	—	—
8th	+4	+2	+2	+6	Cloaked casting (+2 to overcome SR)	6	6	6	5	3	—	—	—	—	—
9th	+4	+3	+3	+6	—	6	6	6	6	4	—	—	—	—	—
10th	+5	+3	+3	+7	Still Spell	6	6	6	6	5	3	—	—	—	—
11th	+5	+3	+3	+7	Advanced learning	6	6	6	6	6	4	—	—	—	—
12th	+6/+1	+4	+4	+8	—	6	6	6	6	6	5	3	—	—	—
13th	+6/+1	+4	+4	+8	—	6	6	6	6	6	6	4	—	—	—
14th	+7/+2	+4	+4	+9	Cloaked casting (+2 DC)	6	6	6	6	6	6	5	3	—	—
15th	+7/+2	+5	+5	+9	Advanced learning	6	6	6	6	6	6	6	4	—	—
16th	+8/+3	+5	+5	+10	—	6	6	6	6	6	6	6	5	3	—
17th	+8/+3	+5	+5	+10	—	6	6	6	6	6	6	6	6	4	—
18th	+9/+4	+6	+6	+11	—	6	6	6	6	6	6	6	6	5	3
19th	+9/+4	+6	+6	+11	Advanced learning	6	6	6	6	6	6	6	6	6	4
20th	+10/+5	+6	+6	+12	Cloaked casting (overcomes SR)	6	6	6	6	6	6	6	6	6	5

Class Skills (6 + Int modifier per level, ×4 at 1st level): Appraise, Balance, Bluff, Climb, Concentration, Decipher Script, Diplomacy, Disable Device, Disguise, Escape Artist, Forgery, Gather Information, Hide, Jump, Knowledge (arcana), Knowledge (local), Listen, Move Silently, Open Lock, Profession, Search, Sense Motive, Sleight of Hand, Speak Language, Spellcraft, Spot, Swim, Tumble, Use Magic Device.

list. You also have the option of adding to your existing spell list through your advanced learning class feature (see below) as you increase in level.

To cast a beguiler spell, you must have an Intelligence score of 10 + the spell's level (Int 10 for 0-level spells, Int 11 for 1st-level spells, and so forth). The Difficulty Class for a saving throw against a beguiler's spell is 10 + the spell's level + the beguiler's Int modifier. Like other spellcasters, a beguiler can cast only a certain number of spells of each spell level per day. The base daily spell allotment is given on Table 1–1. In addition, you receive bonus spells for a high Intelligence score (PH 8).

A beguiler need not prepare spells in advance. You can cast any spell you know at any time, assuming you have not yet used up your spells per day for that spell level.

Armored Mage (Ex): Normally, armor of any type interferes with an arcane spellcaster's gestures, which can cause your spells to fail if those spells have a somatic component. A beguiler's limited focus and specialized training, however, allow you to avoid any chance of arcane spell failure as long as you restrict yourself to light armor. This training does not extend to any other form of armor, nor does this ability apply to spells gained from other spellcasting classes.

Trapfinding: Beguilers can use the Search skill to locate traps when the task has a Difficulty Class higher than 20. Finding a nonmagical trap has a DC of at least 20, or higher if it is well hidden. Finding a magic trap has a DC of 25 + the level of the spell used to create it.

Beguilers can use the Disable Device skill to disarm magic traps. A magic trap typically has a DC of 25 + the level of the spell used to create it.

A beguiler who beats a trap's DC by 10 or more with a Disable Device check can study a trap, figure out how it works, and bypass it (with his allies) without disarming it.

Cloaked Casting (Ex): Starting at 2nd level, a beguiler's spells become more effective when cast against an unwary foe. You gain a +1 bonus to the spell's save DC when you cast a spell that targets any foe who would be denied a Dexterity bonus to AC (whether the target actually has a Dexterity bonus or not).

At 8th level, you gain a +2 bonus on rolls made to overcome the spell resistance of any affected target.

At 14th level, the bonus to your spell's save DC increases to +2.

At 20th level, you become able to automatically overcome the spell resistance of any affected target.

Surprise Casting (Ex): Starting at 2nd level, when you successfully use the Bluff skill to feint in combat, your target is denied its Dexterity bonus (if it has one) to AC for the next melee attack you make against it or the next spell you cast. You must remain in melee with the target, and the attack must be made or the spell cast on or before your next turn. The target is not considered flat-footed and therefore can make attacks of opportunity against you if you do not cast defensively.

At 6th level, you gain the ability to feint in combat as a move action instead of a standard action. If you have the Improved Feint feat, you can now feint in combat as a swift action.

Advanced Learning (Ex): At 3rd level, you can add a new spell to your list, representing the result of personal study and experimentation. The spell must be a sorcerer/wizard spell of the enchantment or illusion school and of a level no higher than that of the highest-level spell you already know. Once a new spell is selected, it is forever added to your spell list and can be cast just like any other spell on your list.

You gain another new spell at 7th, 11th, 15th, and 19th level.

Silent Spell: At 5th level, you gain Silent Spell as a bonus feat.

Still Spell: At 10th level, you gain Still Spell as a bonus feat.

PLAYING A BEGUILER

Truth lies in the eye of the beholder. Manipulation of truth—and others' visions of it—is a part of life. Everyone does it; you just do it better than everyone else. If you nudge someone into doing something he otherwise wouldn't have done, that person still did the actual deed, and some part of him must have wanted it done. You trick fools, charm egocentrics, influence schemers, and control the weak-willed. In a way, you're doing them a favor. If they're clever enough to figure out they've been manipulated, they'll be better prepared to defend themselves against the later manipulations of those who mean them harm. If they don't figure it out, they'll get tricked again, but that's no concern of yours. Life is a game that you win by coming out on top, and the best way to do that is to convince others to give you a boost.

You might adventure because you desire excitement. Someone with your smarts gets bored with mundane pursuits. Alternatively, you might have set off on a life of adventure after some trick or manipulation gone wrong. You have to keep moving, and adventuring offers you a regular change of scenery. In any case, a life of adventure allows you to see new things, meet interesting people, and garner a name for yourself. Of course, it might not be your real name, but fame is fame.

You always look to expand your knowledge and increase your power. You are clever enough to know there's always more to learn. Although you tend to be self-reliant, you understand the value of friendship and allies in your pursuits. Truth might be mutable, but friends value honesty and trust, so you make sure not to entangle your allies in your webs of lies and trickery.

Religion

Beguilers favor deities who share their unfettered outlook and who would seem to appreciate their schemes and strategies. Most beguilers look to Olidammara for obvious reasons, but others prefer Fharlanghn since he shares their love of new beginnings and travel. Gnome beguilers largely put their faith in Garl Glittergold, and some nongnome beguilers follow suit. Many also follow Boccob; the Lord of All Magics cares little to what use beguilers put their spells, and beguilers prefer it that way. Evil beguilers often join Vecna's fold—the Master of All that Is Secret and Hidden welcomes beguilers, manipulating them toward ever greater acts of villainy even as they take advantage of their victims.

Other Classes

Few know of characters such as yourself because many beguilers pretend to be something other than what they are, and you can easily pass as a rogue, bard, wizard, or sorcerer. Those who learn of the class often have a poor impression of beguilers unless they call one a friend. Wizards consider characters such as you to be undisciplined and limited in their

Anastria and Korrik, beguilers

Illus. by S. Prescott

magic. Knights, paladins, and monks rightly think of you as untrustworthy. Rangers, dragon shamans, barbarians, and druids rarely have patience for your prevarications and your enjoyment of civilized society. Rogues, duskblades, sorcerers, and fighters tend to be more practical: If your abilities make their jobs easier, then you find a welcome reception. Bards often find the life led by beguilers fascinating and are intrigued by a beguiler's exploits.

Combat

You're at your best when you can catch foes unaware. Use your spells to hide and disguise yourself and your allies so that you can employ surprise tactics. If you get into melee, use the Bluff skill to feint in combat and thus get the drop on your enemy with cloaked casting or surprise casting. Control the terrain with spells such as *grease* and *fog cloud*. Control foes with *charm person* and *dominate monster* spells.

Advancement

Remaining a beguiler typically presents the best course of advancement. The rogue class might seem like a natural choice for multiclassing, but you don't gain much from taking levels in it. Although it gives you the sneak attack ability, it detracts from your spellcasting prowess.

You should assign skill points according to your role in your adventuring group. If the group already has a rogue who is good at finding traps and sneaking about, boost your ranks in social skills such as Diplomacy and Gather Information. Remember that you can use spells such as *invisibility* and *silence* for stealth, and spells such as *knock* and *spider climb* to do things for which rogues must use skills. High bonuses in Bluff and Concentration are a must if you're going to use the surprise casting ability.

You have many good options for feats, but be sure to take Combat Casting, Combat Expertise, and Improved Feint to get the most from surprise casting and cloaked casting. *Complete Adventurer* offers Mobile Spellcasting, a feat that allows you to cast a spell and move as a single standard action. Combining this with the benefits provided to you by Improved Feint and the Tumble skill, you could move into melee, feint, and cast a spell that gets the benefit of cloaked casting or surprise casting. You should also consider taking the Battle Caster feat from *Complete Arcane*, which allows a beguiler to wear medium armor without spell failure. Combining it with the Armor Proficiency (medium) feat gives you much greater protection. If you're interested in having a lot of feats, it might be worthwhile to take a level of fighter, since the 1st level of the fighter class gives you proficiency with all types of armor and a bonus feat you could use for Combat Expertise or Improved Feint.

STARTING PACKAGES

Package 1: The Controller
Human Beguiler

Ability Scores: Str 8, Dex 14, Con 12, Int 15, Wis 10, Cha 13.
Skills: Bluff, Concentration, Disable Device, Hide, Move Silently, Open Lock, Search, Sense Motive, Spot.
Languages: Common, Goblin, Orc.
Feat: Improved Initiative, Spell Focus (enchantment).
Weapons: Short sword (1d6/19–20),
Armor: Chain shirt (+4 AC).
Other Gear: Standard adventurer's kit, spell component pouch, thieves' tools, 20 gp.

Package 2: The Investigator
Half-Elf Beguiler

Ability Scores: Str 8, Dex 14, Con 10, Int 15, Wis 12, Cha 13.
Skills: Bluff, Gather Information, Hide, Move Silently, Open Lock, Search, Sense Motive, Spot.
Languages: Common, Dwarven, Elven, Goblin.
Feat: Spell Focus (enchantment)
Weapons: Rapier (1d6/18–20), shortbow with 20 arrows (1d6/×3, 60 ft.).
Armor: Studded leather (+3 AC).
Other Gear: Standard adventurer's kit, spell component pouch, thieves' tools, 23 gp.

Package 3: The Trickster
Gnome Beguiler

Ability Scores: Str 10, Dex 14, Con 12, Int 15, Wis 8, Cha 13.
Skills: Bluff, Disguise, Escape Artist, Hide, Move Silently, Search, Spot, Use Magic Device.
Languages: Common, Giant, Gnome, Goblin.
Feat: Spell Focus (illusion).
Weapons: Morningstar (1d6), light crossbow with 20 bolts (1d6/×3, 60 ft.).
Armor: Scale mail (+4 AC), heavy steel shield (+2 AC).
Other Gear: Standard adventurer's kit, spell component pouch, thieves' tools, 40 gp.

BEGUILERS IN THE WORLD

"Just wait 'till I get my hands on her. No one makes a fool of Obramus Tumbor!"
　　—Obramus Tumbor, being made a fool of by a beguiler

The beguiler class gives players a chance to play the archetypal trickster. The class provides the skill set of a rogue and a selection of arcane spells without the complications of balancing multiple classes. Beguilers also make great villains. By manipulating NPCs and situations the PCs encounter, an evil beguiler can operate behind the scenes and trick the adventurers to his own ends.

Daily Life

The way a beguiler behaves depends on his or her individual sense of morality. Some think nothing of adopting false identities or impersonating others as a matter of course. They rely on their spells and their charm to get others to give them what they want. Other beguilers find themselves driven to use their powers of persuasion to help people. They see the daily troubles of others and can't help getting involved in solving arguments, matchmaking, and ending feuds. Regardless of outlook, a beguiler in a civilized area rarely gets bored. There's always something to meddle in or some grand scheme to enact.

Beguilers can become great leaders. With their sharp minds and great charisma, beguilers would be natural leaders were it not for their inconstancy. Beguilers regularly devise brilliant plans for espionage or trickery—plans that usually require them to play a major role—but their natural penchant for improvisation and secrecy often means that such plans possess unpredictable elements or key parts hidden from all other participants. If a beguiler earns the trust of companions, they value her leadership. Lacking that trust, a beguiler rarely leads for long.

Notables

Beguilers often gain notoriety for their deeds, although usually under a false identity. They earn fame, rather than infamy, when they use their abilities to serve a greater good. Anastria Nailo did so when she tricked an entire orc army into a box canyon where it could be ambushed, and again when she charmed a leader of a city and learned that he had already been charmed by a mind flayer. Since she was pretending to be a famous elf bard at the time, Anastira can still maintain a low profile despite her famous deeds, which is just the way she likes it.

Organizations

Beguilers don't organize together, but they often join other organizations, especially thieves guilds and secret political groups. A beguiler joining an organization probably has a specific goal in mind and takes a position that best allows her to attain it. A long-term commitment to such a group rarely appeals to a beguiler, but if the organization champions a cause close to the beguiler's heart, it can count on her very best efforts.

NPC Reactions

Few common folk understand beguilers to be different from sorcerers or wizards who have some rogue training, and many more mistake them for bards. Beguilers further confuse the issue by regularly adopting false identities and hiding their varied abilities. Thus, the reaction a beguiler gets from those she meets depends on what she is pretending to be at the time. Individuals who know about the beguiler class and the outlook common to its members greet beguilers with an attitude one step more hostile than normal. Paladins and knights in particular look poorly upon beguilers, as does anyone who puts great importance in forthrightness.

BEGUILER LORE

Characters with ranks in Knowledge (arcana) can research beguilers to learn more about them. When a character makes a skill check, read or paraphrase the following, including the information from lower DCs.

DC 15: Beguilers are arcane spellcasters who focus on illusions and enchantments. They employ deception and compulsory magic to get what they want.

DC 20: Beguilers can cast spells in light armor, and they have many of the skills of rogues.

BEGUILERS IN THE GAME

Beguilers fit smoothly into any ongoing game, since they are little known and don't require the insertion of an organization into the world or the addition of lots of new mechanics to the game. You can have a beguiler first appear as a villain when players discover a secret manipulator behind foul deeds they have been investigating. A beguiler might first appear as a foe and end up an ally, or the reverse could happen. A PC beguiler can be introduced to the party just as any rogue, bard, or wizard would be.

Think of a beguiler as similar to Loki of Norse myth or the Coyote in Native American tales. The player of a beguiler wants her to be smooth, sly, smart, likable, and light on her feet. Keeping this player happy is a matter of helping the player to feel that way. You might be tempted to make the player's schemes go awry because that seems more interesting to you, but instead you should allow good schemes to work most of the time. Let a player with a beguiler character feel empowered to try crazy ideas and dangerous plans. If it becomes too much of a good thing, then that's when the guards see through her disguise or the villain allows the unwitting PCs to infiltrate their way into his clutches.

Adaptation

When adapting the beguiler to your campaign, look at how rogues and bards fit into your game. The beguiler fills a similar niche, and any organizations that cater to such classes likely prove helpful for beguilers. A thieves' guild might have a small cabal of beguilers associated with it. The beguilers aid the guild on any missions that require their magical talents. In return, the beguilers receive protection, a share of the loot, and a headquarters. Young thieves who show a knack for magic might be shepherded into the beguiler class.

In a kingdom or land where magic is common, beguilers might replace the typical rogue, diplomat, or spy. A bandit gang might consist of several beguilers and a number of fighters. In such lands, magic supersedes a rogue's talent with skills.

With their talent for deception, a beguiler might have a reputation similar to the ninja. The common folk fear the beguilers for their ability to bend minds and to use magic to slip away from the authorities. Every royal court employs a few mages charged with using their spells to ferret out beguilers. In this case, the beguilers are secretive, clannish, and difficult to find. They gather in secret societies and never reveal their lore to those whom they do not trust. Becoming a beguiler is a process of winning the trust of one's master, not simply mastering a few simple spells.

Sample Encounter

An encounter with a beguiler should highlight her use of surprise tactics and manipulation of others to do her bidding. In addition to charmed or dominated minions, a beguiler often gathers allies under false pretenses. Fighting a villainous beguiler should be tricky for the PCs, because they will be forced to figure out who their real enemies are while trying to avoid hurting innocents whom the beguiler has dragged into the fight. The PCs might even have to figure out who the beguiler is, since disguises and hidden spellcasting come easily to such a character.

EL 9: Unlike many half-elves, Anastria Nailo always found it easy to live in either human or elf communities. Quick-witted, perceptive, and naturally empathetic, she could slip from an elf's detached interest to a human's focused drive as easily as she could switch speaking their languages. Always a mischievous charmer, Anastria found the beguiler's abilities came easily to her and allowed her to do more than play at being a human or elf. With the spells she learned, she could pretend to be anyone and anything from a dwarf miner to a goblin shaman. For a time she lived as a gadabout, adopting the lives of the wealthy while they were away or impersonating loyal retainers to gain the patronage of important people. After foiling the plans of an orc warlord and the plot of a mind flayer accidentally while in the guise of a famous bard, Anastria has gained a taste for heroics, and now she's looking to make a name for herself by helping people—even if she's the one who put those people in trouble in the first place.

ANASTRIA NAILO   CR 9
Female half-elf beguiler 9
CN Medium humanoid (elf)
Init +2
Senses low-light vision; Listen +6, Spot +7
Languages Common, Dwarven, Elven, Gnome, Halfling, Orc

AC 18, touch 12, flat-footed 16
  (+2 Dex, +6 armor)
hp 43 (9 HD)
Immune sleep
Fort +5, **Ref** +6, **Will** +7 (+9 against enchantments)

Speed 30 ft. (6 squares)
Melee +1 rapier +7 (1d6/18–20) or
Melee touch +6 (spell)
Ranged mwk light crossbow +7 (1d8/19–20)
Base Atk +4; **Grp** +3
Atk Options Combat Expertise, Improved Feint, Still Spell, surprise casting*
Combat Gear potion of bless weapon, potion of shield of faith +3
Beguiler Spells Known (CL 9th):
   4th (5/day)—Chosen from beguiler spell list
   3rd (7/day)—Tasha's hideous laughter, plus others chosen from beguiler spell list
   2nd (7/day)—Chosen from beguiler spell list
   1st (7/day)—Nystul's magic aura, plus others chosen from beguiler spell list
   0 (6/day)— Chosen from beguiler spell list

Abilities Str 8, Dex 14, Con 12, Int 18, Wis 10, Cha 14
SQ advanced learning* (Nystul's magic aura, Tasha's hideous laughter), armored mage*, cloaked casting*, trapfinding*
Feats Combat Expertise, Improved Feint, Silent Spell[B], Spell Focus (enchantment), Weapon Finesse
Skills Balance +3, Bluff +14, Concentration +13, Diplomacy +20, Disguise +13 (+15 acting), Gather Information +11, Handle Animal +3, Intimidate +4, Jump +5, Listen +6, Search +9, Sense Motive +10, Sleight of Hand +9, Spot +7, Tumble +15
Possessions combat gear plus +2 chain shirt, +1 rapier, masterwork light crossbow with 20 bolts, cloak of resistance +1, headband of intellect +2, disguise kit
*Class features described on page 7

BEGUILER SPELL LIST

The beguiler's spell list appears below. Spells printed in this book are marked with an asterisk.

0 Level: dancing lights, daze, detect magic, ghost sound, message, open/close, read magic.

1st Level: charm person, color spray, comprehend languages, detect secret doors, disguise self, expeditious retreat, hypnotism, mage armor, obscuring mist, rouse*, silent image, sleep, undetectable alignment, whelm*.

2nd Level: blinding color surge*, blur, daze monster, detect thoughts, fog cloud, glitterdust, hypnotic pattern, invisibility, knock, minor image, mirror image, misdirection, see invisibility, silence, spider climb, stay the hand*, touch of idiocy, vertigo*, whelming burst*.

3rd Level: arcane sight, clairaudience/clairvoyance, crown of veils*, deep slumber, dispel magic, displacement, glibness, halt*, haste, hesitate*, hold person, inevitable defeat*, invisibility sphere, legion of sentinels*, major image, nondetection, slow, suggestion, vertigo field*, zone of silence.

4th Level: charm monster, confusion, crushing despair, freedom of movement, greater invisibility, greater mirror image*, locate creature, mass whelm*, phantom battle*, rainbow pattern, solid fog.

5th Level: break enchantment, dominate person, feeblemind, friend to foe*, hold monster, incite riot*, mind fog, Rary's telepathic bond, seeming, sending, swift etherealness*.

6th Level: greater dispel magic, mass suggestion, mislead, overwhelm*, repulsion, shadow walk, true seeing, veil.

7th Level: ethereal jaunt, greater arcane sight, mass hold person, mass invisibility, phase door, power word blind, project image, spell turning.

8th Level: demand, discern location, mind blank, moment of prescience, power word stun, scintillating pattern, screen.

9th Level: dominate monster, etherealness, foresight, mass hold monster, power word kill, time stop.

DRAGON SHAMAN

"I possess a dragon's power. Beware lest you awaken that dragon's wrath."

—Kalia, last and greatest dragon shaman of the Blackspear tribe

Empires crumble, eons pass, and even gods wither and die, but dragons remain. Mortal but eternal, the races of true dragons weather the roll of the ages because of their unsurpassed might. Few creatures can match a dragon in its full fury, whether in a combat of arms or battle of wits. Dragon shamans recognize this fact and see true dragons as more than powerful beings. To a dragon shaman, the passing shadow of a dragon flying overhead isn't a sign that invokes fear; it's a blessing that reveals you to be in the presence of greatness.

Dragon shamans respect true dragons as power incarnate. Some worship dragons, but most simply aspire to gain dragon powers for themselves. In assuming the abilities and the likeness of a dragon, a dragon shaman seeks to emulate that might and embody that power within himself.

TABLE 1–2: THE DRAGON SHAMAN   **HIT DIE: d10**

Level	Base Attack Bonus	Fort Save	Ref Save	Will Save	Special	Draconic Auras Known
1st	+0	+2	+0	+2	Draconic aura +1, totem dragon	3
2nd	+1	+3	+0	+3	Skill Focus	3
3rd	+2	+3	+1	+3	Draconic adaptation	4
4th	+3	+4	+1	+4	Breath weapon (2d6; 15-ft. cone or 30-ft. line), draconic resolve	4
5th	+3	+4	+1	+4	Draconic aura +2	5
6th	+4	+5	+2	+5	Breath weapon (3d6), touch of vitality (heal wounds)	5
7th	+5	+5	+2	+5	Natural armor +1	6
8th	+6/+1	+6	+2	+6	Breath weapon (4d6), Skill Focus	6
9th	+6/+1	+6	+3	+6	Energy immunity	7
10th	+7/+2	+7	+3	+7	Breath weapon (5d6), draconic aura +3	7
11th	+8/+3	+7	+3	+7	Touch of vitality (remove conditions)	7
12th	+9/+4	+8	+4	+8	Breath weapon (6d6; 30-ft. cone or 60-ft. line), natural armor +2	7
13th	+9/+4	+8	+4	+8	Draconic adaptation (share with allies)	7
14th	+10/+5	+9	+4	+9	Breath weapon (7d6), commune with dragon spirit	7
15th	+11/+6/+1	+9	+5	+9	Draconic aura +4	7
16th	+12/+7/+2	+10	+5	+10	Breath weapon (8d6), Skill Focus	7
17th	+12/+7/+2	+10	+5	+10	Natural armor +3	7
18th	+13/+8/+3	+11	+6	+11	Breath weapon (9d6)	7
19th	+14/+9/+4	+11	+6	+11	Draconic wings	7
20th	+15/+10/+5	+12	+6	+12	Breath weapon (10d6; 60-ft. cone or 120-ft. line), draconic aura +5	7

Class Skills (2 + Int modifier per level, ×4 at 1st level): Climb, Craft, Intimidate, Knowledge (nature), Search (plus others depending on the chosen totem dragon).

If you gaze at dragons with awe and aspire to share their power and majesty, then the dragon shaman is the class for you. By choosing a totem dragon, you partake of a true dragon's power and take on aspects of a particular kind of dragon.

MAKING A DRAGON SHAMAN

As a dragon shaman, you primarily act as a melee combatant, but your class features also allow you to grant benefits to those fighting around you. In a standard group of adventurers, you can stand in for the fighter or the cleric. Your combat prowess isn't quite as great as a fighter's, but you can employ special attacks and special defenses a fighter can't access. Although you lack many of the cleric's specialized spells, you do possess the ability to heal and remove negative conditions. As a dragon shaman, you can grow tough scales, breathe fire or another type of energy, and soar on dragon wings—and that barely scratches the surface of the powers at your command.

Abilities: As with any melee-oriented class, Strength is a key ability for dragon shamans. Constitution provides you with increased hit points as usual, and it also increases the save DC of your breath weapon. If you want to make good use of the dragon shaman's ability to heal and remove negative conditions, you'll need a high Charisma.

Races: Although humans make up the majority of dragon shamans, any community of people with a close connection to true dragons can produce dragon shamans. Typically, dragon shamans come from savage societies that live near the lairs of dragons, but even highly civilized populations can produce dragon shamans. In any race or society, dragon shamans tend to dedicate themselves to the dragons native to the area. Thus, elf dragon shamans from a forest nation often aspire to the qualities of a green dragon, whereas the dwarf dragon shamans of a high mountain citadel would seek to gain the qualities of a silver dragon.

Alignment: Attaining the abilities of a true dragon requires a deep understanding of the chosen kind of dragon. An aspiring dragon shaman must make a study of the dragon's typical mindset and emotions; adopting these for himself opens the door to the dragon's power. Thus, dragon shamans align their morals to suit the outlook of the color of true dragon to which they dedicate themselves. Each kind of metallic or chromatic dragon has a particular alignment with which it is associated. A dragon shaman who turns away from the alignment of his chosen dragon type loses many of his powers unless he can successfully adopt another dragon type as his chosen dragon (see Ex-Dragon Shamans, below). Neutral individuals with no preference for law, chaos, good, or evil cannot properly attain the outlook of a true dragon and therefore cannot become dragon shamans.

Starting Gold: 4d4×10 gp (100 gp).

Starting Age: As druid (PH 109).

CLASS FEATURES

As a dragon shaman, you function most effectively on the front lines of any combat. Your class abilities allow you to boost your combat effectiveness and that of your party, and the touch of vitality ability provides you with the power to heal others and remove negative conditions that affect them, giving you more reason to take the fight to your foes and stay close to those melee-oriented allies most likely to need your aid.

Weapon and Armor Proficiency: Dragon shamans are proficient with simple weapons, with light and medium armor, and with shields (except tower shields).

Bonus Languages: A dragon shaman's bonus language options include Draconic.

Draconic Aura (Su): You can channel the mighty powers of dragonkind to project an aura that grants you and nearby allies a special benefit.

Projecting an aura is a swift action (see page 4), and you can only project one draconic aura at a time. An aura remains in effect until you use a free action to dismiss it or you activate another aura in its place. You can have a draconic aura active continually; thus, an aura can be in effect at the start of an encounter even before you take your first turn.

Unless otherwise noted, your draconic aura affects all allies within 30 feet (including yourself) with line of effect to you. Your aura is dismissed if you become unconscious or are slain, but otherwise it remains in effect even if you are incapable of acting.

The bonus granted by your aura begins at +1 and increases to +2 at 5th level, +3 at 10th level, +4 at 15th level, and +5 at 20th level. As a 1st-level dragon shaman, you know how to project three auras chosen from the list below. At every odd-numbered level after that, you learn one additional draconic aura of your choice, until all seven auras are known at 9th level. Each time you activate a draconic aura, you can choose from any of the auras that you know.

Energy Shield: Any creature striking you or your ally with a natural attack or a nonreach melee weapon is dealt 2 points of energy damage for each point of your aura bonus. The energy type is that of your totem dragon's damage-dealing breath weapon (see below).

Power: Bonus on melee damage rolls equal to your aura bonus.

Presence: Bonus on Bluff, Diplomacy, and Intimidate checks equal to your aura bonus.

Resistance: Resistance to your totem dragon's energy type equal to 5 × your aura bonus.

Senses: Bonus on Listen and Spot checks, as well as on initiative checks, equal to your aura bonus.

Toughness: DR 1/magic for each point of your aura bonus (up to 5/magic at 20th level).

Vigor: Fast healing 1 for each point of your aura bonus, but only affects characters at or below one-half their full normal hit points.

Totem Dragon: You must choose a totem dragon from among the true dragons appearing in the *Monster Manual* (black, blue, brass, bronze, copper, gold, green, red, silver, or white).

You must choose a dragon whose alignment is within one step of yours, as described in the following table. You gain additional class skills and a particular sort of breath weapon based on the dragon you select as your totem.

Skill Focus: At 2nd level, you gain Skill Focus as a bonus feat. You must apply the feat to one of the three class skills granted by your chosen totem dragon. For example, a blue dragon shaman can select Skill Focus (Bluff), Skill Focus (Hide), or Skill Focus (Spellcraft).

At 8th level, and again at 16th level, you gain Skill Focus in another of the class skills granted by your chosen totem dragon. If you already have Skill Focus in all three of the skills associated with your totem dragon, you gain Skill Focus in any other dragon shaman class skill.

Draconic Adaptation (Ex or Sp): At 3rd level, you take on an aspect of your totem dragon. Some adaptations are

Totem Dragon	Acceptable Alignment	Class Skills	Breath Weapon Energy Type
Black	NE, CE, CN	Hide, Move Silently, Swim	Line of acid
Blue	NE, LE, LN	Bluff, Hide, Spellcraft	Line of electricity
Brass	NG, CG, CN	Bluff, Gather Information, Survival	Line of fire
Bronze	NG, LG, LN	Disguise, Survival, Swim	Line of electricity
Copper	NG, CG, CN	Bluff, Hide, Jump	Line of acid
Gold	NG, LG, LN	Disguise, Heal, Swim	Cone of fire
Green	NE, LE, LN	Bluff, Hide, Move Silently	Cone of acid
Red	NE, CE, CN	Appraise, Bluff, Jump	Cone of fire
Silver	NG, LG, LN	Bluff, Disguise, Jump	Cone of cold
White	NE, CE, CN	Hide, Move Silently, Swim	Cone of cold

extraordinary abilities that are always active; others are spell-like abilities that you can activate at will. Spell-like abilities have a caster level equal to your class level and a save DC equal to 10 + spell level + Cha modifier.

Black—Water Breathing (Ex): You can breathe underwater indefinitely and can freely use spells and other abilities underwater (always active).

Blue—Ventriloquism (Sp): As the spell (at will).

Brass—Endure Elements (Sp): As the spell, except you can only target yourself (at will).

Bronze—Water Breathing (Ex): You can breathe underwater indefinitely and can freely use spells and other abilities underwater (always active).

Copper—Spider Climb (Sp): As the spell, except you can only target yourself (at will).

Gold—Water Breathing (Ex): You can breathe underwater indefinitely and can freely use spells and other abilities underwater (always active).

Green—Water Breathing (Ex): You can breathe underwater indefinitely and can freely use spells and other abilities underwater (always active).

Red—Treasure Seeker (Ex): You gain a +5 competence bonus on Appraise and Search checks (always active).

Silver—Feather Fall (Sp): As the spell, except you can only target yourself (at will).

White—Icewalker (Ex): You can walk across icy surfaces without reducing your speed or making Balance checks (always active).

At 13th level, you can choose as a swift action (see page 4) to share the effect of your draconic adaptation with any or all allies within 30 feet. In the case of spell-like abilities, you must make this decision when you activate the ability. The benefit lasts until you spend a free action to rescind it or (if the effect has a limited duration) the effect ends, whichever comes first.

Breath Weapon (Su): At 4th level, you gain a breath weapon corresponding to your totem dragon. Regardless of the area one affects or the type of energy damage it deals, all breath weapons deal 2d6 points of damage, plus an extra 1d6 points of damage for every two additional class levels (3d6 at 6th level, 4d6 at 8th level, and so forth). A successful Reflex save halves the damage dealt; the save DC is equal to 10 + 1/2 your dragon shaman level + your Con modifier. Just like a true dragon, once you breathe you must wait 1d4 rounds before you can use your breath weapon again.

Cone-shaped breath weapons extend out to 15 feet at 4th level, increasing to 30 feet at 12th level and to 60 feet at 20th level. Line-shaped breath weapons are 30 feet long at 4th level, increasing to 60 feet at 12th level and to 120 feet at 20th level.

Draconic Resolve (Ex): At 4th level, you gain immunity to paralysis and sleep effects. You also become immune to the frightful presence of dragons.

Touch of Vitality (Su): At 6th level, you can heal the wounds of living creatures (your own or those of others) by touch. Each day you can heal a number of points of damage equal to twice your class level × your Charisma bonus. For example, a 7th-level dragon shaman with a Charisma score of 14 (+2 bonus) can heal 28 points of damage. You can choose to divide your healing among multiple recipients, and you don't have to use it all at once. Using your touch of vitality is a standard action. It has no effect on undead.

Beginning at 11th level, you can choose to spend some of the healing bestowed by your touch of vitality to remove other harmful conditions affecting the target.

For every 5 points of your healing ability you expend, you can cure 1 point of ability damage or remove the dazed, fatigued, or sickened condition from one individual.

For every 10 points of your healing ability you expend, you can remove the exhausted, nauseated, poisoned, or stunned condition from one individual.

For every 20 points of your healing ability you expend, you can remove a negative level or the blinded, deafened, or diseased condition from one individual.

You can remove a condition (or more than one condition) and heal damage with the same touch, so long as you expend the required number of points. For example, if you wanted to heal 12 points of damage and remove the blinded and exhausted conditions from a target, you would have to expend 42 points (12 hit points restored plus 20 points for blinded plus 10 points for exhausted).

Natural Armor (Ex): At 7th level, your skin thickens, developing faint scales. Your natural armor bonus improves by 1. At 12th level, this improvement increases to +2, and at 17th level to +3.

Energy Immunity (Ex): At 9th level, you gain immunity to the energy type of the breath weapon you gained at 4th level.

Commune with Dragon Spirit (Sp): At 14th level, you gain the ability to contact your dragon totem directly to ask questions of it. This is the equivalent of casting a *commune* spell, except that it has no material component, focus, or XP cost and allows only one question per three class levels. After using this ability, you cannot use it again for seven days.

Draconic Wings (Ex): At 19th level, you grow a pair of wings that resemble those of your totem dragon. They allow flight at a speed of 60 feet (good maneuverability). You can even fly while carrying a medium load, though your fly speed drops to 40 feet in this case.

If you already have wings, you can choose whether these draconic wings replace your own.

PLAYING A DRAGON SHAMAN

As a dragon shaman, you believe the acquisition of power is a worthy end in itself. By having power, you can effect your will in the world, be it beneficent or malign. Those who have or seek power deserve your respect, while those who have power but fail to use it earn your derision.

Your strength comes from devoting yourself to dragons, the primal embodiment of the principle of power, but you worship dragons in the abstract, honoring them much as a cleric might honor light as a symbol of purity and goodness. Dragons gather power to themselves simply by living and aging, but you must actively seek the influence and might you desire. As a dragon hungers for flesh to feed itself or for treasure to enlarge its hoard, so you hunger for power.

You adventure out of a desire to test yourself and prove your worth; whatever the specific inducement, the urge to gain more power underlies every quest. Drawn by your power, others follow your lead, and you are happy to command them. Being a great leader is just one of the many ways you can manifest your power.

Religion

Dragon shamans can worship any deity, but most worship divine powers that encourage their worshipers to be proactive in pursuit of the deity's goals. Dragon shamans often worship Erythnul, Gruumsh, Heironeous, Hextor, Kord, or St. Cuthbert, as well as dragon deities such as Bahamut and Tiamat. They rarely find much to admire in more passive or protective deities such as Boccob, Ehlonna, Fharlanghn, and Yondalla.

Dragon shamans from more primitive societies sometimes worship true dragons. These savage dragon shamans might worship all true dragons, assigning each color or metallic hue its own place in a crude pantheon of totemic spirits. Or they might worship a single color or metal as the best among all the true dragons, finding it the most representative of pure power. In rare cases, a dragon shaman worships and serves a particular true dragon. How the dragon reacts to such worship depends on that individual dragon; even good dragons might take advantage of a dragon shaman's worship to achieve their own aims.

Other Classes

You work well with melee-oriented allies such as fighters, duskblades, barbarians, rogues, and even druids. Those characters value the benefits a dragon shaman can grant them and rarely make an issue of their source. Clerics, paladins, monks, and knights are often suspicious of your moral outlook unless you have dedicated yourself to a kind of dragon that associates itself with a code of ethics similar to their own. Wizards, bards, and beguilers view you indifferently, whereas sorcerers might seek you out to learn more of the source of your power and your connection to dragons. Rangers might or might not take issue with your abilities; a ranger whose favored enemy is dragons might attack you on sight.

Combat

Dragon shamans lead from the front, rather than directing battles from a safe position behind others. Keep as many allies as possible within the range of your draconic aura, but focus on those in melee with your foes. Pick a draconic aura that grants your allies the best benefit for the situation, and don't hesitate to switch it during the fight should conditions change and another aura prove more useful. Outside combat, employ the senses or presence aspects of your draconic aura. If you have a cleric or other healer in your group, save your touch of vitality for removing conditions or for emergency healing. If no other healer is present, use it to heal yourself and your allies after combat.

Advancement

You profit most from remaining a dragon shaman throughout your advancement, so that your breath weapon and draconic aura continue to improve as you gain levels. If you do multiclass, a level of barbarian is an excellent choice; the benefits it grants help you in combat regardless of when you take that 1st level. Alternatively, you might consider beginning your career as a 1st-level barbarian for the greater hit points and skill points that option offers, then multiclassing into the dragon shaman class at 2nd level. The fighter class might seem like a strong second choice, but unless you need a fighter bonus feat for a particular kind of character, you'll see better long-term advantages from the barbarian class. The bard class can be an interesting multiclass option, since the benefits provided by bardic music stack with those provided by your draconic aura.

STARTING PACKAGES

Package 1: The Defender
Dwarf Dragon Shaman (Gold)
 Ability Scores: Str 14, Dex 12, Con 15, Int 8, Wis 10, Cha 13.
 Skills: Heal.
 Feat: Shield Specialization (heavy)*.
 Weapons: Morningstar (1d8), five javelins (1d6, 30 ft.).

Armor: Scale mail (+4 AC), heavy wooden shield (+3 AC [includes Shield Specialization]).
 Other Gear: Standard adventurer's kit, 15 gp.

Package 2: The Destroyer
Half-Orc Dragon Shaman (Red)
 Ability Scores: Str 16, Dex 12, Con 13, Int 6, Wis 10, Cha 13.
 Skills: Intimidate.
 Feat: Power Attack.
 Weapons: Morningstar (1d8), five javelins (1d6, 30 ft.).
 Armor: Scale mail (+4 AC), heavy wooden shield (+2 AC).
 Other Gear: Standard adventurer's kit, 10 gp.

Package 3: The Second-Rank Warrior
Human Dragon Shaman (Copper)
 Ability Scores: Str 15, Dex 14, Con 12, Int 8, Wis 10, Cha 13.
 Skills: Hide, Jump.
 Feat: Combat Reflexes, Power Attack.
 Weapons: Longspear (1d8/×3), light crossbow with 20 bolts (1d6/×3, 60 ft.).

Illus. by L. Parrillo

Thane and Iskara, dragon shamans

Armor: Studded leather (+3 AC).
Other Gear: Standard adventurer's kit, 8 gp.

DRAGON SHAMANS IN THE WORLD

"There are differences from one to another, based on the dragon each shaman honors, but the main thing to remember is this: The whole lot of them are mad for power."

—Durven Ironscale, a dwarf sorcerer
instructing the young of the Ironscale clan

Dragon shamans put the power and appeal of dragons in players' hands while providing DMs with a new way to put dragons in the D&D game. The class provides an uncomplicated way to have a new play experience, and each NPC dragon shaman could provide the nucleus for an interesting cult or villainous organization the PCs must face.

Daily Life

A dragon shaman remains ever ready to face the challenges of a new day. Without the need to rest, study, or pray for their powers, dragon shamans can leap up in pursuit of power whenever they desire. This capability causes most dragon shamans to be decisive and swift to act. Chaotic dragon shamans are often impetuous and energetic, while lawful dragon shamans tend to be more ready to improvise and less rigid in their thinking than some might expect. Dragon shamans desire power and constantly seek the means to gain it. To dragon shamans, life and adventure are one and the same.

Dragon shamans often possess the charisma and take-charge attitude required of great leaders, but many suffer from an inability to empathize with those they lead. Dragon shamans respect the pursuit of might and its use, and they often minimize the value of those who adhere to other philosophies. Even among themselves, dragon shamans tend to be contentious, and a single dragon shaman rarely takes a leadership role over a group of his fellows for any length of time. Although dragon shamans give great respect to one another, each is always trying to outdo the others in all pursuits. The most powerful dragon shaman leaders arise among savage tribes that worship dragons, where a single dragon shaman relies on his forceful personality and impressive powers to win the hearts of comrades.

Notables

The pursuit of power garners notoriety for a dragon shaman, but it also can bring about his death or force him into exile. A powerful dragon shaman warlord might suddenly arise and terrorize an area for a time, only to fall from power as swiftly as he appeared. A case in point would be the history of a barbaric human named Kalia. Under her leadership, her tribe of red dragon worshipers raided and razed hundreds of elf and human towns on the border between two nations. Then she vanished, and soon afterward her leaderless tribe was caught in an ambush and exterminated. Some say she died in a squabble with a fellow dragon shaman, but other believe she left her tribe to directly serve a red dragon wyrm that laired in distant mountains.

Organizations

Dragon shamans rarely work together for long unless they are led by a dragon of the type to which all the shamans present have dedicated themselves. In such cases, the dragon is either worshiped or leads because the dragon shamans see it as the embodiment of all they seek; thus, obeying the dragon's edicts presents the swiftest path to that desired goal. Rank and privilege rarely have much meaning in such groups. Instead, the dragon decides each shaman's duties according to his or her merit, changing such assignments as necessary. Such a group exists among the Ironscale clan. Tied to a long-dead silver dragon by blood, the dwarf clan fosters sorcerers and is led by a half-dragon. Despite these firm ties to dragonkind, the clan views its dragon shaman members with some suspicion, since they follow the orders of an unrelated silver dragon that lairs near the clan home.

NPC Reactions

Dragon shamans who don't show aspects of their affiliation with dragons rarely elicit an unusual reaction from others. To most they seem like simple warriors or perhaps barbarians. Those who know of their pursuit of draconic power or who see evidence of it, such as scales or a dragon shaman's breath weapon, react depending on their attitude toward the dragon shaman's totem dragon. This reaction is one step closer to hostile if the dragon is of a kind feared or hated by that individual. The reaction is one step closer to friendly if that individual is directly associated with a dragon of that kind. Clerics, paladins, and others who are deeply entrenched in a particular moral outlook view the dragon shaman's devotion with suspicion, and their reaction is one step closer to hostile regardless of the dragon shaman's totem dragon.

DRAGON SHAMAN LORE

Characters with ranks in Knowledge (arcana) can research dragon shamans to learn more about them. When a character makes a skill check, read or paraphrase the following, including the information from lower DCs.

DC 10: Dragon shamans devote themselves to dragons and aspire to their power.

DC 15: A dragon shaman devotes himself to a particular kind of true dragon and gains powers based on the dragon chosen. He can use the dragon's breath weapon and grow dragonlike scales. Very powerful dragon shamans can grow dragon wings and fly.

DC 20: In addition to the details above, this result allows the PC to know that a dragon shaman projects an aura that can bolster himself and his allies in a number of ways and can heal damage or remove negative conditions somewhat like a paladin.

DRAGON SHAMANS IN THE GAME

Dragon shamans fit easily into any ongoing campaign because true dragons are a cornerstone of nearly every DUNGEON & DRAGONS game. The PCs might first learn of dragon shamans by encountering a cult of dragon worshipers near a dragon's lair. Alternatively, a more civilized group of dragon shamans might serve a dragon who rules a city. A lone dragon shaman

Adventurers face off
against a black dragon

makes an excellent new villain, a powerful temporary ally, or an eager participant in an ongoing plot because his focused pursuit of power can get him involved in anyone's scheme to gain it.

Dragon shaman PCs should present no more difficulty than introducing a monk or cleric of a lesser-known deity. Although the character's abilities might be somewhat foreign, the idea that an individual is so dedicated to one philosophy that it grants him powers should be easily understood. The player of a dragon shaman usually finds the character's association with dragons to be the most entertaining part of the class. Before featuring adventures that deal with dragons, ask that player about her character's philosophy concerning dragons. Does the character admire dragons in the abstract, worship them as living gods, or hold to a philosophy between these extremes? The answer should inform your adventure planning and inspire new adventure ideas. Be careful about using the PC's dedication to dragons to manipulate the character's actions: Occasional use of this idea might provoke some interesting roleplaying, but the player won't enjoy your game if a dragon shows up every session to boss her PC around.

Adaptation

You can alter the dragon shaman to suit your game in a number of ways. You could decide that all dragon shamans are barbaric, or that all them are civilized and sophisticated disciples of dragons who prefer to work behind the scenes through such agents. You might decide that only good dragons are available to your players for their totem dragons, or that a particular organization fosters dragon shamans devoted to a single kind of dragon. If you feature other dragons prominently in your game, such as the gem dragons from *Monster Manual II* or the deep dragon and the shadow dragon from *Monsters of Faerûn*, you might consider changing the class's features to allow a dragon shaman to follow other kinds of dragons as well.

Sample Encounter

Dragon shamans make excellent villains and tricky allies. As a villain, a dragon shaman dedicated to an evil dragon can be paired with a cult of followers, half-dragons, and dragons of all ages to make for exciting themed encounters. As an ally, a dragon shaman's blind pursuit of power could create interesting friction with the PCs and turn an ally into an enemy. A dragon shaman might become embroiled in the PCs' pursuits if they come into possession of an item of great power, if both the PCs and dragon shaman seek the same source of power, or if the dragon shaman's attempts to gather power endanger the PCs or those they care about.

EL 7: Thane has admired blue dragons ever since he witnessed a blue dragon's attack on his city when he was a child. The power of the dragon and the futility of the defenders' efforts against it frightened him, but he also found the spectacle strangely thrilling. When he was older, Thane learned all he could about blue dragons. With each new bit of knowledge, his respect for them grew. In his search for information he met a dragon shaman, and that encounter changed his life. Now a dragon shaman himself, Thane seeks ever greater power and hopes one day to have enough to challenge the dragon that laid waste to his childhood home and prove himself the stronger of the two. Thane seems single-minded and focused. He always has a mental list of goals he wants to achieve in any situation and doggedly pursues them. Although outwardly calm and cold, he explodes into action in an instant when thwarted.

THANE   CR 7

Male human blue dragon shaman 7
LN Medium humanoid
Init +1
Senses Listen +2, Spot +2
Aura draconic aura* +2
   *Class feature described on page 13
Languages Common, Draconic

AC 21, touch 11, flat-footed 20
   (+1 Dex, +6 armor, +3 shield)
hp 57 (7 HD)
Immune paralysis, sleep, frightful presence (dragons)
Fort +8, **Ref** +6, **Will** +6

Speed 20 ft. (4 squares)
Melee +1 morningstar +9 (1d8+3)
Ranged +1 light crossbow +7 (1d8+1/19–20)
Base Atk +5; **Grp** +7

EX-DRAGON SHAMANS

Dragon shamans who change alignment could lose their powers. If a dragon shaman changes to an alignment still appropriate to the dragon to which he is already dedicated, nothing happens. However, if the dragon shaman changes to an alignment inappropriate for his chosen dragon, he immediately loses all abilities granted by the dragon shaman class and becomes an ex-dragon shaman.

An ex-dragon shaman can choose a new color or metallic hue of true dragon to emulate and thus regain the powers granted by the class. To switch to a new totem dragon, he must find a dragon shaman of higher level who is dedicated to that dragon type. The higher-level dragon shaman must willingly expend all her touch of vitality on the ex-dragon shaman each day for a week. At the end of the week, the ex-dragon shaman gains the class features of a dragon shaman dedicated to the newly chosen totem dragon, including exchanging the focus of any class-granted Skill Focus feats. Most dragon shamans who are asked to perform this service demand payment in the form of some great deed. This deed might be a demand that the ex-dragon shaman retrieve magic items that will add to his sponsor's power or simply a short quest to prove the ex-dragon shaman's worth.

Dragon shamans can go through the same process to switch chosen totem dragons even if they don't change alignment. If a dragon shaman has an alignment appropriate for a different true dragon color or hue, the shaman can switch to that kind of dragon through a process identical to the one described above for ex-dragon shamans.

Special Actions breath weapon

Abilities Str 15, Dex 12, Con 14, Int 8, Wis 10, Cha 14
SQ touch of vitality (28 points)
Draconic Auras Known Energy Shield, Power, Presence, Resistance, Senses, Vigor
Spell-Like Abilities (CL 7th):
  At will—*ventriloquism* (DC 13).
Feats Ability Focus (breath weapon), Alertness, Lightning Reflexes, Skill Focus (Bluff)[B], Weapon Focus (morningstar)
Skills Bluff +10, Climb +1, Diplomacy +4, Disguise +2 (+4 acting), Intimidate +9, Knowledge (nature) +4, Listen +2, Speak Language +0, Spot +2, Survival +0 (+2 in aboveground natural environments)
Possessions +1 breastplate, +1 heavy wooden shield, +1 morningstar, +1 light crossbow, cloak of resistance +1, 37 gp

Breath Weapon (Su) 30-ft. line, once every 1d4 rounds, 3d6 electricity, Reflex DC 17 half

DUSKBLADE

"My blade and my magic are one and the same."

—Yele, elf duskblade

The duskblade blurs the line between spellcaster and warrior, marrying the power of magic with hand-to-hand combat prowess.

A student of ancient elven spellcasting techniques, the duskblade combines arcane spellcasting with the combat skills of a fighter. While the ability to cast arcane spells in armor originated with the elves, over the millennia the secrets of the duskblade have been disseminated to the other races, and today members of any race can become a duskblade.

If you find you can't choose between being an arcane spellcaster who zaps your enemies with powerful spells and a nimble, powerful front-line melee character who lays them low with a sword, the duskblade is the perfect class for you. Combining arcane magic with melee prowess, you're prepared in any situation. Enemies who underestimate you never get a second chance, since you don't even have to switch back and forth between hands-on combat and spellcasting; you can do both simultaneously.

MAKING A DUSKBLADE

The duskblade is a quintessential hybrid character, simultaneously a potent spellcaster and an effective melee combatant.

The original duskblades were elite guardians in an ancient elf empire, duelmasters and arcane spellcasters beyond compare. Historical accounts vary on why they were called duskblades; some say the name is symbolic of how they combined swordplay and arcane magic—a night-and-day combination. Others contend that the duskblades earned their name when they were charged with preserving the elf race in the face of a tide of darkness and evil.

The most powerful duskblades can duel a fighter to a standstill and match a wizard spell for spell—for a while, at least. But the class really comes into its own when you embrace your hybrid nature, using a quick-cast spell to supplement your melee attacks or combining a touch spell with a devastating sword strike.

The duskblade is a good choice for players who know they want a sword-wielding arcane spellcaster from the beginning. By contrast, multiclass fighter/wizard combinations and prestige classes such as the eldritch knight are better suited for characters who begin their careers as fighters or arcane spellcasters and only later contemplate embracing their opposite.

Abilities: Your Intelligence and Strength scores should be as high as possible, since your spellcasting and melee combat depend upon them. Your Constitution is also important, because you need all the hit points you can get.

Races: The duskblade class originated among the ancient elves, and to this day most duskblades are elves. However, some humans and half-elves also have proved adept at mastering the class's dual focus on combat and spellcasting. Halflings, gnomes, dwarves, and half-orcs rarely enter this class.

Alignment: Since the duskblade class originated among the elves, those who undergo the intense training required to master the class abilities at the hands of an elf mentor often end their apprenticeship sharing the chaotic good alignment of most elves. However, duskblades are highly individualist and can be of any alignment.

Starting Gold: 6d4×10 gp (150 gp).

Starting Age: As wizard (PH 109).

CLASS FEATURES

Your class features are simple to characterize: constant improvement in your spellcasting, a fighter's base attack bonus progression, and ever-increasing mastery of arcane magic in melee combat.

Weapon and Armor Proficiency: Duskblades are proficient with all martial weapons, as well as all armors and shields (except tower shields).

Spells: You cast arcane spells, which are drawn from the duskblade spell list on page 98. You can cast any spell you know without preparing it ahead of time.

To learn or cast a spell, you must have an Intelligence score equal to at least 10 + the spell level (Int 10 for 0-level spells, Int 11 for 1st-level spells, and so forth). The Difficulty Class for a saving throw against your spell is 10 + the spell level + your Int modifier.

You can cast only a certain number of spells of each spell level per day. Your base daily spell allotment is given on Table 1–3. In addition, you receive bonus spells per day if you have a high Intelligence score (see Table 1–1: Ability Modifiers and Bonus Spells, page 8 of the *Player's Handbook*.)

Spells Known: You begin play knowing two 0-level spells and two 1st-level spells, chosen from the duskblade spell list. You also know one additional 0-level spell for each point of Intelligence bonus.

Each time you gain a new class level, you learn one additional spell of any level you can cast, chosen from the duskblade spell list.

Upon reaching 5th level, and at every subsequent odd-numbered level, you can choose to learn a new spell in place of one you already know. In effect, you lose access to the old spell in exchange for gaining the new one. The new spell's level must be the same as that of the spell being exchanged, and it must be at least two levels lower than the highest-level spell you can cast. For instance, upon reaching 9th level, you could trade in a single 1st-level spell (two levels below the highest-level spell you can cast, which is 3rd) for a different 1st-level spell. You can swap only a single spell at any given level and must choose whether or not to swap the spell at the same time that you gain new spells known for the level.

You need not prepare spells in advance. You can cast any spell you know at any time, assuming you have not yet used up your spells per day for that spell level.

Arcane Attunement (Sp): You can use the spell-like powers *dancing lights*, *detect magic*, *flare*, *ghost sound*, and *read magic* a combined total of times per day equal to 3 + your Int modifier. These spell-like powers do not count against your total of spells known or spells per day.

Armored Mage (Ex): Normally, armor of any type interferes with an arcane spellcaster's gestures, which can cause spells to fail if those spells have a somatic component. A duskblade's limited focus and specialized training, however, allows you to avoid arcane spell failure so long as you stick to light armor and light shields. This training does not extend to medium or heavy armors, nor to heavy shields. This ability does not apply to spells gained from a different spellcasting class.

At 4th level, you learn to use medium armor with no chance of arcane spell failure.

At 7th level, you learn to use a heavy shield with no chance of arcane spell failure.

Combat Casting: At 2nd level, you gain Combat Casting as a bonus feat.

Arcane Channeling (Su): Beginning at 3rd level, you can use a standard action to cast

any touch spell you know and deliver the spell through your weapon with a melee attack. Casting a spell in this manner does not provoke attacks of opportunity. The spell must have a casting time of 1 standard action or less. If the melee attack is successful, the attack deals damage normally; then the effect of the spell is resolved.

At 13th level, you can cast any touch spell you know as part of a full attack action, and the spell affects each target you hit in melee combat that round. Doing so discharges the spell at the end of the round, in the case of a touch spell that would otherwise last longer than 1 round.

Quick Cast: Beginning at 5th level, you can cast one spell each day as a swift action, so long as the casting time of the spell is 1 standard action or less.

You can use this ability twice per day at 10th level, three times per day at 15th level, and four times per day at 20th level.

Spell Power (Ex): Starting at 6th level, you can more easily overcome the spell resistance of any opponent you successfully injure with a melee attack. If you have injured an opponent with a melee attack, you gain a +2 bonus on your caster level check to overcome spell resistance for the remainder of the encounter. This bonus increases to +3 at 11th level, to +4 at 16th level, and to +5 at 18th level.

Tele and Hallia, duskblades

TABLE 1–3: THE DUSKBLADE   **HIT DIE: d8**

Level	Base Attack Bonus	Fort Save	Ref Save	Will Save	Special	Spells per Day					
						0	1st	2nd	3rd	4th	5th
1st	+1	+2	+0	+2	*Arcane attunement, armored mage (light)*	3	2	—	—	—	—
2nd	+2	+3	+0	+3	Combat Casting	4	3	—	—	—	—
3rd	+3	+3	+1	+3	Arcane channeling	5	4	—	—	—	—
4th	+4	+4	+1	+4	Armored mage (medium)	6	5	—	—	—	—
5th	+5	+4	+1	+4	Quick cast 1/day	6	5	2	—	—	—
6th	+6/+1	+5	+2	+5	Spell power +2	6	6	3	—	—	—
7th	+7/+2	+5	+2	+5	Armored mage (heavy shield)	6	6	5	—	—	—
8th	+8/+3	+6	+2	+6		6	7	6	—	—	—
9th	+9/+4	+6	+3	+6		6	7	6	2	—	—
10th	+10/+5	+7	+3	+7	Quick cast 2/day	6	8	7	3	—	—
11th	+11/+6/+1	+7	+3	+7	Spell power +3	6	8	7	5	—	—
12th	+12/+7/+2	+8	+4	+8		6	8	8	6	—	—
13th	+13/+8/+3	+8	+4	+8	Arcane channeling (full attack)	6	9	8	6	2	—
14th	+14/+9/+4	+9	+4	+9		6	9	8	7	3	—
15th	+15/+10/+5	+9	+5	+9	Quick cast 3/day	6	9	8	7	5	—
16th	+16/+11/+6/+1	+10	+5	+10	Spell power +4	6	9	9	8	6	—
17th	+17/+12/+7/+2	+10	+5	+10		6	10	9	8	6	2
18th	+18/+13/+8/+3	+11	+6	+11	Spell power +5	6	10	9	8	7	3
19th	+19/+14/+9/+4	+11	+6	+11		6	10	10	9	7	5
20th	+20/+15/+10/+5	+12	+6	+12	Quick cast 4/day	6	10	10	10	8	6

Class Skills (2 + Int modifier per level, ×4 at 1st level): Climb, Concentration, Craft, Decipher Script, Jump, Knowledge (all skills taken individually), Ride, Sense Motive, Spellcraft, Swim.

PLAYING A DUSKBLADE

A duskblade can take the fighter's place in the front ranks of a party or ensorcel his foes from a distance like a wizard. While you aren't quite as good as either a dedicated fighter or a dedicated wizard or sorcerer in those roles, you're reasonably effective in either, and you can change roles on a round-by-round basis as needed.

Choosing the path of the duskblade means you don't have to choose between being a combat specialist and a spellcaster. You enjoy the best of both worlds, and you'll undertake any quest that promises to improve either your spellcasting or your melee prowess. Driven to simultaneously master both swordplay and spellcasting, you might devote yourself to delving into ancient ruins to learn more about the original duskblades or wander far and wide looking for other duskblades interested in restoring the class to its previous glory.

Religion

The demands of martial and arcane discipline don't leave much room for religion in the typical duskblade. Good-aligned duskblades typically venerate Corellon Larethian, even if they aren't elves, because he supposedly taught the first duskblades the secret of combining melee combat with arcane casting. A few worship Boccob as the personification of their own mastery of magic, while more honor Wee Jas, who exemplifies both the magic they wield and also the death that they deal.

Other Classes

You get along well with members of other classes who share a rigorous devotion to a chosen path, such as paladins, dragon shamans, and monks. You are the object of envy to sorcerers and of admiration to bards, who sometimes try to emulate your abilities (often with disastrous results). Among members of the two classes whose portfolios you draw from, fighters and wizards, some view you with disdain while others are fascinated by your unique meld of melee combat and arcane spellcasting. Barbarians, clerics, and knights tend to distrust you, while rogues, rangers, druids, and beguilers view you and other duskblades with indifference.

Combat

You might sometimes feel you have too many options, too many things you can do in a single round. Use that flexibility to confound your enemies, outfighting what you can't outspell and outspelling what you can't outfight. The monster that engages you in melee, hoping to get an attack of opportunity that spoils your next spell, is in for a surprise—a surprise consisting of three feet of razor-sharp steel.

Most of a duskblade's spells target a single creature or have a range of touch, so you are most effective when you single

NEW ARMOR SPECIAL ABILITY: TWILIGHT

This armor special ability, which first appeared in the *Book of Exalted Deeds* supplement, is of particular use to duskblades. Such armor becomes translucent when donned and possesses a faint sunset-colored sheen. Twilight armor reduces the chance of arcane spell failure by 10%.

Faint abjuration; CL 5th; Craft Magic Arms and Armor; Price +1 bonus.

out and focus upon defeating a single opponent. Your spells that affect areas are limited mostly to cones, which means you need to be on or near the front lines to get the greatest effect from them. Even if you come close to being as effective as a fighter or a sorcerer in his chosen field, you're certainly not as effective as a fighter *and* a sorcerer. You'll occasionally cast a spell and strike with your blade in the same round, but pure spellcasters such as the sorcerer are more able to affect a crowd of foes or blast a group of opponents. That said, actions are the D&D game's most fundamental currency, and you'll be able to take advantage of additional actions in the round, as you combine spellcasting with melee attacks and eventually gain the ability to cast any spell you know as a swift action a number of times per day.

Advancement

Like the sorcerer, you face a crucial decision: which spells to put on your spells known list. The offensive spells on your spell list fall into three primary categories: touch spells, single-target ranged spells, and short-range cones. Choose at least one touch spell, such as *shocking grasp*, to take advantage of your arcane channeling ability. You should also take a movement spell, such as *swift expeditious retreat*, and an attack-enhancing spell such as *true strike* or *magic weapon*. Future spell selections can tailor your repertoire to the role you find yourself most commonly filling, whether it be a front-line fighter or a finesse caster.

Assign as many skill points as possible to Concentration, Knowledge (arcana), and Sense Motive. For feats, take the Weapon Focus (longsword) feat and also consider sudden metamagic feats, such as Sudden Silent and Sudden Empower, both from the *Complete Arcane* supplement.

Do not neglect to put some thought into your gear as well. Spend 30% of your wealth on the heaviest armor you can manage without risking arcane spell failure chance (often mithral and/or having the twilight special ability). Spend 20% on your primary weapon and 20% on items that improve your Intelligence, Strength, and saving throws. Spend 20% on wands and scrolls and the remaining 10% on miscellaneous items and a basic adventuring package.

Your spellcasting and fighting prowess also allow you the opportunity to enter into prestige classes that are suited to either melee or spellcasting.

STARTING PACKAGES

Package 1: The Blaster
Human Duskblade

Ability Scores: Str 15, Dex 13, Con 12, Int 14, Wis 10, Cha 8.

Skills: Climb, Concentration, Jump, Knowledge (arcana), Spellcraft.

Languages: Common, Draconic, Elven.

Feat: Point Blank Shot, Weapon Focus (ranged spell).

Weapon: Greataxe (1d12/×3), 3 javelins (1d6, 30 ft.).

Armor: Chain shirt (+4 AC).

Other Gear: Spell component pouch, standard adventurer's kit, 10 gp.

Spells Known: 1st—*Kelgore's fire bolt, ray of enfeeblement;* 0—*acid splash, disrupt undead, ray of frost, touch of fatigue.*

Package 2: The Defender
Dwarf Duskblade

Ability Scores: Str 15, Dex 13, Con 14, Int 14, Wis 10, Cha 6.

Skills: Concentration, Decipher Script, Knowledge (arcana), Spellcraft.

Languages: Common, Dwarven, Goblin, Orc.

Feat: Toughness.

Weapon: Dwarven waraxe (1d10/×3).

Armor: Scale mail (+4 AC), light wooden shield (+1 AC).

Other Gear: Spell component pouch, standard adventurer's kit, 22 gp.

Spells Known: 1st—*lesser deflect, resist energy;* 0—*acid splash, disrupt undead, ray of frost, touch of fatigue.*

Package 3: The Skirmisher
Elf Duskblade

Ability Scores: Str 15, Dex 15, Con 10, Int 14, Wis 10, Cha 8.

Skills: Climb, Concentration, Jump, Spellcraft, Spot (cc).

Languages: Common, Draconic, Elven, Sylvan.

Feat: Dodge.

Weapons: Glaive (1d10/×3), five javelins (1d6, 30 ft.).

Armor: Studded leather (+3 AC).

Other Gear: Spell component pouch, standard adventurer's kit, 42 gp.

Spells Known: 1st—*swift expeditious retreat, true strike;* 0—*acid splash, disrupt undead, ray of frost, touch of fatigue.*

DUSKBLADES IN THE WORLD

"Your spells cannot penetrate my magical defenses. You are helpless, wizard!"

—Last words of Zufir Halaq, rakshasa lord

The duskblade combines the best features of the fighter and wizard. Duskblades make dangerous foes because they have so many options, magical and martial, available to them every round; their ability to deliver touch spells through a melee attack is particularly potent.

Daily Life

The life of a duskblade is one of constant training. Each duskblade must simultaneously be a swordmaster, a deft spellcaster, and an expert in the esoteric techniques of arcane channeling. Each of those elements requires years to master; put them together, and you have a training regimen that only the most driven characters can maintain. The typical duskblade is doing calisthenics in the castle courtyard before the other characters wake up in the morning and practicing somatic gestures long after everyone else has gone to sleep in the evening. Exceptions exist, of course, but in general duskblades have a reputation as driven, focused individuals.

Notables

Since duskblades are few and far between, they are natural loners, wandering far and wide in search of adventures that will prove a suitable challenge for their unique combination of abilities. Such is the case with Gwilor the Swift, a wild elf who adventured in the woodlands of his people for a century or so before he committed himself entirely to a crusade against the duergar and spent the rest of his long career on extended forays into the underground.

Other duskblades join like-minded adventuring groups. Given their own mix of melee and spellcasting abilities, duskblades are willing to try unusual combinations, such as in the case of Taiglin the Fair, a gray elf duskblade who formed a highly successful party with a human hexblade and a halfling warmage.

Still others are restless, moving from group to group and area to area in search of new challenges. For example, Hallia Yelebane, a self-taught half-elf duskblade, rarely stays in the same country more than a month or two. She arrives, seeks out a suitable challenge for her talents, throws herself into that adventure, and then moves on. In the course of her career (brief by elven standards), she has rescued a halfling metropolis from a cabal of mind flayers who were "farming" the small humanoids for their brains, teamed with a githzerai monk to defeat a famed githyanki knight (and claimed his silver sword as her own), and exposed malenti infiltrators in an aquatic elf community and thus turned back a sahuagin invasion, along with other exploits. Hallia's nickname derives from her unexpected victory, early in her career, over one of her fellow duskblades, the elf Yele, who until then had boasted that he had never been defeated in a one-on-one duel. The two became fast friends and now make a point to duel at least once every year.

Organizations

Because of the elven heritage of the class, many duskblades gravitate toward the elf lands even if they aren't elves themselves. Knowledge of duskblade fighting techniques is sufficiently rare that no large company of duskblades exists—or, if one does, it's a well-kept secret. For centuries, the class has been sustained by nothing more than solitary masters who teach duskblade skills and spells to worthy apprentices, and by those who have taught themselves the techniques from long-neglected tomes and training manuals. More recently, some self-taught duskblades have appeared who master the difficult techniques required by the class through some innate instinct. No matter what their origin, all are equals in the eyes of their fellow duskblades.

Duskblades love to test themselves against each other; on the rare occasions when the paths of two duskblade adventurers happen to cross, they will always make time for a friendly duel before they part. Given elf life spans, some duskblades maintain friendly rivalries that can last for centuries.

NPC Reactions

Few common folk understand who or what duskblades truly are, and most assume those duskblades they happen to meet are simply fighters with a bit of sorcerer ability (or vice versa). Legends speak of elf heroes skilled with both blade and spell, but these tales do little to inform anyone of the specific abilities of the duskblades. Most adventurers react to duskblades with some wariness because a duskblade's combination of abilities makes it very hard to judge how powerful or capable such a character is in any situation.

DUSKBLADE LORE

Characters with ranks in Knowledge (arcana) can research duskblades to learn more about them. When a character makes a skill check, read or paraphrase the following, including the information from lower DCs.

DC 10: Some elves have the ability to cast arcane spells while engaged in melee combat; such elves are known as duskblades.

DC 15: Not all duskblades are elves; sometimes members of other races master the class's special techniques of spellcasting in melee.

DC 20: Duskblades preserve an ancient tradition that enables them to deliver spell damage through weapon strikes.

DUSKBLADES IN THE GAME

Duskblades fit easily into an ongoing game because of their small numbers and enigmatic mix of abilities. The presence of the class is easily explained as your players explore more of the world—they simply hadn't encountered any duskblades until now, or had mistaken those they did encounter for multiclass fighter/wizards. Now that they've discovered this aspect of the setting, however, they're free to multiclass into the duskblade class or to begin a new character with levels only in the new class.

Adaptations

One of the more interesting ways to adapt this class to your campaign is to keep the class abilities more or less the same but to change the race involved. For example, the githyanki have a tradition of multiclass fighter/wizards known as gish; these individuals could easily be reconceived as a gith duskblade class. Unexpected combinations would be the most striking, such as a previously unrevealed halfling duskblade class. After all, few expect halflings to engage in melee except when making sneak attacks, but when magically boosted by *bull's strength* and the like and fighting with oversized weapons, they could prove unexpectedly deadly against those who underestimate them—which, after all, is the essence of the duskblade class.

Sample Encounter

An encounter with a duskblade should highlight his combined use of spells and melee abilities. The duskblade should use his spells to force the PCs to close into melee with him, and then he should batter them with a barrage of touch spells delivered through his melee attacks. Fighting a villainous duskblade should be tricky, because he'll use the tools that are most effective against each character (for example, spells requiring Reflex saves against the fighter and powerful melee attacks against the wizard).

EL 7: Yele has always been drawn to both physical combat and the study of magic. As a duskblade, he combines the two into one seamless fighting style. An adventurer by trade, Yele could encounter the characters as a friend or a foe. If as a foe, it is because some enemy of the adventurers has encouraged Yele to go after them for some reason, perhaps to gain some magical treasure currently in their possession that would significantly boost either his swordplay or his spellcasting.

If as a friend, Yele could join with the adventurers to search for some lost piece of arcane lore or because their quest strikes him as likely to prove an interesting challenge for his talents.

YELE
CR 7

Male elf duskblade 7
NG Medium humanoid
Init +6
Senses low-light vision; Listen +2, Spot +2
Languages Common, Elven, Gnoll, Sylvan

AC 21, touch 13, flat-footed 19
hp 35 (7 HD)
Immune sleep
Fort +6, **Ref** +7, **Will** +6 (+8 against enchantments)

Speed 20 ft. (4 squares)
Melee +1 longsword +11/+6 (1d8+4/19–20)
Base Atk +7; **Grp** +10
Atk Options arcane channeling*, quick cast*

Abilities Str 16, Dex 14, Con 11, Int 14, Wis 10, Cha 8
SQ able to notice secret or concealed doors, armored mage*, spell power*
Spell-Like Abilities (CL 7th):
    5/day—dancing lights, detect magic, flare, ghost sound, read magic
Duskblade Spells Known (CL 7th):
    2nd (6/day)—ghoul touch (+10 melee touch, DC 14), scorching ray (+9 ranged touch), swift fly
    1st (7/day)—ray of enfeeblement (+9 ranged touch), resist energy, shocking grasp (+10 melee touch), swift expeditious retreat, true strike
    0 (6/day)—acid splash, disrupt undead, ray of frost (+9 ranged touch), touch of fatigue (+10 melee touch, DC 12)
Feats Combat Casting[B], Combat Expertise, Improved Initiative, Lightning Reflexes
Skills Concentration +10 (+14 casting defensively), Knowledge (arcana) +12, Knowledge (the planes) +12, Listen +2, Sense Motive +10, Spot +2
Possessions +1 breastplate, +1 light shield, +1 longsword, cloak of resistance +1, ring of protection +1
*Class features described on page 20

Duskblade Spell List

The duskblade's spell list appears below. Spells printed in this book are marked with an asterisk.

    0 Level: acid splash, disrupt undead, ray of frost, touch of fatigue.

    1st Level: Bigby's tripping hand*, blade of blood*, burning hands, cause fear, chill touch, color spray, jump, Kelgore's fire bolt*, lesser deflect*, magic weapon, obscuring mist, ray of enfeeblement,
resist energy, rouse*, shocking grasp, stand*, swift expeditious retreat, true strike.

    2nd Level: animalistic power*, bear's endurance, Bigby's striking fist*, bull's strength, cat's grace, darkvision, deflect*, dimension hop*, ghoul touch, Melf's acid arrow, scorching ray, see invisibility, seeking ray*, spider climb, stretch weapon*, sure strike*, swift fly, swift invisibility, touch of idiocy.

    3rd Level: crown of might*, crown of protection*, dispelling touch*, doom scarabs*, energy aegis*, energy surge*, greater magic weapon, halt*, keen edge, protection from energy, ray of exhaustion, regroup*, vampiric touch.

    4th Level: Bigby's interposing hand, channeled pyroburst*, dimension door, dispel magic, enervate, fire shield, phantasmal killer, shout, toxic weapon*.

    5th Level: Bigby's clenched fist, chain lightning, disintegrate, hold monster, polar ray, slashing dispel*, sonic shield*, waves of fatigue.

SWIFT EXPEDITIOUS RETREAT, SWIFT FLY, AND SWIFT INVISIBILITY

Three spells on the duskblade's spell list—swift expeditious retreat, swift fly, and swift invisibility—appear in Spell Compendium. If you do not have that book, treat these spells as their nonswift versions, except that their casting time is 1 swift action and the duration of each spell is 1 round.

KNIGHT

"I offer you surrender or an honorable death in battle. The choice is yours."

—Archibold the Impetuous

A knight is a proud, skilled melee combatant who fights in the name of honor and chivalry. A knight relies on more than a sharp sword and a stout suit of armor to defeat her foes. Her drive, determination, and fighting spirit allow her to control the battlefield in ways that others cannot match. A knight can challenge an opponent to a duel, calling upon the foe's pride and ego to force his hand. The knight's talent with heavy armor, shields, and defensive tactics grant her the ability to disrupt her foe's plans. Only the most talented rogues and monks can slip past a knight's defenses to strike at her allies. An adventuring group with wizards, sorcerers, and other lightly armored members thrives with the assistance of a knight. While the knight keeps enemies occupied, her allies can use their talents and abilities without fear of attack or harassment.

The knight class is a great choice if you want to play a tough, durable melee combatant whose strong personality allows you to manipulate your foes. Weaker foes cower in fear before you, while stronger foes move to strike you rather than your allies when you play on their egos and challenge them to duels. Your expertise in using armor and carrying a shield allows you to form an impregnable defensive line. Once you engage a foe, he has difficulty moving away to threaten your allies. If you want to be a front-line melee combatant who defends the rest of the party and manipulates opponents, the knight is a good choice.

MAKING A KNIGHT

A low-level knight is similar to a cross between a fighter and a bard. You have many hit points, a high Armor Class, and an ability similar to bardic music (the knight's challenge class feature). You can pick a single foe, usually the one who poses the most dangerous physical threat, and gain a bonus on attack rolls and damage rolls against that opponent. You must pay close attention to the knight's code of conduct, since it forbids you from taking advantage of several tactically useful situations.

You excel in combat in a manner similar to a fighter—but while a fighter can slay a monster, your primary talent is your ability to keep that monster away from your allies while you battle it. It might take you longer to win the day, but your many hit points and strong defensive abilities help preserve you. Best of all, your defense enables your allies to function at full capacity without being subject to the monster's attacks. Any sorcerer or wizard in the party thrives when you are there to absorb attacks and hold back your mutual foes.

As you advance in level, you gain the ability to dictate a foe's actions, forcing him to attack you instead of other targets. Weaker opponents, which typically appear in numbers too large for you to hold them all back, quail in terror when you menace them. Even if they slip past you, they take penalties when they attack your allies. Your knight's challenge and shield block class features combine to let you excel in one-on-one melee, granting you a bonus on attack rolls, damage rolls, and Armor Class against a single foe of your choice. If the group faces a mighty villain or a single, overwhelming physical threat, it's up to you to keep the monster occupied while your allies cast their spells or maneuver for position.

Abilities: You benefit from a high Charisma score, since it determines how often you can use some of your abilities and the save DC of those abilities. A high Constitution allows you to increase your already impressive hit point total, thus bolstering your capacity to defend your allies. Strength improves your combat abilities, making you more effective as a front-line character.

Races: The majority of knights are dwarves, humans, and half-elves. The dwarf's tendency toward order, combined with that race's militaristic bent, gives rise to fighting orders dedicated to upholding justice and obeying an honorable code. Dwarf knights also serve as wandering dispensers of justice between isolated settlements who enforce the rule of law and protect small clanholds. Humanity, with its sprawling kingdoms and empires, produces many knights who fight as much for king and country as for personal honor and monetary rewards. Some half-elves enter into such service as well and can rise to high ranks within such orders. Gnomes and halflings rarely become knights, since the knight's straightforward code of conduct runs counter to the small races' reliance on trickery and clever planning. Few half-orcs have the opportunity to become knights, but when they do their natural strength serves them well. Elf knights are rare, since elves prefer freedom and flexibility over the rigid code of honor all knights must follow.

Alignment: Knights are always lawful. Their dedication to a code of conduct is but one expression of their devotion to order. Most knightly orders arise as institutions forged to protect a kingdom from invaders or to enforce the law against chaos from within.

While knights value order, they tend in equal numbers toward good, evil, and neutrality. Lawful good knights see order as a tool to protect the innocent and weak from evil. Lawful evil knights believe that the social order serves to reward the strong. Lawful neutral knights abhor the destruction and suffering that chaos can bring and so uphold order for its own sake.

Starting Gold: 6d4×10 gp (150 gp).
Starting Age: As paladin (PH 109).

CLASS FEATURES

Your class features involve mastering the use of armor and shields and learning how to manipulate your foes so that melee combat takes place on your terms, not theirs.

Weapon and Armor Proficiency: Knights are proficient with all simple and martial weapons and with all armor (heavy, medium, and light) and all shields (except tower shields).

Knight's Challenge: Your dauntless fighting spirit plays a major role in your fighting style, as important as the strength of your arm or the sharpness of your blade. In battle, you use the force of your personality to challenge your enemies. You can call out a foe, shouting a challenge that boosts his confidence, or issue a general challenge that strikes fear into weak opponents and compels strong opponents to seek you out for personal combat. By playing on your enemies' ego, you can manipulate your foes.

You can use this ability a number of times per day equal to 1/2 your class level + your Charisma bonus (minimum once per day). As you gain levels, you gain a number of options that you can use in conjunction with this ability.

Even if you and your foes lack a shared language, you can still effectively communicate through body language, tone, and certain oaths and challenges you learn from a variety of different tongues.

Fighting Challenge (Ex): As a swift action, you can issue a challenge against a single opponent. The target of this ability must have an Intelligence of 5 or higher, have a language of some sort, and have a CR greater than or equal to your character level minus 2. If it does not meet these requirements, a use of this ability is expended without effect.

If the target does meet the conditions given above, you gain a +1 morale bonus on Will saves and a +1 morale bonus on attack rolls and damage rolls against the target of this ability. You fight with renewed vigor and energy by placing your honor and reputation on the line. If your chosen foe reduces you to 0 or fewer hit points, you lose two uses of your knight's challenge ability for the day because of the blow to your ego and confidence from this defeat.

The effect of a fighting challenge lasts for a number of rounds equal to 5 + your Charisma bonus (if any).

If you are capable of issuing a knight's challenge more than once per day, you can use this ability more than once in a single encounter. If your first chosen foe is defeated or flees the area, you can issue a new challenge to a different foe. You cannot switch foes if your original target is still active.

At 7th level, the bonus you gain from this ability increases to +2. At 13th level, it rises to +3. At 19th level, it increases to +4.

TABLE 1–4: THE KNIGHT   **HIT DIE: d12**

Level	Base Attack Bonus	Fort Save	Ref Save	Will Save	Special
1st	+1	+0	+0	+2	Fighting challenge +1, knight's challenge, knight's code
2nd	+2	+0	+0	+3	Mounted Combat, shield block +1
3rd	+3	+1	+1	+3	Bulwark of defense
4th	+4	+1	+1	+4	Armor mastery (medium), test of mettle
5th	+5	+1	+1	+4	Bonus feat, vigilant defender
6th	+6/+1	+2	+2	+5	Shield ally
7th	+7/+2	+2	+2	+5	Fighting challenge +2
8th	+8/+3	+2	+2	+6	Call to battle
9th	+9/+4	+3	+3	+6	Armor mastery (heavy)
10th	+10/+5	+3	+3	+7	Bonus feat
11th	+11/+6/+1	+3	+3	+7	Shield block +2
12th	+12/+7/+2	+4	+4	+8	Daunting challenge
13th	+13/+8/+3	+4	+4	+8	Fighting challenge +3
14th	+14/+9/+4	+4	+4	+9	Improved shield ally
15th	+15/+10/+5	+5	+5	+9	Bonus feat
16th	+16/+11/+6/+1	+5	+5	+10	Bond of loyalty
17th	+17/+12/+7/+2	+5	+5	+10	Impetuous endurance
18th	+18/+13/+8/+3	+6	+6	+11	—
19th	+19/+14/+9/+4	+6	+6	+11	Fighting challenge +4
20th	+20/+15/+10/+5	+6	+6	+12	Loyal beyond death, shield block +3

Class Skills (2 + Int modifier per level, ×4 at 1st level): Climb, Handle Animal, Intimidate, Jump, Knowledge (nobility and royalty), Ride, Swim.

Test of Mettle (Ex): Starting at 4th level, you can shout a challenge to all enemies, calling out for the mightiest among them to face you in combat. Any target of this ability must have a language of some sort and an Intelligence score of 5 or higher. Creatures that do not meet these requirements are immune to the test of mettle. You must have line of sight and line of effect to the targets of this ability.

As a swift action, you can expend one use of your knight's challenge ability to cause all your enemies within 100 feet with a CR greater than or equal to your character level minus 2 to make Will saves (DC 10 + 1/2 your class level + your Cha modifier). Creatures that fail this save are forced to attack you with their ranged or melee attacks in preference over other available targets. If a foe attacks by casting a spell or using a supernatural ability, he must target you with the attack or include you in the effect's area.

An opponent compelled to act in this manner is not thrown into a mindless rage and does not have to move to attack you in melee if doing so would provoke attacks of opportunity against him. In such a case, he can use ranged attacks against you or attack any opponents he threatens as normal. If anyone other than you attacks the target, the effect of the test of mettle ends for that specific target.

If you are reduced to 0 or fewer hit points by an opponent forced to attack you due to this ability, you gain one additional use of your knight's challenge ability for that day. This additional use comes from increased confidence and the knowledge that you have proved your mettle as a knight against your enemies by calling out foes even against overwhelming odds. This additional use disappears if you have not used it by the start of the next day. You can only gain one additional use of your knight's challenge ability in this manner per day.

The effect of a test of mettle lasts for a number of rounds equal to 5 + your Charisma bonus (if any). Whether a creature fails or succeeds on its save against your test of mettle, it can only be targeted by this effect once per day.

Call to Battle (Ex): Starting at 8th level, you become an inspiring figure on the battlefield. When all seems lost, you are a beacon of hope who continues to fight on despite the odds. No cause is yet lost when a knight still battles on its name.

As a swift action, you can expend one use of your knight's challenge ability to grant an ally another save against a fear effect. The target gains a bonus on this save equal to your Charisma bonus (if any). If the target succeeds on this save, he gains the benefit for a successful save against the attack or spell. This ability reflects your talent to inspire your allies in the face of a daunting foe.

For example, Lidda fails her save against a lich's *fear* spell. On his next action, Sir Agrivail uses his call to battle ability to grant Lidda another save. If she succeeds, she immediately shrugs off the effect of the *fear* spell.

Daunting Challenge (Ex): Starting at 12th level, you can call out opponents, striking fear into the hearts of your enemies. In this manner you separate the strong-minded from the weak-willed, allowing you to focus on opponents that are worthy foes.

As a swift action, you can expend one use of your knight's challenge ability to issue a daunting challenge. This ability affects all creatures within 100 feet of you that have a CR less than your character level minus 2. Targets must be able to hear you, speak or understand a language of some sort, and have an Intelligence score of 5 or more. All targets who meet these conditions must make Will saves (DC 10 + 1/2 your class level + your Cha modifier) or become shaken.

Whether a creature fails or succeeds on its save against your daunting challenge, it can only be targeted by this effect once per day.

Bond of Loyalty (Ex): Starting at 16th level, your loyalty to your comrades endures even in the face of powerful magic. You can expend one use of your knight's challenge ability to make an additional saving throw against a mind-affecting spell or ability. You can use this ability once per round as a free action and can continue to use it even if an opponent is controlling your actions with a mind-affecting spell or ability.

Loyal Beyond Death (Ex): At 20th level, if you are reduced to 0 or fewer hit points by an effect that otherwise leaves your body intact, you can expend one use of your knight's challenge ability to remain conscious and continue to act for 1 more round before dying. You can use this ability even if your hit point total is –10 or lower. If your body is somehow destroyed before your next action (such as by *disintegrate*), then you cannot act. You can continue to expend uses of your knight's challenge ability to survive from round to round until you run out of uses. If you receive healing that leaves you with more than –10 hit points, you survive (or fall unconscious, as appropriate to your new hit point total) when you stop using this ability. Otherwise, death overtakes you when you run out of uses of your knight's challenge ability.

The Knight's Code: You fight not only to defeat your foes but to prove your honor, demonstrate your fighting ability, and win renown across the land. The stories that arise from your deeds are just as important to you as the deeds themselves. A good knight hopes that her example encourages others to lead righteous lives. A neutral knight wishes to uphold the cause of his liege (if he has one) and win glory. An evil knight seeks to win acclaim across the land and increase her own personal power.

The knight's code focuses on fair play: A victory achieved through pure skill is more difficult, and hence wins more glory, than one achieved through trickery or guile.

- A knight does not gain a bonus on attack rolls when flanking. You still confer the benefit of a flanking position to your ally, but you forgo your own +2 bonus on attack rolls. You can choose to keep the +2 bonus, but doing so violates your code of honor (see below).
- A knight never strikes a flat-footed opponent. Instead, you allow your foe to ready himself before attacking.
- A knight never deals lethal damage against a helpless foe. You can strike such a foe, but only with attacks that deal nonlethal damage.

If you violate any part of this code, you lose one use of your knight's challenge ability for the day. If your knight's challenge ability is not available when you violate the code (for example, if you have exhausted your uses for the day), you take a –2 penalty on attack rolls and saves for the rest of that day. Your betrayal of your code of conduct undermines the foundation of confidence and honor that drives you forward.

While you cleave to your view of honor, chivalry, and pursuit of glory, you do not force your views on others. You might chide a rogue for sneaking around a battlefield, but you recognize (and perhaps even feel a bit smug about) the reality that not everyone is fit to follow the knight's path.

Mounted Combat: At 2nd level, you gain Mounted Combat as a bonus feat.

Shield Block (Ex): Starting at 2nd level, you excel in using your armor and shield to frustrate your enemy's attacks. During your action, designate a single opponent as the target of this ability. Your shield bonus to AC against that foe increases by 1, as you move your shield to deflect an incoming blow, possibly providing just enough protection to turn a telling swing into a near miss.

Sir Agrivail and Lady Sorra, knights

Illus. by E. Polak

This shield bonus increases to +2 at 11th level and +3 at 20th level.

Bulwark of Defense (Ex): When you reach 3rd level, an opponent that begins its turn in your threatened area treats all the squares that you threaten as difficult terrain. Your strict vigilance and active defensive maneuvers force your opponents to move with care.

Armor Mastery (Ex): Starting at 4th level, you are able to wear your armor like a second skin and ignore the standard speed reduction for wearing medium armor. Starting at 9th level, you ignore the speed reduction imposed by heavy armor as well.

Bonus Feat: At 5th level, you gain a bonus feat chosen from the following list: Animal Affinity, Diehard, Endurance, Great Fortitude, Iron Will, Quick Draw, Ride-By Attack, Spirited Charge, Trample, or Weapon Focus (lance). You must still meet any prerequisites for the feat. You gain an additional bonus feat from this list at 10th level and again at 15th level.

Vigilant Defender (Ex): Starting at 5th level, you stand your ground against all enemies, warding the spot where you make your stand to prevent foes from slipping past and attacking those you protect. If an opponent attempts to use the Tumble skill to move through your threatened area or your space without provoking attacks of opportunity, the Tumble check DC to avoid your attacks of opportunity increases by an amount equal to your class level.

Shield Ally (Ex): Starting at 6th level, as an immediate action you can opt to absorb part of the damage dealt to an adjacent ally. Each time this ally takes damage from a physical attack before your next turn, you can take half this damage on yourself. The target takes the other half as normal. You can only absorb damage from physical melee attacks and ranged attacks, such as an incoming arrow or a blow from a sword, not from spells and other effects.

Improved Shield Ally (Ex): At 14th level, your ability to absorb damage increases. Once per round you can absorb all the damage from a single attack directed against an adjacent ally. In addition, you continue to absorb half the damage from other physical attacks on an adjacent ally, if you so choose. You must decide whether to use this ability after the attacker determines that an attack has succeeded but before he rolls damage.

Impetuous Endurance (Ex): Starting at 17th level, your fighting spirit enables you to push your body beyond the normal limits of endurance. You no longer automatically fail a saving throw on a roll of 1. You might still fail the save if your result fails to equal or beat the DC.

PLAYING A KNIGHT

As a knight, you are driven to prove your abilities, showcase the code of chivalry as a proper way to live, and defend your allies. You are impetuous and brave, never backing down from a challenge. When you face a mighty foe, you take a moment to call out a challenge to him, salute his fighting ability, or list his crimes that you seek to avenge.

Religion

Knights value order and honor in all things. They worship lawful gods, though whether their patrons are good, neutral, or evil depends solely on the knight's preferences. Good knights favor Heironeous, while neutral ones follow St. Cuthbert. Evil knights, if they venerate a god, offer prayers to Hextor. Knights of Heironeous and Hextor are renowned for the epic duels they have fought against each other. Opposing armies sometimes halt their advance to allow these sworn enemies to duel to the death before the rest of the battle is joined.

Other Classes

You respect paladins for their skill in combat and devotion to a code of conduct, although their path is somewhat different from your own. You see wizards, sorcerers, clerics, and bards as useful allies who should stay back away from combat; individual knights sometimes travel partnered with a member of one of these classes. Most knights consider barbarians to be crazed lunatics who lack the honor, self-control, and training to fight in a proper civilized manner, yet a skilled barbarian can earn a knight's grudging respect through deeds in battle. You have little regard for rogues, beguilers, or others who rely on stealth or deceit. In general, you have no feeling one way or the other toward druids, monks, and rangers. You distrust the duskblade's mix of melee combat and spellcasting but can empathize with the dragon shaman's devotion to his totem dragon, though you might be wary of particular shamans (those devoted to chaotic dragons). In general, you feel protective (but with a touch of condescension) toward adventurers who cannot handle heavy armor and weapons.

Combat

You serve two basic roles in battle. You excel at dominating the field of battle, since your defensive abilities make it difficult for opponents to move past you and strike vulnerable members of your party. You believe that the best way to face an enemy is to challenge him to an honorable duel and kill him fair and square, claiming all the glory for yourself. When faced with multiple foes, you can strike fear into some and goad others into attacking you rather than your allies. You are the sorcerer's, wizard's, or bard's best friend. Your commanding presence draws attacks to you, while your hit points and heavy armor make you ideally suited to absorb blows. While you are engaging foes in combat, your allies can use their spells and special abilities without interference.

Advancement

When looking at feats to select as you gain levels, you have two basic paths. You can focus on your fighting skill, or you can attempt to expand your capabilities to serve as the party's spokesman. The former option is best when you are the group's primary combat specialist. If the party includes a barbarian, paladin, fighter, ranger, or duskblade, you can afford to dabble in feats that improve your Charisma-based skills. Although Diplomacy is not a class skill for you, the Skill Focus feat combined with your superior Charisma and a few cross-class ranks makes you a serviceable emissary.

When it comes to combat feats, look to ones that improve your ability to deal damage. Your class features already enhance your defense, making feats such as Power Attack,

Weapon Focus, and so forth excellent options to boost your offense. Alternatively, you could focus on crippling your foe's ability to deal damage. Combat Expertise combined with Improved Disarm and Improved Trip form a potent combo. When you lure a foe into attacking you, you can pluck his weapon from his hand or knock him to the ground. In either case, your opponent is neutralized as a threat to you or your allies.

Improved Initiative is a critically important feat, since it allows you to act first, move forward, and defend your allies. The sooner you find a place at the front line, the longer you can hold back the monsters.

STARTING PACKAGES

Package 1: The Cavalier
Human Knight

Ability Scores: Str 15, Dex 12, Con 13, Int 10, Wis 8, Cha 14.
Skills: Diplomacy, Knowledge (nobility and royalty), Ride.
Feats: Mounted Combat, Skill Focus (Ride).
Weapons: Lance (1d8/×3), longsword (1d8/19–20), three javelins (1d6, 30 ft.).
Armor: Chain shirt (+4 AC), heavy wooden shield (+2 AC).
Other Gear: Standard adventurer's kit, 11 gp.

Package 2: The Defender
Dwarf Knight

Ability Scores: Str 15, Dex 12, Con 15, Int 10, Wis 8, Cha 12.
Skills: Diplomacy, Ride.
Feat: Shield Specialization (heavy).
Weapons: Dwarven waraxe (1d10/×3), warhammer (1d8/×3), 5 javelins (1d6, 30 ft.)
Armor: Scale mail (+4 AC), heavy steel shield (+2 AC).
Other Gear: Standard adventurer's kit, 18 gp.

Package 3: The Destroyer
Half-Orc Knight

Ability Scores: Str 16, Dex 12, Con 13, Int 8, Wis 8, Cha 13.
Skill: Intimidate.
Feat: Power Attack.
Weapons: Battleaxe (1d8/×3), five javelins (1d6, 30 ft.).
Armor: Scale mail (+4 AC), heavy steel shield (+2 AC).
Other Gear: Standard adventurer's kit, 50 gp.

KNIGHTS IN THE WORLD

"I like having a knight in front of me in a fight. He holds the line and allows me to work my spells in peace. Best of all, so long as he has his back to me I can't hear him prattling on about honor, strength, and chivalry."

—Vaarlis Runespeaker, mage-initiate of Wee Jas

The concept of the knight, or cavalier, or chevalier has arisen in many cultures that used mounted warriors in their armies. Typically, knights were members of the rich, land-owning upper class who could afford to buy and maintain heavy armor and a horse. Such individuals served an elite role in the military not only for their fighting talents and ability to ride over and smash through infantry who lacked polearms but also for their social standing. For the historical knight,

his status as a rich landowner was the basis of his superiority to others. Legend transformed the concept of the knight to focus on one who sets forth searching for deeds that will win him glory, drawing on his code of conduct and charismatic personality to defeat his enemies. Since a character who owns land and sits on a fortune in gold makes for a poor adventurer in a traditional D&D game, the knight character class focuses on the concept of a heavily armored melee combatant who fights according to a strict code of conduct. Fidelity to that code grants the knight the confidence and fighting spirit to excel on the battlefield and hence the glory he or she seeks.

Daily Life

A knight adventures to prove her skill at arms, to advance the cause of whatever lord she might serve, and to further her own aims. She rides forth from her lord's castle to right wrongs, quest in her lord's name, and prove herself worthy of knighthood. By actively seeking fame, glory, and acclaim, the knight brings praise and respect to the code of honor that she fights under.

Some knights are lone wanderers with neither castle nor king. A bloody war might leave a knight without a master. Homeless and with little more than her armor and weapons, this knight adventures to further the cause she still holds dear. She could work to bring down the enemies who defeated her lord or attempt to do as much good across the land as possible, winning glory all the while. She might seek for a new cause worthy of her devotion. The knight's order might fall, but the concepts of honor and chivalry endure so long as one knight holds them dear.

Other knights are similar to paladins in that they place their faith in a cause, though for a knight this cause is rooted in the world rather than a divine power. A knight might fight against oppression and brutality in all its forms, such as when a dwarf knight ventures into the underground with his companions on a crusade to defeat drow, duergar, and other horrors before they can threaten the surface. Such a knight doesn't need a lord or an order. All he needs is a sharp sword, a stout shield, and an indomitable belief in his cause.

The knight of the D&D game is a wanderer who hunts down the red dragon that has despoiled the countryside, or the hero who mans the walls and rallies the town guard when a horde of orcs appears on the horizon. The knight fights for a cause, and it matters not whether that cause is upholding the crown or a ceaseless desire to bring justice and hope to the land.

Notables

Knights gain notoriety for their deeds, whether triumphs in combat or selfless acts of great honor. Many an adventurer grew up on stories such as that of Archibold the Impetuous, who after the defeat of his liege's army stood alone to block pursuit on a narrow bridge while his allies withdrew to safety. The bards claim that Sir Archibold slew more than a hundred hobgoblins before he finally fell, by which time his allies had reached the safety of a nearby fortress.

Another legend tells of Lady Attis, an evil but brave knight who drove off a rampaging red dragon that had terrorized the region, not from any beneficence toward the inhabitants but to win the fame of defeating a foe no one else dared face.

Organizations

Knights often band together into orders of knighthood, and many of these organizations have storied histories. Knightly orders typically allow their members to spend much of their time on individual quests, requiring only that the knight live by the code of the order and be willing to return to the order's headquarters when called upon. Knightly orders have a proud tradition of using heraldic symbols to identify themselves, and knights who belong to the order often carry these symbols on their shields and armor to identify their affiliation.

NPC Reactions

Individuals react to knights based on their previous interactions with other members of the class. A heroic knight meets stony silence and suspicion in a land where evil knights oppress the poor. By the same token, a villainous knight finds that folk who assume knights are chivalrous, fair, and honorable are quick to trust her and willing to believe the best about her. Such trust might indeed bring out the best in her, or it might lead swiftly to disaster, depending on the knight.

A knight who has retired from adventuring typically acquires some position of authority, with commensurate political power, whether as general, king's champion, or ruler of some city or outpost. People's opinions of knights are thus often the same as their views of authority in general.

KNIGHT LORE

Characters with ranks in Knowledge (nobility and royalty) can research knights to learn more about them. When a character makes a skill check, read or paraphrase the following, including the information from lower DCs.

DC 10: Knights are skilled mounted fighters who specialize in defensive combat.

DC 15: Knights are combat-oriented characters adept at protecting their companions and stopping foes from getting past them. They follow a strict code of honor.

DC 20: Knights are masters of armor and shield use. They can lure foes into one-on-one combat through sheer force of will.

KNIGHTS IN THE GAME

Because of their obvious place in real-world history, knights fit well into any campaign with a medieval setting. The class can be available to characters of almost any race or origin, or you can tie the class to a specific kingdom or group of cultures in your campaign world. Either way, the knight provides an exciting option for players interested in a melee-oriented character capable of holding a line of combat and really protecting her allies, as well as challenging monsters in single combat.

Adaptation

This class can fit in a campaign in many ways—to serve a specific plot need, you can tie its history to a race or add a connection to a mysterious organization. The class description assumes that many races and cultures produce knights, but in your world perhaps only lawful societies might field knights as part of their armed forces, creating an instant and flavorful difference between lawful and chaotic culture groups. If you take this route, create a chaotic-oriented group of hexblades, rangers, or scouts who oppose the order of knights.

Sample Encounter

A knight can be encountered anywhere her quest for glory might take her: at the head of an enemy army, on a lone mission into the underground, or simply wandering the countryside looking for suitable challenges. A knight often appears partnered with an arcane or divine spellcaster, since the knight's class features work best in conjunction with an unarmored or lightly armored partner.

EL 7: Lady Sorra adheres to the code of knighthood for one reason: it seems the fastest way to gain power in a world where those of common birth lack opportunity. She could make a temporary ally or suitable antagonist for any adventuring group, perhaps first appearing as an ally in one adventure and then again later in another as an antagonist. In the latter case, she is likely to be found serving as the personal bodyguard of a powerful evil spellcaster.

LADY SORRA   CR 7

Female human knight 7
LE Medium humanoid
Init +5; **Senses** Listen +0, Spot +0
Languages Common

AC 21, touch 12, flat-footed 20; shield block* +1
hp 65 (7 HD)
Fort +7, **Ref** +4, **Will** +8

Speed 30 ft. (6 squares)
Melee +1 longsword +11/+6 (1d8+4/19–20)
Base Atk +7; **Grp** +10
Atk Options Cleave, Power Attack, fighting challenge* +2, test of mettle

---

Abilities Str 16, Dex 13, Con 14, Int 8, Wis 10, Cha 12
SQ armor mastery*, knight's challenge* 4/day, knight's code*, shield ally*, vigilant defender*, wall of steel*
Feats Cleave, Great Fortitude[B], Improved Initiative, Iron Will, Mounted Combat[B], Power Attack
Skills Handle Animal +11, Intimidate +11
Possessions +1 breastplate, +1 heavy shield, +1 longsword, cloak of resistance +1, ring of protection +1
*Class features described on pages 25–28

EX-KNIGHTS

A knight who is no longer lawful loses the benefits of her knight's challenge ability. As a result, she cannot use class features that require her to expend uses of the knight's challenge ability, such as fighting challenge, test of mettle, and call to battle. She no longer takes penalties for violating her code of conduct.

A knight can regain her status by returning to a lawful alignment.

Illus. by R. Horsley

he choice of a class delineates some of the most important aspects of a D&D character. With a class comes a specific role in the party, baseline mechanical attributes such as base attack and base save bonuses, and a host of special abilities that define the character. To complement the eleven standard classes presented in the *Player's Handbook*, supplements such as the *Complete* series have introduced additional classes. This chapter provides advice and insight on eighteen classes that fit well within most D&D games and presents a set of options to enhance characters of that class.

Each class presentation in this chapter includes sample character themes that help define a character's role and personality. These are not intended as an exhaustive catalog, and you are not required to adopt any of them. Each class entry also includes suggested backgrounds and suggested personality archetypes; see Chapter 5 for more information on these elements.

In addition to this roleplaying advice, each presentation offers one or more alternative class features and a set of alternative starting packages.

Alternative class features replace class features found in the original class description. If you have already reached or passed the level at which you can take the feature, you can use the retraining option described on page 192 to gain

an alternative class feature in place of the normal feature gained at that level.

The format for alternative class features is summarized below.

ALTERNATIVE CLASS FEATURE NAME

A general description of the ability and why you might want to consider it.

Level: You can select the alternative class feature only at this level (unless you are using the retraining option described in Chapter 8).

Replaces: This line identifies the ability that you must sacrifice to gain the alternative class feature.

Benefit: This section describes the mechanical effects of the new ability.

NEW STARTING PACKAGES

The final section of each of the presentations in this chapter is a set of three new starting packages for each class, each one designed for a character that fills a particular role in the adventuring party. For details about how to use these starting packages (and to modify them, if you desire), see page 5.

BARBARIAN

All stand in awe at the berserker fury you tap at will, enhancing your strength and toughness at the expense of reason. But what do cultured people know of the frozen wastes or hellish jungles that forged your earliest experiences? The cruel vicissitudes of growing up "savage" were normal to you. When your older brother was lost on a bear hunt one day, and your younger sister died of disease in the howling dark late one night, how could you know that in other places, they might not have had to die? These and other experiences marked you, and you stand apart from those born into the comforts of civilization.

Suggested Backgrounds (choose one): Gladiator, Mariner, Tribal Origin.

Suggested Personality Archetypes (choose one): Challenger, Explorer, Mercenary, Orphan, Renegade, Savage, Seeker, Simple Soul, Wanderer.

CHARACTER THEMES

One or both of the following character themes could apply to you.

Fearless: You are made of stern stuff. You're not foolish, but you're not afraid to test your mettle and resourcefulness against any foe. If you are told a foe is beyond your ability to defeat, you need more evidence than merely the claim. You do not boast, but make bold statements that echo your experiences and resolve.

Once you are actually embroiled in a conflict, you prefer a quick, urgent battle cry. A battle cry is a yell intended to rally your allies while putting fear into the hearts of enemies. See the Barbarian Battlecries sidebar and create a few of your own battlecries tailored to your experience.

"Fear cannot thwart my will."

"I braved the deadly glacier's darkest, coldest crevasse [/disease-rotted deep jungle] for three days—this trial cannot compare with that feat."

"If you fear to cross swords with the foe, pray for a quick death, for you'll never find fulfillment in this life."

"It is in hours such as these that heroes are born!"

"Fear breeds fear!"

Krusk the Conqueror, barbarian warlord

Tattooed: Your flesh is scribed with one or more pictures or symbols that signify your connection with the ancient principles of your barbarian past. One or more of the following tattoos adorn your body.

Arrowhead: You wear this simple pointed tattoo on your forehead. You believe that it lends you alertness in your dealings, both in combat and in your perception of the lies others tell you. Most people are certainly distracted by it.

Bear: Across your chest is tattooed a mighty bear, whose inexhaustible strength is your strength, and whose capacity to keep fighting even when sorely wounded is a quality you also possess.

Butterfly: This stylistically rendered winged thing is (you claim) a butterfly, and you tell all who admire it that it signifies everlasting life.

Circle: This tattooed open circle (or hoop) is the universal symbol of wholeness, female power, and infinity. If you are female, you have this emblem tattooed on your forehead, and all who see it know that you are an avatar of the feminine spirit.

Crossed Swords: The weapons you choose to wield say a lot about you, but they gain greater significance when their representations are tattooed upon your flesh. Such tattoos are tokens of good luck, and as long as they are visible, you know that you cannot suffer lasting defeat.

Demon: By tattooing a demonic image on your chest (instead of a bear), you indicate to others that you have no love for piety, show no mercy to your enemies, and don't care the least bit for propriety.

Dragon Scales: Your cheeks are tattooed with radiant dragon scales, which indicate the position of authority that was yours prior to your leaving your savage land, or the chiefdom that awaits you when you one day return to forge a mighty barbarian horde.

Lightning: Jagged lines scribed down your lower jaw and neck represent bolts of swift lightning, and you believe their presence lends you swiftness of pace and possibly of thought.

Mask: In lieu of other facial tattoos, you've chosen to cover your face with a single tattoo representing a fierce animal or monster, a nature spirit, or an ancestor. Your tribal shaman convinced you that the application of such a painful and encompassing (and disfiguring!) tattoo would allow you to more easily contact the spirit world and gain the power of the spirit or animal represented by the mask. Alternatively, you were shunned or cast out by your tribe. The tattoo covering your face forever marks you as an outcast to your tribe, unworthy to associate with the people of your birth.

Naga: Instead of snakes spiraling up your arms, you have tattooed human-headed nagas! The nagas represent anarchy and indicate to others who understand the symbol that you follow no law but your own, civilization be damned.

Snake: Tattooed snakes coil around your upper arms, simple but colorful. Their heads point toward your head, imparting their wisdom to you in spirit, if not in voice.

Spider: On the palm of one of your hands, hidden in normal dealings with strangers, the tattoo of a night-dark spider lurks with five of its legs extending up onto the undersides of your fingers. To you (and others familiar with the symbology), the spider represents trickery and even death, though others might say treachery instead of trickery. When engaged in trickery (or treachery), it is your habit to reveal your open palm to the victim of your trick (or double-cross) as the nature of your action becomes apparent to them.

Sun Rays: On the backs of your hands are tattooed the long rays of the golden sun. Just like you can count on the sun rising daily, people can count on you, as this tattoo signifies.

Toad: You believe that this minor tattoo you wear on one shoulder helps protect you from witchcraft, evil spells, and demonic influences.

BERSERKER STRENGTH

The decision of when to rage is one of the toughest faced by a barbarian. Selecting the berserker strength class feature in place of rage removes the need for this often complicated tactical decision, replacing it with an automatically activated boost to your combat prowess and durability. In short, when the going gets tough, you get tougher.

Level: 1st.

Replaces: If you select this class feature, you do not gain rage (or any later improvements to that class feature).

BARBARIAN BATTLECRIES

Below are a few battle cries you enjoy screaming out to mark the beginning of a conflict, or into an enemy's face in the midst of battle.

[a shriek like a high-pitched yowl of a wildcat]
Blood for the Blood God!
Break the bones, hew the flesh!
Death to the city dwellers!
For the North! [or your tribe name]
Scream your last!
Your guts for a garter!
Your skin for a shawl!
Your skull for a cup!

Benefit: Whenever your current hit point total is below 5 × your barbarian level, your berserker strength automatically activates. You gain a +4 bonus to your Strength score, a +2 bonus on saves, damage reduction 2/—, and a –2 penalty to your AC. The damage reduction granted by berserker strength stacks with any similar kind of damage reduction.

There is no limit to the number of times per day your berserker strength can activate. While berserker strength is active, you have the same limitation on actions as a barbarian in rage (PH 25). You cannot voluntarily end your berserker strength, although you automatically drop out of it while unconscious, helpless, or (most likely) when you receive healing to bring your current hit points above the threshold.

At 11th level (or if you would gain the greater rage class feature from any class), your berserker strength improves instead. The bonus to your Strength score improves to +6, your bonus on saves improves to +3, and you gain damage reduction 3/— (or your existing damage reduction of the same kind improves by 3).

At 20th level (or if you would gain the mighty rage class feature from any class), your berserker strength instead improves again. The bonus to your Strength score improves to +8, your bonus on saves improves to +4, and you gain damage reduction 4/— (or your existing damage reduction of the same kind improves by 4).

Any effect that would normally apply only during your rage applies whenever your berserker strength is active.

STARTING PACKAGES

Package 1: The Destroyer
Half-Orc Barbarian
> *Ability Scores:* Str 17, Dex 13, Con 14, Int 8, Wis 12, Cha 6.
> *Skills:* Climb, Jump, Swim.
> *Feat:* Power Attack.
> *Weapons:* Greataxe (1d12/×3), five javelins (1d6, 30 ft.).
> *Armor:* Scale mail (+4 AC).
> *Other Gear:* Standard adventurer's kit, 9 gp.

Package 2: The Hunter
Elf Barbarian
> *Ability Scores:* Str 15, Dex 16, Con 10, Int 10, Wis 13, Cha 8.
> *Skills:* Climb, Handle Animal, Listen, Survival.
> *Feat:* Track.
> *Weapons:* Battleaxe (1d8/×3), shortbow with 20 arrows (1d6/19–20, 60 ft.).
> *Armor:* Studded leather (+3 AC), heavy steel shield (+2 AC).
> *Other Gear:* Standard adventurer's kit, 1 gp.

Package 3: The Whirlwind
Human Barbarian
> *Ability Scores:* Str 14, Dex 15, Con 13, Int 10, Wis 12, Cha 8.
> *Skills:* Climb, Intimidate, Jump, Listen, Swim.
> *Feat:* Two-Weapon Fighting, Weapon Focus (kukri).
> *Weapons:* Two kukris (1d4/18–20), five javelins (1d6, 30 ft.).
> *Armor:* Scale mail (+4 AC).
> *Other Gear:* Standard adventurer's kit, 4 gp.

BARD

You roam the bright kingdoms and less savory regions of the world alike, amassing lore, negotiating tricky deals, scouting, gambling, spying, relaying messages, and telling epic stories. You work magic with your music, influencing the hearts and minds of both friends and foes. In the end, the best stories end up being about you.

Suggested Backgrounds (choose one): Artisan, Drifter, Mariner, Noble Scion.

Suggested Personality Archetypes (choose one): Agent, Daredevil, Explorer, Innocent, Mercenary, Orphan, Rebel, Renegade, Royalty, Trickster, Wanderer.

CHARACTER THEMES

One or more of the following character themes could apply to you.

Military Historian: This character theme requires you to have at least one rank in Knowledge (history). You are a student of conflict, an expert on the subject of the famous battles between prehistoric tribes, ancient militaries, and modern armies between kings and necromancers.

Now and then, you regale your friends with snippets of these histories. You find it all so interesting that you know everyone else would feel the same way, if only they were exposed to the sagas.

"We could learn something from the Battle of Rakdar, fought three hundred years ago. When the army of King Yria encountered an allied army of eight kings at Rakdar, it was utterly decimated by the much larger force. King Yria learned the value of alliances then."

"The Battle of Ceschremi sent ten thousand warriors to their graves, because reinforcements didn't arrive when Emperor Drezzar ordered. Over the years, his generals had taken the money meant to keep reinforcements at the ready and instead bought fine mansions for themselves in the countryside. Those were later burned by the Ceschremi army, which advanced unopposed."

Negotiator: In some groups, your diplomatic skills will exceed those of all your friends. To be a good negotiator, you must be fair, but stern. While the Diplomacy skill provides the mechanical resolution of a scene, DMs enjoy hearing the gist of your negotiating points as a precursor to attempting the skill check.

Really, it's all about the "spin." With the proper spin, even a three-day-dead orc can be made to sound enticing. For example, if you are attempting to explain to a city official why your group was responsible for so much destruction in a recent street altercation, you might say:

"Your honor, consider the devastation that would have otherwise been wrought. Consider the buildings unburnt, lives saved, and money still safely in coffers precisely because of our actions!"

On the other hand, if you are trying to trade in an unneeded magic weapon for some other trifle that you or a friend would prefer, try:

"Your eyes miss nothing, madam, but of course you couldn't know that this blade was once the boyhood dagger of the playwright Isheuan. Indeed, his honeyed words are a delight to all. And this blade was grasped in that same hand that also takes so ably to the pen. Consider its value now!"

Riddlemaster: You absorb stories, but you collect riddles. A good riddle is a treasure in itself, and "a thorough knowledge of riddles keeps the intellect flexible and sharp," as you are fond of saying. More than that, a knowledge of riddles can prove useful in negotiations with certain enigmatic beasts, prideful kings, or any foe whose conceit compels it to agree to test of riddles to resolve a dispute.

Every bard knows at least a few riddles. Beyond these beginning few, you are constantly on the lookout for more, whether through research in dusty tomes, or by riddling with strangers and friends, ally or foe, even when there is nothing at stake. In this way, you are able to collect ever more riddles for your growing repertoire. You are also adroit at creating your own riddles.

How To Write A Riddle: Use three rules when writing a riddle.

1) Pick an word or phrase as the answer to your riddle.

2) Turn the word or phrase over and over in your head, free-associating and making note of any unusual or off-the-wall idea that comes to mind.

3) Come up with clues about these ideas you've just generated.

Put it all together, tidy it up, and you might have just created a riddle that will last the ages.

Spy: Even if you don't have a commission, you can play up the fact that you *might* be working under official authority—after all, you've (supposedly) done so in the past.

Purchase a leather-bound journal (in game), and keep copious notes about all your surroundings, exploits, and the doings of your acquaintances. At some later point, your habits could reveal an important clue that was missed earlier. To prevent anyone else from gleaning the same information, you keep this journal in a cipher.

Ciphers: A cipher is a way to record information in such a way that it is obscured to those without special knowledge. In most cases, this special knowledge is a key (for simple ciphers) that provides the necessary insight for rearranging letters into their proper order or otherwise rendering a message legible.

If you end up *actually* acting as a spy for a merchant guild, temple, or other organization, you can pass a note every few sessions to the DM using a simple cipher—assuming the DM aids you in this endeavor.

One of the simplest ciphers replaces each letter of the alphabet with a different letter that is a certain number of letters away. For instance, if the cipher is "letter +1" (replace each letter with the one that follows it in the alphabet), then the message "J bn b tqz," when decrypted, reads "I am a spy."

Storyteller: You are a repository of stories both ancient and contemporary. From the wealth of stories at your disposal, the lessons of history and adages of past bards and sages are at your fingertips. Use this knowledge to your advantage when you wish to influence an ally's (or foe's) opinion about something, such as a plan of action or a proposed agreement. By preceding your point with a reference to a story (real or made up), you lend additional weight to the point you make immediately afterward. Most sentient creatures feel the pressure of precedent of others' past experience on a similar matter, even if you've invented the story on the spot (as long as they don't know you're making it up). Of course, it's better if you actually have a story, or a piece of history told as a story, in mind before you attempt this tactic.

For example, when confronted with a particular thorny problem, especially if you see a solution, stroke your chin and say:

"This reminds me of the time Prince Voltred tried to enter his falcon in the archery contest. Funny thing about that. . . ."

Or, when you disagree with a conclusion, try:

"The slave Medricar thought the same thing, when he once escaped his master to live in the forest. He figured he could survive on the wild herbs and honey he would find. Good thing he changed his mind. . . ."

Or, when you believe not enough forethought has gone into an ally's proposed course of action:

"Might work, yes, but you remember Darvn, who rushed into the Cave of the Yellow Skull? If he had just watched a little longer, he'd have seen the giant sleeping behind the stone."

BARDIC KNACK

Wandering bards learn more mundane skills and less esoteric knowledge on their travels. If you select this class feature, you have done a little bit of everything; maybe you spent a few months as a wilderness guide, and you also had a cousin in an ambassador's retinue who regaled you with tales of courtly intrigue.

The bardic knack class feature makes you more capable of accomplishing simple tasks with a wide variety of skills. You don't need to dabble in noncritical skills (unless you want to be considered trained in their use), freeing up your skill points to focus on a small range of crucial skills.

Level: 1st.

Replaces: If you select this class feature, you do not gain bardic knowledge.

Benefit: When making any skill check, you can use 1/2 your bard level (rounded up) in place of the number of ranks you have in the skill (even if that number is 0).

For example, a 5th-level bard would have the equivalent of 3 ranks in Appraise, Balance, Bluff, and so on (but only for the purpose of making skill checks).

You can't take 10 on checks when you use bardic knack (to take 10 you have to use your actual ranks). If the skill doesn't allow untrained checks, you must have at least 1 actual rank to attempt the check.

STARTING PACKAGES

Package 1: The Controller
Half-Elf Bard

Ability Scores: Str 10, Dex 14, Con 13, Int 12, Wis 8, Cha 15.

Skills: Bluff, Diplomacy, Disguise, Gather Information, Knowledge (local), Perform, Sense Motive.

Languages: Common, Elven, Celestial.

Feat: Skill Focus (Perform).

Weapons: Longsword (1d8/19–20), shortbow with 20 arrows (1d6/×3, 60 ft.).

Armor: Studded leather (+3 AC).

Other Gear: Common musical instrument, spell component pouch, standard adventurer's kit, 9 gp.

Spells Known: 0—detect magic, lullaby, mage hand, prestidigitation.

Package 2: The Problem Solver
Gnome Bard

Ability Scores: Str 8, Dex 14, Con 10, Int 12, Wis 13, Cha 15.

Skills: Bluff, Concentration, Craft (alchemy), Listen, Perform, Spellcraft, Use Magic Device.

Languages: Common, Gnome, Goblin.

Feat: Arcane Flourish*.

Weapons: Longsword (1d6/19–20), shortbow with 20 arrows (1d4/×3, 60 ft.).

Armor: Studded leather (+3 AC),

Other Gear: Common musical instrument, spell component pouch, standard adventurer's kit, 4 gp.

Spells Known: 0—dancing lights, detect magic, mage hand, read magic.

Package 3: The Vanguard
Human Bard

Ability Scores: Str 10, Dex 14, Con 13, Int 12, Wis 8, Cha 15.

Skills: Concentration, Diplomacy, Escape Artist, Listen, Perform, Spot, Tumble.

Languages: Common, Draconic.

Feats: Combat Expertise, Still Spell.

Weapons: Rapier (1d6/18–20), five javelins (1d6, 30 ft.).

Armor: Studded leather (+3 AC), light wooden shield (+1 AC, 5% arcane spell failure).

Other Gear: Common musical instrument, spell component pouch, standard adventurer's kit, 22 gp.

Spells Known: 0—detect magic, ghost sound, light, message.

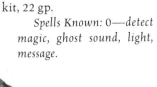

Gimble, Herald of the High Crown

Illus. by S. Belledin

CLERIC

You are a representative of an almighty deity's authority in the mortal world. You give thanks daily to the good fortune that put you in such an enviable position. You know firsthand that the places of natural beauty, the structure of societies, and even existential cosmic laws would falter and perhaps collapse altogether without divine influence and intervention.

However, deities work through agencies other than mere divine decree. In fact, gods prefer to work through intermediaries such as you when possible. You use the power of your deity to make your god's will manifest. In doing so, your lot improves, as you are raised slowly up in the eyes of the deity you serve with each deed you accomplish in your god's name.

Suggested Backgrounds (choose one): Artisan, Ascetic, Noble Scion.

Suggested Personality Archetypes (choose one): Agent, Companion, Crusader, Innocent, Leader, Martyr, Orphan, Prophet, Royalty, Sage, Seeker, Simple Soul, Theorist.

CHARACTER THEMES

One or more of the following character themes could apply to you.

Giver of Blessings: Since you are an instrument of your deity's will, you often find yourself (along with your companions) in tight spaces. In such circumstances, it is customary for you to bless yourself and your companions with your god's beneficence immediately prior to taking desperate action.

Keeping such blessings to a minimum number of words is a good idea, given that you are usually only moved to give a blessing when circumstances are dire.

You are partial to one or more of the following blessings (substituting your deity's name for Pelor):

"Refresh and gladden our spirits.
Purify our hearts.
Illumine our powers.
We lay our hope in Pelor's hands."

"Bless us, oh Pelor,
and these thy weapons which
we are about to deploy in thy name,
through your beneficence."

"We humbly beseech you from the bottom of
our hearts to succor us in our necessity."

Missionary: You believe without question that others would benefit by conversion to the worship of your deity. You have taken it upon yourself to be a propagator of your religion, and draw upon one of the following methods of proselytization.

Conversion through Exhortation: You are a strident evangelist who exhorts others to consider your deity's worship at every opportunity. For instance, whenever you heal a companion, you murmur:

"Through Pelor's grace, be healed. If your belief were greater, how much greater would the relief from your wounds be?"

On the other hand, when smiting enemies, you scream (regardless of whether your friends have yet converted):

"When you cross me, you cross the great god Pelor and earn his wrath, and the wrath of all his disciples!"

Conversion by Example: You never exhort your companions to convert, but instead serve your deity lovingly and well. You heal your companions at need, smite enemies, and accomplish other duties required by the company you keep.

After months of showing how the grace of Pelor helps you through example, you are ready to choose your moment. At some point your aid, healing prayer, or other good work will come at just the precise moment to save or renew one of your companions. This is the time to whisper persuasively in his or her ear:

"Consider what Pelor has done for you—it is through his aid that I have aided you. If you say so now, I will tell you more of Pelor later."

In this way, you can slowly bring one or more of your companions into the fold.

Prayerful: You know that maintaining the channels of communication between yourself and your deity is necessary, not just when your god grants your spells, but all day through. However, the adventuring life being what it is, your prayers are short and sweet, and you drop them into conversation when possible.

For instance, whenever you make a particularly forceful assertion, you append one of the following phrases (substituting your deity's name for Pelor):

Jozan, High Priest of Pelor

". . . as Pelor's grace demands."
". . . just as Pelor sweeps aside foes."
". . . so that Pelor may smile upon us."
". . . in Pelor's name, let it be so."
". . . in this we ask Pelor's aid."
". . . and in so doing we will be instruments of Pelor's peace."
". . . and in this we shall have Pelor's divine aid."
". . . for behold, Pelor has smiled on us from the very beginning."
". . . and may all sin in Pelor's eyes be washed from our souls, so that our purposes are pure."

Illus. by H. Lyon

Sermonizer: You are familiar with the trials and travails of your deity, especially if your god or one of his saints or other associated entities was forced to undergo a great trial to reach a higher spiritual understanding or vision.

You are given to dropping in bits and pieces of this story prior to expressing your point. You hope that by being made aware of holy example, your companions will see the wisdom of your words.

For instance, you might say as part of your arguments (substituting your deity's name for Pelor):

"... but as the One Hundred Writs of Pelor tell us ..."

"... lest we suffer as Pelor suffered in his many trials ..."

"... but even the purest hearts can fall. Remember Eyria, the devoted paladin of Pelor? Renowned for her piety and courage, she was slain in battle with a death knight, but in her destruction she was victorious."

"... long before you were born and long after you've become but dust, Pelor's disciples will continue their good works and see to it that Pelor's will is accomplished.

Soldier of Divinity: You stand a little closer to the paladin ideal than other clerics. You disdain blessings and prayers, and you avoid healing your compatriots except in the direst of circumstances. Instead, you select your spells, feats, and magic items so that your deity's divine grace directly infuses your strength at arms and defense. If you pray for just the right combination of aid, your ability to fight your god's battles comes close to equaling any warrior's combat ability, and in some cases exceeds those capabilities.

Of course, being a soldier of your deity doesn't mean that you can't be prayerful (see above), though your pleas to your god take on a much more military context:

"Move, infidel, or feel divine wrath."

"Kill them all, Pelor commands it!"

SPONTANEOUS DOMAIN CASTING

After a while, clerics can start looking very similar. Even with a variety of domains to choose from, domain spells take up such a small portion of the average cleric's repertoire that they don't have much effect on the overall feel of the character. With spontaneous domain casting, though, your domain choice becomes a more important element of your character. You won't be able to provide as much healing to your party as a typical cleric, but the ability to prepare *cure* or *inflict* spells in your domain spell slots keeps you from falling too far behind in that area.

Level: 1st.

Replaces: If you select this class feature, you do not gain the ability to spontaneously convert prepared spells into *cure* or *inflict* spells.

Benefit: You can convert stored spell energy into the spells of one of your domains. Pick one of your two domains. You can "lose" any prepared spell (other than a domain spell) to cast any spell of the same level or lower on that domain list. Your choice is permanent unless an alignment change, deity change, or other dramatic event leaves you incapable of accessing the domain.

In addition, when preparing spells you can choose to fill any or all of your domain spell slots with either *cure* or *inflict* spells (depending on whether you would normally convert prepared spells to *cure* or *inflict* spells) of the same level.

Example: Crucius is a cleric of Heironeous with the Good and War domains. At 1st level, he chooses to spontaneously cast War domain spells. Thereafter, he can lose a prepared 1st-level spell to cast *magic weapon*, a prepared 2nd-level spell to cast *spiritual weapon* (or *magic weapon*), and so on. Furthermore, in each domain spell slot he can prepare a spell from the Good domain, a spell from the War domain, or a *cure* spell of the same level.

STARTING PACKAGES

Package 1: The Defender

Dwarf Cleric of Moradin

Ability Scores: Str 12, Dex 8, Con 16, Int 10, Wis 15, Cha 11.

Skills: Concentration, Knowledge (religion).

Feat: Improved Turning.

Weapons: Morningstar (1d8), light crossbow with 20 bolts (1d8/19–20, 80 ft.).

Armor: Scale mail (+4 AC), heavy wooden shield (+2 AC).

Other Gear: Spell component pouch, standard adventurer's kit, wooden holy symbol, 2 gp.

Class Features: Channels positive energy; Good and Protection domains.

Spells Prepared: 1st—*command, protection from evil*D, *shield of faith*; 0—*detect magic, light, resistance.*

D: Domain spell.

Package 2: The Destroyer

Half-Orc Cleric of Heironeous

Ability Scores: Str 16, Dex 10, Con 12, Int 6, Wis 15, Cha 11.

Skill: Concentration.

Feats: Divine Justice*, Martial Weapon Proficiency (longsword), Weapon Focus (longsword).

Weapons: Longsword (1d8/19–20), 2 javelins (1d6, 20 ft.).

Armor: Scale mail (+4 AC), heavy wooden shield (+2 AC).

Other Gear: Spell component pouch, standard adventurer's kit, wooden holy symbol, 5 gp.

Class Features: Channels positive energy; Good and War (longsword) domains.

Spells Prepared: 1st—*bless, divine favor, magic weapon*D; 0—*guidance, resistance, virtue.*

D: Domain spell.

Package 3: The Healer

Human Cleric of Pelor

Ability Scores: Str 14, Dex 8, Con 12, Int 10, Wis 15, Cha 13.

Skills: Concentration, Diplomacy, Heal.

Feats: Combat Casting, Sacred Healing*.

Weapons: Longspear (1d8/×3), light crossbow with 20 bolts (1d8/19–20, 80 ft.).

Armor: Scale mail (+4 AC).

Other Gear: Spell component pouch, standard adventurer's kit, wooden holy symbol, 12 gp.

Class Features: Channels positive energy; Healing and Sun domains.

Spells Prepared: 1st—*endure elements*D, *protection from evil, sanctuary*; 0—*detect magic, detect poison, light.*

D: Domain spell.

DRUID

Your secret instruction occurred in caves and forests sacred to life. You learned clandestine verses, the names of stars and constellations, the cycle of the seasons, sacred songs, formulas for prayers and incantations, rules of divination and magic, and the language of animals. To this day, you still learn; as a druid, you are a lifelong student of the natural world.

Why isn't everyone? After witnessing the fury of a storm, the splendor of the setting sun, and the spirit-cleansing power of a grove of aspen trees, only the most stone-hearted would not be moved to protect and conserve them, and what's more, rejoice and cherish the slow-growing, natural elements of the world that form the foundation of everything else. Without the web of sun, rain, growth, death, and rebirth in nature, the vaunted civilizations of men, elves, dwarves, and other creatures would crumble like dust.

Suggested Backgrounds (choose one): Ascetic, Farm Hand, Tribal Origin.

Suggested Personality Archetypes (choose one): Agent, Crusader, Explorer, Innocent, Martyr, Orphan, Prophet, Renegade, Sage, Savage, Wanderer.

CHARACTER THEMES

One or more of the following character themes could apply to you.

Conservationist: You espouse a philosophy you like to call the "conservation ethic." The conservation ethic promotes the measured use, allotment, and protection of natural lands and waters. You employ your ethic as an aid in your efforts to sustain the natural world: its forests, lakes, seas, and all the strange and wondrous creatures that live within it.

In order to engender a similar ethic in your companions and others that you meet, you offer poetic references to nature when traveling, when first seeing a new vista, or when you otherwise deem appropriate:

"Spend a heartbeat and notice every waving leaf, every tendril of mist in the dark woods, and every humming insect."

"The deer, the wolf, the oak, the fish, and the great birds are our fellows, and they can be wronged, just as you can be wronged."

"An unchecked and untempered appetite will devour green plains and leave behind only a barren wasteland."

"What soul can't find peace and spiritual renewal in the forlorn cry of the whippoorwill or the arguments of the frogs around a pond at night?"

"Whatever happens to the wild places, the pure waters, and the teeming beasts soon happens to us. An invisible web connects all things."

Friend of Animals: Small and relatively defenseless animals have no greater friend than you. While you know that nature is not merciful, and that the weak and old are destined to be food for young, strong predators, you also know that mercy can selectively apply to nature.

To this end you know by sight dozens, if not hundreds, of individual small animals such as birds, gophers, and rabbits. You don't bore your humanoid companions with all the names you've given all the little creatures that you recognize, unless asked.

You always carry with you a small bag in which you keep crumbs, old bones, jerky, grain, thistle, or other treats that animals enjoy, and leave them as small offerings when convenient.

"See that one? Hawks rarely live as long as Shrieker. He's a tough old bird."

"Sometimes my friends find me around the campfire at night, and tell me stories of their day."

Hunter: You are displeased when those who should know better exploit nature. But you retain a burning hatred for those things that are nature's bane by virtue of their mere existence; you hate that which is unnatural, including aberrations (such as beholders and carrion crawlers) and undead (such as zombies and vampires).

From time to time, you lead raids against such creatures, especially when they encroach on natural wonders and lands that you revere. Even while such creatures are still contained, it is better to excise them before they can cause damage to the natural world, rather than wait for the damage to happen as it inevitably will.

Undead in particular have no connection to nature—they exist apart from it, a mockery of the normal cycles of life. Nature cries out each moment they are suffered to exist.

"Those not of creation deserve no part in it."

"This aberration's body must be displayed as a warning to the others."

Judge: You are the guardian of unwritten ancient laws inspired by nature. As someone with such knowledge, you believe you have the power to judge those who have sinned against the natural order. When you judge, you can sentence the malefactor to be excommunicated from sacred groves, the deep woods, and all other places where nature still reigns supreme.

To the extent you are able to communicate your judgments to other druids, wild animals, treants, and other creatures of the wild, your judgments stand. Of course, the easiest way to ensure your judgment is to take matters into your own hands against those who have sinned most heinously (such as undead, through their mere existence).

In most cases, other druids are willing to abide by your judgments, if you show through your actions that you are willing to abide by theirs.

However, no civilized court of law, whether a council of village elders or a king's tribunal, recognizes the right of druids and their judgments. That's all right with you—neither do you recognize their right over sovereign nature.

"Primeval justice is the first arbiter and final authority."

"The laws of man pale before the law of nature."

Philosopher: Nature is red in tooth and claw, regardless of what the sentimental philosophies of so-called civilization might claim. To truly cherish all life, you embrace the fact that bad things and good are all part of the evolving environment. When events unfold that seem initially bad or ruinous, you philosophically attempt to provide perspective to your companions.

"In the landscape of spring, there is neither better nor worse. The flowering branches grow naturally, some long, some short."

"Nature's tranquility comes like a fresh wind that blows away cares like autumn leaves."

"There are no sermons in stones. It is easier to get a spark out of a stone than a moral."

"We cannot command nature except by obeying her."

"Nature teaches us to either adapt or perish."

Teacher: Unlike many druids, who can come across as sullen and rough (albeit steadfast in their beliefs), you enjoy teaching others just why it is so important that nature have a protector such as yourself. After all, it is not obvious to the casual observer that life exists only through a subtle connection and deep interaction with all other living things.

Think about it—where does the food you eat come from? We eat meat, and we eat greens. If we kill all the meat animals, or the land where the animals graze, what are you going to eat? If we build over all the farms with sprawling cities, who is going to grow your potatoes and barley?"

"There is power in nature apart from what magic or resources we can extract from it. Sure, a grove of trees will build a house—but it can also house a spirit."

"Consider the herders and shepherds who conserve their cattle and sheep from season to season, extracting milk, wool, and even meat while ensuring the health of the overall herd. It is no different with the plains, forests, and lakes. We need to be tree stewards, grass shepherds, and lake wardens if we want to continue to enjoy the bounty nature provides year after year."

Star Watcher: You spend so much time in the wild that you recognize the stars and constellations of the night sky as easily as you note the smell of flame on the wind or the spoor of a mountain cat about to give birth.

You know the various epicycles and positions of the celestial bodies, but more important, you hold that your knowledge of the positions of stars, comets, moons, and planets is useful in understanding, interpreting, and organizing knowledge about what has come before, what's going on now, and what will one day come to pass. You like to say to your companions concerning your predilection for the stars:

". . . by looking up I see downward."

Vadania, hierophant druid of the Tall Forest

In addition, you make a point to see the stars at least once a week, and more often if possible. If you are prevented from seeing the open sky, you at least have your personally constructed star chart, a scroll of paper on which you've inked the various stars, planets, and other celestial bodies important to you. You can while away long hours poring over your charts and drawing complicated designs meant to unleash your intuitive side, so that visions of the future might become clear.

"I saw a comet once that was part of no star chart I had studied. I named it after my secret desire."

"The stars are wise beyond all else. They looked on as this world formed, and they'll look on after this world has run through its history to the end."

SPONTANEOUS REJUVENATION

By selecting the spontaneous rejuvenation alternative class feature, you can provide the party with plenty of healing without trampling on the cleric's role.

Level: 1st.

Replaces: If you select this class feature, you do not gain the ability to spontaneously convert prepared spells into *summon nature's ally* spells.

Benefit: You can transform the stored energy of a spell you have prepared to invigorate you and your allies.

To use spontaneous rejuvenation, you must spend a standard action and sacrifice a prepared spell. All allies within 30 feet of you (including yourself) gain fast healing for 3 rounds. The fast healing amount is equal to the spell's level. For example, if you sacrifice *remove disease*, a 3rd-level spell, each ally gains fast healing 3 for 3 rounds.

The fast healing granted by this class feature doesn't stack with itself or with fast healing from other sources.

SHAPESHIFT

Taking the shapeshift alternative class feature means you can focus on your actions in combat (rather than worrying about your animal companion) while still unleashing nature's fury upon your foes.

Level: 1st.

Replaces: If you select this class feature, you do not gain an animal companion at 1st level, nor do you gain the wild shape class feature at 5th level (or any variation of that class

Illus. by R. Spencer

feature at later levels, such as the ability to wild shape into an elemental at 16th level).

Benefit: You can shapeshift at will into powerful animal or nature-oriented forms. Each time you use this ability, you can choose the exact look that your shapeshifted form takes. Druids pick animals from the terrain and climate they're most familiar with. For example, a druid from a jungle might adopt the form of a black panther when in predator form, while one from the taiga might shapeshift into a white wolf. The two forms look different, but functionally they're identical. This is a supernatural ability.

It requires only a swift action to shapeshift. If you are capable of taking more than one form, you can shapeshift directly between two forms without returning to your normal form. There's no limit to the number of times per day you can change forms, nor to the amount of time you can spend in a shapeshifted form.

You retain your normal Hit Dice, hit points, base attack bonus, base saving throw bonuses, and skill ranks regardless of your form. You also retain your normal ability scores, though each form grants a bonus to your Strength score.

You keep all extraordinary, supernatural, and spell-like special attacks and qualities of your normal form, except for those requiring a body part your new form does not have.

All your held, carried, or worn gear melds into your new form and becomes nonfunctional until you return to your normal form. You cannot speak in shapeshifted form, and your limbs lack the precision required to wield a weapon or perform tasks requiring fine manipulation. You can't cast spells or activate magic items while in shapeshifted form, even if you have the Natural Spell feat or other ability that would allow you to cast spells while wild shaped.

Unless otherwise noted in the descriptions below, you retain your size and space when you adopt a new form. You always retain your type and subtypes, regardless of the nature of the form assumed. You don't gain any special attacks or qualities while shapeshifted except as described below.

When you shapeshift into a form other than your own, you gain natural weapons (and reach with those weapons) as described below. These natural weapons gain an enhancement bonus on attack rolls and damage rolls equal to 1/4 your druid level, and at 4th level and higher they are treated as magic weapons for the purpose of overcoming damage reduction. The damage dice given are for Medium druids; smaller or larger druids should adjust those values according to the table on page 28 of the *Dungeon Master's Guide*.

If knocked unconscious or slain in shapeshifted form, you revert to your original form.

Predator Form: This form, traditionally that of a wolf, panther, or other predatory mammal, is the first one a shapeshifting druid learns.

While in predator form, you gain a primary bite attack that deals 1d6 points of damage. You have the reach of a long creature of your size (5 feet for Small or Medium). You gain a +4 enhancement bonus to Strength, and your natural armor bonus improves by 4. Your base land speed becomes 50 feet.

At 4th level, you gain Mobility as a bonus feat whenever you are in predator form (even if you don't meet the prerequisites).

Aerial Form: At 5th level, you can shapeshift into a flying creature. Traditionally resembling an eagle, vulture, or bat, the aerial form enables fast travel and the ability to soar out of harm's way.

While in aerial form, you gain a primary talon attack that deals 1d6 points of damage. You have the reach of a long creature of your size (5 feet for Small or Medium). You gain a +2 enhancement bonus to Strength and a +2 enhancement bonus on Reflex saves, and your natural armor bonus improves by 2. You gain a fly speed of 40 feet (good maneuverability).

At 7th level, you gain Flyby Attack as a bonus feat whenever you are in aerial form.

Ferocious Slayer Form: At 8th level, you can shapeshift into a large and fierce predatory form, such as a tiger, brown bear, or dire wolf.

While in ferocious slayer form, you gain a primary bite attack that deals 1d8 points of damage and two secondary claw attacks that each deal 1d6 points of damage. Your size increases by one category (to a maximum of Colossal), and you have the reach of a long creature of your size (5 feet for Medium or Large). You gain a +8 enhancement bonus to Strength and a +4 enhancement bonus on Fortitude saves, and your natural armor bonus improves by 8. Your base land speed changes to 40 feet.

At 10th level, you gain Improved Critical (bite) and Improved Critical (claw) as bonus feats whenever you are in ferocious slayer form.

Forest Avenger Form: At 12th level, you can take the form of a massive plantlike creature, similar to a shambling mound or a treant. (Druids not native to forest terrains typically rename this form to fit their environment.)

While in forest avenger form, you gain a pair of primary slam attacks that deal 1d8 points of damage each. Your size increases by one category (to a maximum of Colossal) and you have the reach of a tall creature of your size (5 feet for Medium, 10 feet for Large). You gain a +12 enhancement bonus to Strength and a +4 enhancement bonus on Fortitude and Will saves, and your natural armor bonus improves by 12. Your base land speed becomes 20 feet.

You gain damage reduction 5/slashing while in forest avenger form.

At 14th level, you gain Improved Overrun as a bonus feat while in forest avenger form (even if you don't meet the normal prerequisites).

Elemental Fury Form: At 16th level, you can shapeshift into a giant form of air, earth, fire, or water (your choice each time you shapeshift).

While in elemental fury form, you gain a pair of primary slam attacks that deal 2d6 points of damage each. Your size increases by two categories (to a maximum of Colossal), and you have the reach of a tall creature of your size (10 feet for Large, 15 feet for Huge). You gain a +16 enhancement bonus to Strength and a +4 enhancement bonus on Fortitude, Reflex, and Will saves, and your natural armor bonus improves by 16. You do not gain any new modes of movement in elemental fury form, nor does your base land speed change.

You gain immunity to extra damage from critical hits while in elemental form. You also gain immunity to an energy type related to the element chosen (air = electricity, earth = acid, fire = fire, water = cold). You don't need to breathe while in elemental fury form.

At 18th level, you gain Great Cleave as a bonus feat while in elemental fury form (even if you don't meet the normal prerequisites).

STARTING PACKAGES

Package 1: The Beastmaster
Halfling Druid

Ability Scores: Str 8, Dex 14, Con 14, Int 8, Wis 15, Cha 13.
Skills: Handle Animal, Ride, Survival.
Languages: Common, Druidic, Halfling.
Feat: Animal Affinity.
Weapons: Longspear (1d6/×3), sling with 20 bullets (1d3, 50 ft.).
Armor: Hide (+3 AC).
Other Gear: Spell component pouch, standard adventurer's kit, 9 gp, 8 sp.
Class Feature: Riding dog animal companion.
Spells Prepared: 1st—*cure light wounds, speak with animals;* 0—*cure minor wounds* (2), *detect magic.*

Package 2: The Feral Beast
Elf Druid

Ability Scores: Str 13, Dex 14, Con 12, Int 8, Wis 15, Cha 10.

Skills: Listen, Spot, Survival.
Languages: Common, Druidic, Elven.
Feat: Alertness.
Weapon: Spear (1d8/×3), sling with 20 bullets (1d4, 50 ft.).
Armor: Hide (+3 AC).
Other Gear: Spell component pouch, standard adventurer's kit, 12 gp, 8 sp.
Class Feature: Hawk animal companion.
Spells Prepared: 1st—*cure light wounds, longstrider;* 0—*cure minor wounds, know direction, light.*

Package 3: The Warden
Human Druid

Ability Scores: Str 10, Dex 12, Con 14, Int 8, Wis 15, Cha 13.
Skills: Concentration, Knowledge (nature), Spot, Survival.
Languages: Common, Druidic.
Feats: Augment Summoning, Spell Focus (conjuration).
Weapons: Scimitar (1d6/18–20), sling with 20 bullets (1d4, 50 ft.).
Armor: Leather (+2 AC), light wooden shield (+1 AC).
Other Gear: Spell component pouch, standard adventurer's kit, 1 gp, 8 sp.
Class Feature: Wolf animal companion.
Spells Prepared: 1st—*cure light wounds, entangle;* 0—*cure minor wounds, detect magic, flare.*

ANIMAL COMPANIONS

The list below is a compilation of all terrestrial animals eligible to be chosen as animal companions, organized by minimum druid level required. Apply the parenthetical adjustment to the druid's level for purposes of determining the companion's characteristics and special abilities.

If the campaign takes place wholly or partly in an aquatic environment, consult *Stormwrack* for a list of additional appropriate animal companions.

1st Level
Badger
Brixashulty†[RW]
Camel
Caribou[F]
Chordevoc†[RW]
Climbdog[AE]
Dire rat
Dog
Dog, riding
Eagle
Hawk
Horse, light
Horse, heavy
Jackal[S]
Owl
Pony
Serval[S]
Snake, Small viper
Snake, Medium viper
Swindlespitter[M3]
Vulture[S]
Wolf
†Halfling druids only

4th Level (–3)
Ape
Axebeak[AE]
Badger, dire
Bat, dire
Bear, black
Bison
Boar
Brixashulty†[RW]
Cheetah
Chordevoc†[RW]
Fleshraker[3]
Hawk, dire††[M2, RW$]
Jackal, dire[S]
Leopard
Lizard, monitor
Snake, constrictor
Snake, Large viper
Toad, dire[M2]
Weasel, dire
Wolverine
†Nonhalfling druids only
††Raptoran druids only

7th Level (–6)
Ape, dire
Ankylosaurus, cave[MH]
Bear, brown
Boar, dire
Crocodile, giant
Deinonychus
Eagle, dire[RS]
Hawk, dire††[M2, RW$]
Lion
Megaloceros[F]
Protoceratops[S]
Rhinoceros
Snake, Huge viper
Terror bird[FF]
Tiger
Wolf, dire
Wolverine, dire
††Nonraptoran druids only

10th Level (–9)
Allosaurus[M2, A$]
Bear, polar
Bloodstriker[M3]
Glyptodon[F]

Hippopotamus[S]
Horse, dire[M2]
Lion, dire
Megaraptor
Puma, dire[S]
Snake, dire[M2]
Snake, giant constrictor
Tiger, saber-toothed[F]
Tortoise, dire[S]
Triceratops, cave[MH]
Tyrannosaurus, cave[MH]
Vulture, dire[S]

13th Level (–12)
Ankylosaurus[M2, A$]
Bear, dire
Diprotodon[S]
Elephant
Elk, dire[M2]
Fhorge[FF]
Lizard, giant banded[S]

16th Level (–15)
Bear, dire polar[F]
Elephant, dire[M2]
Hippopotamus, dire[S]

Indricothere[FF]
Mammoth, woolly[F*]
Mastodon[M3]
Mastodon, grizzly[M2]
Megatherium[FF]
Quetzalcoatlus[M2, A$]
Rhinoceros, dire[FF]
Tiger, dire
Triceratops
Tyrannosaurus

*Listed in previous source as available at a different level.
A: See *D&D v.3.5 Accessory Update* for new statistics
AE: *Arms & Equipment Guide*
F: *Frostburn*
FF: *Fiend Folio*
M2: *Monster Manual II*
M3: *Monster Manual III*
MH: *Miniatures Handbook*
RS: *Races of Stone*
RW: *Races of the Wild*
S: *Sandstorm*

FAVORED SOUL

You are a free agent of your deity, unfettered by the strictures of a clerical hierarchy. You wander from place to place, wielding your power to advance the causes you deem worthy in the eyes of your god, or else you choose a great crusade against that which offends your deity, requiring a lifelong commitment and unswerving purpose. While the cleric comes to his power through study and discipline, you are the recipient of a great gift—or, as some perceive it, a terrible curse. How you wield the divine power burning in your heart is up to you.

This class appears in the *Complete Divine* supplement.

Suggested Backgrounds (choose one): Ascetic, Drifter, Noble Scion.

Suggested Personality Archetypes (choose one): Companion, Crusader, Innocent, Martyr, Prophet, Seeker, Wanderer.

CHARACTER THEMES

One or more of the following character themes could apply to you.

Mystic: You aspire to the divine in every aspect of your life. The difficulties and dangers around you are only temporary; you keep your eyes firmly fixed on matters of the spirit, which are all that truly matter. You have little interest in wealth, fame, or creature comforts, since these things are transitory too. Instead, you seek enlightenment, understanding, and spiritual growth.

Some might see you as oblivious or irrational, but those are unfair characterizations. You simply have the ability to look past fear, pain, and suffering to the eternal rewards that will surely follow. You possess moral and physical courage in abundance, because you do not fear death or injury. You don't go out of your way to get hurt or killed, of course, but there is no point in fearing pain or death when you know that your spirit will survive.

While your comrades might not always appreciate your detachment from matters of the physical world, you are compassionate (or careful, at least, if you are evil) and fearless. Nothing discourages you.

Seek out adventures for the right reasons—aiding others, gaining knowledge, advancing the cause of your deity, or (if you are not good) hardening your soul and accruing power for the day when you leave your fleshly existence behind. Monetary gain for its own sake interests you little, but the growth you experience in taking on any challenging experience—such as recovering an ancient treasure—means

Sorra the blessed

that you do not necessarily spurn your companions' quests for material gain.

When circumstances permit, contemplate decisions carefully. You are not given to hasty action or impetuousness. Even in combat, you remain calm and deliberate. Speak slowly and thoughtfully; avoid undue excitement. When you encourage your friends, remind them that very little in the world around them has the power to do them true and lasting injury.

"Courage, friends; all this has happened before, and will happen again."

"Pain is illusory! It exists only in the mind."

"True strength lies within."

"Death is a doorway, nothing more. Fear it not."

Prophet: The hand of a deity is upon you, and you are not always in control of your words or actions. From time to time you give yourself over completely to the will of your deity, and say or do things that you had no intention of saying or doing. Driven by impulses you cannot control or understand, you might be capable of astonishing acts of courage or awful treachery—it all depends on the whim of your deity.

When you play a prophetic character, you do not surrender control of your character to the Dungeon Master. However, you should ask your DM to look for the occasional opportunity to communicate unusual information through your character's words or actions. When confronting an evil lord, your comrades might be inclined to guard their words and avoid a fight in the middle of his castle—but the prophet might suddenly blaze forth with a ringing condemnation of the lord's secret wickedness, possibly enumerating crimes you and the other players had no direct knowledge of beforehand.

Even if your Dungeon Master does not provide you with *ex cathedra* material for the game session, you should listen to your intuition. Don't watch your words and don't rethink impetuous actions. Take these impulses as signs that your character is caught in the grip of her deity, and let the chips fall where they may.

Work with your Dungeon Master to create a few interesting prophecies for the campaign. The best prophecies are ones that can come true in unexpected ways.

"The third moon draws nigh; beware!"

"One of you will fall tonight."

"We shall triumph, and yet we shall fail."

"I cannot see all that follows from the deeds of this day."

Scourge of Unbelievers: You are your deity's chosen instrument of vengeance, punishment, and righteous wrath.

It falls to you to defend the innocent and harry the iniquitous. You are driven, never able to rest as long as your deity's enemies remain at large. Since you have an inclusive view of who might be considered an enemy of your deity, that means you rarely rest at all.

Examine your deity's alignment, description, and dogma or credo and create a list of the creatures or people you need to smite first. Anybody not on that list is irrelevant ... unless, of course, they can be recruited as allies in your ongoing crusade. When your adventures pit you against foes that your deity has no special distaste for, you chafe for the opportunity to finish up and return to what's truly important: bringing the wrath of your deity down upon his or her enemies.

You are frequently inspired to scream or snarl imprecations, letting your foes know exactly who you are and exactly why you are punishing them.

"*Pelor's light will sear you, spawn of darkness!*"

"*Pelor commands your destruction, infidel!*"

"*Naught shall avail you against the might of Pelor, demon! I will hurl you screaming back into the Abyss!*"

DEITY'S FAVOR

The favored soul enjoys the flexibility of spontaneous spellcasting, but her limited spell selection can hinder her ability to provide the healing expected from a divine caster. Choosing the deity's favor class feature means you'll be a bit less potent in combat, but lets you use the spells you're already casting to help you and your allies last longer in a fight. Favored souls who choose this option should expect a lot of requests for support spells such as *bless*, *bull's strength*, and *prayer*, but remember that your *cure* spells gain this benefit as well.

Level: 3rd.

Replaces: If you select this class feature, you do not gain the deity's weapon focus or deity's weapon specialization class features (you still gain proficiency with your deity's favored weapon).

Benefit: Beginning at 3rd level, whenever you cast a favored soul spell, you can choose any one ally affected by that spell (including yourself) to gain temporary hit points equal to three times the spell's level. These temporary hit points last for up to 1 minute per level of the spell. If the spell would also grant temporary hit points, use only the larger value and its duration.

If you use this ability on a creature that is still under the effect of a previous use, the new temporary hit points overlap (do not stack with) the temporary hit points the creature had remaining.

Beginning at 12th level, you can choose to grant these temporary hit points to any number of allies affected by the spell.

STARTING PACKAGES

Package 1: The Defender

Dwarf Favored Soul of Moradin

    Ability Scores: Str 13, Dex 10, Con 14, Int 8, Wis 15, Cha 12.

    Skills: Concentration.

    Feat: Shield Specialization* (heavy).

    Weapon: Warhammer (1d8/×3), five javelins (1d6, 30 ft.).

    Armor: Scale mail (+4 AC), heavy wooden shield (+2 AC).

    Other Gear: Spell component pouch, standard adventurer's kit, 31 gp.

Package 2: The Healer

Halfling Favored Soul of Yondalla

    Ability Scores: Str 12, Dex 12, Con 12, Int 8, Wis 15, Cha 13.

    Skills: Heal.

    Feat: Spontaneous Healer (*Complete Divine*).

    Weapons: Short sword (1d4/19–20), five javelins (1d4, 30 ft.).

    Armor: Scale mail (+4 AC), heavy wooden shield (+2 AC).

    Other Gear: Spell component pouch, standard adventurer's kit, 33 gp.

Package 3: The Vanguard

Human Favored Soul of Kord

    Ability Scores: Str 14, Dex 10, Con 12, Int 8, Wis 15, Cha 13.

    Skills: Concentration, Diplomacy.

    Feats: Combat Casting, Combat Focus*.

    Weapons: Greatsword (1d12/19–20), five javelins (1d6, 30 ft.).

    Armor: Scale mail (+4 AC).

    Other Gear: Spell component pouch, standard adventurer's kit.

MAKING A PROPHECY

What's the point of being a prophet if you never get anything right? The trick in creating a prophecy is to bury it in symbols or metaphors that, after the fact, become perfectly obvious. The more specific you are, the more likely it is that you will get something wrong.

Don't use names, use titles. Instead of saying, "King Derath of Veronia," say something like, "Veronia's lord"—or better yet, "the Lion of Veronia," or even "the Lion of the East."

Don't use dates that occur once; use times of year, seasons, or celestial events. So, instead of saying "March 15th of the year 635," say something like "beneath the third moon," or "when winter's grip weakens in the fifth year."

Use metaphors instead of clear statements. Don't say "dies," or "is killed;" say "falls into darkness," "stands before his fathers," or "goes into the night."

Add a random, unconnected remark, such as "The traitor sees it all," or "Now the door stands open to the night."

Here's an example:

When rises the red moon above the North,
The Lion of Veronia ceases his roar.
Three times three are the slain.
Rose petals fall from the elf maiden's hands.

These images could mean almost anything. The red moon might be a specific season or celestial phenomena, or a metaphor for "war." The Lion of Veronia might be its king or a Veronian-born hero. The rose petals could be flowers strewn on a grave, or perhaps drops of blood—so was the elf maiden grieving for the slain, or was she actually their murderer? It worked for Nostradamus; you can make it work for you.

FIGHTER

You are an adventuring opportunist, willing to go wherever the next fight leads you. You'll take up quests, you'll accept commissions, and you'll even consider taking on leadership roles, as long as you can practice your warrior's craft. You know fighting—none know it better. Other combatants with exotic martial styles or those who mix spells with swords obscure what is most important—who's the best? Who can put their sword in an enemy's guts first? You, that's who. You are a straight-up, no-nonsense person, and you know the value of your hard-won, long practiced skills. While you take great risks in hopes of receiving an equally big payout, for you the thrill of combat is at least as compelling as the loot at adventure's end.

The alternative class features presented here provide alternatives to the traditional full attack routine. The fighter who takes one or more of these options seeks the flexibility to alter his tactics based on the situation he faces. Against a foe that has a high AC or damage reduction, trading less useful second, third, or fourth attacks for tangible benefits represents a significant boon to the fighter.

Suggested Backgrounds (choose one): Gladiator, Guttersnipe, Noble Scion, Soldier.

Suggested Personality Archetypes (choose one): Challenger, Companion, Leader, Martyr, Mercenary, Orphan, Rebel, Renegade, Royalty, Seeker, Simple Soul, Strategist, Theorist.

CHARACTER THEMES

One or more of the following character themes could apply to you.

Comrade in Arms: In a fight, your best weapons are your friends. Your skill in arms can get you only so far, but without a friend to screen attacks while you drink down a potion of curing and an ally with whom you can flank a monster, your ability to win in the face of any odds would be greatly diminished. Though you're not ordinarily a sentimental person, the bonds of warfare link you with your companions, and you consider them brothers and sisters to a significant degree. You regularly put yourself in harm's way for their sake, and you like to believe they'd do the same for you.

"We can take them if we work as a team!"

"I'll charge straight in--you take the left flank, and you the right. And how about some archery to distract them?"

FIGHTER BATTLECRIES

Differentiating between friend and foe is a vital part of any fight. In the heat of the battle visual recognition of friend and foe can be difficult; a predefined shouted cry or motto can promote recognition, as well as unnerve your foes.

Clear the way!	Warriors, forward!
To arms!	All together!
To battle!	Blades and blood!
To the end!	[[Home city name]]!
To me!	[[mercenary company name]]!

Formally Trained: Unlike many fighters, you have a special pedigree—your skill in the craft comes from formal training in an academy. Your academy training imparted to you all the right-of-way rules in regard to attacks and defenses, should you ever be called upon to fight in a noble tournament, as opposed to the desperate battles below the ground in which you usually find yourself embroiled.

You know all the proper terms for swordsmanship, and know that all blades fall into four major categories: foils, epees, sabers, and longswords (which are either one- or two-handed affairs). Your knowledge of all the specializations and names of the thousands of blade types is nearly encyclopedic, especially with regard to the more obscure types of blades utilized by swordsmen of distant countries. While this knowledge has little practical application, you do enjoy showing it off to your companions.

"The difference between the bokuto, a wooden training sword, and the suburito is actually very small—the suburito is slightly heaver."

"The dao is like a saber—but the dao lacks a hand guard, which somewhat limits your options in a fight."

"If it's a sword, it has a tip, a blade, a fuller, and a hilt made up of the guard, grip, and pommel."

"A fuller? A fuller is a rounded groove on the flat side of a blade. Although sometimes called 'blood grooves,' their purpose is really to lighten the blade."

"Kukri is actually pronounced khu-khoo-ree."

Practice Makes Perfect: For you, daily exercise is more than something to get your blood running—you see it as a requirement of your craft. With first light, you're up doing pushups, stomach crunches, running in place, and then the all-important swordplay, whether with a comrade or practicing forms on your own. Afterward, you spend time oiling your equipment against rust and sun, and of course give your blade a little time with the whetstone. You certainly won't go more than a week without your practice, and you prefer a daily regimen.

Self-Taught: Your academy was the street, and your craft is unpolished but well tested. You don't know and don't care for all the "jargon" a few who claim to be warriors spout. You know swords, you know bows—you know how to use them, who cares what they're called? The information doesn't help you in a fight, and it might get you killed if you worry too much about the cutting edge versus the thrusting tip and the rest of that sort of nonsense.

"I know swords--that's all I need."

"I knew a fellow who liked to talk fancy, just like you. He's dead now."

ELUSIVE ATTACK

You know that the key to winning any fight is not getting hit, so you trade offensive power for a steadier defense.

Level: 6th.

Replaces: If you select this class feature, you do not gain the fighter bonus feat at 6th level.

Benefit: At 6th level, you master a technique of combining offense and defense. As a full-round action, make one attack at your highest base attack bonus. Until the start of your next

Tordek Brighthammer, Warchief of the Iron Halls

turn, you gain a +2 dodge bonus to AC. This bonus improves to +4 at 11th level and to +6 at 16th level.

COUNTERATTACK

Every offensive move creates an opening for a counterattack, and you know how to exploit this facet of combat to its fullest.

Level: 12th.

Replaces: If you select this class feature, you do not gain the fighter bonus feat at 12th level.

Benefit: At 12th level, you learn to hold back some of your offensive prowess to enable a potent counterattack. As a full-round action, make one melee attack at your highest base attack bonus. At any time before the start of your next turn, you can use an immediate action to make a melee attack (using your highest base attack bonus) against an enemy that attacks you in melee.

OVERPOWERING ATTACK

You never waste time wounding your opponent, instead concentrating on delivering one solid strike.

Level: 16th.

Replaces: If you select this class feature, you do not gain the fighter bonus feat at 16th level.

Benefit: At 16th level, you can focus your attention in combat to deliver a single deadly attack. As a full-round action, make one attack at your highest base attack bonus. That attack deals double damage, as do any other attacks you make before the start of your next turn.

STARTING PACKAGES

Package 1: The Archer
Elf Fighter

 Ability Scores: Str 15, Dex 15, Con 12, Int 10, Wis 12, Cha 8.

 Skills: Jump, Spot (cc).

 Feats: Point Blank Shot, Precise Shot.

 Weapons: Spear (1d8/×3), dagger (1d4/19–20, 10 ft.) longbow with 40 arrows (1d8/×3, 100 ft.).

 Armor: Chain shirt (+4 AC).

 Other Gear: Standard adventurer's kit, 4 gp.

Package 2: The Defender
Dwarf Fighter

 Ability Scores: Str 15, Dex 13, Con 16, Int 10, Wis 12, Cha 6.

 Skills: Craft (weaponsmithing), Intimidate.

 Feats: Iron Will, Weapon Focus (dwarven waraxe).

 Weapon: Dwarven waraxe (1d10/×3), shortbow with 20 arrows (1d6/×3, 60 ft.).

 Armor: Scale mail (+4 AC), heavy steel shield (+2 AC).

 Other Gear: Standard adventurer's kit, 4 gp.

Package 3: The Destroyer
Human Fighter

 Ability Scores: Str 15, Dex 13, Con 14, Int 10, Wis 12, Cha 8.

 Skills: Climb, Intimidate, Jump.

 Feats: Cleave, Power Attack, Weapon Focus (greatsword).

 Weapons: Greatsword (2d6/19–20), shortbow with 20 arrows (1d6/×3, 60 ft.).

 Armor: Scale mail (+4 AC).

 Other Gear: Standard adventurer's kit, 4 gp.

Illus. by S. Ellis

SCARS

Every scar has a story, and your body tells many tales.

Jagged Scar Running from Eye to Jaw: "A guy at the Rolling Rock Alehouse got in a lucky shot with a broken whisky bottle."

Raking Scars Down Arm and Chest: "Yeah, turns out this girl I was seeing was actually a werewolf."

Huge Halfmoon Scar on Forearm: "Damn shark man got a bite out of me."

Ragged Circle Scar on Stomach: "See this? A salamander stuck me with a flaming spear. You haven't felt pain until you've had a yard of burning metal shoved into your guts."

Serrated Scar on Brow: "The lich said 'run' and I ran—right into its sarcophagus. Knocked me silly, but the pain washed away the fear."

Half-healed Scar on Palm: "When I grabbed that demon, it burned my hand with hellish cold fire. The damn thing still hasn't healed! Sometimes, when I wake from a nightmare I can't remember, the wound is oozing a strange, green fluid. . . ."

Mystery Scar: "It's something I want to forget and that you don't want to know about."

HEXBLADE

Nothing fazes you. Like the warlock, you are a son of darkness, gifted with powers that others find unnerving (at best) or outright evil (the usual case). Your adventures carry you far and wide, because you rarely find it easy to stay in the same place for long. Sooner or later the whispers and guarded glances begin again, and it is time to move on. No one understands your powers, and most people you meet wonder exactly how you're going to stab them in the back when you finally show your true colors. Hexblades have a bad reputation in many quarters, but whether you're the exception or the rule is up to you.

This class appears in the *Complete Warrior* supplement.

Suggested Backgrounds (choose one): Artisan, Drifter, Guttersnipe, Soldier.

Suggested Personality Archetypes (choose one): Daredevil, Mercenary, Orphan, Rebel, Renegade, Wanderer.

CHARACTER THEMES

One or more of the following character themes could apply to you.

Darkhunter: Sometimes evil is the best weapon to wield against evil. You are a grim and dark avenger, using your baleful abilities to hunt down and slay villains and monsters more evil than yourself. Even if your methods and motivations are not particularly pure, who can question your results?

As a sworn enemy of evil, you do not hesitate before taking on a quest to destroy or drive off even the most horrible monster. You commit to the hunt with little expectation of reward. But once you've chosen an enemy to defeat, you'll stop at nothing to come out on top. Bargain away your orc captives to the mind flayers to gain passage through their territory to the place where your true adversary lairs? No problem. Sanitize an outbreak of lycanthropy by killing all the bitten villagers? It's hard, but necessary. You rarely indulge in cruelty or excess, but you can be a remorseless foe indeed.

You are absolutely convinced that you are the only person who really knows what's going on in most situations. Cut off people who talk too much, before they waste more of your time. Don't bother to tell people what you are going to do, and never explain your actions afterward. Your companions don't have the stomach for the work at hand, so it would be better if they didn't get in your way or question your methods. You can always find new allies.

Darkhunters are silent, nameless figures who do not deign to speak to their foes—or their allies, for that matter. When they do, they tend to be terse, grim, and blunt.

"Enough talk. Now it's time to die."

"Go home, bar your door, and ignore anything you hear outside from sundown to sunup. You may live to see the dawn."

"Do not follow me. I will kill anyone who does."

"I've seen worse."

Sellsword: You are a sword for hire—nothing more, nothing less. You judge the worthiness of a cause by the amount of money it can put in your pocket. While you always look out for number one, you do recognize the value of loyalty to your comrades—you don't have many friends in this world, so it's smart to stay on the good side of the few you have.

Since your powers are poorly understood, you go to some lengths to hide them from people you don't know. Let them think you're simply a fighter, or perhaps a fighter-sorcerer. Witch-hunts, sinister rumors, and ugly accusations are all bad for business.

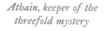

Athain, keeper of the threefold mystery

DOESN'T PLAY WELL WITH OTHERS

Sometimes, the most interesting characters are those with the worst attitude problems. They're just not team players. You can seriously annoy the other players at the game table by playing this role to the hilt, so be careful when you adopt a persona that is hard to get along with. A little bit of attitude goes a very long way. Instead of starting a fight when your friends are trying to roleplay a conversation with a NPC, you could simply adopt a sullen silence or utter dark, cryptic warnings. Rather than derail a well-worked out plan to defeat a particular monster by not doing your part, negotiate an assignment that doesn't tie you to the rest of the party, such as scouting, sneaking up behind the foe, or distracting another enemy nearby. In short, you should still be a team player, even if your character isn't.

Besides, it's useful to keep a few tricks up your sleeve; you never know when a surprise hex might be the only way to save your skin.

You rarely get worked up over the opposition, because to you, it's all business. Ogres rampaging through the province? You can fix that. Demons murdering the priests of Pelor? You'll adjust your rates and take your best shot at stopping them. You need a record for reliability and success if you're going to make any real money.

Others might view you as cold or heartless, but you know that it's wisest to avoid emotional entanglements. You can't stand it when people start acting against their self-interest in the name of a nebulous "cause," and you detest deal-breakers. When dealing with potential employers, look them right in the eye and state your terms.

"What's in it for me?"

"I'm not getting paid to do that."

"The dragon wasn't in the contract. If you want the dragon taken care of, you're going to have to up your offer."

"Nothing personal. It's just business."

"Sounds like you have a real problem. It's going to cost you."

Tormented Champion: Dark powers manipulate you. People you love get hurt, causes you support founder and collapse, and places you visit fall into ruin. You have been marked for a tortured and restless existence, and your fate is to be a harbinger of doom and woe.

You swing from morose depression to desperate acts of blazing anger. Most of the time, you struggle with despondency and gloom. Make dark pronouncements and dire predictions about things you observe, and point out flaws in your your allies' plans.

Sometimes you are moved to rail against your fate and lash out with blind, unreasoning anger at whatever obstacle or foe frustrates you. You might leap headlong into a throng of enemies, heedless of your safety. Or you might shake your fist at the gods and curse them bitterly.

"The vampire's been watching us the whole time. We're doing exactly what he wants."

"Some of us aren't getting out of this alive."

"You'll get halfway across, the rope will break, and you'll fall into the river there and be swept away into some black, airless cavern where you'll die trying to claw your way through cold, hard stone."

"Is that all you've got?"

DARK COMPANION

By mixing arcane spells with martial talents, the hexblade blurs the traditional line between fighter and sorcerer. Replacing the familiar—a link to traditional forms of arcane magic—with a unique fighting companion helps establish the hexblade's difference from the sorcerer.

In combat, a dark companion functions like a floating hex that you can place upon your foes. By weakening the defenses of enemies, your dark companion makes your spells and attacks (and those of your allies) more powerful.

Level: 4th.

Replaces: If you select this class feature, you do not gain a familiar.

Benefit: At 4th level, you can create an illusory companion resembling a panther, spun from the darkness of the night. Doing so takes 24 hours and uses up magic materials that cost 100 gp. Once created, your dark companion stands with you in battle, hindering your enemies' defenses.

Any enemy adjacent to your dark companion takes a –2 penalty on its saves and to its AC. Your companion's speed is equal to yours (including all modes of movement you possess) and it acts during your turn each round. It follows your mental commands perfectly—in effect, it is merely an extension of your will.

Your dark companion has no real substance, and thus can't attack or otherwise affect creatures or objects. It occupies a 5-foot space. Even though any creature can enter a dark companion's 5-foot space without restriction, it must occupy its own space in order to have any effect on enemies. It is immune to any damage or other effects that might harm creatures, though it can be dispelled or suppressed just like a spell effect. Your dark companion is treated as a spell whose level is equal to 1/4 your hexblade level. If it is dispelled, it automatically reforms at your side 24 hours later.

A dark companion can't create flanking situations, nor does it provoke attacks of opportunity from movement, because enemies automatically recognize it as an illusion. If it is more than 120 feet from you at the start of your turn, or if you ever lose line of effect to it, it instantly reappears adjacent to you.

STARTING PACKAGES

Package 1: The Defender
Gnome Hexblade

    Ability Scores: Str 13, Dex 13, Con 14, Int 10, Wis 8, Cha 14.

    Skills: Bluff, Spellcraft.

    Feat: Armor Proficiency (medium).

    Weapons: Greatsword (1d8/19–20), short bow with 20 arrows (1d4/×3, 60 ft.).

    Armor: Scale mail (+4 AC).

    Other Gear: Standard adventurer's kit, 4 gp.

Package 2: The Destroyer
Human Hexblade

    Ability Scores: Str 15, Dex 13, Con 12, Int 10, Wis 8, Cha 14.

    Skills: Concentration, Intimidate, Spellcraft.

    Feat: Power Attack, Cleave.

    Weapons: Greataxe (1d12/×3), five javelins (1d6, 30 ft.).

    Armor: Chain shirt (+4 AC).

    Other Gear: Standard adventurer's kit, 10 gp.

Package 3: The Skirmisher
Elf Hexblade

    Ability Scores: Str 15, Dex 15, Con 10, Int 10, Wis 8, Cha 14.

    Skills: Diplomacy, Knowledge (arcana).

    Feat: Dodge.

    Weapons: Glaive (1d10/×3), warhammer (1d8/×3), longbow with 20 arrows (1d8/×3, 100 ft.).

    Armor: Studded leather (+3 AC).

    Other Gear: Standard adventurer's kit, 14 gp.

MARSHAL

War is your true calling. You follow the shrill ring of steel on steel and the harsh cries of the carrion birds, for it is on the battlefield that you demonstrate your true worth. When the specter of war is far away, you take service with a strong lord, state, or cause, training other warriors and preparing your warband for the day when battle finally comes to the land in which you reside. Or, if that does not suit you, you search out combat wherever it awaits—perhaps you skirmish against orc raiders threatening the kingdom's frontier, fight for a rebellious duke who is trying to throw off the king's rule in his lands, or travel abroad to far and exotic lands in search of a battle worthy of your talents. When you take up the haphazard career of an adventurer, you're only passing the time until something big comes along.

This class appears in the *Miniatures Handbook* supplement.

Suggested Backgrounds (choose one): Artisan, Mariner, Noble Scion, Soldier.

Suggested Personality Archetypes (choose one): Challenger, Crusader, Leader, Mercenary, Royalty, Strategist, Theorist.

CHARACTER THEMES

One or both of the following character themes could apply to you.

Black Knight: You are a hero of the first rank, a bold and inspiring leader of men—but you do not want to be recognized. Knights entering the lists sometimes cover their heraldic devices with sable cloths to keep their identities a secret; you likewise do not display the emblems you have won, and adopt a simple nom de guerre so that no one will know who you are.

Decide why you desire anonymity. You could be a noble of high birth, expected to spend your days engaged in statecraft instead of roaming the land as a nameless adventurer. You adopt your guise so that you will be free to aid people with the point of your sword instead of wasting time with the intrigues of the court. You might have a fearsome enemy that you cannot defeat, and so you remain hidden so that the people around you will not become the victims of your adversary. Or perhaps you are actually infamous, known for a terrible defeat on a distant battlefield. You carry the guilt of hundreds of lost lives, even though you might not have ever had any chance to triumph.

If your DM agrees, you are a member of the nobility. Design your house's heraldic insignia and motto, so that you can describe what you reveal when you finally choose to unmask your shield.

Since you are trying to remain mostly anonymous, you don't view it as your role to be the bold and inspiring leader of your party. Instead, you are satisfied to be a stalwart comrade and loyal follower, using your abilities to help your friends defeat their foes. You do your best to avoid the spotlight and give credit to your allies for your successes.

"I may have struck the last blow, but the troll was dead on its feet by then. Mialee's fireball made all the difference."

"Valor is its own reward."

"I was there, certainly, and I suppose I played a small part. But my companions deserve the credit for defeating the dragon."

"Give my share to the temple of St. Cuthbert."

"Who I am is not important. What is important is that the werewolf has been slain. Your town should be safe now."

Leader of the Company: A marshal combines personal charisma, leadership, and tactical acumen like no other character. You are a born leader, the equal of a paladin. Everyone expects flowery speech from the bard or persuasive words from the sorcerer, but the marshal and the paladin are heroes

TAKING CHARGE AT THE TABLE

If your character is the "leader" of the adventuring party, you've got a hard but rewarding bit of roleplaying ahead of you. Most people at the gaming table don't want to be bossed around; we all get enough of that in our real lives, after all. Even if you think your character would be a hard-nosed drill sergeant who barks orders at everyone around him, you'd better not try that at the table.

So how do you lead in the game without stepping on everyone else's ability to make choices? You need to be a democratic leader, not an autocratic one. To that end, try these techniques.

Ask for ideas: Solicit suggestions from the other players, even if it's something as simple as "Anybody got half an idea of what this monster can do?" Recognize other characters' areas of expertise and ask for their help. For example, if the party is facing a magical phenomenon, make a point of asking the player running the arcane spellcaster what he thinks the party should do.

Be the chooser of plans: Make a point of trying other players' suggestions instead of issuing your orders without their input. Don't go with the same player's idea each and every time—everybody at the table should have an opportunity to see their ideas tested by the party. It's okay to choose your own plan, but make that the exception, not the rule.

Encourage initiative: Look for ways to put decision-making in the hands of your comrades. For example, if you want the rogue to scout ahead, don't provide exacting instructions for how far ahead you'd like her to be or what she should do if she gets in trouble. If the party needs information about the location of a villain's lair, look over to the bard and say, "Devis, you're in charge of finding out where Talthon is hiding. We'll follow your lead."

Be generous with praise: Cheer the successes of other players in character. Your leader should shout out a "Well done!" or "Huzzah!" or "By the gods, you fight like a lion today!" when other characters do well.

Avoid criticizing others: Here's a place where game leadership takes a sharp turn from real-world leadership. In real life, a leader needs to let his or her subordinates know if they're falling short of the mark—preferably without humiliating them in public, but that depends on the setting. It's not your job to make the other people at the table better D&D players or more thoughtful followers, and they'll resent it if you try. As a "leader" in the game, you have to be exceedingly careful about criticizing other players. Nobody wants to come to a game to be chewed out or cut down by a sarcastic remark. An absence of praise speaks volumes, if you've been generous with your encouragement previously.

that warriors want to follow. You possess sincerity, purpose, and valor, and your potent auras allow you to manifest these virtues for your allies.

Not only are you a skilled diplomat, but you are the absolute best choice for the job of battle commander. Since you can easily change the benefit your aura provides, it behooves your allies to follow your lead. They'll do better in the fight if they take actions that make use of your aura. For example, if you choose the minor auras *over the top* or *master of opportunity*, you provide a real incentive for your friends to charge or move past enemies to reach the foe you want them to fight. When you use your auras this way, say something inspirational!

You should strongly consider the Leadership feat if you are roleplaying a marshal of this type. If the other players at the table don't listen to you, at least your cohort or followers will.

"Ignore the lizardfolk! The druid is our true foe!"

"Surround the gray render and strike from the flank! That is the quickest path to victory!"

"Stand your ground here, and let the orcs come to us! We'll cut them down as they climb the rampart!"

"Follow me! Now is the time to strike!"

ADRENALINE BOOST

As a marshal, you make everyone on your team more effective at what they do. While the traditional marshal accomplishes some of that by improving his allies' mobility, by choosing adrenaline boost you instead to take on some of the cleric's ability to bolster the health of your allies. It's particularly effective in rallying injured comrades, making it a good ability to save until things start looking grim.

Level: 4th.

Replaces: If you select this class feature, you do not gain the grant move action class feature.

Benefit: Starting at 4th level, you can exhort your allies to discover a reservoir of energy they didn't think they had. Once per day, as a standard action, you can grant temporary hit points equal to your marshal level to any or all of your allies within 30 feet (but not to yourself). If the ally's current hit point total is no more than half his full normal hit points, the number of temporary hit points granted to that character is doubled (to twice your marshal level).

This ability only affects allies with an Intelligence score of 3 or higher who can hear you and understand your language. The temporary hit points last for up to 1 minute per marshal level.

At 8th level, you can use this ability twice per day. You can use it three times per day at 12th level, four times per day at 16th level, and five times per day at 20th level.

If you use this ability on a creature that is still under the effect of a previous use, the new temporary hit points overlap (do not stack with) the temporary hit points the creature had remaining.

STARTING PACKAGES

Package 1: The Defender
Dwarf Marshal

Ability Scores: Str 14, Dex 13, Con 14, Int 8, Wis 10, Cha 13.

Skills: Intimidate, Listen, Spot.

Feat: Shield Specialization (heavy).

Weapons: Dwarven waraxe (1d10/×3), warhammer (1d8/×3), 5 javelins (1d6, 30 ft.)

Armor: Scale mail (+4 AC), heavy wooden shield (+2 AC).

Other Gear: Standard adventurer's kit, 6 gp.

Aura: Force of Will.

Package 2: The Second-Rank Warrior
Elf Marshal

Ability Scores: Str 14, Dex 15, Con 10, Int 10, Wis 8, Cha 15.

Skills: Diplomacy, Listen, Sense Motive, Spot.

Feat: Combat Reflexes.

Weapons: Glaive (1d10/×3), shortbow with 20 arrows (1d8/×3, 100 ft.).

Armor: Scale mail (+4 AC).

Other Gear: Standard adventurer's kit, 26 gp.

Aura: Master of Tactics.

Package 3: The Vanguard
Human Marshal

Ability Scores: Str 14, Dex 13, Con 12, Int 10, Wis 8, Cha 15.

Skills: Diplomacy, Intimidate, Knowledge (nobility and royalty), Sense Motive, Spot.

Feats: Battlefield Inspiration (*Miniatures Handbook*), Improved Initiative.

Weapons: Longsword (1d8/19–20), five javelins (1d6, 30 ft.).

Armor: Scale mail (+4 AC), heavy steel shield (+2 AC).

Other Gear: Standard adventurer's kit, 20 gp.

Aura: Motivate Dexterity.

Illus. by H. Lyon

Korrin, Protector of the Crown

MONK

You were introduced to martial techniques in a distant, hard-to-reach monastery. You first learned the eighteen basic empty-hand techniques. You learned the "heart-mind-fist" kata, you learned how to swing an eyebrow-height staff, and you finally learned how to deliver the potent cannon punch.

After that, you were ready to begin actual training in the truly deadly martial arts.

Years later you emerged, a champion of your martial style, but still a student seeking continual improvement and perfection through martial discipline. One day you hope to join the great masters of your art, focusing your *ki* so precisely that you transcend the mortal realm altogether and partake of immortality.

Suggested Backgrounds (choose one): Artisan, Ascetic, Gladiator.

Suggested Personality Archetypes (choose one): Agent, Challenger, Companion, Crusader, Innocent, Martyr, Orphan, Prophet, Seeker, Wanderer.

*Ember, Mistress of the
Four Winds*

CHARACTER THEMES

One or more of the following character themes could apply to you.

Enlightened One: You follow a meditative way of life considered by some a religion, by others a profound philosophy, and by the uninformed simply a routine. You regard your constant search for enlightenment as a way of life, work, and an art form.

One of the precepts of your philosophy is "sitting meditation" in which you sit quietly once a day, directing your awareness toward your core and breathing deeply for at least 5 minutes.

As an "enlightened one," you know many parables, called *koans*, that teach wisdom if considered long enough.

"An enlightened one lived a simple life in a hut at the foot of a mountain. One evening a thief visited the hut only to discover there was nothing to steal. The enlightened one caught him and told the rogue, 'You've traveled far to find me, so you should not leave empty-handed. Here, have my robe as a gift.' Confused, the thief nevertheless took the robe. Nude, his eyes on the full moon, the enlightened one said, 'I wish I could have given him this beautiful moon.'"

"An enlightened one visited a terminally ill man and asked, "Shall I lead you on?' The sick man replied, 'I came here alone and I go alone. What help could you be?' The enlightened one answered, 'If you think you really come and go, that is your delusion. Let me show you the path on which there is no coming and no going.' These words revealed the true path so clearly that the sick man smiled and passed on."

History Keeper: Every monastery has its own story of origin, describing where it gained its particular style and what ancient master popularized the particular specialized form of martial arts taught there. Every monastery puts in a claim as the oldest, or alleges to teach the most "pure" form of the martial arts.

You don't fret about it because you know your monastery is actually the oldest and the most authentic. You like to tell the story of how your monastery learned the secrets of its current style.

"The ancient and legendary master Chandharma founded our temple five hundred years ago, and the monks took him in. In thanks, Chandharma trained the monks in the original, true forms and katas. I know the very style that ancient Chandharma once taught my forebears."

"Northern" Stylist: Your monastery taught a particular style of martial arts referred to as the northern style. This style features long steps, extended postures and wide stances, jumping, kicking, and dramatic acrobatic flourishes. The northern style is known for a great variety of attack forms. When you use any one of these forms, you call out the attack name in a strong, confident voice, which steadies you and frightens your enemies with your poise.

"Long Fist!" You use this punch attack to spear past your foe's guard when least expected.

"Tumbling Fist!" A tumbling fist is the strike you make after you've tumbled into the perfect position to strike at your foe.

"Quivering Palm!" This famous strike needs no explanation. Even if you're not powerful enough to use the discipline, the name alone inspires fear in your enemies.

"Red Fist!" Whenever you draw first blood, you like to scream this out, just to unnerve your foe.

"Flood Fist!" When you use a flurry of blows, you are using the famous flood fist, where you seek to overwhelm your foe's defenses under a flood of staggering blows.

"Flower Fist!" This disingenuous, fast and deceptive blow is made whenever you foe is off guard, whether he is surprised, flanked, or otherwise not effectively defending himself.

"Southeastern" Stylist: Your monastery taught a particular style of martial art referred to as the southeastern style. This style features fists, elbows, shins, feet, and knees to strike at opponents, as well as briefly held grapples that set an opponent up for a particularly egregious elbow or knee attack. Unlike other martial styles, the southeastern style is specifically designed to incorporate fitness and toughness, which allows a southeastern style fighter the endurance to accept pain and ignore fatigue in a fight. When you use a southeastern style attack form, you call out the attack name in a strong, confident voice, which steadies you and frightens your enemies with your poise.

"*Kao Dode!*" As part of an attack, you jump and bring your knee up into your opponent's stomach, side, or if low enough, your opponent's head.

"*Kao Loi!*" You spring up off one leg and switch in midair to strike with the knee of the other leg. This confusing strike is dramatic when successful.

"*Kao Tone!*" The simplest knee strike, you simply bring one knee up directly into your foe's stomach, side, or head (if low enough). Sometimes this is aided if you grab your foe by the head and jerk him forward at the same time.

"Southern" Stylist: Your monastery taught a particular style of martial art referred to as the southern style. This style features short steps and close fighting, with arms close to the chest, elbows held low and ready to offer protection against blows to the stomach or sides. Most important, the southern style is distinguished by five animals.

When you use any one of these styles, you call out the animal you are emulating in a strong, confident voice, which steadies you and frightens your enemies with your poise.

"*Tiger!*" You emulate the tiger to express qualities of fearlessness and aggression. The tiger attacks in a straight line. When you charge, you are emulating the tiger, the most aggressive of the five "southern" animals.

"*Crane!*" You emulate the crane to avoid your enemies' attacks, no matter how they come at you. When fighting defensively, you are emulating the crane.

"*Leopard!*" You emulate the leopard to maximize your agility. After all, pound for pound the leopard is one of the strongest animals, and also the fastest. When you tumble into position to attack your opponents, you are emulating the leopard.

"*Snake!*" You adopt the fluidity of snakes to better close with your opponents and hurt them from positions they are unready to defend against. When you grapple an opponent, you imitate the sinuous, fluid motion of the snake.

"*Dragon!*" You emulate the dragon for a broad array of needs. When you attack under the guise of the dragon, your attacks are strong and hard. When you make a stunning attack, you are emulating the dragon.

A signature attack is the three-finger claw ("*Dragon Claw!*")—the index, thumb and middle fingers make hard pinching attacks to your foe's muscles and tendons. When striking with the dragon claw, you have incredible stunning power because the blow originates in your stomach and hips, then flows up as you rotate forward into the blow, which culminates in the stunning claw.

Staffmaster: While you are adept at closed and open hand styles of martial arts, you are particularly skilled with the use of a long quarterstaff. Instead of the standard length quarterstaff, you prefer a 7- to 8-foot-long, flexible staff that you refer to as your "flowing water staff" or sometimes your "dragon pole."

Instead of attacking with either end, you usually grasp one end of the staff and use it to make devastating thrust attacks, diversionary "slap" attacks, and to deflect the blows of your foes, letting them slide off your staff like water.

DECISIVE STRIKE

Flurry of blows can be exciting to use—just look at all the attack rolls you can make—but in practice it can lead to a flurry of misses. The decisive strike alternative class feature turns your typical combat maneuver from a whirl of action into a methodical and devastating attack.

Level: 1st.

Replaces: If you select this class feature, you do not gain flurry of blows (or any later improvements to that class feature).

Benefit: As a full-round action, make one attack with an unarmed strike or a special monk weapon, using your highest base attack bonus but taking a –2 penalty on this attack roll. If the attack hits, it deals double damage (as does any other attack you make before the start of your next turn). If you use this strike to deliver a stunning attack, increase the save DC to resist the stun by 2. This is an extraordinary ability.

At 5th level, the penalty on the attack roll lessens to –1, and at 9th level it disappears.

At 11th level, you can make two attacks when using this class feature, though no more than one attack can target a single creature. Both attacks use your highest base attack bonus.

STARTING PACKAGES

Package 1: The Defender

Human Monk

Ability Scores: Str 13, Dex 15, Con 12, Int 10, Wis 14, Cha 8.

Skills: Balance, Listen, Sense Motive, Spot, Tumble.

Feats: Combat Focus*, Dodge, Stunning Fist.

Weapon: Unarmed strike (1d6), sling with 10 bullets (1d4, 50 ft.).

Armor: None.

Other Gear: Standard adventurer's kit (without sunrods), 1 gp, 3 sp.

Package 2: The Destroyer

Half-Orc Monk

Ability Scores: Str 15, Dex 15, Con 12, Int 8, Wis 14, Cha 6.

Skills: Climb, Jump, Tumble.

Feat: Improved Grapple, Improved Natural Attack, Weapon Focus (unarmed strike).

Weapon: Unarmed strike (1d8), sling with 10 bullets (1d4, 50 ft.).

Armor: None.

Other Gear: Standard adventurer's kit (without sunrods), 1 gp, 3 sp.

Package 3: The Skirmisher

Elf Monk

Ability Scores: Str 13, Dex 17, Con 10, Int 10, Wis 14, Cha 8.

Skills: Hide, Listen, Move Silently, Tumble.

Feat: Ability Focus (stunning fist), Stunning Fist.

Weapon: Unarmed strike (1d6), sling with 10 bullets (1d4, 50 ft.).

Armor: None.

Other Gear: Standard adventurer's kit (without sunrods), 1 gp, 3 sp.

PALADIN

You have power over evil, given you by your glorious, almighty deity. Your devotion and pure, unwavering desire provides strength that illuminates the darkest souls, saving some and punishing those that can't be redeemed. Your faith wards you from harm, inoculates you from fear, and gives you the hands of a healer—but your hands are equally dynamic on the hilt of an avenging sword pledged to divinity.

When wizards scheme, you pray. When dragons roar, you take up your sword, fearless. When devils from the Hells steal innocent souls, you respond with sacred vengeance and send them fleeing back to the pit whence they came.

Suggested Backgrounds (choose one): Ascetic, Noble Scion, Soldier.

Suggested Personality Archetypes (choose one): Agent, Companion, Crusader, Leader, Martyr, Prophet, Royalty, Strategist.

CHARACTER THEMES

One or more of the following character themes could apply to you.

Bound in Honor: You follow a strict code of honor. Whenever a situation arises that might touch upon your code, you voice the particular precept of your code, as if part of a prayer to your deity. In doing so, you hope that others will be inspired by your good example, and perhaps begin to follow parts of the code themselves.

Your code includes two or more of the following principles. You might enunciate additional principles not described here, depending on the deity or cause you serve.

"*Before all else, a paladin is faithful.*" The faith of a paladin requires no proof—it is a heartfelt knowledge that the goodness you do, or the evil you allow to flourish, is all that you take from this world to the next.

"*A paladin's valor is a measure of her faith.*" When things begin to go bad, your valor proves itself. When knocked low, you get up. You do not run from conflict if it can be won, and most especially, you never leave compatriots to a fight that is yours to win. Fear is something that only less valorous men and women experience.

"*Humility in all things.*" You are modest regarding your own importance and always submit to your deity's will. You know your place, but your place is important. You are not proud

or arrogant, though you challenge the unenlightened with your creed.

"*Patience outlasts all.*" You understand that it might take your entire life span to make a difference in the world—you don't hurry, you persevere. You have the god-supported tenacity not to quit your tasks, once taken up.

"*Loyalty to true friends, vengeance to betrayers and foes.*" You know that strength flows from solidarity, and solidarity only comes when all trust each other. Defeating the evils that plague the world is possible if all are loyal. Those who betray loyalty must be dealt with swiftly.

"*Benevolence is a balm to all souls.*" A paladin is charitable and desires to safeguard others from influences that would destroy their innocence or end their lives. Benevolence is no less a tool of your deity than your sword.

"*Integrity is the foundation on which all things of value are built.*" You adhere to the ethical and moral standards of your deity, acting in all ways as a beacon of truthfulness that others might emulate. Your character and sense of self relies upon your honesty. How can one be truthful "to a fault"?

"*Mercy for those that deserve mercy.*" Sometimes even the righteous can stray from the true path, and thus you must occasionally show compassion. However, mercy for unrepentant evildoers is tantamount to doing evil yourself.

"*Generosity is the left hand of [your deity].*" When you are willing to give of your wealth, or even more important, your time, you show the real strength and depth of your belief in your deity. Only someone truly comfortable with her faith has the spiritual reserve to be generous.

Chivalrous: You seek to be a paragon of the concepts of justice and morality in behavior between people. As such, you are brave in battle, loyal to your deity, and willing to sacrifice yourself for that belief (see Bound in Honor, above). Toward your fellows you are merciful, humble, and courteous.

Most important, you are gracious and gentle to those worthy of high regard, and you might even seek to court someone you admire. If that person is unavailable and married to someone else, especially if he or she is of higher status, your chivalry leads you into a type of "courtly love." You dedicate your life to the object of your affection, expressing your appreciation from afar through an intricate system of colors and ribbons worn on behalf of your beloved and favors done in his or her name. It's an elaborate dance,

Illus. by D. Hudnut

Alhandra, Commander of the Shining Crusade

a game that the players freely enjoy without expectation of commitment.

"For the Lady who has my heart, I dedicate this quest."

"Leave this to me--honor commands that the final blow be mine."

Merciless: Do any deserve mercy? No.

Leniency and compassion are words used to describe weak dealings toward those who have been judged and found wanting. This doesn't mean that you seek to kill all those who, in your judgment, are weak and faithless, but it does mean that such creatures do not deserve your respect.

"There is no mercy, there is only judgment."

Moral Philosopher: Moral conduct, morality, and the correctness of moral thought are paramount to you; however, you know that morals vary by culture. Is one moral code better than another? Is an ethical code better, or as your brothers and sisters in your order claim, are ethics a mortal-contrived sham that hides the true reach of morals? You don't know, but you wonder.

"An ethical code establishes tradeoffs toward the greater good, and weighs all the negative and positive results of an action, apart from moral absolutes. Thus, decisions are based upon the greatest good for the greatest number."

Reverent: You begin almost every utterance with a reference to your god.

"As the truth of [your deity] tells us . . ."

"If [your deity] allows . . . ."

"In the name of [your deity], the beneficent, the merciful . . ."

If you do not begin an utterance with a reference to your deity, you wrap up with one.

". . . as [your deity] commands."

". . . may [your deity] light and guard me."

". . . that all may know the wisdom and majesty of [your deity]."

Zealous: You are a fervent servant of your deity. You are diligent in your duties, show enthusiasm in performing them on your deity's behalf, and display a powerful interest in anything related to your deity, whether it's support or opposition.

You show your zeal to your friends and foes in one or more of the following ways.

Exultant: You are joyful and proud when you think of your deity, and are given to rejoicing and triumphal shouts. See the Paladin Battlecries sidebar.

Disciple: You know the history of your deity, and those saints and other people important to your deity. You know the trials and tribulations of your deity and/or your deity's saints, and you reenact those trials in a yearly ceremony. Moreover, you dress according to a strict interpretation of any doctrine your deity dispenses.

Missionary: You know with your gut that others would be happier if they worshiped your deity as you do. To this end you consistently (though not constantly—annoyance isn't a tool of conversion) exhort friends and strangers to convert.

Tattooed: You've shaved your head and proudly display a tattoo of your deity's holy symbol across your brow and naked head.

Tract Giver: You always carry with you several tracts that describe the glories of your deity, and pass these out (or leave them to be found) wherever you think they'll do the most good. (To this end, you have an arrangement with a printer, or

at least a letterist.) You are not a vocal missionary, preferring to work in more subtle ways.

"Consider the benefits that would be yours if you find grace with [your deity]—surety, confidence, and comradeship, at the very least!"

CHARGING SMITE

Despite the glorious vision of a shining knight atop a warhorse charging into combat, the reality in the D&D game is that it's far from easy (and sometimes impossible) to bring a big animal along on your dungeon crawl. To avoid the drain on time and resources created by a special mount you might not even be able to use, you can select the charging smite alternative class feature instead. You still leap into the fray, taking the fight to the enemy, but you do so in a manner that better matches the typical combat found in a D&D game.

Level: 5th.

Replaces: If you select this class feature, you do not gain a special mount.

Benefit: Beginning at 5th level, if you smite evil on a charge attack, you deal an extra 2 points of damage per paladin level to any evil creature you hit (in addition to the normal bonus damage dealt by a smite). If the charge attack misses, the smite ability is not considered used. This is a supernatural ability.

STARTING PACKAGES

Package 1: The Cavalier
Elf Paladin

Ability Scores: Str 13, Dex 12, Con 12, Int 8, Wis 12, Cha 15.

Skill: Ride.

Feat: Mounted Combat.

Weapons: Longsword (1d8/19–20), lance (1d8/×3), shortbow with 20 arrows (1d6/×3, 60 ft.).

Armor: Scale mail (+4 AC), heavy wooden shield.

Other Gear: Standard adventurer's kit, wooden holy symbol, 21 gp.

Package 2: The Destroyer
Dwarf Paladin

Ability Scores: Str 13, Dex 8, Con 16, Int 10, Wis 12, Cha 13.

Skills: Knowledge (nobility and royalty), Sense Motive.

Feat: Power Attack.

Weapons: Greataxe (1d12/×3), five javelins (1d6, 30 ft.).

Armor: Scale mail (+4 AC).

Other Gear: Standard adventurer's kit, wooden holy symbol, 34 gp.

Package 3: The Vanguard
Human Paladin

Ability Scores: Str 12, Dex 8, Con 14, Int 10, Wis 13, Cha 15.

Skills: Diplomacy, Heal, Sense Motive.

Feats: Improved Initiative, Shield Specialization (heavy).

Weapons: Longsword (1d8/19–20), two javelins (1d6, 30 ft.)

Armor: Chain shirt (+4 AC), heavy wooden shield (+2 AC).

Other Gear: Standard adventurer's kit, wooden holy symbol, 10 gp.

RANGER

You travel to places where few others dare to tread. Relying on a potent combination of stealth, woodcraft, magic, and fighting skill, you are the master of the wilderness. Where others see a trackless forest, you see an impenetrable refuge. Where others see a burning desert, you see a deadly trap for enemies you lure within. Where others see impassable mountains, you see high roads to new lands. You are the ultimate explorer, self-reliant and adaptable. No other adventurer comes close to your independence and sheer versatility.

Suggested Backgrounds (choose one): Drifter, Farm Hand, Mariner, Soldier, Tribal Origin.

Suggested Personality Archetypes (choose one): Agent, Explorer, Orphan, Rebel, Renegade, Savage, Seeker, Wanderer.

CHARACTER THEMES

One or more of the following character themes could apply to you.

Bounty Hunter: Unlike other rangers, you are equally at ease in the wilderness or in the cities and towns of humankind. You hone your woodcraft and tracking skills to use them against other people instead of forest-dwelling monsters. You might be a cold-hearted mercenary, an intrepid tracker, or even an outlaw or highwayman who uses woodcraft to get close to your quarry. For you, the lore of the wilderness is a tool that you employ for your particular ends.

Your choice of favored enemy makes you more effective at tracking (and defeating) particular quarries, so choose wisely. It's not unusual for a bounty hunter to choose his own race as a favored enemy—not because you're a misanthropic killer, but simply because you want to be especially good at following villains who happen to be of your race through the wilderness.

Keep a record of each quarry you stalk over the course of your career, and preferably a trophy or souvenir from each success. Show off your trophies and boast a little about your victories when you have the chance. You want word to get around about who you are and what you do, so that villains who find you on their trail will be more likely to panic, slip up, and make a fatal mistake.

"The price is 100 gold—no less, no more."

"Only one bounty has ever escaped me—so far. I keep a constant eye out, just in case."

Driven Avenger: When you were a child, your town was burned to the ground by orcs, or displacer beasts devoured your family, or a dragon hunted your tribe to extinction. Whatever the tragedy, you have been left with an endless thirst for vengeance against the monster or monsters that ruined your life.

The monsters responsible for your loss are at the top of your list of favored enemies. Your back-story prominently features a tragic loss at the hands, claws, talons, or fangs of these monsters. Create a suitable tale of woe and suffering, and write it down—you'll tell it over and over again to anyone who asks.

In any situation or challenge you confront, look for signs that your mortal enemies are somehow involved. For example, if drow enslaved your village, you should suspect drow involvement in almost any problem you encounter.

"The drow are behind this. You'll see."

"Only drow attack with such precision."

"I didn't like the way that innkeeper was watching us. I bet he's secretly in league with the drow, spying on us for them!"

"The only good drow is a dead drow."

Master of Beasts: You have allies everywhere you go. The birds and beasts are your friends, and even the fiercest creatures suffer your presence. While your animal companions do not help you in battle like the druid's help her, you value them for more than their fighting skill. Animals give you senses that you otherwise would not possess, allow you to keep watch over vast areas without being seen, and can carry messages over great distances.

Avoid fighting naturally occurring animals if possible. Instead of killing a cave-dwelling brown bear in your path, see if you can lure it away from its lair or merely frighten it off. Sometimes you have to resort to lethal methods to fight off dangerous animals, but there is no honor in such a battle; you should help your companions to avoid encounters of this sort instead of killing animals that are only acting as their nature dictates.

It's not unusual for a ranger of this sort to be uncomfortable around other people. Keep your thoughts to yourself, and don't use two words when one will do. People are cruel and deceitful, but you can always trust an animal to act in accordance with its nature. When you have to interact with humanoids, stay short and to the point, and speak bluntly. When you can, use animal metaphors to make your point.

"If you hope to catch Drethaas, you must run like the deer all day and through the night. Can you keep up with me?"

"The ogre is licking its wounds in its den. Now we can finish the monster."

"We have his scent now. He won't get away."

"I have the eyes of an eagle. No orc will pass by this place unseen."

Wayfinder: You live for the opportunity to tread new lands and see things no one has seen before. You measure yourself against the raw power of nature by crossing unfordable rivers, climbing impassable mountains, and mastering uncrossable deserts. The lure of treasure and the challenge of fearsome

DO ONE JOB, AND DO IT WELL

While rangers have a lot of skill points to spend, you will find that it's just not possible to maximize your skill ranks in all the things that rangers do. Depending on your particular character theme, you might need to prioritize your skill purchases as follows.

Bounty Hunter: Craft (trapmaking), Ride, Search, Survival, Use Rope. Survival is the most important of these for a tracker.

Cross-class skills such as Gather Information and Intimidate can be useful, too.

Driven Avenger: Hide, Listen, Move Silently, Spot.

Master of Beasts: Handle Animal, Knowledge (nature), Ride.

Wayfinder: Climb, Knowledge (geography), Survival, Swim, Use Rope.

foes serve only as excuses for you to head out on your next journey. Before you die, you want to see more of the world than anyone before you has seen.

You are restless and uneasy in times of idleness. You chafe at long delays, because when you're waiting for something to happen you're stuck in one spot. Urge your companions to push on another mile, venture into just one more room, or at least give you a chance to scout just over the next hill before stopping for the night. Keep a journal of your travels, noting the weather, the creatures you encountered, the places you visited, and the spot where you camped for each night.

Overland travel is your special area of expertise, so make sure you voice your opinion when the party debates the question of how to move from one place to another. If your friends are wise, they'll listen to you.

Because you are widely traveled and interested in a variety of things, you naturally relate new experiences to things you've seen or done before.

"This cave's a little bit like that second chamber in the Caverns of Creeping Shadows. You remember, the one with the weird green-glowing fungus-balls and the gricks? Do you think we might find gricks here too?"

"Let's find a safer place to cross. In my experience, this is just the sort of mountain stream that will batter you to pieces and carry you over a waterfall if you fall in. I don't want to have to go looking for your body."

"This desert's got nothing on the Anvil of Searing Pain. Now that was a desert."

"Careful! I'll bet you these orcs are headhunters, like those Blood Moon warriors we ran into a few months back. Look, they've got kukris just like those Blood Moon orcs."

DISTRACTING ATTACK

A ranger's animal companion isn't nearly as tough as a druid's, and thus works best as a scout or occasional flanker in combat. If your ranger would prefer to avoid the hassle of taking care of an animal companion, you can get some of the same benefit with the distracting attack alternative class feature. Though not as effective as an actual flanker, the ability to spread out your attacks to affect multiple enemies is a nice side effect.

Level: 4th.

Replaces: If you select this class feature, you do not gain an animal companion.

Benefit: Beginning at 4th level, whenever you hit an enemy with a weapon attack (whether melee or ranged), that enemy is considered flanked by you for the purpose of adjudicating your allies' attacks. For example, if your rogue ally attacked that enemy, not only would she gain a +2 bonus on her melee attack roll but she could also add her sneak attack damage to a successful melee attack.

This flanked condition lasts until either the enemy is attacked by one of your allies or until the start of your next turn, whichever comes first. This is an extraordinary ability.

This ability has no effect on creatures that can't be flanked.

Soveliss, Ranger of the Solstice Glade

Illus. by C. Frank

STARTING PACKAGES

Package 1: The Archer

Elf Ranger

　　Ability Scores: Str 12, Dex 17, Con 12, Int 10, Wis 13, Cha 8.

　　Skills: Climb, Hide, Listen, Move Silently, Spot, Survival.

　　Feat: Point Blank Shot, Track.

　　Weapons: Longsword (1d8/19–20), longbow with 20 arrows (1d8/×3, 100 ft.).

　　Armor: Studded leather (+3 AC).

　　Other Gear: Standard adventurer's kit, 19 gp.

Package 2: The Hunter

Half-Elf Ranger

　　Ability Scores: Str 12, Dex 15, Con 14, Int 10, Wis 13, Cha 8.

　Skills: Hide, Knowledge (nature), Listen, Move Silently, Spot, Survival.

　Feat: Alertness, Track.

　Weapons: Longsword (1d8/19–20), dagger (1d4/19–20, 10 ft.), longbow with 20 arrows (1d8/×3, 100 ft.).

　Armor: Studded leather (+3 AC).

　Other Gear: Standard adventurer's kit, 17 gp.

Package 3: The Skirmisher

Human Ranger

　Ability Scores: Str 12, Dex 15, Con 14, Int 10, Wis 13, Cha 8.

　Skills: Climb, Heal, Hide, Jump, Move Silently, Spot, Survival.

　Feats: Dodge, Mobility, Track.

　Weapon: Longsword (1d8/19–20), short sword (1d6/19–20), 3 javelins (1d6, 30 ft.)

　Armor: Chain shirt (+4 AC).

　Other Gear: Standard adventurer's kit, 5 gp.

ROGUE

The world owes you a living.

You are the ultimate opportunist, keeping your eyes open for the next big chance to come your way. Fortune favors the bold, and while you might not always fight with noteworthy valor, you certainly have the boldest of aspirations.

You are a trickster, a rapscallion, a scoundrel. You don't fight fair, and if you can help it, you don't fight at all. Stealth, guile, and daring are your weapons. Why fight when another act of daring—such as an impossible climb or a brazen bluff—might serve to help you pass an obstacle and deliver the prize into your hands?

Suggested Backgrounds (choose one): Artisan, Drifter, Guttersnipe, Mariner.

Suggested Personality Archetypes (choose one): Agent, Challenger, Daredevil, Explorer, Mercenary, Orphan, Rebel, Renegade, Simple Soul, Strategist, Trickster, Wanderer.

CHARACTER THEMES

One or more of the following character themes could apply to you.

Braggart: You have a true gift for self-aggrandizement and letting your mouth run away from you. Sometimes this can lead to trouble, but let's face it: Anyone as clever, quick, and good-looking as you *should* be renowned for her deeds, and shouldn't knuckle under in the face of so-called authority. If some jumped-up constable or high so-called noble doesn't like the way you carry yourself, it's his problem, not yours. He probably wishes he had half your charm and style.

Take every opportunity to insult, belittle, and deride your enemies. What better way to show off your wit and inventiveness, while entertaining your friends? Don't let a combat pass without a quip.

"Are you trying to kill me with your axe or your breath, you malodorous fiend?"

"Hey, you dried-up old husk of a wizard! You wanted to live forever looking like that?"

"Where's the evil plan? Come on, you've got to have an evil plan! How can you call yourself a crazed cultist if you don't have an evil plan?"

Make sure stories told about your deeds reflect well on you; if part of the story is a little boring or doesn't cast you in a good light, there's no harm in adding some embellishment. There's no conversation that can't be improved by talking about yourself a little—or a lot. You're the most interesting person around, after all.

"Was Lord Gerrat there when I stole the Dragon Egg Ruby from under a demilich's skull? Did he stand next to me when I faced down the frost giant jarl with nothing but this kukri so that my friends could get away? Then Lord Gerrat can wait a few hours, because I'm not leaving this tavern while the music's still playing and everyone is dancing."

"Yes, yes, that's all very interesting, but let's talk about me."

Above all, maintain your self-confidence! If you don't believe in yourself, who will? People exaggerate their troubles, so you should feel free to whittle them back to size.

"Oh, sure I've fought dragons before! Great big ones, fire-breathing of course, bigger than castles! They're not so tough."

"They just call it the Tomb of Horrors to scare off the morons. It's a sham, a put-on! We'll walk right in and steal every last copper from the place, just you wait and see!"

Common-Born Hero: You view yourself as a champion of the people, fighting against injustice and tyranny with a sly sense of humor, a larcenous streak, and an intuitive grasp of the art of derring-do. You can't stand to let a bully go unpunished, and most monsters and villains are nothing more than particularly big and scary bullies.

While you are certainly happy to profit from your adventures, you live for the gratitude and appreciation of the common folk. Returning a stolen treasure to its rightful owner—especially an owner who is otherwise impoverished—is more satisfying than simply enriching yourself. Even if it's difficult to part with a hard-won prize, you trust that suitable rewards will follow when you do the right thing. You don't have to give away everything you find, but you should see to it that your successful adventures help as many people as possible.

More so than most other characters, you take an interest in the common people you encounter in your travels. Keep a list of the minor NPCs you encounter, as well as what they need or what they want. Ask your DM to provide your character with opportunities to meet and help common folk if these are not a feature of his game. (DMs will appreciate it if you don't pester them for details on every person in the village, though.)

"Madam, why so sad? Here, take this gold coin and buy your family a feast!"

"I swear on the blood of my mother, there will be justice in this town!"

Skulk: You're an artist, not a common thief. You are a bold and daring warrior, but instead of putting your faith in iron-mongery and clumsy charges, you seek victory in the shadows. You have no battle cry or trademark move—you don't want to be seen or heard before you strike. Some might question your courage, but none can doubt your effectiveness.

Surprise is your biggest asset, so you are a master of skills and talents that let you creep into places where you can take your enemy unaware. Seek out opportunities to scout out the lay of the land and locate potential enemies without a big, noisy party of adventurers at your heels, giving away your position and waking up every monster in the dungeon. If you can silently take out a weak or unsuspecting foe on your own, great—but remember, it's your job to avoid giving the villains a chance to strike back. Make sure you can handle anything you start when your allies aren't at hand.

You are rarely loud or boastful; you know what you can do, and that's the only measure that counts. You find it easier to speak little and hear much, keeping your opinions to yourself. When you do voice an opinion, you tend to be terse and offer little or no explanation.

"I'll take care of the sentries."

"Give me ten minutes to get into position before the rest of you storm in."

"Five ogres ahead—two sleeping, three more awake. I don't want to leave them behind us."

Specialist: You are a consummate professional. Master of a set of rare and valuable skills, you view adventures as jobs—nothing more and nothing less. You don't accompany adventuring parties to test yourself against ferocious monsters or to halt the depredations of murderous villains. You go along for your fair cut of the loot, and you have no use for the thickheaded heroics of muscle-bound sword swingers or crusading zealots. If you wind up in a fight, you probably bungled the job.

Rogue specialists come in four basic flavors: lockpicks (who concentrate on Open Lock), trapfinders (who need Search and Disable Device), swindlers (who use Bluff, Disguise, and Gather Information), and acrobats (who rely on Balance, Jump, Climb, and Tumble). In each case, the key to success is your ability to amass a lot of ranks in key skills other characters are unlikely to duplicate. Magic can eventually obviate the usefulness of a swindler, lockpick, or acrobat thanks to spells such as *charm person* or *levitate*, but trapfinders provide a capability that is very hard to replace. If you are going to be a specialist, consider being a trapfinder first.

Keep notes on various obstacles you encounter, especially the ones you can't get around or through on your first try. Someday you're going to go back with the right tools (or perhaps a little more training) and defeat each and every one.

You can be opinionated, and you believe that most obstacles can be overcome through the use of your special skills. You are confident and pragmatic.

"I never met a lock I couldn't open."

"Better let me go first. Otherwise someone's likely to get killed."

"Hmmmph. Goblin-work. Shoddy."

DISRUPTIVE ATTACK

More than perhaps any other character, a rogue's ability to fully contribute to a fight varies dramatically based on the enemies she faces. Against a mummy, flesh golem, or shambling mound, the rogue's damage-dealing drops precipitously. The disruptive attack alternative class feature allows a rogue to be effective in combat against such creatures by making them vulnerable to the attacks of her and her allies. It's also useful against creatures vulnerable to your sneak attacks, creating interesting tactical decisions for you in such fights.

Level: 4th.

Replaces: If you select this class feature, you do not gain uncanny dodge at 4th level. Instead, you gain uncanny dodge at 8th level (when you would normally gain improved uncanny dodge).

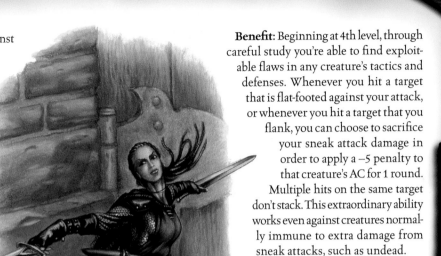

Lidda the Sparrowhawk, grandmaster of the Red Knives thieves guild

Benefit: Beginning at 4th level, through careful study you're able to find exploitable flaws in any creature's tactics and defenses. Whenever you hit a target that is flat-footed against your attack, or whenever you hit a target that you flank, you can choose to sacrifice your sneak attack damage in order to apply a –5 penalty to that creature's AC for 1 round. Multiple hits on the same target don't stack. This extraordinary ability works even against creatures normally immune to extra damage from sneak attacks, such as undead.

STARTING PACKAGES

Package 1: The Archer
Halfling Rogue

Ability Scores: Str 6, Dex 17, Con 12, Int 13, Wis 14, Cha 10.

Skills: Climb, Disable Device, Hide, Listen, Move Silently, Open Lock, Search, Spot, Tumble.

Languages: Common, Goblin, Halfling.

Feat: Point Blank Shot.

Weapon: Morningstar (1d6/×3), light crossbow with 20 bolts (1d6/19–20, 80 ft.).

Armor: Studded leather (+3 AC).

Other Gear: Standard adventurer's kit, thieves' tools, 10 gp.

Package 2: The Duelist
Elf Rogue

Ability Scores: Str 10, Dex 17, Con 10, Int 14, Wis 8, Cha 13.

Skills: Balance, Bluff, Disable Device, Hide, Listen, Move Silently, Open Lock, Search, Spot, Tumble.

Languages: Common, Draconic, Elven, Orc.

Feat: Combat Expertise.

Weapons: Rapier (1d6/18–20), dagger (1d4/19–20, 10 ft.), shortbow with 20 arrows (1d6/×3, 60 ft.).

Armor: Studded leather (+3 AC).

Other Gear: Standard adventurer's kit, thieves' tools, 6 gp.

Package 3: The Explorer
Human Rogue

Ability Scores: Str 13, Dex 15, Con 12, Int 14, Wis 10, Cha 8.

Skills: Climb, Disable Device, Gather Information, Hide, Jump, Listen, Move Silently, Open Lock, Search, Spot, Tumble.

Languages: Common, Goblin, Undercommon.

Feat: Alertness, Combat Reflexes.

Weapons: Longspear (1d8/×3), morningstar (1d8), light crossbow with 20 bolts (1d8/19–20, 80 ft.).

Armor: Studded leather (+3 AC).

Other Gear: Standard adventurer's kit, thieves' tools, 5 gp.

Illus. by R. Spencer

SCOUT

You navigate difficult terrain as easily as a commoner walks down a cobbled lane. Your natural talent and intensive training forged you into the ideal investigator of both the green wilds and the dark depths. Where your compatriots find themselves caught on brambles, tripped up on potholes, and wounded by caltrops, you flow, jump, and sweep through all distractions offered by the mute landscape.

Your ability to travel into difficult-to-reach locations complements your ability to evade the eyes of both friend and foe. You are seen only where and when you choose to be.

Quick, trackless, difficult to pin down, and able to pierce both physical barriers and lightless expanses, you are lethal when you decide to make your presence known, whether in a direct attack or when you make your report to the eager company ready to act on the intelligence you gathered.

This class appears in the *Complete Adventurer* supplement.

Suggested Backgrounds (choose one): Drifter, Mariner, Soldier.

Suggested Personality Archetypes (choose one): Agent, Daredevil, Explorer, Orphan, Rebel, Renegade, Seeker, Wanderer.

Deruwyn, Scout Captain of the Mithral Delvers

CHARACTER THEMES

One or more of the following character themes could apply to you.

Game Hunter: You eat what you kill, and you're none too fond of fancy meals served in taverns. To you, hunting animals for food in their proper season, by climate, and factoring in animal diversity is a philosophy and even a way of life. You'd never eat a spawning fish out of season, and you recoil in disgust at the thought of dining on veal or herded animals.

This means you're kept busy hunting for your sustenance, but luckily you know how to prepare and preserve large catches in ways that ensure you can comfortably eat for a month or more between big hunts. Of course, you prefer fresh game to preserved, so whenever you can give jerky a rest in favor of quail, squab, or coney, you take time to set up a snare or head into the brush, only to emerge an hour later with your fresh prize in hand.

You are not stingy with freshly caught game, and you know many different ways of preparing your catch. You cook for your compatriots as much as they'll allow, and you enjoy trying new preparations with natural spices, seasonings, and novel presentations.

"I know a recipe for coney better than anything you'll ever taste in town."

"It's not the season for salmon—don't insult me by trying to serve it."

Military Heritage: You come from a military tradition, having served either in the king's army or in a large, respected mercenary company. You distinguished yourself, though you never achieved high rank. On the other hand, you were a noncommissioned officer, and those who outranked you depended upon your scouting expertise.

Because of your military heritage, you are familiar with military jargon, and speak of *"flanking maneuvers"* and how *"strategy is large scale while tactics are small scale."* Moreover, you like to assess all adventuring (and perhaps even social) situations in terms of seven strategic principles that served you well while you were *"in service."*

"Figuring out the objective is half the battle." Once you throw out all distracting factors, what are you really hoping to achieve?

"With enough munitions, we can mount a credible offense." You're not afraid to pay for magic arrows and other high-quality offensive "hardware."

"Without cooperation, we have nothing." You know the value that teamwork and mutual aid adds to any dangerous situation. You like to work out tactics ahead of time, and to establish who in the party is responsible for what duty.

"We have to concentrate our attacks!" It's foolish to scatter attacks across multiple enemies—if members of your party concentrate their attacks on a dangerous foe, that foe would be brought down quicker, and thus unable to deal its own damage as long. Then, on to the next foe.

"Always look for tactical advantage, then maneuver to reach those positions." You point out to others in your party where each might be positioned for best possible effect. See Tactician on page 58 under the warmage character themes.

"Surprise is one of my favorite weapons." You like to sneak ahead and get the lay of the land before engaging enemies.

"Keep it simple!" Plans are well and good, but complicated schemes go out the window the moment the first arrow is fired. Plans that are too involved almost always collapse.

Sniper: You are especially skilled in field craft and marksmanship, allowing you to target selected enemies from concealment at range. Ideally, you move into a position against a foe unaware of your presence, use as few

Illus. by E. Fiegenschuh

attacks as possible to down the target, then withdraw without being seen.

Of course, in a conflict when you support a larger party of adventurers, you do not withdraw, but instead rely on your comrades to keep the foe or foes from attacking you directly. In return, you concentrate your fire against foes most dangerous to your party.

You developed your field skills on your own, or perhaps you were trained in a military detachment of the king's guard or in a special unit fielded by a large mercenary company.

World Traveler: You've seen it all. Well, you've seen a lot in your travels, and you don't mind audibly comparing the place where you currently find yourself with other places you've allegedly traveled to. Even when you haven't physically traveled to a locale you like to brag about, you indicate (if pinned down) that you've read all about the locale in question; after all, a scout has to keep on top of these sorts of things.

"The way this tower is laid out reminds me of Tarmind Spire. Tarmind—the spire was named after the sorcerer who built it—was a demonbinder. Tarmind Spire was where he caged all the demons he bound. Anyway, keep an eye out for demons."

"This waterfall puts me in mind of the Falls of Shandarm. Those falls plunge a hundred feet in a roaring cascade of white whose thunder can be heard for miles. Local tribes cast coins, gems, even magic items into it, thinking that their sacrifice will grant them fortune and long life. I don't know if that's true, but there's a fortune hidden below the cataract. Maybe we should search the basin here?"

"Whenever I travel through a mine, I think of the Mines of Minwray. The dwarves found the Minwray mine—they didn't delve it themselves. It was a great barrow of interconnected passages, following the vein of some mysterious mineral, delved by a vanished race. By the time the dwarves found it, the mineral was completely exhausted. But the dwarves expanded the dig, hoping to find some trace of what the mysterious Minwray had mined so assiduously."

"I hate these deep ravines—did I ever tell you about the Skarvos Ravine? Twenty miles long and half a mile deep, the ravine shelters a sprawling citadel of crude dark stone in the deepest, darkest root of the fissure. No one's ever returned from the citadel who explored it, so no one knows what is inside."

DUNGEON SPECIALIST

The scout's mobility gives her a significant advantage over foes in combat. While any scout can hold her own in an underground setting, some specifically train for the dark, enclosed spaces found in dungeon environments. If you select the dungeon specialist alternative class feature, you give up some of your speed to turn the dungeon into a three-dimensional combat environment. You'll shine in small rooms and tight corridors, though area spells become a bit more dangerous for you.

Level: 3rd.

Replaces: By choosing the dungeon specialist alternative class feature, you give up both fast movement (normally gained at 3rd level and improved at 11th level) and evasion (normally gained at 5th level).

Benefit: At 3rd level, you gain a climb speed equal to one-half your base land speed (rounded down to the next 5-foot increment), and you can attack with a light weapon normally while climbing. At 11th level, your climb speed improves to equal your base land speed.

Having a climb speed grants you a +8 racial bonus on Climb checks and allows you to take 10 on Climb checks even if rushed or threatened. You also retain your Dexterity bonus to AC while climbing, and enemies gain no special bonus on attacks against you while you are climbing. See Movement Modes, *MM* 311, for more details.

At 5th level, you learn to use confining areas to your advantage. Whenever you are standing on the ground and adjacent to a wall, you gain a +2 bonus to AC and opponents gain no bonus on their attack rolls when flanking you.

This is an extraordinary ability. You lose both of these benefits when wearing medium or heavy armor or when carrying a medium or heavy load.

STARTING PACKAGES

Package 1: The Archer
Halfling Scout

Ability Scores: Str 12, Dex 17, Con 12, Int 10, Wis 13, Cha 8.

Skills: Climb, Disable Device, Hide, Listen, Move Silently, Open Lock, Search, Spot.

Feat: Point Blank Shot.

Weapons: Spear (1d6/×3), dagger (1d3/19–20), shortbow with 20 arrows (1d4/×3, 60 ft.)

Armor: Studded leather (+3 AC).

Other Gear: Standard adventurer's kit, thieves' tools, 20 gp.

Package 2: The Hunter
Elf Scout

Ability Scores: Str 14, Dex 17, Con 10, Int 10, Wis 13, Cha 8.

Skills: Disable Device, Hide, Listen, Move Silently, Open Lock, Search, Spot, Survival.

Feat: Track.

Weapons: Spear (1d8/×3), throwing axe (1d6, 10 ft.), shortbow with 20 arrows (1d6/×3, 100 ft.).

Armor: Studded leather (+3 AC).

Other Gear: Standard adventurer's kit, thieves' tools, 15 gp.

Package 3: The Skirmisher
Human Scout

Ability Scores: Str 14, Dex 15, Con 12, Int 10, Wis 13, Cha 8.

Skills: Disable Device, Hide, Jump, Listen, Move Silently, Open Lock, Search, Spot, Tumble.

Feats: Dodge, Two-Weapon Fighting.

Weapons: Two short swords (1d6/19–20), 5 javelins (1d6, 30 ft.).

Armor: Studded leather (+3 AC).

Other Gear: Standard adventurer's kit, thieves' tools, 30 gp.

SORCERER

You weave spells like poets compose sonnets. You require no dusty tomes, no grueling apprenticeships, no protracted study of arcane phenomena—all you need is your inborn talent to wield raw magic.

As a child, you knew you were different from others, and when you uttered your first spontaneous spell, your suspicions were confirmed—sorcery infused your blood!

But where did this awesome gift arise from? Could it be a mere knack, or is it true that you can claim dragons as ancestors? It might be that your ability to manifest magic through mere force of will is your inheritance from those ancient creatures.

Suggested Backgrounds (choose one): Artisan, Ascetic, Drifter, Noble Scion.

Suggested Personality Archetypes (choose one): Companion, Daredevil, Innocent, Mercenary, Orphan, Renegade, Royalty, Sage, Seeker, Simple Soul, Wanderer.

CHARACTER THEMES

One or more of the following character themes could apply to you.

Mysterious Stranger: No one knows the real you, and you prefer to keep it that way. Though you have allies, and might even have a few friends, your background is a mystery to all.

Of course, in the absence of fact, rumor and legend rush to fill the void. While you might not actively spread misinformation, it pleases you to hear others tell fantastic stories about where (and how) you were born or raised, your exploits, and the true extent of your powers.

When other characters ask about your background, don't ever give a straight reply. Dance around the truth, making ominous statements in place of answers. Let them believe what they would like—and let your actions give them every reason to believe the most fantastic possibilities.

A few ranks of Bluff (and/or cross-class ranks of Intimidate) are particularly useful for pulling off this theme. In keeping your secrets, it's useful to be able to lie directly to someone's face, or to stare someone in the face until he or she slinks away nervously.

"Many before you have pondered my origin. Your questions, like those, must remain unanswered . . . for your own safety."

"You wouldn't be the first to make the mistake of underestimating my power."

Hennet, master sorcerer of the Emerald Flame

Genealogist: You amass oral histories, search records, and seek out family stories to discover the truth about your ancestors and living relatives. Though your overall goal is to prove that you are indeed descended from dragons, you've acquired a lot of secondary knowledge concerning now-defunct kingdoms, the movement of people across the landscape, great wars and philosophical movements, and other historical curiosities.

While still ongoing, your search of your family history has led you to uncover distant cousins and even a few buried family secrets. For instance, you learned that your great grandfather didn't die in service to the king's guard as everyone believes. It turns out he shipped to sea with a privateer. Over the course of decades, he worked to become the captain of his own ship. You've never been able to discover the final fate of your grandfather's ship, but you are constantly on the lookout for fresh information.

Despite the interesting revelations you discover and the people you now know you can count as distant relatives, your true quest remains: You've never once turned your mind from the thought of your dragon ancestry.

"My grandfather had secrets that no one could have guessed. I wonder if he had a hidden hoard?"

"You'd do well to learn your own ancestry. How do you truly know what you are if you don't know from where you've come?"

Misunderstood Rebel: You've never fit in. No one understands you, and truth to tell, you don't care anymore. Your dark, brooding clothing, pale features, and much-tattooed flesh is part of who you are, and if people can't accept that, it's their problem, not yours. Moreover, you relish locations that others find horror-inducing, including necropolises, haunted citadels, and cursed cathedrals. Though you still draw breath, you feel as if you have something in common with ghosts, vampires, and other humanoid-shaped undead—although none have yet seemed overly interested in doing anything other than attempting to kill you.

You have a knack for writing dark and dismal tales, and whether with pen or out loud, you have composed several stories featuring cursed families, being buried alive, and the fall of cities into hellish rifts.

"Who cares?"

"I wrote a story once about a girl who was dead for a year and never knew it. . . ."

Pretender: This character theme relies on you having taken 1 or more ranks in Bluff. Your natural charisma leads you into making preposterous, but somehow reasonable-sounding claims regarding a wide variety of topics.

You most effectively use this talent when playing games of chance, especially cards. For instance, when playing the high-stakes game of three-dragon ante, your ability to bluff effectively is a tactic you've come to rely on when you want to make the other players believe your weak hand is strong, or that your strong hand is weak, depending on how the dragons fall.

However, when you are faced with stressful situations, your propensity to invent answers to hard questions out of whole cloth could get you into trouble at least as often as it helps. For example, when challenged by guards asking for credentials necessary to allow you and your friends past some threshold, you launch into a song-and-dance meant to distract:

"Well, of course I'd normally give you the countersign, but didn't you get the news? Spies are about, invisible, just waiting to overhear someone give the countersign at this entry. Can you imagine if they learned the countersign? Can you imagine if it was because you required me to give it to you now?"

"The Grand Duke sent for me. Don't give me any claptrap about not knowing who I am or that I am not on the list—the Grand Duke asked for me by name! If you don't let me past RIGHT now, I can guarantee that when I finally do see the Duke a half-hour from now because you've delayed me, I'll tell him right off I was delayed because of YOU! What's your name, guard?"

METAMAGIC SPECIALIST

With a limited selection of spells at his fingertips, it's natural for a sorcerer to turn to metamagic feats to gain flexibility in effects. If the idea of playing a sorcerer who efficiently twists his spells into new shapes and sizes excites you, the metamagic specialist alternative class feature is the way to go. Though you must forgo the benefits of a familiar to pursue this path, some sorcerers relish not having to keep track of such a vulnerable accessory.

Level: 1st.

Replaces: If you select this class feature, you do not gain a familiar.

Benefit: You can apply metamagic feats that you know to sorcerer spells without increasing the casting time. This benefit even lets you quicken your sorcerer spells with the Quicken Spell feat.

You can use this class feature a number of times per day equal to 3 + your Int modifier (minimum 1). This is an extraordinary ability.

STARTING PACKAGES

Package 1: The Battle Mage

Gnome Sorcerer

Ability Scores: Str 10, Dex 13, Con 16, Int 8, Wis 10, Cha 15.

Skills: Concentration.

Feat: Toughness.

Weapon: Spear (1d6/×3), dagger (1d3/19–20, 10 ft.), light crossbow with 20 bolts (1d6/19–20, 80 ft.).

Armor: None.

Other Gear: Spell component pouch, standard adventurer's kit, 14 gp.

Spells Known: 1st—*mage armor, ray of enfeeblement, shocking grasp;* 0—*acid splash, daze, detect magic, read magic, touch of fatigue.*

Package 2: The Blaster

Halfling Sorcerer

Ability Scores: Str 6, Dex 15, Con 14, Int 12, Wis 10, Cha 15.

Skills: Bluff, Concentration, Knowledge (arcana).

Languages: Common, Draconic, Halfling.

Feat: Spell Focus (evocation).

Weapons: Longspear (1d6/×3), dagger (1d3/19–20, 10 ft.), light crossbow with 20 bolts (1d6/19–20, 80 ft.).

Armor: None.

Other Gear: Spell component pouch, standard adventurer's kit, 11 gp.

Spells Known: 1st—*color spray, magic missile, obscuring mist;* 0—*acid splash, detect magic, disrupt undead, light, ray of frost.*

Package 3: The Infernal Summoner

Human Sorcerer

Ability Scores: Str 8, Dex 13, Con 14, Int 12, Wis 10, Cha 15.

Skills: Bluff, Concentration, Knowledge (arcana), Spellcraft.

Languages: Common, Infernal.

Feats: Infernal Sorcerer Heritage, Infernal Sorcerer Howl.

Weapons: Longspear (1d6/×3), dagger (1d3/19–20, 10 ft.), light crossbow with 20 bolts (1d6/19–20, 80 ft.).

Armor: None.

Other Gear: Spell component pouch, standard adventurer's kit, 11 gp.

Spells Known: 1st—*grease, mage armor, summon monster I;* 0—*acid splash, detect magic, daze, message, read magic.*

SWASHBUCKLER

You'll do nearly anything on a dare, going so far as to risk your life to prove your panache. You have a style all your own. Agile and swift, witty and charming, you are the toast of the town wherever you go, although sometimes your antics earn you the displeasure of authority figures and the annoyance of your more conservative compatriots.

Luckily, you excel both with your swift blade and your equally agile tongue. You can charm even the most stone-hearted long enough to make your getaway.

Seeking fame, praise, and perhaps hoping to right the occasional injustice, you leap into action, glorying in the life of a famous hero.

This class appears in the *Complete Adventurer* supplement.

Suggested Backgrounds (*choose one*): Drifter, Gladiator, Mariner, Noble Scion.

Suggested Personality Archetypes (*choose one*): Challenger, Daredevil, Rebel, Trickster, Wanderer.

CHARACTER THEMES

One or more of the following character themes could apply to you.

Avenger: Someone wronged you in the past, and you've made it your mission to put that misdeed right and bring justice, or at least vengeance, to bear. You can be heard frequently muttering the name of the person whom you blame for your present state. You keep your blade especially sharp, you like to explain to anyone who will listen, so that when the time comes for you to exact justice, your foe's blood will soak the earth. See the Driven Avenger on page 54 under the ranger character themes.

"I keep a special blade as sharp as a dragon's tooth for the final blow I'll strike."

"If justice can't be mine, then I claim vengeance."

Braggart: You are given to making incredible claims and boasts. See the rogue character theme of the same name on page 56.

Clothes Horse: You dress in conspicuous, flashy clothes. Dun-colored leather, gray, and tan—these are colors for dullards. You prefer brilliant red, hunter green, navy blue, snowy white, and coal black, but color alone doesn't make the ensemble—it is the fashion!

Though a courtier's outfit will set you back 30 gold pieces, you own several widely different sets. On the days when you are less likely to soil your clothing in sewer water or in the blood of your foes, you trot out your finest noble outfits, made pricier by your personalized touches.

"Take a care you don't get any of your blood on my new silk doublet, you knave!"

Daredevil: Your audacity sometimes leads you to perform dangerous stunts merely to prove to others that few things are beyond your reach, when you set your mind to them. Sometimes, with enough time and resources, you can rig a stunt so that it looks dangerous to onlookers, but actually includes hidden safety features. However, your stunts are frequently as dangerous as they appear.

Baiting a Monster: While you are adventuring, sometimes a dangerous beast needs to be lured into a particular location so it can be dealt with more easily, while other times a monster is in too formidable a tactical location to attack. That's when you shine. You declare straightaway that you're up to baiting the creature so that it'll move in the desired direction. Invective works, as does a swift attack and retreat, but sometimes you end up snatching a valuable item and running.

"You call that a monster? I've seen more dangerous claws in a barnyard!"

Master Magician: You claim you can endure anything, even being buried alive. Why, you've gone a full seven days being buried alive in a coffin under 6 feet of earth, or so you claim. If secretly allowed to make preparations to obtain food (and air), or if you can make a deal with a friend with the right spells to check up on you now and then, you might just take another dare to try eight days!

"It's true, that one time I almost died, but that was just to impress the ladies."

Escapist: You brag that there is no restraint from which you can't free yourself (to employ this character theme, you should have 1 or more ranks in Escape Artist). Whether manacles, chains, ropes, or other restraint devices, you claim you've never been foiled. To keep your record safe, you take extensive precautions, including keeping "rigged" sets of manacles and stocks to practice with, and as an extreme, occasionally swallowing a skeleton key good for unlocking many types of manacles and vaults. When necessary, you can regurgitate the key, though it's an unpleasant process.

"The Tarterian Depths of Carceri couldn't hold me. Do you think your puny cell has a chance?"

Leaping a Pit: Ten feet? No problem. Twenty? Just as easy. Your friends know that fissures are your specialty and rarely dare you to span them, although on occasion putting on a little paying show by jumping a horse across a river isn't out of the question. You take it in stride that it's best to have several extra healing potions on hand during such an event—after all, you've learned that your fame actually increases after a failed attempt if you are terribly injured.

"It's okay . . . it's not as far across as it looks."

Humorist: Your natural charisma leads you to entertain your friends and larger groups by making them laugh. You employ a wide variety of tools toward this end, including jokes, relating amusing situations (sometimes with comedic embellishment), or acting the fool.

"What do you do if an orc attacks you with a crossbow? Pick up the crossbow and shoot the orc."

"Two orc mercenaries are walking down the street when one collapses. He doesn't seem to be breathing and his eyes are glazed. The other rushes up the steps of a nearby temple and finds a cleric. He gasps: 'My friend is dead! What can I do?' The cleric says: 'Calm down, I can help. First, let's make sure he's dead.' The orc rushes away, then returns a moment later, cleaning blood off his blade. He says, 'Okay, now what?'"

"At dinner one night, the goblin child cries, 'Mommy, Mommy! When are we going to have Aunt Gruma for dinner?' The mother replies, 'Quiet, we haven't even finished your grandmother yet.'"

Negotiator: In some groups, your diplomatic skills exceed those of your friends. See the bard character theme of the same name on page 34.

Pretender: Your natural charisma leads you to make preposterous, but somehow reasonable-sounding claims regarding a wide variety of topics. See the sorcerer character theme of the same name on page 61.

SHIELD OF BLADES

The typical swashbuckler is best suited to fighting a single foe. Some, however, practice using a pair of light weapons to fend off attacks from all around them. The shield of blades alternative class feature is designed for swashbucklers who fight with two weapons. Though it requires a full attack action to use the ability, the AC bonus applies against all attackers (even invisible ones), unlike the dodge bonus gained by the traditional swashbuckling style.

Level: 5th.

Replaces: If you select this class feature, you do not gain the dodge bonus class feature (or its improvements at 10th, 15th, and 20th level).

Benefit: Beginning at 5th level, you become adept at defending yourself when wielding a pair of light weapons. You gain a +2 shield bonus to your AC whenever you attack with at least two light weapons during your turn. (Despite the name of this class feature, you can use any light weapon to gain the benefit, even unarmed strikes or natural weapons.) This AC bonus lasts until the start of your next turn. This is an extraordinary ability.

This bonus increases by 1 for every five levels beyond 5th (+3 at 10th level, +4 at 15th level, and +5 at 20th level). You lose this bonus when wearing medium or heavy armor or when carrying a medium or heavy load.

STARTING PACKAGES

Package 1: The Destroyer
Half-Orc Swashbuckler

Ability Scores: Str 15, Dex 15, Con 10, Int 12, Wis 8, Cha 10.

Skills: Climb, Escape Artist, Jump, Tumble, Swim.

Languages: Common, Abyssal, Orc.

Feats: Two-Weapon Fighting, Weapon Finesse.

Weapons: Two short swords (1d6/19–20), dagger (1d4/19–20, 10 ft.).

Armor: Chain shirt (+4 AC).

Other Gear: Standard adventurer's kit, 13 gp.

Meara Swiftblade, Queen's champion

Package 2: The Duelist
Human Swashbuckler

Ability Scores: Str 13, Dex 15, Con 10, Int 14, Wis 8, Cha 12.

Skills: Balance, Bluff, Diplomacy, Escape Artist, Jump, Sense Motive, Tumble.

Languages: Common, Elven, Goblin.

Feats: Combat Expertise, Weapon Finesse, Weapon Focus (rapier).

Weapons: Rapier (1d6/18–20), dagger (1d4/19–20, 10 ft.).

Armor: Chain shirt (+4 AC).

Other Gear: Standard adventurer's kit, 13 gp.

Package 3: The Skirmisher
Elf Swashbuckler

Ability Scores: Str 13, Dex 17, Con 10, Int 14, Wis 8, Cha 10.

Skills: Balance, Bluff, Climb, Escape Artist, Jump, Tumble.

Languages: Common, Elven, Orc, Sylvan.

Feats: Dodge, Weapon Finesse.

Weapons: Rapier (1d6/18–20), dagger (1d4/19–20, 10 ft.), two javelins (1d6, 30 ft.).

Armor: Chain shirt (+4 AC).

Other Gear: Standard adventurer's kit, 11 gp.

WARLOCK

You deal with things other people cannot even imagine. Only through your determination and willpower do you resist being utterly consumed by the dark power you wield. You walk the earth, free to work good or evil with your so-called gift. But even if you choose to resist evil's lure, it is a struggle you must win each and every day of your life.

Magic is a part of your being in a way that not even the most powerful sorcerer or wizard will ever know. In your heart burns a strange and terrible font of power, giving you the ability to perform uncanny feats with only a flick of the wrist or a wave of the hand to show for it. You are capable enough in battle, but your real strength lies in your ability to bedevil and blight your enemies with a variety of noxious curses and sinister tricks. Few people care to associate with you—but those who do find you to be a capable companion indeed.

This class appears in the *Complete Arcane* supplement.

Suggested Backgrounds (choose one): Ascetic, Drifter, Guttersnipe.

Suggested Personality Archetypes (choose one): Challenger, Daredevil, Orphan, Renegade, Strategist, Theorist, Trickster, Wanderer.

CHARACTER THEMES

One or more of the following character themes could apply to you.

Hellion: You are an *enfant terrible*, a troublemaker who cares nothing for the expectations or sensibilities of the people around you. You delight in scandalizing those who seek to censure your behavior.

Never apologize for your actions or conceal your true nature. If the common folk are frightened of warlocks, let them be frightened! You savor the taste of their fear. When dealing with the powerful, dispense with etiquette and tact and speak your mind. You take pleasure in the gasps of shock and daggerlike glances of those who think you're uncouth. The unwritten rules of discourse and behavior are silly and outmoded anyway, so you flaunt them at every opportunity. You don't need to be obscene, vile, or gross, but you feel no need to moderate your behavior or watch your words.

"All power is evil. Haven't you learned that yet?"

"Stand aside, constable! No one stops me from going where I like and doing what I please! Or would you prefer to be a toad?"

"You'd like my head on a pike, would you? Well, here it is—come take it if you can! Otherwise, leave me be!"

Possessed: You are a plaything for the sinister powers that created you. Several different spirits or personas constantly vie for control of your body. Your own persona rarely loses control outright, but its dominance is shaky enough that other personas can speak, gesture, or even force you to begin various actions before you manage to regain control.

For example, you find yourself leveling your *wand of lightning bolt* at your ally's back before you drag down your wand hand with your other arm. You threaten yourself with vile oaths and imprecations. You might even wake up to find that you are far from the place where you went to sleep, and people tell you that you did and said things you have no memory of. All in all, you present a profoundly unnerving spectacle.

Make strange, unconnected gestures at the gaming table. Point a pencil or pen at one of your fellow players, and then suddenly "notice" that your hand is doing something you didn't want it to and pull it down. Create several distinct voices that argue with each other. Make sure the other players know what you're doing so they don't have you committed; remember, a little bit of this sort of behavior goes a long way.

When roleplaying a warlock with this trait, you don't have to betray your friends or take actions harmful to yourself or your allies. But you should certainly say things that are incongruous with the actions you perform.

"I can hold off the ogres, but only if the elf dies first. No, wait, he's my friend. Definitely the ogres first."

Reformed: You have done terrible wrongs in your life. You have mocked the holy, plundered the weak, harried the just, and murdered the innocent. But now you repent of the evil you inflicted on the world, and earnestly strive to atone for your many crimes. By turning the powers of darkness against other evildoers, you hope to make amends as best you can.

In your travels, you might encounter those who know of your evil past. Such people might assume that your reformation is nothing more than a cynical attempt to escape justice, or perhaps a cruel sham designed to provide you with opportunities to indulge in even greater wickedness than before. In some lands you are reviled, and you walk abroad at no small risk of imprisonment or execution. In all fairness, you deserve such treatment after what you did.

"I've done . . . great evil. Those deeds darkened my soul, and every day I do all I can to erase that stain."

Morthos, warlock of the Ebon Tower

Supernatural Stricture: You are a supernatural creature, and you are subject to laws and strictures that other adventurers never experience. Others might think of these as superstitions or taboos, but for you they are immutable laws. For instance, you must choose a random way to go anytime you encounter a crossroads, unless someone tells you the way. (City streets and dungeon corridors don't usually count as crossroads.) You refuse to enter a home without an invitation. Domestic animals panic at your approach. You refuse to set foot on sacred ground, or you cannot look a blue-eyed person in the face. Whatever your stricture is, it rarely puts your life in danger, but it is occasionally inconveniencing to you, and memorable to anyone who witnesses your odd behavior.

There are three basic ways to handle this sort of limitation in play.

Voluntary Compliance: You observe the stricture through roleplaying alone.

Compliance to Avoid a Penalty: You observe the stricture because violating it would bring about a minor penalty.

Inviolable Law: You are absolutely incapable of defying the stricture.

Ideally, a supernatural stricture should, on rare occasions, force you to choose or avoid an action that most other characters would not give a second thought. If you get lost at crossroads, you might have to wait for hours at a lonely intersection in the countryside for someone to come along and show you which way to go. If you make domestic animals panic, you might find it impossible to ride a horse, and thus walk instead of ride when traveling overland.

"I'm sorry, but I may not cross this threshold without an invitation. Won't you invite me in?"

FIENDISH FLAMEWREATH

By their very nature, a warlock's powers are unusual and unpredictable. Some warlocks manifest a visible sign of their fiendish prowess, developing the ability to wreathe themselves in burning flames to deal damage to attackers. Giving up your fast healing means you're less capable of bouncing back after a fight, but the deterrence factor of the fiendish flamewreath alternative class feature might result in you taking less damage entirely.

Level: 8th.

Replaces: If you select this class feature, you do not gain the fiendish resilience class feature normally gained at 8th level (or the improvements to that class feature gained at 13th and 18th level).

Benefit: Beginning at 8th level, you know the trick of fiendish flamewreath. Once per day you can immolate yourself in

wispy flames that don't hurt you but deal 1d6 points of fire damage to any creature striking you with its body or a hand-held weapon. Creatures wielding weapons with exceptional reach, such as longspears, are not subject to this damage if they attack you.

Activating your fiendish flamewreath is a free action; it lasts for 2 minutes or until you take another free action to end it. The flames provide light equivalent to a torch, but can't be extinguished except by you. This is a supernatural ability.

At 13th level, your fiendish flamewreath deals 2d6 points of fire damage. At 18th level, the damage improves to 5d6 points.

STARTING PACKAGES

Package 1: The Blaster

Halfling Warlock

    Ability Scores: Str 8, Dex 14, Con 13, Int 12, Wis 10, Cha 15.

    Skills: Concentration, Knowledge (arcana), Spellcraft.

    Languages: Common, Goblin, Halfling.

    Feat: Point Blank Shot.

    Weapons: Longspear (1d6/×3), dagger (1d4/19–20, 10 ft.).

    Armor: Studded leather (+3 AC).

    Other Gear: Standard adventurer's kit, 28 gp.

    Invocations: Least—*eldritch blast, frightful blast.*

Package 2: The Controller

Elf Warlock

    Ability Scores: Str 8, Dex 14, Con 13, Int 12, Wis 10, Cha 15.

    Skills: Bluff, Concentration, Intimidate.

    Languages: Common, Elven, Orc.

    Feat: Necropolis Born (Complete Arcane).

    Weapon: Morningstar (1d8).

    Armor: Studded leather (+3 AC).

    Other Gear: Standard adventurer's kit, 29 gp.

    Invocations: Least—*eldritch blast, miasmic cloud.*

Package 3: The Problem Solver

Human Warlock

    Ability Scores: Str 8, Dex 14, Con 13, Int 12, Wis 10, Cha 15.

    Skills: Bluff, Concentration, Spellcraft, Use Magic Device.

    Languages: Common, Infernal.

    Feats: Communicator (Complete Arcane), Skill Focus (Use Magic Device).

    Weapons: Longspear (1d8/×3), morningstar (1d8), two daggers (1d4/19–20, 10 ft.).

    Armor: Studded leather (+3 AC).

    Other Gear: Standard adventurer's kit, 20 gp.

    Invocations: Least—*devil's sight, eldritch blast.*

SUPERNATURAL PENALTIES AND BONUSES

Talk with your DM about whether or not you should be subject to a penalty for breaking a stricture, and if so, what the right sort of penalty should be. Generally, a –1 penalty on caster level or saving throws for 24 hours is not unreasonable for breaking a stricture.

If you are liable to a penalty for your supernatural stricture, you are accepting a penalty that offers no benefit other than an interesting roleplaying hook. To balance this out, you should have a supernatural gift that occasionally provides a modest bonus (+1 bonus on caster level or saving throws for 24 hours). The gift should be something that is not under your control. For example, you might receive the benefit of your gift on the night of the new moon, during a thunderstorm, or when you carry a lock of hair from a man hanged for murder. Work with your DM to create a flavorful and appropriate gift for your warlock.

WARMAGE

Magic's application to warfare is more than an academic's theory—it is your life! You dream of blasts of devastating magic, spells of steel, and the clarion horn calling the warriors to battle. The stamp of marching troops is the sound dearest to your ears, though the blast of a fireball ripping through the ranks of massed line of enemies has its place.

You graduated near the top of your class from the war college, where every day you drilled in the dark predawn light, through through the heat of the day, until the bugle played its nightly signal that today's training was done. The magic of war is ingrained in you, and you ache to release it on the battlefield, or in a smaller skirmish where your skills will be all the more visible.

This class appears in the *Complete Arcane* supplement.

Suggested Backgrounds (*choose one*): Gladiator, Noble Scion, Soldier.

Suggested Personality Archetypes (*choose one*): Agent, Challenger, Leader, Royalty, Strategist.

CHARACTER THEMES

One or more of the following character themes could apply to you.

Foul-Tempered: A student of hard knocks, you are given to bouts of abusive or venomous language, though you pepper your speech with choice bits of invective even when you're not blaming a subordinate, censuring a compatriot, or expressing your bitter and deep-seated ill will regarding all that walk on two and four legs.

Though you've been known to swear a blue streak, you've also learned that using foul language is far more effective if rationed—a choice curse or shout at just the right moment has far more impact than a constant stream of epithets . . . though on occasion the situation calls for just such a string of slurs and imprecations. You've also found that it helps company unity if you swear mostly at foes and restrain from applying your venomous tongue to your compatriots.

"What are you looking at, cave creeper?"

"Where to, chief?"

"Idiocy drips from the fool's mouth."

Military Heritage, High Rank: You come from a military tradition, having served either in the king's army or in a large, respected mercenary company. You distinguished yourself and even achieved a reasonably high rank. When you emerged from your war college you were commissioned as a company grade officer and thus began your service as a lieutenant, but soon advanced to captain.

You still proudly wear the rank insignia of a captain, despite having been discharged from the company you originally served. You wear the insignia as a shoulder patch. Others who served recognize your insignia, and you recognize theirs.

Because of your military heritage, you are familiar with military jargon and make use of it, as well as elements of military strategy. See the Military Heritage entry on page 58 under the scout character themes.

Military Historian: This character theme requires you to have at least 1 rank in Knowledge (history). You are a student of conflict, an expert on the subject of the famous battles between prehistoric tribes, ancient militaries, and modern armies between kings and necromancers. See the bard character theme of the same name on page 34.

Tactician: While a military strategy is an overall plan for a large conflict, tactics are the actual means used to attain a goal in a particular fight. As someone who achieved the rank of captain, you know effective tactics and like to employ them in a fight, depending on the situation.

Camouflage: When at all possible, you attempt to hide the presence of yourself and your party from potential enemies, hoping to discourage ranged weapon accuracy and targeting until you can close, or even completely hide from an enemy force until you are ready to attack.

"Change into your darkest clothes, and don't forget to rub charcoal across your faces."

Decoy: One of your favorite tactics is the use of a decoy. Whether a spell that provides the illusion of a powerful heroic ally or a monster in your thrall, or just a loud noise or fabricated conversation, you use a decoy to distract a foe or foes from what is truly important—usually you and your group's true position and strength.

"We need the illusion of dragon charging their line—then we can sneak in around back."

Arthon, destroyer of hordes

Ambush: When possible, you prefer to attack your foes from concealment when they least expect such an assault. Good options include striking from dense underbrush or firing ranged weapons from a high position.

"We have to establish a killing ground, position two groups to cut off any escape, and post someone to keep watch so we know when to launch the ambush."

Frontal Assault: Sometimes, the best tactic is a direct, hostile advance toward the foe. The hope is to overwhelm the enemy with your strength. However, you know that it's rank stupidity to call for a frontal assault against a foe in a fortified position.

"We've run out of options. Time for a suicide strike . . . er, frontal assault!"

Pincer Movement: If you are with a group large enough to pull it off, and if you're fighting a foe in numbers large enough for it to matter, you like to employ a tactic called the pincer movement, where you attack the massed flanks of the opponent simultaneously in a pinching motion after your foe has committed forward. Your forces ideally respond by moving out to surround the foes.

"Surround them, envelop them, don't let any escape!"

Flying Wedge: In some ways like a frontal assault but more refined, a flying wedge is a charge where all your allies are arrayed in a V shape. You put a bruiser at the point of the V, hoping to breach the foe's line; then the following attackers can widen the gap. This maneuver carries a certain risk: If the foe can slow or pause the wedge, you've given your foe an opportunity to try a pincer movement of its own.

"Beat him down, break the line, bowl them over!"

ECLECTIC LEARNING

Some warmages find the limited range of their spell selection chafing. These characters yearn for the sorcerer's or wizard's utility spells, such as *invisibility, dimension door,* or even the humble *detect magic.* While you will never have as wide an access to such spells as other arcane casters, the eclectic learning alternative class feature gives you at least a taste of what your fellow arcanists already enjoy (without significantly watering down your battlefield focus).

If you take this option, choose carefully which spells to learn. Focus on spells that will remain useful as long as possible—while *eagle's splendor* might seem like a good choice at 6th level, by the time you can afford a good *cloak of Charisma* you might regret that earlier choice.

Level: 3rd, 6th, 11th, or 16th.

Replaces: If you select this class feature, you do not gain the advanced learning class feature normally gained at a particular level. The choice you make at one level has no bearing on the choice you make at a later level—you could choose eclectic learning at 3rd and 6th level, advanced learning at 11th level, and then eclectic learning again at 16th level.

Benefit: At 3rd, 6th, 11th, or 16th level, you can choose to add a new spell to your list that would normally be outside your area of expertise. The spell must be a sorcerer/wizard spell, but it can be from any school. The spell is treated as being one level higher than normal (for example, *invisibility*, a 2nd-level sorcerer/wizard spell, would be treated as a 3rd-level warmage spell for you). You must be capable of casting spells of the new spell's adjusted level—for instance, you can't choose a 3rd-level sorcerer/wizard spell at 6th level, because the spell is treated as a 4th-level spell for you.

STARTING PACKAGES

Package 1: The Battle Mage
Gnome Warmage

    Ability Scores: Str 8, Dex 14, Con 15, Int 12, Wis 8, Cha 15.

    Skills: Concentration, Intimidate, Spellcraft.

    Languages: Common, Gnome, Goblin.

    Feat: Battle Caster (*Complete Arcane*).

    Weapon: Longspear (1d6/×3).

    Armor: Scale mail (+4 AC).

    Other Gear: Spell component pouch, standard adventurer's kit.

Package 2: The Blaster
Human Warmage

    Ability Scores: Str 8, Dex 14, Con 13, Int 12, Wis 10, Cha 15.

    Skills: Concentration, Intimidate, Knowledge (arcana), Spellcraft.

    Languages: Common, Draconic.

    Feats: Lightning Reflexes, Spell Focus (evocation).

    Weapons: Spear (1d8/×3), light crossbow with 20 bolts (1d8/19–20, 80 ft.).

    Armor: Leather (+2 AC).

    Other Gear: Spell component pouch, standard adventurer's kit, 1 gp.

Package 3: The Sharpshooter
Halfling Warmage

    Ability Scores: Str 6, Dex 16, Con 13, Int 12, Wis 10, Cha 15.

    Skills: Concentration, Spellcraft, Spot (cc).

    Languages: Common, Elven, Halfling.

    Feat: Point Blank Shot.

    Weapons: Spear (1d8/×3), light crossbow with 20 bolts (1d8/19–20, 80 ft.).

    Armor: Leather (+2 AC).

    Other Gear: Spell component pouch, standard adventurer's kit, 1 gp.

Illus. by S. Prescott

WIZARD

Given time enough, you hope to discover every secret of magic ever penned. The arcane secrets of the world excite you like nothing else, and the discovery of a new tome, scroll, or magical treatise makes your heart skip a beat, your face flush, and your breath come quick. Each new libram of spells you discover is another intellectual fortune, and the anticipation of what you'll find is nearly as satisfying as the actual identification of a spell wholly new to your library.

While you hate leaving your sanctum with its library and arcane equipment that you use to determine the magical secrets of magic items and artifacts, it is good to now and then venture from the laboratory and actually utter the incantations, hexes, and powerful spells that you prepare daily. The craft you pursue is an art, and like any pursuit, it requires practice.

Suggested Backgrounds (choose one): Artisan, Ascetic, Noble Scion.

Suggested Personality Archetypes (choose one): Agent, Challenger, Crusader, Innocent, Mercenary, Renegade, Royalty, Sage, Seeker, Strategist, Theorist, Trickster.

CHARACTER THEMES

One or more of the following character themes could apply to you.

Doting Master: Your familiar is more than a mere adjunct of your power—it is your companion, friend, and confidant. Whenever you eat, whether informally, or at an inn or even at a formal party, you always make certain that your familiar samples the best tasting portions of the meal.

You worry about your familiar's ability to stay warm, or at least fashionable, and so you've ordered a few custom pieces of clothing with which to outfit your familiar, including a vest, paw (or talon) gloves, and goggles. Whether or not your familiar is smart enough to respond, you ask its opinion on weighty matters.

While you are immensely proud of your familiar, you cast a critical eye at the familiars of other wizards and arcanists who keep pets. You know that your bond with your familiar, and better yet the skill your familiar displays, is a reflection of your worth.

"Never mind them, Piggin. We know we're right, even if they choose not to bow to our superior knowledge of things arcane."

"This pie is succulent! Come, get a taste, Little Browning! Where are you?"

"Look there, Tibb. A raven! So bedraggled, so thin. Poor thing looks like it's on its last feathers, doesn't it?"

Evil Curious: You've always told yourself that you merely enjoy magic—who wouldn't? It's the best thing about living, isn't it? But you've recently realized that your impulse control might not be what it should when it comes to the discovery of new tomes and items. No matter how evil the previous owner of the item or tome, you can't help but be curious about the spells within.

However, you also know that true evil is a lure that can cage your mind and will just as effectively as an illithid can, and it can consume all your good works and past accomplishments. To avoid that fate, you constantly look for items and or spells that might serve as an "insulator" so that you can study evil tomes and items with some amount of spiritual protection. You've heard that such spells exist, however fallible, and you intend to find them.

"I have safeguards to protect me against any influences beyond my own will!"

"We must understand this if we are going to learn what we need to defeat the threat!"

Knowledgeable: As a master wizard, steeped in the arts arcane, you know a lot about a lot, much of which is esoteric to your comrades unschooled in wizardry. That is no reason not make regular use of your large and mysterious vocabulary in day-to-day conversation, or to reference various entities of great power and or wizardly significance when you are surprised or otherwise disturbed.

You are also familiar with a great many tomes and don't mind referencing them in regular conversation, especially if you claim to have penned a few of your own.

"By the silver scales of the Denebic Water Dragon!"

"Just as the gaze of Shandalfar pierces any murk . . ."

"If the dread power of the Spell of Utter Ruination could be used as a measure . . ."

"If I knew the words to the Citrine Wall of Finality, things would be different here, but . . ."

"This path reminds me of the Twelve Unsolvable Mazes of the Demon King Tatharok."

"Oh ho! You'd argue with the author of The Power of the Wizard— The Earth, The Planes, and the Magical Path to Enlightenment?"

"I don't hold too much with the mysticism infused with the spells discussed in Drawing Down the Moon, or any mysticism, really. I'm more about the art, not the theory."

"Well, according to what I've read in Magical Monsters: A Bestiary of Fearsome Creatures . . ."

IMMEDIATE MAGIC

Other than having a single additional spell of each spell level, a specialist wizard functions like any other wizard. Your evoker's *fireball* spell deals as much damage as that of a conjurer, diviner, or necromancer, and doesn't look any different. By taking the immediate magic alternative class feature, you gain a useful trick that sets you apart from other specialists. Though giving up your familiar is a hardship, it means you have one less thing to worry about in a fight.

Level: 1st.

Replaces: If you select this class feature, you do not gain a familiar.

Benefit: You gain a spell-like ability that reflects your chosen school of magic. Activating this ability is an immediate action, and you can use this spell-like ability a number of times per day equal to your Intelligence bonus (minimum 1). Its equivalent spell level is equal to one-half your wizard level (minimum 1st), and the caster level is your wizard level. The save DC (if any) is equal to 10 + 1/2 your wizard level + your Int modifier. This is an extraordinary ability.

You can't activate this ability in response to an attack that you aren't aware of. For instance, if an invisible rogue strikes at you, you can't activate urgent shield to gain a bonus to your AC against the attack. All effects last until the start of your next turn unless otherwise noted.

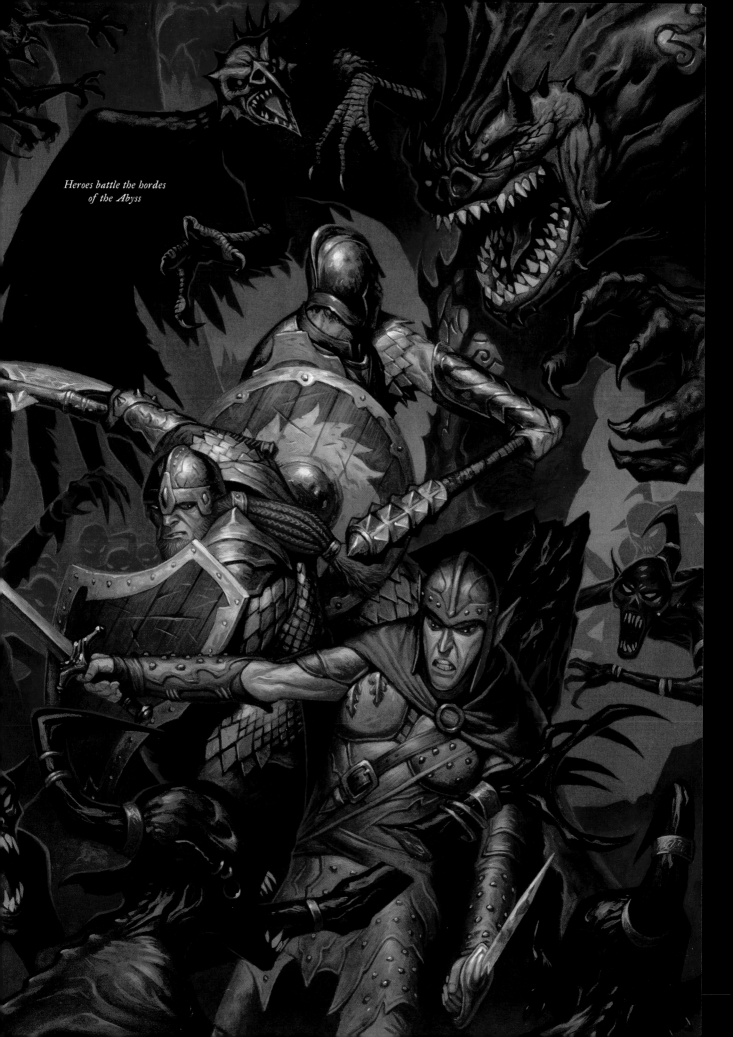

Heroes battle the hordes
of the Abyss

To select this ability, you must also choose to specialize in a school of magic. The spell-like ability gained depends on your specialty (see below).

Urgent Shield (abjuration): You create a temporary shield of force that grants you a +2 shield bonus to AC.

Abrupt Jaunt (conjuration): You teleport up to 10 feet. You can't bring along any other creatures.

Glimpse Peril (divination): You get a flash of foresight into the danger lying in your future. You gain a +2 insight bonus on the next saving throw you make before your next turn.

Instant Daze (enchantment): When an enemy that has HD equal to or less than your wizard level makes a melee attack against you, you can render him dazed (Will negates). This is a compulsion, mind-affecting ability.

Counterfire (evocation): When a visible enemy within 60 feet targets you with a ranged attack or spell, you can respond with a glowing arrow of force. This requires a ranged touch attack to hit and deals 1d6 points of damage per three wizard levels. Both attacks resolve simultaneously (neither can disrupt the other).

Brief Figment (illusion): You create a figment double of yourself (similar to *mirror image*). The image lasts until it is struck or until the start of your next turn.

Cursed Glance (necromancy): When a visible enemy within 60 feet targets you with an attack or spell, you can respond with a curse. If the enemy fails a Will save, he takes a –2 penalty to AC and on saving throws.

Sudden Shift (transmutation): You temporarily change your form to grant yourself a climb, fly, or swim speed equal to your current land speed. If you activate this ability during your turn, it lasts until the end of that turn; otherwise it lasts until the end of your next turn.

STARTING PACKAGES

Package 1: The Blaster

Elf Wizard (Evoker)

Ability Scores: Str 8, Dex 15, Con 12, Int 15, Wis 12, Cha 10.

Skills: Concentration, Knowledge (arcana), Knowledge (the planes), Spellcraft.

Languages: Common, Draconic, Elven, Orc.

Feats: Scribe Scroll, Spell Focus (evocation).

Weapons: Quarterstaff (1d6), shortbow with 20 arrows (1d6/×3, 60 ft.).

*Archmage Mialee
of the Seven Stars*

Armor: None.

Other Gear: Spell component pouch, spellbook, standard adventurer's kit, 4 gp.

Spells Prepared: 1st—*burning hands, magic missile, shield;* 0—*detect magic, light, ray of frost.*

Spellbook: All 0-level spells plus *burning hands, mage armor, magic missile, obscuring mist, shield.*

Specialty School: Evocation (prohibited schools: enchantment, illusion).

Package 2: The Controller

Gnome Wizard (Enchanter)

Ability Scores: Str 6, Dex 13, Con 14, Int 15, Wis 10, Cha 14.

Skills: Bluff (cc), Concentration, Knowledge (local), Spellcraft.

Languages: Common, Draconic, Gnome, Goblin.

Feats: Scribe Scroll, Spell Focus (enchantment).

Weapons: Club (1d4), light crossbow with 20 bolts (1d6/19–20, 80 ft.).

Armor: None.

Other Gear: Spell component pouch, spellbook, standard adventurer's kit, 3 gp.

Spells Prepared: 1st—*charm person, sleep;* 0—*daze, light, read magic.*

Spellbook: All 0-level spells plus *charm person, expeditious retreat, silent image, sleep, shield.*

Specialty School: Enchantment (prohibited schools: conjuration, necromancy).

Package 3: The Problem Solver

Human Wizard (Diviner)

Ability Scores: Str 8, Dex 13, Con 14, Int 15, Wis 12, Cha 10.

Skills: Concentration, Craft (alchemy), Decipher Script, Knowledge (arcana), Spellcraft.

Languages: Common, Draconic, Elven.

Feats: Combat Familiar, Grenadier, Scribe Scroll.

Weapons: Quarterstaff (1d6), dagger (1d4/19–20, 10 ft.), light crossbow with 20 bolts (1d8/19–20, 80 ft.).

Armor: None.

Other Gear: Spell component pouch, spellbook, standard adventurer's kit, 1 gp.

Spells Prepared: 1st—*cause fear, comprehend languages, protection from evil;* 0—*detect magic, light, read magic.*

Spellbook: All 0-level spells plus *cause fear, comprehend languages, enlarge person, protection from evil, summon monster I.*

Specialty School: Divination (prohibited school: evocation).

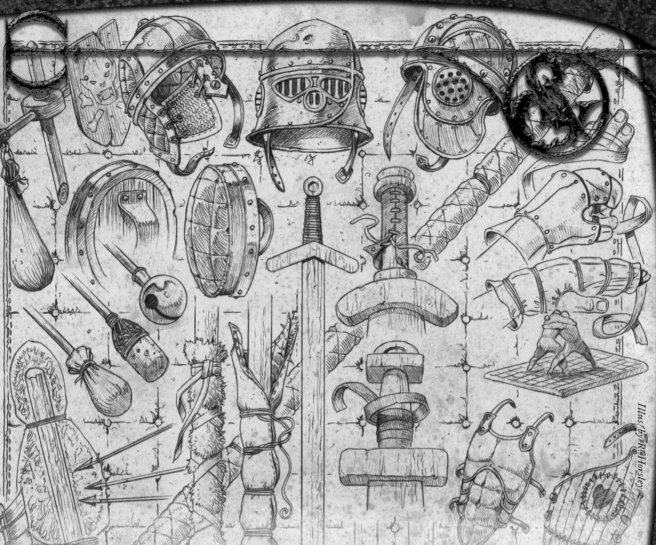

Illus. by R&H Horsley

F eats are one of the best ways to customize your character. A fighter with Exotic Weapon Proficiency (spiked chain), Combat Expertise, and Improved Trip operates in a completely different manner than one with Point Blank Shot, Precise Shot, and Shot on the Run. Feats give you the opportunity to create a unique character by supplementing your class's core abilities or expanding your PC in a new direction.

The following feats supplement those found in Chapter 5 of the *Player's Handbook*. Many of them have feats from that book as prerequisites.

GENERAL FEATS

The feats described below are all general feats. Their prerequisites and benefits are summarized on Table 3–1.

ACROBATIC STRIKE

Your dexterous maneuvers and skilled acrobatics allow you to slip past a foe's defenses and deliver an accurate strike against him.

Prerequisite: Tumble 12 ranks.

Benefit: If you succeed in using Tumble to avoid an opponent's attack of opportunity, you gain a +4 bonus on the next attack that you make against that foe as long as the attack occurs before the end of your current turn.

Special: A fighter can select Acrobatic Strike as one of his fighter bonus feats.

ACTIVE SHIELD DEFENSE

Your expert use of your shield allows you to strike at vulnerable foes even when you forgo your own attacks in favor of defense.

Prerequisites: Proficiency with shields, Shield Specialization.

Benefit: When fighting defensively and using a shield, you do not take the standard fighting defensively penalties on attacks of opportunity.

When using the total defense action and a shield, you still threaten the area around you as normal. You can make attacks of opportunity with a –4 penalty.

Normal: You take a –4 penalty on all attacks while fighting defensively. You cannot attack while using the total defense action.

Special: A fighter can select Active Shield Defense as one of his fighter bonus feats.

ADAPTABLE FLANKER

When you and an ally team up against a foe, you know how to maximize the threat your ally poses to ruin your target's defenses.

Prerequisites: Combat Reflexes, Vexing Flanker, base attack bonus +4.

TABLE 3–1: GENERAL FEATS

Feat	Prerequisites	Benefit
Acrobatic Strike	Tumble 12 ranks	+6 on next attack against opponent you tumble past
Arcane Flourish	Perform 4 ranks, arcane caster level 1st	Expend spell to gain bonus on Perform check
Arcane Accompaniment	Perform 4 ranks, Arcane Flourish, arcane caster level 1st, bardic music	Expend prepared spell or spell slot to extend duration of bardic music
Arcane Thesis	Knowledge (arcana) 9 ranks, ability to cast arcane spells	+2 caster level, cheaper metamagic with one spell
Arcane Toughness	Toughness, arcane caster level 3rd	Expend prepared spell or spell slot to heal when at or below 0 hit points
Arcane Consumption	Arcane Toughness, Toughness, arcane caster level 6th	+2 save DC for one spell, Con penalty for 12 hours and fatigued
Armor Specialization	Proficiency with selected armor type, base attack bonus +12	DR 2/– with chosen armor
Battle Dancer	Base attack bonus +2, bardic music	+2 on attacks while moving and using bardic music
Bonded Familiar	Familiar	You and familiar shift damage after deadly attack
Bounding Assault	Dex 13, Dodge, Mobility, Spring Attack, base attack bonus +12	Attack twice while using Spring Attack
Rapid Blitz	Dex 13, Bounding Assault, Dodge, Mobility, Spring Attack, base attack bonus +18	Make third attack as part of Spring Attack
Brutal Strike	Str 13, Power Attack, base attack bonus +6	Daze opponent with successful bludgeoning attack
Combat Acrobat	Balance 9 ranks, Tumble 9 ranks	Gain new uses for Balance skill
Combat Familiar	Arcane caster level 1st, familiar	Familiar enters foe's square without provoking attack
Lurking Familiar	Combat Familiar, arcane caster level 6th	Familiar can hide in your square
Combat Tactician	Dex 13, Dodge, base attack bonus +12	+2 on damage against foe you approach and attack
Cometary Collision	Str 13, Improved Bull Rush, Power Attack	Ready action to slam into charging foe
Companion Spellbond	Animal companion	Share spells with companion at greater range
Crossbow Sniper	Proficiency with hand, heavy, or light crossbow, Weapon Focus with hand, heavy, or light crossbow, base attack bonus +1	Half Dexterity bonus on crossbow damage, 60 ft. skirmish or sneak attack
Cunning Evasion	Hide 9 ranks, evasion	Hide and move immediately after using evasion
Dampen Spell	Improved Counterspell	Reduce your save DC against foe's spell by expending spell or slot as immediate action
Deadeye Shot	Point Blank Shot, Precise Shot, base attack bonus +4, skirmish or sneak attack ability	Ready action to fire, denying foe Dex bonus to AC on your attack after ally hits foe
Defensive Sweep	Base attack bonus +15	Foe must move or provoke attack
Elven Spell Lore	Int 17 or elf, Knowledge (arcana) 12 ranks	Bonus on dispel attempts, alter energy type of spell
Fade into Violence	Bluff 6 ranks, Hide 6 ranks	Foe strikes ally, not you, if your Bluff check succeeds
Fiery Fist	Dex 13, Wis 13, Improved Unarmed Strike, Stunning Fist, base attack bonus +8	Expend Stunning Fist use to cloak fists, feet in fiery energy for +1d6 damage
Fiery Ki Defense	Dex 13, Wis 13, Fiery Fist, Improved Unarmed Strike, Stunning Fist, base attack bonus +8	Expend Stunning Fist use to cloak self in flame, damaging any who strike you
Ki Blast	Dex 13, Wis 13, Fiery Fist, Improved Unarmed Strike, Stunning Fist, base attack bonus +8	Expend Stunning Fist uses to throw ball of *ki* energy
Flay	Str 13, Power Attack	Inflict painful wounds on unarmored targets
Grenadier	—	+1 on attacks and damage with splash weapons
Hindering Opportunist	Combat Reflexes, base attack bonus +3	Replace attack of opportunity with aid another
Stalwart Defense	Combat Reflexes, Hindering Opportunist, base attack bonus +9	Foes provoke aid another action from you when they attack allies
Indomitable Soul	Endurance, Iron Will	Roll twice against fear and mind-affecting attacks
Intimidating Strike	Intimidate 4 ranks	Use Intimidate check with attack to shake opponent
Keen-Eared Scout	Listen 6 ranks, Alertness or Skill Focus (Listen)	Listen check reveals extra information about sound
Leap of the Heavens	Jump 4 ranks	Don't double DC for standing jumps, +5 bonus on running jumps
Lunging Strike	Base attack bonus +6	Extend reach of one attack
Mad Foam Rager	Rage or frenzy ability	Once per rage or frenzy, delay spell or attack effect
Master Manipulator	Cha 13, Diplomacy 9 ranks	Gain two new uses of Diplomacy skill
Melee Evasion	Dex 13, Int 13, Combat Expertise, Dodge	While fighting defensively, negate foe's attack
Melee Weapon Mastery	Proficiency with selected weapon, Weapon Focus with selected weapon, Weapon Specialization with selected weapon, base attack bonus +8	Gain Weapon Focus, Weapon Specialization benefits with multiple weapons

Feat	Prerequisites	Benefit
Crushing Strike	Proficiency with a bludgeoning weapon, Weapon Focus with a bludgeoning weapon, Melee Weapon Mastery (bludgeoning), Weapon Specialization with a bludgeoning weapon, base attack bonus +14	+1 on attacks per previous hit with bludgeon
Driving Attack	Proficiency with selected weapon, Weapon Focus with selected weapon, Melee Weapon Mastery (piercing), Weapon Specialization with selected weapon, base attack bonus +14	Bull rush with piercing weapon attack
Slashing Flurry	Proficiency with selected weapon, Weapon Focus with selected weapon, Melee Weapon Mastery (slashing), Weapon Specialization with selected weapon, base attack bonus +14	Gain extra attack with slashing weapon
Weapon Supremacy	Proficiency with selected weapon, Greater Weapon Focus with selected weapon, Greater Weapon Specialization with selected weapon, Weapon Focus with selected weapon, Weapon Specialization with selected weapon, Melee Weapon Mastery with weapon type of selected weapon, fighter level 18th	Gain further abilities with chosen weapon
Overwhelming Assault	Base attack bonus +15	Gain bonus against adjacent foe not attacking you
Penetrating Shot	Str 15, Point Blank Shot, base attack bonus +10	Your ranged attack targets every foe in 60-ft. line
Ranged Weapon Mastery	Proficiency with selected weapon, Weapon Focus with selected weapon, Weapon Specialization with selected weapon, base attack bonus +8	Gain Weapon Focus, Weapon Specialization benefits with multiple weapons
Robilar's Gambit	Combat Reflexes, base attack bonus +12	Grant foes bonus on attacks and damage, but their attacks provoke attacks of opportunity
Shield Specialization	Proficiency with shields	Increase shield bonus by +1
Active Shield Defense	Proficiency with shields, Shield Specialization	Make attacks of opportunity without penalty when fighting defensively
Agile Shield Fighter	Proficiency with shields, Improved Shield Bash, Shield Specialization	Reduce two weapon penalties when using shield bash
Shield Sling	Proficiency with shields, Improved Shield Bash, Shield Specialization, base attack bonus +9	Use shield as ranged weapon
Shield Ward	Proficiency with shields, Shield Specialization	Gain shield bonus to touch AC and against bull rush, disarm, grapple, overrun, and trip
Short Haft	Proficiency with selected weapon, Weapon Focus with selected weapon, base attack bonus +3	Lose reach benefits, attack adjacent foes
Spectral Skirmisher	Base attack bonus +6	Gain bonuses while invisible
Spell-Linked Familiar	Arcane caster level 9th, familiar	Familiar gains limited spellcasting ability
Steadfast Determination	Endurance	Use Constitution to modify Will saves
Telling Blow	Skirmish attack or sneak attack	Gain skirmish or sneak attack damage on critical hits
Trophy Collector	Craft (taxidermy) 6 ranks	Gain bonuses from trophies you create and wear
Tumbling Feint	Bluff 4 ranks, Tumble 4 ranks	+5 on feint attempt after successful Tumble
Two-Weapon Pounce	Dex 15, Two-Weapon Fighting, base attack bonus +6	Attack with both weapons when charging
Two-Weapon Rend	Dex 15, Two-Weapon Fighting, base attack bonus +11	Gain bonus damage if you hit with both weapons
Vatic Gaze	Arcane caster level 9th	Detect magic at will, use Sense Motive to determine foe's highest-level spell
Versatile Unarmed Strike	Improved Unarmed Strike	Deal bludgeoning, piercing, or slashing damage with unarmed strikes
Vexing Flanker	Combat Reflexes	+4 on attacks when flanking
Adaptable Flanker	Combat Reflexes, Vexing Flanker, base attack bonus +4	Flank chosen foe from adjacent square
Wanderer's Diplomacy	Halfling or 4 ranks in Bluff, Diplomacy, and Sense Motive	Gain special social abilities
Water Splitting Stone	Dex 13, Wis 13, Improved Unarmed Strike, Stunning Fist, base attack bonus +9	+4 bonus on damage when striking foe that has DR

Illus. by E. Fiegenschuh

Benefit: As a swift action, you designate a single opponent as the target of this feat. When you are adjacent to the chosen target, you can choose to count as occupying any other square you threaten for purposes of determining flanking bonuses for you and your allies. You also occupy your current square for flanking an opponent.

Special: A fighter can select Adaptable Flanker as one of his fighter bonus feats.

AGILE SHIELD FIGHTER

You are skilled in combining your shield bash attack with an armed strike. When you use your shield in unison with a weapon, your training allows you to score telling blows with both.

Prerequisites: Proficiency with shields, Improved Shield Bash, Shield Specialization.

Benefit: When making a shield bash and armed strike attack as part of a full attack action, you take a –2 penalty on each attack. These penalties replace the normal ones you incur for fighting with two weapons.

Special: A fighter can select Agile Shield Fighter as one of his fighter bonus feats.

ARCANE ACCOMPANIMENT

You infuse your performance with magical energy, allowing its effects to continue even as you attend to other tasks.

Prerequisites: Perform 4 ranks, Arcane Flourish, arcane caster level 1st, bardic music.

Benefit: As a swift action, you can expend a prepared spell or a spell slot to extend the duration of your bardic music ability after you stop performing. You extend the duration a number of rounds equal to the level of the spell used in this manner. This extension is in addition to the normal duration of the effect after you stop your performance.

You can expend only one spell slot to extend the duration of your bardic music.

The slot can come from any of your arcane caster classes, not just bard.

This has no effect on bardic music or similar abilities with a duration of instantaneous or permanent.

ARCANE CONSUMPTION

You can sacrifice your physical health to strengthen a spell. This process leaves you wracked with pain, but the enhanced energy you draw from the spell might provide the margin between victory and defeat.

Prerequisites: Arcane Toughness, Toughness, arcane caster level 6th.

Benefit: Once per day as a swift action, you can grant the next spell you cast a +4 bonus on its save DC. You must cast and complete this spell on the same turn that you use a swift action to activate this feat. In return, you take a –4 penalty to Constitution for 12 hours and are fatigued.

ARCANE FLOURISH

You use your magical abilities to improve your performance talents. By bleeding magical energy into your singing, oratory, or other abilities, you enhance the pitch and sound, project your voice with a more commanding tone, and so forth.

Prerequisites: Perform 4 ranks, arcane caster level 1st.

Benefit: As a swift action, you can expend a prepared spell or spell slot to grant your next Perform check a competence bonus equal to 1 + the level of the spell or slot. You must make a check within 1 minute of using this feat, or the energy you expend dissipates with no effect.

ARCANE THESIS

You have studied a single spell in-depth. Your expertise grants you formidable though narrowly focused arcane mastery.

Prerequisites: Knowledge (arcana) 9 ranks, ability to cast arcane spells.

An elf uses Acrobatic Strike to get the drop on a giant

Benefit: Choose one arcane spell that you can cast to be your thesis spell. When casting that spell, you do so at +2 caster level. When you apply a metamagic feat other than Heighten Spell to that spell, the enhanced spell uses up a spell slot one level lower than normal. For example, an empowered thesis spell uses up a spell slot one level higher than the spell's actual slot (rather than the normal two levels higher).

Special: You can gain this feat multiple times. Its effects do not stack. Each time you take the feat, it applies to a new spell.

ARCANE TOUGHNESS

You draw upon the power of your magic to sustain yourself, allowing you to continue fighting long after your physical body has failed you.

Prerequisites: Toughness, arcane caster level 3rd.

Benefit: You can expend a prepared spell or spell slot as an immediate action when you are reduced to 0 or fewer hit points. You heal a number of points of damage equal to the level of the spell or spell slot used in this manner. You cannot use this ability to negate effects that disable you without causing hit point damage, such as a medusa's ability to turn you to stone. Even if this healing does not bring you above negative hit points, it still stabilizes you.

Using a 0-level spell with this feat grants no benefit.

ARMOR SPECIALIZATION

Through long wear and hours of combat, you have trained your body to believe in its armor. Where others flinch, you confront. When the sword falls, your instincts, born of bruises and rent flesh, present your cuirass, cuisse, helm, or gorget to meet the blade at the perfect angle, causing it to skitter off harmlessly.

Prerequisites: Proficiency with selected armor type, base attack bonus +12.

Benefit: Choose one type of medium or heavy armor with which you are proficient. When wearing masterwork armor (including magic armor) of that type, you gain damage reduction 2/–. Any time you lose your Dexterity bonus to Armor Class, you lose the benefit of this feat, because you cannot properly deflect the blows of the enemy.

Special: You can gain this feat multiple times. Its effects do not stack. Each time you take the feat, it applies to a new type of armor.

A fighter can select Armor Specialization as one of his fighter bonus feats.

BATTLE DANCER

You strike at your foes in time with the music you sing or in cadence with an oration you deliver. The magical power of your bardic performance drives you forward and improves your fighting ability.

Prerequisites: Base attack bonus +2, bardic music.

Benefit: During a round in which you grant any ally a bonus on attack rolls, damage rolls, or saves with one of your bardic music abilities, you gain a +2 morale bonus on your attack rolls if you move at least one square before attacking. You lose this benefit for the remaining duration of your current use of bardic music if you do not move or if you do not attack on your turn. If you stand still and attack (or move without attacking), you do not gain this feat's benefit, but this ability's duration continues.

Special: A fighter can select Battle Dancer as one of his fighter bonus feats.

BONDED FAMILIAR

You enjoy a stronger than normal magical bond with your familiar, granting you access to two special abilities.

Prerequisite: Familiar.

Benefit: As long as your familiar is within 30 feet of you, the two of you can share the damage from a single deadly attack. Once per day, if an attack would drop your familiar to 0 or fewer hit points, you can instead choose to accept that damage. In addition, once per day, your familiar can choose to take the damage from a single attack or effect that would reduce you to 0 or fewer hit points. This ability applies only to attacks or effects that deal hit point damage. You or your familiar could not absorb the effect of a spell such as *flesh to stone*.

BOUNDING ASSAULT

You can move and attack with superior speed and power.

Prerequisites: Dex 13, Dodge, Mobility, Spring Attack, base attack bonus +12.

Benefit: When using the Spring Attack feat, you designate two foes rather than one. Your movement does not provoke attacks of opportunity from either of these foes. While using an attack action with the Spring Attack feat, you can make a second attack with a –5 penalty. You can use both attacks against one of the opponents targeted with this feat, or split your attacks between them.

Illus. by C. Frank

Arcane Accompaniment channels magical energy into Gimble's song

BRUTAL STRIKE

You can batter foes senseless with your mace, morningstar, quarterstaff, or flail. Few victims are willing to stand toe-to-toe with a warrior known for knocking his foes witless with a single strike.

Prerequisites: Str 13, Power Attack, base attack bonus +6.

Benefit: If you use your Power Attack feat to increase your damage with a bludgeoning weapon, you can attempt a brutal strike. You must declare your intention before making your attack. If the attack hits and your opponent takes damage, he must make a Fortitude save (DC 10 + your extra damage from the Power Attack feat on the attack) or be sickened for 1 round.

You can use this feat once per round during your attack action.

Special: This feat cannot be used against a creature that is not subject to extra damage from critical hits.

A fighter can select Brutal Strike as one of his fighter bonus feats.

COMBAT ACROBAT

Your acrobatics and agility in combat allow you to maneuver across the battlefield with ease. You stay on your feet and speed over difficult terrain due to your superior athleticism and acrobatic talents.

Prerequisites: Balance 9 ranks, Tumble 9 ranks.

Benefit: You gain several benefits from this feat to reflect your overall athletic ability and training in the skills vital to an acrobat.

Acrobatic Recovery: If an effect causes you to fall prone, you can make a DC 20 Balance check to remain on your feet.

Sure Footed Maneuver: With a DC 15 Balance check, you can ignore up to 4 squares of difficult terrain while moving. You treat these squares as normal terrain. You still endure any effects or hazards associated with the terrain. For example, a shallow pool of boiling water might deal fire damage and count as difficult terrain. You would still take damage from the water even if your Balance check allowed you to move through it at full speed.

Special: A fighter can select Combat Acrobat as one of his fighter bonus feats.

COMBAT FAMILIAR

Your familiar is skilled in delivering attack spells against your foes. It flits past their defenses to discharge its spell without leaving itself vulnerable to attack.

Prerequisites: Arcane caster level 1st, familiar.

Bounding Assault enables this fighter to target two foes instead of one

Tordek uses Cometary Collision to close quickly with a displacer beast skeleton

Illus. by E. Widermann

Benefit: If your familiar holds the charge for a touch spell, it does not provoke an attack of opportunity for entering an opponent's square.

COMBAT TACTICIAN

You excel at approaching an opponent from an unexpected direction to deliver deadly attacks. As you approach your foe, you duck and weave to confuse his defenses. Alternatively, you draw a weapon and make a quick attack that surprises your foe.

Prerequisites: Dex 13, Dodge, base attack bonus +12.

Benefit: You can designate one specific foe as the target of this feat as a free action. If neither you nor the target threatens each other at the start of your turn, you gain a +2 bonus on melee damage against that target during your turn.

COMETARY COLLISION

You are a thunderbolt of destruction on the battlefield. By carefully timing your charge, you rush forward and slam into an enemy just as he gathers the speed needed to charge you. You turn your opponent's momentum against him.

Prerequisites: Str 13, Improved Bull Rush, Power Attack.

Benefit: You can ready a standard action to use this feat when an opponent charges you or any other target. At any point during your opponent's charge, you can charge him. In place of the normal charge benefits, you gain +2 on your attack roll and +4 on your damage roll. Your foe loses the benefits of charging (but not the penalties) but can still attack you. If the target charged someone else, he can choose to instead attack you. You take the standard –2 penalty to AC for charging.

If you cannot move at least 10 feet or cannot charge due to terrain or other factors, you do not gain this feat's benefit. In either case, you use your readied action to move but do not gain an attack.

Special: A fighter can select Cometary Collision as one of his fighter bonus feats.

COMPANION SPELLBOND

You form a special magical link with your animal companion, allowing you to share spells with it over a greater distance.

Prerequisite: Animal companion.

Benefit: You use your companion's share spells ability out to a range of 30 feet, rather than the standard 5 feet. You can cast touch spells to affect your companion at a greater range than normal. You can change a spell's range from touch to short (range of 25 feet + 5 feet per two caster levels) if the spell targets only your companion.

CROSSBOW SNIPER

You are skilled in lining up accurate, deadly shots with your crossbow. Perhaps you add custom-made sights to your weapon, or you have learned to maximize the stability and precision the weapon offers.

Prerequisites: Proficiency with hand, heavy, or light crossbow, Weapon Focus with hand, heavy, or light crossbow, base attack bonus +1.

Benefit: When using a crossbow for which you have the Weapon Focus feat, you gain a bonus on damage rolls equal to 1/2 your Dexterity bonus.

If you have the skirmish or sneak attack ability, the maximum range at which you can make such attacks increases to 60 feet when you are using a crossbow for which you have the Weapon Focus feat.

Special: A fighter can select Crossbow Sniper as one of his fighter bonus feats.

CRUSHING STRIKE

You wield a bludgeoning weapon with superior power, allowing you to batter aside an opponent's defenses.

Prerequisites: Proficiency with a bludgeoning weapon, Weapon Focus with a bludgeoning weapon, Weapon Mastery (bludgeoning), Weapon Specialization with a bludgeoning weapon, base attack bonus +14.

Benefit: When you use a full attack action while fighting with any bludgeoning weapon, each attack that connects beats down your foe's defenses, granting a cumulative +1 bonus on attack rolls until the end of your current turn.

CUNNING EVASION

When an area attack detonates around you, you use the chaos and flash of energy to duck out of sight.

Prerequisites: Hide 9 ranks, evasion.

Benefit: If you are caught within an area attack whose damage you avoid completely due to your evasion or improved evasion ability, you can make a combined Hide check and a 5-foot step as an immediate action. You can attempt this check only if there is cover suitable for a Hide check, and you can take your 5-foot step into cover before making your Hide attempt.

Special: If you have the hide in plain sight class feature, you do not need cover near you to attempt the Hide check allowed by this feat.

DAMPEN SPELL

From the lowliest prestidigitator to the most august hierophant, spellcasters both arcane and divine recognize the power of counterspelling. You are no exception. You have learned to channel energy into a foe's spell to weaken its effects. Although you fail to nullify the spell, you render it much easier to resist.

Prerequisite: Improved Counterspell.

Benefit: You can use an immediate action to attempt to dampen an enemy's spell. As with counterspelling, you must identify the target spell as it is being cast. If you successfully identify it, you can expend any spell or spell slot to dampen your opponent's incantation. Because of your hasty, immediate casting, you do not fully counter the target spell. Instead, you subtract the level of the spell or spell slot you expend from the save DC of your opponent's spell.

DEADEYE SHOT

You carefully line up a ranged attack, timing it precisely so that you hit your opponent when his guard is down. When your target is busy dealing with an ally's melee attack, you strike.

Prerequisites: Point Blank Shot, Precise Shot, base attack bonus +4, skirmish or sneak attack ability.

Benefit: By firing just as your ally connects with a blow, you take advantage of the distraction to strike the same enemy when his guard is ruined. If you ready a ranged attack to occur when an ally strikes a particular target, and your ally succeeds, that target loses his Dexterity bonus to AC against your attack.

Special: A fighter can select Deadeye Shot as one of his fighter bonus feats.

DEFENSIVE SWEEP

You sweep your weapon through the area you threaten, warding away opponents and forcing them to move away or suffer a fearsome blow.

Prerequisite: Base attack bonus +15.

Benefit: If an opponent begins his action adjacent to you and does not move, he provokes an attack of opportunity from you immediately after his turn ends, provided that you threaten the square that he occupies. Any sort of movement, including a 5-foot step, allows the opponent to avoid provoking this special attack of opportunity. This feat does not give you any ability to make additional attacks of opportunity in a given round.

Special: A fighter can select Defensive Sweep as one of his fighter bonus feats.

DRIVING ATTACK

When you strike an opponent with a piercing weapon, the brutal impact of your strike sends him sprawling.

Prerequisites: Proficiency with selected piercing weapon, Weapon Focus with selected piercing weapon, Weapon Mastery (piercing), Weapon Specialization with selected piercing weapon, base attack bonus +14.

Benefit: If you use a full-round action to make a single melee attack with any piercing weapon and succeed in hitting, you can initiate a special bull rush attempt against the target. This bull rush uses your total bonus on damage rolls in place of your Strength modifier. You do not provoke an attack of opportunity with this bull rush, and you cannot move forward with your opponent.

If you succeed in pushing an opponent back 10 feet or more, you can reduce the distance you push him by 10 feet. In return, your foe falls prone in the square where he ends his movement. Note that by reducing the distance you push your opponent, you can have him fall prone in his current space.

ELVEN SPELL LORE

You have studied the mighty arcane traditions of the elves, granting you insight into the intricate workings of magic and the theoretical structures behind spells.

Prerequisites: Int 17 or elf, Knowledge (arcana) 12 ranks.

Benefit: Your understanding of the elven secrets of magic grants you two benefits. When you cast *dispel magic* or *greater dispel magic*, you gain a +2 bonus on your caster level check. Your understanding of magic allows you to more easily unravel the power that sustains a foe's spell.

In addition, your knowledge of magic grants you rare insights into forgotten spell lore. Choose a single spell in your spellbook when you take this feat. When preparing that spell, you can alter the type of damage it deals to a single type of your choice. You must make this choice when preparing the spell (those who do not prepare spells cannot benefit from this aspect of the feat). You can prepare the spell multiple times, selecting the same or a different energy type for it with each preparation.

You can gain this feat multiple times. The caster level bonus does not stack, and each time you take the feat, a different spell must be chosen.

FADE INTO VIOLENCE

While the chaos of battle swirls around you, you rely on your ability to slip into the background to avoid your enemy's notice. Your frightened demeanor and pitiable appearance causes your opponents to seek out other targets.

Prerequisites: Bluff 6 ranks, Hide 6 ranks.

Benefit: When you wear no armor or light armor and carry nothing in your hands, your opponents might assume that you are an ineffectual fighter. As an immediate action, choose a single target for this feat. If that opponent threatens both you and one of your allies, that foe strikes your ally rather than you unless he succeeds on a Sense Motive check opposed by your Bluff check. If your foe is larger than you, you gain a +4 bonus on your Bluff check. You lose this benefit if you attack any opponent or target an opponent with a spell. This benefit does not apply to ranged attacks or attacks of opportunity that you provoke.

Once you choose a target for this feat, you cannot switch to a new target for the rest of the encounter.

FIERY FIST

By channeling your *ki* energy, you sheathe your limbs in magical fire. Your unarmed strikes deal extra fire damage.

Prerequisites: Dex 13, Wis 13, Improved Unarmed Strike, Stunning Fist, base attack bonus +8.

Benefit: As a swift action, you can expend one of your uses of the Stunning Fist feat to surround your fists and feet in flame. For the rest of your turn, you gain an extra 1d6 points of fire damage on your unarmed strikes.

When you select this feat, you gain an additional daily use of Stunning Fist.

Special: A fighter can select Fiery Fist as one of his fighter bonus feats. A monk with the Stunning Fist feat can select Fiery Fist as her bonus feat at 2nd level, even if she does not meet the other prerequisites.

FIERY KI DEFENSE

You channel your *ki* energy into a cloak of flame that injures all who attempt to strike you.

Prerequisites: Dex 13, Wis 13, Fiery Fist, Improved Unarmed Strike, Stunning Fist, base attack bonus +8.

Benefit: As a swift action, you can expend one of your uses of the Stunning Fist feat to cloak yourself in flame. Any creature that strikes you with a melee attack takes 1d6 points of fire damage. This benefit lasts until the start of your next turn.

Special: A fighter can select Fiery Ki Defense as one of his fighter bonus feats. A monk with the Stunning Fist feat can select Fiery Ki Defense as her bonus feat at 8th level, as long as she also possesses the Fiery Fist feat (other prerequisites can be ignored).

FLAY

When fighting unarmored opponents, you excel at twisting your weapon just before impact. This motion rips and tears at your foe's flesh, causing intense pain. This attack is wholly ineffective against armored foes, but it tears through natural defenses.

Prerequisites: Str 13, Power Attack.

Benefit: When you use your Power Attack feat with a slashing or piercing weapon against a foe who lacks an armor bonus to AC, you inflict horrid pain on your target. If your attack hits, your opponent must make a Fortitude save (DC 10 + your damage bonus from Power Attack on the strike). If this save fails, he takes a –2 penalty on attacks for 1 round.

You can use this feat once per round against a given target.

Special: A fighter can select Flay as one of his fighter bonus feats.

GRENADIER

You are skilled in using grenadelike weapons. You excel at tossing them to just the right spot to maximize the amount of damage they cause as they burst open upon the battlefield.

Benefit: You are an expert with splash weapons and all manner of incendiary mixtures. You gain a +1 bonus on attack rolls with splash weapons and a +1 bonus on the weapon's damage (including splash damage).

Special: A fighter can select Grenadier as one of his fighter bonus feats.

HINDERING OPPORTUNIST

When you have a chance to strike a distracted foe, you instead use that opportunity to aid or protect an ally against him.

Prerequisites: Combat Reflexes, base attack bonus +3.

Benefit: Whenever an opponent provokes an attack of opportunity from you, you can choose to replace that attack with an aid another action targeting that opponent.

INTIMIDATING STRIKE

You make a display of your combat prowess designed to strike terror in your foe. Your stance, attack method, and demeanor demonstrate to your foe that you are capable of defeating him with little effort. Your intent is clear—if you decide to hit your foe, you could easily slay him.

Prerequisites: Intimidate 4 ranks.

Benefit: As a standard action, you make a single melee attack against your foe. You subtract a number from this attack equal to or less than your base attack bonus. If your attack hits, you can make an Intimidate check against the foe you struck, with a bonus equal to the number you subtracted from your attack roll. If this check succeeds, your opponent is shaken for the rest of the encounter. You cannot use this feat to worsen an opponent's fear condition beyond shaken.

Special: A fighter can select Intimidating Strike as one of his fighter bonus feats.

INDOMITABLE SOUL

Your physical toughness translates into greater mental resiliency. Where others cave in to magical effects that alter their minds, you stand resolute.

Prerequisites: Endurance, Iron Will.

Benefit: Whenever you make a Will save against a mind-affecting or fear ability, you can roll 2d20 and use the higher of the two die rolls.

KEEN-EARED SCOUT

Your sharp sense of hearing allows you to determine much more about your surroundings.

Prerequisites: Listen 6 ranks, Alertness or Skill Focus (Listen).

Benefit: When you make a Listen check, you might learn more than normal about a source of noise.

If you beat the Listen DC by 5 or more, you determine the size, speed, and direction of the source of noise.

If you beat the DC by 10 or more, you determine the precise, current position of the creature or object that caused the sound.

If you beat the DC by 15 or more, you determine the type of armor the creature wears and what it carries, if anything.

If you beat the DC by 20 or more, you learn the creature's type and subtypes.

The information you learn is cumulative. For example, if you got a Listen check result of 35 against a DC of 23, you gain the information for beating the check by 10 and by 5. These benefits apply to both standard and opposed Listen checks.

Also, you gain a +5 bonus on Listen checks to pinpoint invisible creatures.

KI BLAST

You focus your *ki* into a ball of energy that you can hurl at an opponent.

Prerequisites: Dex 13, Wis 13, Fiery Fist, Improved Unarmed Strike, Stunning Fist, base attack bonus +8.

Benefit: You can expend two daily uses of your Stunning Fist feat as a move action to create an orb of raw *ki* energy. You can then throw the seething orb as a standard action with a range of 60 feet. This ranged touch attack deals damage equal to 3d6 points + your Wis modifier. The *ki* orb is a force effect.

If you fail to throw the orb before the end of your turn, it dissipates harmlessly.

When you take this feat, you gain an additional daily use of Stunning Fist.

Special: A fighter can select Ki Blast as one of his fighter bonus feats. A monk with the Stunning Fist feat can select Ki Blast as her bonus feat at 8th level, as long as she possesses the Fiery Fist feat and a base attack bonus of +6 (other prerequisites can be ignored).

LEAP OF THE HEAVENS

Your excellent athletic ability and superior conditioning allow you to make near-superhuman leaps.

Prerequisite: Jump 4 ranks.

Benefit: When making a Jump check, the DC for the check doesn't double if you fail to move 20 feet in a straight line prior to jumping. If you do move 20 feet in a straight line before attempting a jump, you gain a +5 competence bonus on your check.

Normal: All Jump checks require a 20-foot running start to avoid doubling the DC of the check.

LUNGING STRIKE

You make a single attack against a foe who stands just beyond your reach.

Prerequisite: Base attack bonus +6.

Benefit: As a full-round action, you can make a single strike with a 5-foot bonus to your attack's reach. This benefit applies to both armed and unarmed attacks, including touch attacks made to deliver spells.

Special: A fighter can select Lunging Strike as one of his fighter bonus feats.

LURKING FAMILIAR

Your familiar hides within the folds of your robe or takes cover behind you as your opponents close in. When it moves to attack, its sudden appearance might catch your foe by surprise.

Prerequisites: Combat Familiar, arcane caster level 6th, familiar.

Benefit: If your familiar occupies your square, it gains cover against all attacks. As a consequence, it can make a Hide check to avoid your foe's notice. If your familiar then leaves your space to attack an opponent, it gains the normal benefit for attacking from a hidden position.

MAD FOAM RAGER

You fight with the rage that only a rabid badger or a beer-addled dwarf can bring to bear. In combat, you shrug off attacks and continue fighting even in the face of horrific injuries and effects.

Prerequisite: Rage or frenzy ability.

Benefit: When fighting, you can endure tremendous blows with little visible effect. As an immediate action, you can choose to delay the effect of a single attack, spell, or ability used against you. The damage or effect does not take hold until the end of your next turn. You can only use this ability while under the effect of your rage or frenzy ability. You can activate it once every time you use your rage or frenzy ability.

MASTER MANIPULATOR

Your words are your weapons. You confuse others with your speech, luring them into giving up vital secrets and leaving them dumbfounded with your carefully constructed, conversational static.

Prerequisites: Cha 13, Diplomacy 9 ranks.

Benefit: This feat grants two new uses for the Diplomacy skill. You must share a language with a creature to use these options against it. Neither ability functions during combat.

Captivating Speech: You can distract a creature with your compelling delivery and witticisms. With a successful Diplomacy check opposed by the target's own Diplomacy check or Will save, you can impose a −4 penalty on the target's Listen, Sense Motive, and Spot checks so long as you continue speaking. You can affect a number of targets equal to 1 + your Cha bonus (if any), as long as they are all within 20 feet.

Trap of Words: If a creature attempts and fails to successfully to use Bluff to lie to you, you skillfully maneuver the conversation to confuse the target or trick him into letting slip a vital clue. After succeeding on your Sense Motive check, you can then engage the target in conversation for at least 1 minute. At the end of this time, make a Diplomacy check opposed by the target's Bluff check. If you succeed, the target inadvertently reveals his lie and the reason behind it.

MELEE EVASION

Your speed, agility, and talent for intelligent fighting allow you to avoid your opponent's blows. You take careful stock of an opponent and slip away from his sword blow just as he commits to the attack.

Prerequisites: Dex 13, Int 13, Combat Expertise, Dodge.

Benefit: While fighting defensively, you can attempt to negate a single attack made by the target of your Dodge feat. If this opponent attacks you, use an immediate action to make a d20 roll modified by your highest base attack bonus. The result is used as your normal AC and touch AC against that single, specific attack from your opponent. You cannot use this feat if your Dexterity bonus to AC does not apply against your opponent's attack.

Special: A fighter can select Melee Evasion as one of his fighter bonus feats.

MELEE WEAPON MASTERY

You have mastered a wide range of weapons. Your training with one specific weapon now extends to other weapons of a similar sort.

A halfling uses Master Manipulator to catch a human in a lie

Prerequisites: Proficiency with selected weapon, Weapon Focus with selected weapon, Weapon Specialization with selected weapon, base attack bonus +8.

Benefit: When you select this feat, choose bludgeoning, piercing, or slashing. You must have Weapon Focus and Weapon Specialization with a melee weapon that deals this type of damage. When using any melee weapon that has the damage type you selected, you gain a +2 bonus on attack rolls and a +2 bonus on damage rolls.

Special: You can select this feat more than once. Each time, you can select a new damage type.

A fighter can choose Melee Weapon Mastery as one of his fighter bonus feats.

OVERWHELMING ASSAULT

If you attack a foe who does nothing to turn aside your attack, you press forward with an indomitable strike. Only a fool ignores the deadly threat you present.

Prerequisite: Base attack bonus +15.

Benefit: As a free action, designate one specific foe as the target of this feat. If this foe begins his turn adjacent to you, ends his turn still adjacent to you, and does not attack you, target you with a spell, or use a special ability against you, you gain a +4 bonus on melee attack rolls against him on your next turn.

PENETRATING SHOT

You send a powerful shot cleaving through your enemies.

Prerequisites: Str 15, Point Blank Shot, base attack bonus +10.

Benefit: When you make a ranged attack with a projectile weapon (such as a bow, crossbow, or sling), you can instead choose to unleash a single, mighty attack that blasts through multiple opponents. This attack requires a standard action, and your shot takes the form of a 60-foot line. Make a separate attack roll against each creature in the line. If struck, creatures along this line take damage from your shot, though any extra damage (such as from a sneak attack or a flaming weapon) is applied only against the first creature struck.

Special: A fighter can select Penetrating Shot as one of his fighter bonus feats.

Illus. by S. Belledin

RANGED WEAPON MASTERY

You have mastered a wide range of weapons. Your training with one specific weapon now extends to other weapons of a similar sort.

Prerequisites: Proficiency with selected weapon, Weapon Focus with selected weapon, Weapon Specialization with selected weapon, base attack bonus +8.

Benefit: When you select this feat, choose bludgeoning, piercing, or slashing. You must have Weapon Focus and Weapon Specialization with a ranged weapon that deals this type of damage. When using any ranged weapon that has the damage type you selected, you gain a +2 bonus on attacks and a +2 bonus on damage. In addition, you increase its range increment by 20 feet.

Special: You can select this feat more than once. Each time, you can select a new damage type.

A fighter can choose Ranged Weapon Mastery as one of his fighter bonus feats.

RAPID BLITZ

You charge across the battlefield, combining your speed and fighting ability to move and attack with unmatched skill.

Prerequisites: Dex 13, Bounding Assault, Dodge, Mobility, Spring Attack, base attack bonus +18.

Benefit: You can designate a third target for your Spring Attack feat. In addition to the second attack you gain from your Bounding Assault feat, you can make a third attack with a −10 penalty.

ROBILAR'S GAMBIT

By offering Robilar's Gambit, you absorb damage to place yourself in an advantageous position. This dangerous sacrifice is not for the unfit or the unwise, for one failed retaliatory strike can undo the advantage gained. Lord Robilar, a rash and impetuous fighter, gained fame using this technique against his enemies.

Prerequisites: Combat Reflexes, base attack bonus +12.

Benefit: At the start of your action, you can adopt a fighting stance that exposes you to harm but allows you to take advantage of your opponents' exposed defenses as they reach in to attack you. Anyone who strikes at you gains a +4 bonus on attack rolls and damage rolls against you. In return, they provoke attacks of opportunity from you each time they swing. Resolve your attack of opportunity after your foe's attack.

Normal: Opponents do not provoke attacks of opportunity by attacking. Further, when an opponent provokes an attack of opportunity, you resolve your attack before he completes the action that provoked the attack of opportunity.

Special: A fighter can select Robilar's Gambit as one of his fighter bonus feats.

SHIELD SLING

You can hurl your shield as a deadly missile, turning it from a defensive item to a crushing, thrown weapon.

Prerequisites: Proficiency with shields, Improved Shield Bash, Shield Specialization, base attack bonus +9.

Benefit: You can wield your light shield or heavy shield as a thrown weapon with a range increment of 20 feet. The shield deals damage as normal for its size (see Table 7–5, PH 116), and you gain your Strength bonus on damage as normal for a thrown weapon. In addition, you can make a ranged touch attack to initiate a trip attempt. Your target resists the trip attempt as normal. You lose your size bonus (though not a size penalty) on your Strength check. If your foe's check succeeds, he cannot attempt to trip you.

You cannot throw a tower shield. You can throw a buckler, but it does no damage, and you cannot use it to trip an opponent.

Special: A fighter can select Shield Sling as one of his fighter bonus feats.

SHIELD SPECIALIZATION

You are skilled in using a shield, allowing you to gain greater defensive benefits from it.

Prerequisite: Proficiency with shields.

Benefit: Choose one type of shield from the following list: buckler, heavy, or light. When using a shield of the appropriate type, you increase its shield bonus to AC by 1.

Special: You can take this feat more than once. Each time you select it, choose a different type of shield.

A fighter can select Shield Specialization as one of his fighter bonus feats.

SHIELD WARD

You use your shield like a wall of steel and wood. When an opponent attempts to draw in close to you, your shield forces him away or ruins his attacks.

Prerequisite: Proficiency with shields, Shield Specialization.

Benefit: You apply your shield bonus to your touch AC, and on checks or rolls to resist bull rush, disarm, grapple, overrun, or trip attempts against you.

Special: A fighter can select Shield Ward as one of his fighter bonus feats.

SHORT HAFT

You have trained in polearm fighting alongside your comrades in arms, sometimes reaching past them while they shield you, and sometimes shielding them while they attack from behind you.

Prerequisites: Proficiency with a reach weapon, Weapon Focus with a reach weapon, base attack bonus +3.

Benefit: As a swift action, you can choose to lose the benefit of wielding any reach weapon other than a spiked chain or a whip. In return, you can use that weapon to threaten and attack spaces adjacent to you. With another swift action, you can give up this feat's benefit in order to regain the use of your weapon's superior reach.

Special: A fighter can select Short Haft as one of his fighter bonus feats.

SLASHING FLURRY

You swing your weapon with uncanny speed, slicing apart a foe in the blink of an eye.

Prerequisites: Proficiency with selected slashing weapon, Weapon Focus with selected slashing weapon, Weapon Mastery (slashing), Weapon Specialization with selected slashing weapon, base attack bonus +14.

Benefit: When you use a standard action to attack with any slashing weapon, you can choose to make a second attack with that weapon. You take a –5 penalty on the first attack, and a –10 penalty on the second.

When you use a full attack action with any slashing weapon, you gain one additional attack at your highest base attack bonus. That attack and all other attacks you make in the current round take a –5 penalty.

SPECTRAL SKIRMISHER

You have trained extensively in the use of magic that renders you invisible. In combat, you use this experience to vex your opponents and increase your survivability.

Prerequisite: Base attack bonus +6.

Benefit: While you are invisible, you gain additional benefits. Creatures unable to see you due to invisibility take a –5 penalty on all Listen checks to detect you. A creature using a melee attack against the square you occupy provokes an attack of opportunity from you. You must choose to make this attack before checking to see if the creature finds you. If you attack and hit, the creature automatically finds you in your square. See page 152 of the *Player's Handbook* and page 295 of the *Dungeon Master's Guide* for the effects of invisibility on combat.

Special: A fighter can select Spectral Skirmisher as one of his fighter bonus feats.

SPELL-LINKED FAMILIAR

You and your familiar can share spell energy, allowing your familiar to cast a limited number of spells each day.

Prerequisites: Arcane caster level 9th, familiar.

Benefit: Your familiar can cast spells that you grant to it. A familiar gains spells based on your arcane caster level, and any spells granted to your familiar are subtracted from your daily allotment.

The maximum number of spells of a certain level that you can grant to your familiar is given on the table below. For example, as a 16th-level arcane caster, you can grant your familiar as many as three 0-level spells, two 1st-level spells, and one 2nd-level spell.

	Spell Level		
Caster Level	0	1st	2nd
9th–11th	1	—	—
12th–14th	2	1	—
15th–17th	3	2	1
18th–20th	4	3	2

The familiar uses 1/2 your caster level as its caster level. It cannot cast spells that have a gp or XP cost, or that require a focus. A familiar does not need somatic, material, or verbal components to cast a spell that was granted to it by this feat.

STALWART DEFENSE

You excel at aiding your allies in battle. When an opponent attempts to strike one of them, you make a quick, distracting motion to ruin the foe's efforts.

Prerequisites: Combat Reflexes, Hindering Opportunist, base attack bonus +9.

Benefit: When an opponent you threaten attempts a melee attack against one of your allies, you can give up one of your attacks of opportunity to attempt an aid another action. You target the attacking opponent with the aid another. The target of your foe's attack gains the benefit of your action in the form of a +2 bonus to AC against the attempted attack. You cannot use this feat against the same opponent more than once per round.

STEADFAST DETERMINATION

Your physical durability allows you to shrug off attacks that would cripple a lesser person. Rather than depend on agility or willpower, you use your raw toughness to survive.

Prerequisites: Endurance.

Benefit: You can use your Constitution modifier in place of your Wisdom modifier on Will saves.

You do not automatically fail Fortitude saves on a roll of natural 1.

TELLING BLOW

When you strike an opponent's vital areas, you draw on your ability to land crippling blows to make the most of your attack.

Prerequisite: Skirmish or sneak attack ability.

Benefit: When you score a critical hit against a target, you deal your skirmish or sneak attack damage in addition to the damage from your critical hit. Your critical multiplier applies only to your normal damage, not your skirmish or sneak attack damage. This benefit affects both melee and ranged attacks.

TROPHY COLLECTOR

A belt of minotaur fur, a hood of cloaker wing-skin, and an amulet fashioned from a petrified dragon's eye—these are the intimidating symbols of your trade. You are skilled in preserving portions of defeated enemies and turning them into trophies. The memory of your past accomplishments drives you onward, instilling in you the confidence needed to face still greater foes.

Prerequisite: Craft (taxidermy) 6 ranks.

Benefit: When you defeat a foe in combat, you can preserve a part of its body and create a trophy that you can wear or brandish. In order to be worthy of your efforts, the opponent must have a CR greater than your current level.

A trophy has a value equal to the defeated creature's CR × 100 gp. You must spend time using the Craft (taxidermy) skill to create the trophy as normal. Once you create a trophy, you can sell it for its market price or wear it. When you create a trophy, you must design it to occupy space on your body as one of these kinds of magic items: amulet, belt, boots, or cloak. You cannot gain the benefit of both a magic item and a trophy if both occupy the same space on your body; in such a case, the object you donned last becomes functional and the other object does not work.

While wearing a trophy, you gain a +2 bonus on Intimidate checks per trophy against creatures of the same type as the trophy, except for outsiders and humanoids. In these two cases, the target must share the same subtype as the creature from which you crafted the trophy. You take a –4 penalty on Diplomacy checks against creatures of the same type or subtype as one or more of your worn trophies.

For each trophy you wear, you gain a +1 bonus on saves against fear effects. Once per day, you gain a morale bonus on a single Will save equal to the number of trophies you wear. In this case, you draw upon the memories of past victories to strengthen your resolve. If you choose to take this morale bonus on a save against a fear effect, it stacks with the usual +1 bonus on saves per trophy worn.

Special: You can only craft trophies from corporeal creatures that you actively helped defeat. You cannot craft trophies from oozes.

Illus. by R. Spencer

Soveliss dispatches a red slaad twice as fast by using Two-Weapon Rend

TUMBLING FEINT

When you move near an opponent, your acrobatic maneuvers leave him confused and unable to properly defend himself.

Prerequisites: Bluff 4 ranks, Tumble 4 ranks.

Benefit: As a swift action at the start of your turn, you designate a single opponent as the target of this feat. If you successfully use your Tumble skill to avoid provoking an attack of opportunity from that opponent, you gain a +5 bonus on your next Bluff check to feint against him. You must use this benefit on or before your next turn.

For example, Lidda designates a nearby ogre as the target of this feat. She tumbles into the ogre's threatened area and continues to tumble past the creature, moving to a square from which she plans to make a melee attack against the ogre. Lidda succeeds on her Tumble check to avoid provoking an attack of opportunity from the ogre, and she moves into her destination square. She can now use a standard action to feint the ogre, applying the benefit of this feat on her Bluff check, or she can take any other sort of standard action, including making a normal melee attack against the ogre. If she chooses

not to feint immediately, she can wait until her next turn and still gain this feat's benefit.

Special: A fighter can select Tumbling Feint as one of his fighter bonus feats.

TWO-WEAPON POUNCE

When you charge an opponent while wielding two weapons, you can make two quick attacks. You trade the momentum and power of the charge for the opportunity to use your second weapon.

Prerequisites: Dex 15, Two-Weapon Fighting, base attack bonus +6.

Benefit: When you are making a charge and wielding weapons in both hands, you can attack with both of your weapons. If you do so, you lose the bonus on attack rolls normally granted by a charge. The –2 penalty to AC from charging still applies.

Normal: When making a charge, you get a single attack at the end of your movement.

Special: A fighter can select Two-Weapon Pounce as one of his fighter bonus feats. A ranger who has chosen the two-weapon combat style can select Two-Weapon Pounce as long as he has a base attack bonus of +6 and is wearing light armor or no armor.

TWO-WEAPON REND

You wield two weapons with an artisan's precision. Each strike builds on the next, allowing you to deal more damage.

Prerequisites: Dex 15, Two-Weapon Fighting, base attack bonus +11.

Benefit: If you successfully hit an opponent with both of the weapons you wield, you deal extra damage equal to 1d6 + 1-1/2 times your Strength bonus. This extra damage is treated as the same type that your off-hand weapon deals normally for the purpose of overcoming damage reduction and other effects related to damage type. You can gain this extra damage once per round against a given opponent.

Special: A fighter can select Two-Weapon Rend as one of his fighter bonus feats. A ranger who has chosen the two-weapon combat style can select Two-Weapon Rend as long as he has a base attack bonus of +11 and is wearing light armor or no armor.

VATIC GAZE

Your arcane studies have brought forth your nascent talent to sense magical auras and the power that others are capable of wielding.

Prerequisite: Arcane caster level 9th.

Benefit: You can use *detect magic* at will.

Also, as a swift action, you can attempt to determine an opponent's spellcasting ability. You make a Sense Motive check (DC 5 + target's caster level). If this check succeeds, you learn the highest-level spells the target is capable of casting. This benefit grants you no insight into spell-like or supernatural abilities.

VERSATILE UNARMED STRIKE

You employ a variety of unarmed fighting styles, allowing you to alter the type of damage your attacks deal.

Prerequisite: Improved Unarmed Strike.

Benefit: As a swift action, you can opt for your unarmed strikes to deal your choice of bludgeoning, piercing, or slashing damage. Once you make this choice, your unarmed strikes continue to deal the chosen damage type until you use another swift action to change it.

Special: A fighter can select Versatile Unarmed Strike as one of his fighter bonus feats.

VEXING FLANKER

You excel at picking apart an opponent's defenses when your allies also threaten him.

Prerequisite: Combat Reflexes.

Benefit: You gain a +4 bonus on your attack rolls when flanking.

Normal: Flanking grants a +2 bonus on attack rolls.

Special: A fighter can select Vexing Flanker as one of his fighter bonus feats.

WANDERER'S DIPLOMACY

Many halflings journey far and wide across the world, spending no more than a few months in one place. You have spent time among the halflings, or you are a halfling yourself. Your exposure to that race's nomadic way of life has taught you several useful methods of dealing with strangers.

Prerequisites: Halfling or 4 ranks in Bluff, Diplomacy, and Sense Motive.

Benefit: You excel in using your words and wit to make your way in the world. This feat grants you three separate abilities.

Canny Merchant: You can make a Diplomacy check to track down an item that is normally too expensive to be purchased in the town or settlement where you are currently located. The DC of this check is 10 + (the item's gp cost minus the community's gp limit, divided by 1,000). If this check succeeds, you learn of a merchant who can supply the item to you. You must still purchase it as normal.

Intuitive Communication: When you are faced with a creature whose language you do not understand, you can attempt to communicate with it by making a successful Sense Motive check. This check requires that you spend at least 1 minute listening to the creature and watching its gestures

and demeanor. The check's base DC is 20. If the creature is not the same type as you, the DC is 30.

With a successful check, you learn the basic gist of the creature's speech. This ability gives you no special talent to speak the creature's tongue.

Social Agility: You can temporarily alter a creature's attitude toward you. You can use Bluff against an unfriendly or less hostile creature in the same way you use Diplomacy. Using Bluff in this manner is a standard action that takes no special penalties. The target's attitude remains changed for 1 minute. After this time, it becomes one grade more hostile than where it started for 10 minutes.

WATER SPLITTING STONE

You channel your *ki* energy to splinter the defenses of creatures whose tough hides or magical natures normally allow them to shrug off your blows.

Prerequisite: Dex 13, Wis 13, Improved Unarmed Strike, Stunning Fist, base attack bonus +9.

Benefit: You gain a +4 bonus on damage rolls when you make an unarmed strike against an opponent whose damage reduction is effective against your unarmed strikes. This feat's benefit does not apply against a target if its damage reduction does not apply to your attacks. For example, a monk with *ki strike* (adamantine) does not gain the bonus on damage rolls against a foe with damage reduction that affects attacks with adamantine weapons.

Special: A fighter can select Water Splitting Stone as one of his fighter bonus feats. A monk with the Stunning Fist feat can select Water Splitting Stone as long as she has a base attack bonus +9 (other prerequisites can be ignored).

WEAPON SUPREMACY

You are a grandmaster in the use of your chosen weapon. When you hold it in your hands, no foe can stand against you.

Prerequisites: Proficiency with selected weapon, Greater Weapon Focus with selected weapon, Greater Weapon Specialization with selected weapon, Weapon Focus with selected weapon, Weapon Specialization with selected weapon, Weapon Mastery with damage type of selected weapon, fighter level 18th.

Benefit: When fighting with the weapon that you choose for this feat, you gain a number of additional advantages.

You gain a +4 bonus on all checks made to resist being disarmed.

You can wield your weapon against a foe who grapples you without penalty and without first making a grapple check. In this situation, you can take a standard action or a full attack action as normal.

When you take a full attack action, you can apply a +5 bonus to any single attack after your first strike.

Once per round before making an attack roll, you can instead choose to treat your d20 result as a 10.

You gain a +1 bonus to AC.

Special: You can choose this feat only once, for a single specific kind of weapon. The dedication and focus it requires makes it impossible to gain this feat for more than one weapon.

CEREMONY FEATS

A ceremony feat grants you the knowledge and training needed to complete several specific ceremonies. Each feat uses the Knowledge (religion) skill to gauge the depth of your study. As you gain more ranks in that skill, the ceremonies available through the feat increase.

A creature can benefit from one ceremony at a time. If you attempt a second ceremony on the same creature, the first ceremony's benefits immediately end and the second ceremony applies.

Each ceremony has a cost in time and resources. The ceremony consumes the materials needed for it when it ends (not when the benefit ends). If the ceremony is disrupted, such as if an opponent attacks before you finish, the material components are not lost.

The two feats described below are ceremony feats. Their prerequisites and benefits are summarized on Table 3–2.

RITUAL BLESSING

You call upon the powers of goodness and light to bless your allies. If your religious studies are advanced enough, the rituals you learn allow you to ward against illness or poison, enhance your healing abilities, and protect against evil.

Prerequisites: Good alignment, Knowledge (religion) 4 ranks.

Benefit: You gain access to rituals based on your ranks in Knowledge (religion).

Anoint (Knowledge [religion] 4 ranks): You speak a blessing over the recipient of this ritual, anoint him with holy water, and say a short prayer for him. When you cast a *cure* spell on the recipient, he heals an extra 2 points of damage.

Performing this ritual requires 5 minutes of incantation and a vial of holy water. Its effects last for 24 hours.

Cleanse (Knowledge [religion] 8 ranks): You sprinkle holy water over the recipient of this ritual and speak a prayer to his health and vigor. The target gains a +2 bonus on saves against disease and poison.

Performing this ritual requires 10 minutes of incantation and a vial of holy water. Its effects last for 24 hours.

Ward (Knowledge [religion] 13 ranks): You use a special combination of powdered silver and holy water to create a mystical ward that offers protection against demons and devils. The recipient of this ritual gains a +1 bonus on saves against spells and special attacks used by evil outsiders.

Performing this ritual requires 10 minutes of work, a vial of holy water, and powdered silver worth 30 gp. Its effects last for 24 hours.

RITUAL BLOOD BONDS

You invest your allies with the mighty power of your totem, god, or similar divine entity. These rituals allow you to forge bonds between warriors that stand the test of combat.

Prerequisites: Orc or half-orc, Knowledge (religion) 4 ranks.

Benefit: You gain access to rituals based on your total ranks in Knowledge (religion).

Blood Brothers (Knowledge [religion] 4 ranks): You gather up to six of your allies together in a circle. Each member of this circle pledges allegiance to the others, cuts himself, and bleeds into a bowl containing holy water or unholy water (as appropriate to your alignment). You then sprinkle this mixture on yourself and the members of the circle. You and everyone else who participated in this ritual gains a +4 morale bonus on Will saves against fear as long as each individual can see one other ally who took part in this ritual.

This ritual requires 10 minutes of incantation and a vial of holy water or unholy water. Its effect lasts for 24 hours.

Vengeful Bonds of Brotherhood (Knowledge [religion] 8 ranks): You create a close, mystical bond between you and your allies. Up to six individuals can participate with you in this ritual. Each participant cuts his hand. Everyone in the ritual then clasps hands in a circle while you stand in the middle. You speak a prayer while sprinkling holy or unholy water on each participant. This ritual grants a benefit to its participants (including you) when an ally falls in battle. If an individual who participated in this ritual sees another participant drop to 0 or fewer hit points due to an opponent's actions, he gains a +2 morale bonus on attack rolls against the foe who dropped his ally. The benefit lasts for 1 minute every time it is triggered. You can gain this bonus against multiple foes during the duration of the effect.

This ritual requires 10 minutes of incantation, a vial of holy water or unholy water, and silver dust worth 10 gp. The ritual's benefit lasts for 24 hours.

COMBAT FORM FEATS

While most warriors draw on their strength, agility, and toughness in battle, a few learn to tap into the true potential of their minds. Somewhat like a monk, such a warrior supplements his physical practice with rigorous mental training to hone his fighting abilities. His mind and body become one as he fights, allowing him to achieve unparalleled levels of combat mastery. Being in this state of perfect mental and physical harmony is known as maintaining a combat focus. (Taking the feat called Combat Focus is how a character learns to achieve this state; all other combat form feats have Combat Focus as a prerequisite.) The task of maintaining a combat focus is both difficult and straining. Thus, a warrior cannot remain in this state for long. While he does, however, he can use any combat form feats he possesses.

The six feats described below are combat form feats. Their prerequisites and benefits are summarized on Table 3–3.

COMBAT AWARENESS

When you maintain your combat focus, you have an uncanny ability to sense the ebb and flow of your opponents' vitality. As you attain greater mastery of this fighting style, you learn to sense a foe's presence even with your eyes closed.

Prerequisites: Wis 13, Blind-Fight, Combat Focus, base attack bonus +12.

Benefit: While maintaining your combat focus, you learn the current hit point total of each adjacent opponent and ally.

Table 3–2: Ceremony Feats

Feat	Prerequisites	Benefit
Ritual Blessing	Good alignment, Knowledge (religion) 4 ranks	Gain warding rituals
Ritual Blood Bonds	Orc or half-orc, Knowledge (religion) 4 ranks	Gain toughening rituals

Table 3–3: Combat Form Feats

Feat	Prerequisites	Benefit
Combat Focus	Wis 13	Enter meditative state to gain +2 bonus on Will saves
Combat Stability	Wis 13, Combat Focus, base attack bonus +3	+4 against bull rush, disarm, grapple, overrun, and trip
Combat Defense	Dex 13, Wis 13, Combat Focus, Dodge, base attack bonus +6	Change target of Dodge feat as immediate action
Combat Vigor	Wis 13, Combat Focus, base attack bonus +9	While in focus, gain fast healing 2
Combat Awareness	Wis 13, Blind-Fight, Combat Focus, base attack bonus +12	Learn hit point totals of all adjacent creatures
Combat Strike	Wis 13, Combat Focus, any two other combat form feats, base attack bonus +15	Expend combat focus to gain bonus on attacks and damage

If you have three or more combat form feats, you gain blindsight out to 5 feet.

Special: A fighter can select Combat Awareness as one of his fighter bonus feats.

COMBAT DEFENSE

The state of keen focus and mental discipline you attain in combat allows you to shift the focus of your defense from one opponent to another with careful, precise maneuvers.

Prerequisites: Dex 13, Wis 13, Combat Focus, Dodge, base attack bonus +6.

Benefit: While you maintain your combat focus, you can change the target of your Dodge feat to a new opponent as an immediate action.

If you have three or more combat form feats, you gain an additional +1 dodge bonus to AC against the target of your Dodge feat.

Normal: Designating or changing the target of your Dodge feat can only be done on your turn as a free action.

Special: A fighter can select Combat Defense as one of his fighter bonus feats.

COMBAT FOCUS

The way of the warrior requires more than simple, brute strength. Some warriors bring their minds to such keen focus during the heat of battle that they can attain superhuman levels of endurance, perception, and mental toughness. Through intense mental exercise and training, you learn to enter a state of perfect martial clarity.

Prerequisite: Wis 13.

Benefit: In battle, you push aside the chaos of the fight and attain a focused state that grants you a keen, clear picture of the battle. Fear and pain ebb away as you focus solely on defeating your enemy. The first time you make a successful attack during an encounter, you gain your combat focus. In this state, your mind and body become one, allowing you to overcome mundane physical limits. You can maintain your combat focus for 10 rounds after entering it, +1 additional round per combat form feat you

possess aside from this one. You can only gain your combat focus once per encounter.

While you are maintaining your combat focus, you gain a +2 bonus on Will saves. If you have three or more combat form feats, this bonus increases to +4.

Special: A fighter can select Combat Focus as one of his fighter bonus feats.

COMBAT STABILITY

When you maintain your combat focus, you become difficult to dislodge. Your muscles lock into an unyielding position, granting you superior ability to resist trip attacks, bull rushes, disarms, and similar effects.

Prerequisite: Wis 13, Combat Focus, base attack bonus +3.

Benefit: You gain a +4 bonus on checks or rolls to resist bull rush, disarm, grapple, overrun, and trip attempts made against you.

If you have three or more combat form feats, the bonus granted by this feat increases to +8.

Special: A fighter can select Combat Stability as one of his fighter bonus feats.

COMBAT STRIKE

Your intense, focused state allows you to see the one critical moment in a battle when you hang suspended between victory and defeat. By pouring the energy required to maintain your focus into your assault, you batter through your foe's defenses.

Prerequisites: Wis 13, Combat Focus, any two other combat form feats, base attack bonus +15.

Benefit: If you choose to end your combat focus as a swift action, you gain a bonus on attack rolls and damage rolls equal to your total number of combat form feats for the rest of your current turn. You immediately lose all benefits of combat form feats that affect you only while you are maintaining your combat focus.

Special: A fighter can select Combat Strike as one of his fighter bonus feats.

Illus. by D. Hudnut

COMBAT VIGOR

When you maintain your combat focus, your clarity of purpose and relentless drive allow you to overcome your body's frailties. Minor wounds heal in a matter of seconds, and you quickly recover from even a grievous blow.

Prerequisites: Wis 13, Combat Focus, base attack bonus +9.

Benefit: While you maintain your combat focus, you gain fast healing 2. You lose this benefit when your combat focus ends.

If you have three or more combat form feats, the benefit of this feat improves to fast healing 4.

Special: A fighter can select Combat Vigor as one of his fighter bonus feats.

DIVINE FEATS

Divine feats are the province of those who are able to turn or rebuke undead. Instead of attempting to affect an undead creature, you expend a turn or rebuke undead attempt to trigger the benefit of a divine feat you have. You can activate only one divine feat per round, though overlapping durations might allow you the benefits of more than one divine feat at a time. Activating a divine feat is a supernatural ability, requires a type of action or an amount of time depending on the feat, and does not provoke attacks of opportunity unless otherwise noted in the feat description. Activating a divine feat is not considered an attack unless doing so would directly cause damage to a target.

The eight feats described below are divine feats. Their prerequisites and benefits are summarized on Table 3–4.

DIVINE ARMOR

You call upon your deity to protect you in your hour of need by wreathing you in divine power that wards off your enemies' attacks.

Prerequisites: Divine caster level 5th, ability to turn or rebuke undead.

Benefit: As a swift action, you can expend a turn or rebuke undead attempt to gain damage reduction 5/– until the start of your next turn.

DIVINE FORTUNE

With a quick prayer, you channel divine energy to help resist a spell, poison, or other deadly effect.

Prerequisites: Divine caster level 5th, ability to turn or rebuke undead.

Benefit: As an immediate action, you can expend a turn or rebuke undead attempt to gain a +4 bonus on your next saving throw. If this benefit is not used immediately, it lasts until the start of your next turn.

DIVINE JUSTICE

You can channel divine energy to turn your foe's strength against him, striking him with the same force that he used against you.

Prerequisite: Ability to turn or rebuke undead.

Benefit: As a swift action, you can expend a turn or rebuke undead attempt to mark an opponent as the target of this feat. The next time this opponent strikes you with an armed melee attack or a natural weapon, record the damage he deals. The next time you strike him in melee, you deal that damage or your weapon's normal damage, whichever is greater. Your weapon's qualities still determine if damage reduction applies to the damage you deal.

You can mark only one opponent at a time with this feat. You must take damage from your foe within 1 minute of using this feat, or your turn or rebuke undead attempt is wasted. After taking damage, you must strike your foe within 1 minute, or you lose this feat's benefit. Until you strike your foe and trigger the feat's benefit, you cannot use this feat again to mark the same or a different opponent.

Regdar practices his combat forms

DIVINE WARD

You create a channel of divine energy between yourself and a willing ally. This link allows you to cast your spells upon him from greater than normal range.

Prerequisite: Ability to turn or rebuke undead.

Benefit: Once every 24 hours, you can spend 10 minutes creating a magical ward between you and one willing target.

TABLE 3–4: DIVINE FEATS

Feat	Prerequisites	Benefit
Divine Armor	Divine caster level 5th, ability to turn or rebuke undead	Expend turn/rebuke attempt to gain DR 5/–
Divine Fortune	Divine caster level 5th, ability to turn or rebuke undead	Expend turn/rebuke attempt for +4 bonus on next save
Divine Justice	Ability to turn or rebuke undead	Expend turn/rebuke attempt, choose foe, deal your damage or his
Divine Ward	Ability to turn or rebuke undead	Increase range of spells from touch to short for ally
Profane Aura	Divine caster level 9th, ability to rebuke undead	Create mist that grants concealment, +2 AC for undead
Sacred Healing	Ability to turn undead	Expend turn attempt for bonus on healing attempts
Sacred Purification	Sacred Healing, ability to turn undead	Expend turn attempt to heal living and harm undead
Sacred Radiance	Divine caster level 9th, ability to turn undead	Expend turn attempt to create radius of light that soothes allies, hampers undead

For the rest of the 24-hour period, you can increase the range of a touch spell to short range (25 feet + 5 feet per two caster levels) if you target the warded creature, and only the warded creature. When you cast a spell in this manner, you must expend a turn or rebuke undead attempt.

You can create a ward between you and more than one target, so long as you expend the necessary time and turning attempts. You must expend a turn or rebuke undead attempt to create each ward beyond the first.

PROFANE AURA

You call upon the dark powers you worship to fill the area around you with a dreadful mist that obscures sight.

Prerequisites: Divine caster level 9th, ability to rebuke undead.

Benefit: As a standard action, you can expend one of your rebuke undead attempts to fill the area around you with a cold, clammy mist. The mist extends out in a 60-foot-radius emanation centered on you and flows through the air as you move, keeping you at the center of its area. The mist provides concealment to creatures within the cloud. While in the mist, creatures (including you) 5 feet away from each other have concealment, and creatures separated by more than 5 feet have total concealment from each other.

In addition, mindless undead creatures within the cloud gain a +2 deflection bonus to AC.

SACRED HEALING

You can channel divine energy to aid in your efforts to tend to a comrade's injuries, sickness, or other conditions.

Prerequisite: Ability to turn undead.

Benefit: As a swift action, you can expend a turn undead attempt to augment your ability to tend to the wounds of others. You gain a +5 bonus on Heal checks and a +2 bonus per die on the damage healed by any conjuration (healing) spells you cast. This benefit lasts until the end of your current turn.

SACRED PURIFICATION

You serve as a conduit of divine energy, filling the area around you with power that aids the living and saps the undead.

Prerequisites: Sacred Healing, ability to turn undead.

Benefit: As a swift action, you can expend a turn undead attempt to create a pulse of divine energy. All living creatures within 60 feet of you heal an amount of damage equal to 1d8 points + your Charisma bonus (if any). All undead creatures in this area take damage equal to 1d8 points + your Charisma bonus.

SACRED RADIANCE

You channel divine energy to fill the area around you with a soothing, gentle radiance.

Prerequisites: Divine caster level 9th, ability to turn undead.

Benefit: As a standard action, you can expend a turn undead attempt to bathe yourself in light. This light provides bright illumination in a 60-foot-radius emanation centered on you and an additional 60 feet of shadowy illumination beyond that area. The light moves as you move, keeping you at the center of its area. It temporarily negates areas of magical darkness created by spells of 3rd level or lower.

Any non-evil creature within 60 feet of you gains a +2 morale bonus on saves against fear, poison, disease, and death effects. Evil creatures take a –2 penalty on saves against fear effects.

This benefit lasts for 10 minutes.

HERITAGE FEATS

A heritage feat signifies a specific ancestry of your character. The heritage feats in this book allow your sorcerer to tap into the celestial or infernal source of his magical power to master new abilities (a sorcerer's draconic heritage source of power is covered in *Complete Arcane*). You and your DM are encouraged to come up with a background story explaining your character's heritage, though the exact source of this ancestral link isn't crucial to the feat's operation (and might remain a mystery to the character).

A character can select a heritage feat at any level. Choosing a heritage feat after 1st level signifies that the ancestral power of the character is only now manifesting itself. (A character's first choice among these heritage feats must be either Celestial Sorcerer Heritage or Infernal Sorcerer Heritage, because all other heritage feats have one of these feats as a prerequisite.)

While different sorts of heritage feats cannot normally be combined (see page 37 of the *Planar Handbook* supplement), a single sorcerer could possess draconic, infernal, and celestial

TABLE 3–5: HERITAGE FEATS

Feat	Prerequisites	Benefit
Celestial Sorcerer Heritage	Sorcerer level 1st	Gain bonus spell and a bonus on saves against electricity and petrification
Celestial Sorcerer Aura	Celestial Sorcerer Heritage, sorcerer level 1st	Expend spell slot to create righteous aura
Celestial Sorcerer Lance	Celestial Sorcerer Heritage, sorcerer level 1st	Expend spell slot to create energy bolt that harms evil creatures
Celestial Sorcerer Wings	Celestial Sorcerer Heritage, sorcerer level 1st	Expend spell slot to fly for short period of time
Celestial Sorcerer Lore	Celestial Sorcerer Heritage, any two other celestial sorcerer heritage feats, sorcerer level 1st	Add *magic circle against evil, tongues, teleport* to list of spells known
Infernal Sorcerer Heritage	Sorcerer level 1st	Gain bonus against fire and poison, +2 caster level with conjuration (summoning)
Infernal Sorcerer Eyes	Infernal Sorcerer Heritage, sorcerer level 1st	Expend spell slot to see in darkness
Infernal Sorcerer Howl	Infernal Sorcerer Heritage, sorcerer level 1st	Expend spell slot to create cone of sonic energy
Infernal Sorcerer Resistance	Infernal Sorcerer Heritage, sorcerer level 1st	Gain acid and cold resistance

sorcerer heritage feats. In this case, the sorcerer claims a truly varied family tree that includes a variety of strange beings. Sorcerers with both infernal and celestial traits are exceedingly rare, however. These casters are tormented souls, pulled between the polar opposites that lurk within their blood.

The nine feats described below are heritage feats. Their prerequisites and benefits are summarized on Table 3–5.

CELESTIAL SORCERER AURA

The power of your sorcerous heritage shines through, allowing you to infuse the area around you with a menacing aura.

Prerequisites: Celestial Sorcerer Heritage, sorcerer level 1st.

A tiefling sorcerer rends the air with her Infernal Sorcerer Howl

Illus. by L.Parillo

Benefit: As a standard action, you can expend a spell slot to generate a righteous aura of menace that affects all hostile creatures in a 20-foot radius around you. All your opponents within this area must make a Will save (DC 10 + the level of the spell slot expended + your Cha modifier). On a failed save, a creature takes a –2 penalty on attack rolls, checks, and saves for 24 hours or until it successfully hits you. A creature that resists or breaks this effect cannot be affected by it again for 24 hours. This is a supernatural ability.

CELESTIAL SORCERER HERITAGE

Your ancestry manifests in the form of several special abilities. You gain access to abilities similar to those of an archon.

Prerequisite: Sorcerer level 1st.

Benefit: You gain a bonus on saves against electricity and petrification equal to the number of celestial sorcerer feats you possess. You also add *protection from evil* to your list of 1st-level sorcerer spells known. This spell is in addition to the spells you gain normally based on your sorcerer level.

CELESTIAL SORCERER LANCE

You can channel your arcane energy into a bolt of power that is baneful to evil creatures.

Prerequisites: Celestial Sorcerer Heritage, sorcerer level 1st.

Benefit: As a standard action, you can expend a spell slot to create a 60-foot line of energy that deals damage only against creatures with an evil alignment. The bolt deals 1d8 points of damage per level of the spell slot spent to activate this ability. A Reflex save (DC 10 + the level of the spell slot expended + your Cha modifier) halves this damage. This is a supernatural ability.

CELESTIAL SORCERER LORE

The power of your ancestry grants you access to a variety of new spells.

Prerequisites: Celestial Sorcerer Heritage, any two other celestial sorcerer heritage feats, sorcerer level 1st.

Benefit: You add *magic circle against evil, tongues,* and *teleport* to your list of spells known. You gain these spells when you gain access to spells of the appropriate level. These spells are in addition to the spells you gain normally based on your sorcerer level.

CELESTIAL SORCERER WINGS

You channel your inborn magical abilities to spawn a pair of spectral, magical wings that glow with majestic power.

Prerequisites: Celestial Sorcerer Heritage, sorcerer level 1st.

Benefit: You can expend a spell slot as a standard action to gain the ability to fly. You fly at a speed equal to twice your base land speed with good maneuverability. This benefit lasts for 1 round per level of the spell slot used to activate it. This is a supernatural ability.

INFERNAL SORCERER EYES

Your eyes glow with infernal fire, allowing you to see through magical darkness.

Prerequisites: Infernal Sorcerer Heritage, sorcerer level 1st.

Benefit: As a swift action, you can expend a spell slot to cause your eyes to emit a spectral red glow. You gain the ability to see perfectly in darkness of any kind, out to the limit of your line of sight. You ignore the concealment provided by darkness spells and effects. This benefit lasts for 10 minutes per level of the spell slot used to activate it.

INFERNAL SORCERER HERITAGE

Your innate magic derives from infernal ancestors. Your blood is thick with their power, allowing you to exhibit a variety of abilities.

Prerequisite: Sorcerer level 1st.

Benefit: You gain a bonus on saves against fire and poison equal to the number of infernal sorcerer heritage feats you possess. When you use a conjuration (summoning) spell to summon an evil outsider, you gain a +2 bonus to your caster level.

INFERNAL SORCERER HOWL

You channel the fury of your infernal ancestors into a thunderous roar that blasts your enemies with sonic power.

Prerequisites: Infernal Sorcerer Heritage, sorcerer level 1st.

Benefit: By expending one of your spell slots, you create a 30-foot cone of sonic energy. All opponents within the cone take 2d6 points of damage per level of the spell slot expended. Each target can attempt a Fortitude save (DC 10 + the level of the spell slot expended + your Cha modifier) for half damage. This is a supernatural ability.

INFERNAL SORCERER RESISTANCE

You are as tough and resilient as an infernal monstrosity, allowing you to shrug off acid and cold damage.

Prerequisites: Infernal Sorcerer Heritage, sorcerer level 1st.

Benefit: You gain resistance to acid and resistance to cold equal to the total number of infernal sorcerer heritage feats you have.

METAMAGIC FEATS

Metamagic feats allow spellcasters to modify the way a spell is cast or the effect a spell has after it is successfully cast. Full information about metamagic feats appears on page 88 of the *Player's Handbook*.

The five feats described below are new metamagic feats. Their prerequisites and benefits are summarized on Table 3–6.

BLISTERING SPELL

Your fire spells sear the flesh from your enemies' bones, leaving them wracked with pain.

Benefit: This metamagic feat can be applied only to a spell that has the fire descriptor. A blistering spell deals an extra 2 points of fire damage per level of the spell. In addition to the spell's normal effect, any creature that fails its save against a blistering spell takes a –2 penalty on attack rolls and checks until the beginning of your next turn. A blistering spell uses up a spell slot one level higher than the spell's actual level.

EARTHBOUND SPELL

You bind a spell into the rock and soil, leaving it there until an opponent stumbles across it. At that time, the spell releases its energy.

Benefit: When you cast an earthbound spell, you place it within a square adjacent to you. You must specify all effects, options, and other relevant variables when you cast the spell. The next creature to enter the warded square triggers the spell. If the spell affects an area, that square is the center of the area or the point at which the area begins. For a cone, line, or similar area, you must designate the direction in which the cone or line extends. An earthbound spell that does not affect an area targets the creature that triggered it. You cannot apply the Earthbound Spell metamagic feat to a spell with a range of personal.

An earthbound spell remains in place for 1 hour or until it is triggered. A Search check (DC 25 + the spell's level) reveals its presence, as does *detect magic* and similar abilities. A character with trapfinding can make a Disable Device check (DC 25 + the spell's level) to remove an earthbound spell (as if it is a magic trap). A *dispel magic* effect can also remove an earthbound spell, thus preventing it from functioning.

An earthbound spell uses up a spell slot two levels higher than the spell's actual level.

FLASH FROST SPELL

Your spells that use cold and ice to damage your foes leave behind a thin layer of slippery frost.

Benefit: This metamagic feat can be applied only to spells that have the cold descriptor and that affect an area. A flash frost spell deals an extra 2 points of cold damage per level of the spell to all targets in the area. When you cast such a spell, the area of the spell is covered with a slippery layer of ice for 1 round. Anyone attempting to move through this icy area must make a DC 10 Balance check or fall prone. A creature that runs or charges through the area must make a DC 20 Balance check to avoid falling. A flash frost spell uses up a spell slot one level higher than the spell's actual level.

IMBUED SUMMONING

Your summoning spells gain an element of surprise. You can summon creatures that come into existence with the benefit of a spell such as *invisibility* or *bull's strength*.

Prerequisites: Augment Summoning, Spell Focus (conjuration).

Benefit: When you cast a spell from the summoning subschool, you can choose to grant the summoned creature the benefit of any spell of 3rd level or lower you can cast that has a range of touch. You cast the spell you wish to grant the creature (using a prepared spell or a spell slot) at the same time you cast your summoning spell. The creature gains the benefit of the spell when it appears.

An imbued summoning spell uses up a spell slot one level higher than the spell's actual level.

SMITING SPELL

You can channel the energy of a touch spell into a weapon, causing the spell to discharge when you strike an opponent.

Prerequisites: Base attack bonus +1, caster level 1st.

Benefit: You can alter a spell with a range of touch to transfer its energy from your hand to a weapon that you hold. The next time you strike an opponent with that weapon, the spell discharges. The target takes the normal damage and effects of a successful attack in addition to the spell's effect. Once you place a spell into a weapon, you must discharge it within 1 minute, or its energy dissipates harmlessly.

You can place a smiting spell on a piece of ammunition or a projectile, such as a sling bullet, an arrow, or a crossbow bolt. In such a case, the spell dissipates if the attack misses. The spell cannot be placed on a bow, crossbow, sling, or similar weapon that uses ammunition.

A smiting spell uses up a spell slot one level higher than the spell's actual level.

TACTICAL FEATS

Tactical feats allow characters to perform a number of powerful maneuvers.

If you are playing a character who has one or more tactical feats, you are responsible for keeping track of the actions needed to set up the feat's maneuver. It's also a good idea to briefly mention to the DM that you're working toward a tactical maneuver—a remark along the lines of "I'm using my spiked rebuke maneuver this round. I'll let you know if I gain my attack bonus against any opponents who attack and miss me" is appropriate.

Some descriptions of tactical feats refer to the first round, second round, and so on. These terms are related to the timing of the maneuver, not the encounter as a whole. For instance, if you have the Combat Cloak Expert feat, you don't have to move adjacent to an opponent in the first round of combat to utilize the cloaked strike maneuver during that combat. Any round when you move adjacent to an opponent for the purpose of utilizing this maneuver is considered the first round of the maneuver.

The six feats described below are tactical feats. Their prerequisites and benefits are summarized on Table 3–7.

BLOOD-SPIKED CHARGER

You throw yourself into the fray, using your spiked armor and spiked shield to tear your opponents to pieces.

Prerequisites: Str 13, proficiency with spiked armor and spiked shields, Power Attack, Weapon Focus (spiked armor), Weapon Focus (spiked shield), base attack bonus +6.

Benefit: The Blood-Spiked Charger feat grants you access to three special tactical maneuvers.

Spiked Avalanche: When you are using the charge action while wearing spiked armor and carrying either a spiked shield or nothing in your hands, you throw yourself into the air, transforming yourself into a deadly, spiked projectile. A successful attack with either your spiked shield or your

TABLE 3–6: METAMAGIC FEATS

Feat	Prerequisites	Benefit
Blistering Spell	—	Fire spells cause –2 penalty for 1 turn on failed save
Earthbound Spell	—	Cast spell into ground as a trap
Flash Frost Spell	—	Cold spells coat area of effect with slippery ice
Imbued Summoning	Augment Summoning, Spell Focus (conjuration)	Summoned creature arrives with beneficial spell
Smiting Spell	Base attack bonus +1, caster level 1st	Place touch spell in weapon

TABLE 3–7: TACTICAL FEATS

Feat	Prerequisites	Benefit
Blood-Spiked Charger	Str 13, proficiency with armor spikes and shield spikes, Power Attack, Weapon Focus (armor spikes), Weapon Focus (shield spikes), base attack bonus +6	Gain armor and shield spike maneuvers
Combat Cloak Expert	Dex 15, Int 13, Combat Expertise, Dodge, base attack bonus +6	Gain cloak maneuvers
Combat Panache	Bluff 8 ranks, Intimidate 8 ranks, Perform 8 ranks	Gain charismatic combat maneuvers
Einhander	Tumble 6 ranks, base attack bonus +6	Gain one-handed weapon combat maneuvers
Mad Alchemist	Grenadier, Craft (alchemy) 6 ranks	Gain thrown item combat maneuvers
Shadow Striker	Hide 12 ranks, Move Silently 12 ranks	Gain stealthy combat maneuvers

spiked armor deals extra damage equal to twice your Strength bonus. You can attack with both your spiked armor and a spiked shield on this charge, each one benefiting from the Strength bonus, but you take the normal penalties for using two weapons.

Spiked Rebuke: When you are fighting defensively and carrying a spiked shield, you lash out at your foes with your shield in response to their attacks. Determine what your AC would be without your spiked shield and the AC bonus for fighting defensively. If an opponent's attack hits against this lower AC but misses against your actual AC, the foe strikes your shield, allowing you to deflect his attack in such a way as to leave him vulnerable to your counter. On your next action, you gain a +2 bonus on attack rolls against your chosen foe with your spiked shield.

Spiked Slam: As a full-round action when you are wielding a spiked shield, you can opt to make only a single attack at your best base attack bonus. You brace yourself behind your spiked shield, drive yourself forward, and slam into your foe. You enter your foe's space, which provokes attacks of opportunity. In return, your attack deals extra damage equal to twice your Strength and an additional amount based on your size (see below). After making this attack, you stumble back into the square you occupied just before making this attack. Until the start of your next turn, you do not threaten any squares.

Size	Additional Damage
Small	1d4
Medium	1d6
Large	1d8
Huge	2d6
Gargantuan	2d8
Colossal	3d6

Special: A fighter can select Blood-Spiked Charger as one of his fighter bonus feats.

COMBAT CLOAK EXPERT

You are adept at turning your cloak into a vital part of your combat repertoire. By twirling it about you, sweeping it over enemies, and using it to conceal your weapon, you can catch an opponent by surprise.

Prerequisites: Dex 15, Int 13, Combat Expertise, Dodge, base attack bonus +6.

Benefit: The Combat Cloak Expert feat grants you access to three special tactical maneuvers. You must wear a cloak in order to utilize them.

Cloak Defense: While you are fighting defensively, you can use your cloak to confuse your foes. You hold it before your chest like a curtain, making it difficult for enemies to read your defensive moves. Your cloak grants you a +1 shield bonus to AC. If you use the total defense action, your cloak's shield bonus improves to +2. (Shield bonuses do not stack, making it likely that this maneuver is a poor option if you already carry a shield.)

Cloaked Strike: You can use your cloak to hide a light weapon. To utilize this maneuver, on the first round you must move adjacent to an opponent while you do not have a weapon in either hand. On the second round, you make a Bluff check opposed by your foe's Sense Motive check as you use a move action to draw your weapon. If this check succeeds, your opponent loses either his Dexterity bonus to AC or his shield bonus to AC (your choice) until the end of your current turn.

Whirling Cloak: You can attempt to use your cloak to confuse your opponent. As a move action after successfully striking an opponent in melee, make a melee touch attack against that foe. If this attack hits, you whirl your cloak around him, temporarily ruining his defenses. Your opponent cannot make attacks of opportunity against a particular ally of your choice until the start of his next turn.

Special: A fighter can select Combat Cloak Expert as one of his fighter bonus feats.

COMBAT PANACHE

Your glowing personality and sharp performance abilities allow you to navigate the battlefield on sheer chutzpah alone. While others rely on swords and armor, you use your cutting wit and ability to manipulate others.

Prerequisites: Bluff 8 ranks, Intimidate 8 ranks, Perform 8 ranks.

Benefit: The Combat Panache feat grants you access to three special tactical maneuvers.

Fortuitous Tumble: For a brief moment, you appear to let your guard down. As your foe swings at you, you slip out of the way, causing his attack to slam into one of his allies. By positioning yourself correctly and making yourself an appealing target, you dupe your foe into making a critical blunder.

To use this maneuver, you must be successfully attacked by a foe. On your next turn, you can take a move action to make a Bluff check opposed by his Sense Motive check. If you succeed on the check, you can take an immediate action at the start of your foe's next turn and designate a different target for your opponent's next melee attack (which must be a creature it threatens).

Play Dead: You crumple to the ground as if slain, luring your opponent into a false sense of security. As an immediate action after you are hit for at least 10 points of damage by a single attack, you can attempt to play dead. You drop prone and make a Bluff check opposed by your attacker's (or any other relevant observer's) Sense Motive check. If you succeed on this check, the observer assumes you are dead. If you subsequently rise and attack him in the same round, he loses any attack of opportunity he might have been entitled to against you, and he loses his Dexterity bonus to AC against the first attack that you make.

You can use this ability once per encounter. Standing up after playing dead does not provoke attacks of opportunity.

Sneering Glower: With just the right mix of your intimidating presence and your martial talents, you strike such fear into your target that he has difficulty fighting you effectively. On your next turn after you deal at least 1 point of damage to your opponent, you can make an Intimidate check against him as a move action. If you succeed on this check, your foe takes a penalty on his attack rolls against you equal to your Charisma bonus. You can gain this benefit against only one foe at a time; it lasts for the duration of the encounter or until you switch targets. If you designate a new target for this ability (by attempting a new Intimidate check against a different creature), the previous target no longer takes the penalty on his attack rolls against you. Opponents that are immune to the effects of the Intimidate skill, such as mindless creatures and those with immunity to fear, are immune to this maneuver.

Special: A fighter can select Combat Panache as one of his fighter bonus feats.

EINHANDER

You excel at wielding a one-handed weapon while carrying nothing in your off hand.

Prerequisites: Tumble 6 ranks, base attack bonus +6.

Benefit: If you are fighting with a one-handed weapon or a light weapon and carrying nothing in your off hand, the Einhander feat grants you access to three special tactical maneuvers.

Narrow Profile: You can tuck your arm behind your back and offer a narrow profile when you concentrate on defense rather than offense. You gain an additional +2 dodge bonus to AC when fighting defensively or using the total defense action.

Off-Hand Balance: You use your off hand to balance yourself while performing acrobatic maneuvers. After you successfully strike an opponent, you gain a +2 bonus on Tumble checks to avoid his attacks of opportunity until the start of your next turn. When you flip and roll out of harm's way, you use one hand to keep your balance and your other hand to keep your weapon trained on your foe.

Off-Hand Swap: With a flourish, you flip your weapon into the air, catch it in your off hand, and continue to press the attack. When you use this maneuver, you must first take a full attack action to strike an opponent at least twice. On your next turn, you can make a special feint as a free action, using Sleight of Hand rather than Bluff. Your opponent uses the standard rules for resisting a feint. Once you use this maneuver against a particular opponent, whether it succeeds or fails, you cannot use it against him again.

Special: A fighter can select Einhander as one of his fighter bonus feats.

MAD ALCHEMIST

You are an expert at using alchemical items. Through experimentation, research, and your careful study of the art of alchemy, you have learned to make the most of items such as alchemist's fire.

Prerequisites: Craft (alchemy) 6 ranks, Grenadier.

Benefit: The Mad Alchemist feat grants you access to three special tactical maneuvers.

Distracting Blast: If you ready an action to throw a thunderstone at the square an opponent occupies, you can disrupt his actions. The sudden bang from the stone's detonation ruins your foe's concentration, possibly spoiling his attack or his attempt to cast a spell. If the target of this blast was casting a spell when you threw the thunderstone, he must make a Concentration check opposed by your Craft (alchemy) check. If you succeed on this check, his spell is ruined. If the target was not casting a spell, he must make a Will save opposed by your Craft (alchemy) check or take a –2 penalty on attack rolls, checks, and saves until the beginning of your next turn.

Fiery Blaze: To use this maneuver, you must first strike a creature with a container of lantern oil or alchemist's fire. On your next turn, you must strike the creature with a spell or weapon attack that deals fire damage. If you do so, the creature takes an extra 1d6 points of fire damage and catches on fire if it is not already in flames.

Tanglefoot Defense: By tearing open a tanglefoot bag and spreading its contents across an area, you can create a vexing barrier that hinders an opponent's approach. As a standard action, you can transform a single square of clear terrain into difficult terrain through the use of a tanglefoot bag. This effect persists for 10 minutes before the tanglefoot bag loses its potency.

SHADOW STRIKER

You melt into the shadows, hiding from your enemies until the time is right. Your cunning, guile, and stealth allow you to pick the most opportune moment to strike.

Prerequisites: Hide 12 ranks, Move Silently 12 ranks.

Benefit: The Shadow Striker feat grants you access to three special tactical maneuvers.

Evade Notice: If both you and an ally threaten an opponent, you can attempt to slip beneath your opponent's notice. On your turn, if you take no hostile actions, such as attacking, casting an offensive spell, and so forth, you can make a Hide check opposed by the threatened foe's Spot check. If you succeed on this check, your foe cannot attack you on his next turn as long as he threatens another active opponent. If you attack your foe for any reason before or during his next turn, you lose this maneuver's benefit.

Fade Away: To use this maneuver, you must first attack an opponent as a standard action, then move away and attempt a Hide check as part of your move action for the turn. If your attack hits, it creates a momentary diversion, granting you a +5 bonus on this Hide check.

Ghost Strike: You use an ally's distraction and your talent to move noiselessly and slip out of your opponent's field of vision for a single, crucial moment. To use this maneuver, both you and an ally must threaten a single foe. As a standard action, you make a Move Silently check opposed by your foe's Listen check. If you succeed on this check, you gain this maneuver's benefit. On the next round, your target loses his Dexterity bonus to AC against your first attack of the round so long as your ally still threatens him.

Special: A fighter can select Shadow Striker as one of his fighter bonus feats.

Illus. by R. Horsley

This chapter presents new tools and weapons for spellcasters of all types. The spells range in power and utility, from a handful of direct- and indirect-damage spells to spells that move the caster and his allies or enemies across the battlefield and those that allow the caster to act on borrowed time. Some spells call or summon new allies for the spellcaster. Channeled spells are a new type of spell that have a greater effect the longer you spend casting. Other spells, such as the various *crown* spells, have an ongoing effect that can be discharged for a more powerful result.

The chapter begins with the spell lists for the spellcasting classes, including the new classes in Chapter 1 of this book. An M or F appearing at the end of a spell's name denotes a spell with a material or focus component, respectively, that is not normally included in a spell component pouch. An X denotes a spell with an XP component paid by the caster.

After the spell lists, the new spells appear in alphabetical order by spell name (with the exception of those whose names begin with "greater," "mass," or "swift"; see Order of Presentation, PH 181). For explanation of spell terminology, see Chapter 10 of the *Player's Handbook*.

DUAL-SCHOOL SPELLS

Dual-school spells, featured in this book for the first time, have effects that encompass two distinct schools of magic. In all cases, treat these spells as if they belonged to both schools simultaneously. Effects that prevent a spellcaster from accessing one school of a dual-school spell prevent all access to that spell. For example, a specialist wizard cannot learn a dual-school spell if either of the spell's schools is one of his prohibited schools. Benefits that apply to a school of magic do not stack with themselves even if the spellcaster can apply them to both schools of magic. For example, if a spellcaster has the Spell Focus feat for either school, it applies to the dual-school spell normally. However, spellcasters who have taken the Spell Focus feat for both of a dual-school spell's associated schools only increase the DC of the dual-school spell by +1.

THE POLYMORPH SUBSCHOOL

Another feature new in *Player's Handbook II* is the polymorph subschool, defined and explained below.

A spell of the polymorph subschool changes the target's form from one shape to another. Unless stated otherwise in the spell's description, the target of a polymorph spell takes on all the statistics and special abilities of an average member of the new form in place of its own except as follows:

• The target retains its own alignment (and personality, within the limits of the new form's ability scores).

• The target retains its own hit points.

• The target is treated has having its normal Hit Dice for purpose of adjudicating effects based on HD, such as the *sleep* spell, though it uses the new form's base attack bonus, base save bonuses, and all other statistics derived from Hit Dice.

- The target retains the ability to understand the languages it understands in its normal form. If the new form is normally capable of speech, the target retains the ability to speak these languages as well. It can write in the languages it understands, but only if the new form is capable of writing in some manner (even a primitive manner, such as drawing in the dirt with a paw).

In all other ways, the target's normal game statistics are effectively replaced by those of the new form. The target loses all of the special abilities it has in its normal form, including its class features (even if the new form would normally be able to use these class features).

If the new form's size is different from the target's normal size, its new space must share as much of the original form's space as possible, squeezing into the available space (see PH 148) if necessary. If insufficient space exists for the new form, the spell fails.

Any gear worn or carried by the target melds into the new form and becomes nonfunctional. When the target reverts to its true form, any objects previously melded into the new form reappear in the same location on its body they previously occupied and are once again functional. Any new items worn in the assumed form fall off and land at the target's feet.

The spellcaster can freely designate the new form's minor physical qualities (such as hair color and skin color) within the normal ranges for a creature of that kind. The new form's significant physical qualities (such as height, weight, and gender) are also under the spellcaster's control, but they must fall within the norms for the new form's kind. The target of a polymorph spell is effectively camouflaged as a creature of its new form, and gains a +10 bonus on Disguise checks if it uses this ability to create a disguise.

If the target of a polymorph spell is slain or rendered unconscious, the spell ends. Any part of the body that is separated from the whole remains polymorphed until the effect ends.

Incorporeal or gaseous creatures are immune to polymorph spells, as are creatures of the plant type. A creature with the shapechanger subtype (such as a lycanthrope or doppelganger) can revert to its natural form as a standard action.

Spells That Have Come Before

For the purpose of adjudicating effects that apply to polymorph spells, any spell whose effect is based on either *alter self* or *polymorph* should be considered to have the polymorph subschool. However, note that the spells' existing rules text takes priority over that of the subschool. *Alter self*, for instance, does not change the target's ability scores (unlike normal for spells of the polymorph subschool).

ASSASSIN SPELLS

1st-Level Assassin Spell

Blade of Blood: Weapon deals +1d6 damage, or +3d6 if you take 5 points of damage.

2nd-Level Assassin Spell

Increase Virulence: Poison's DC increases by 2.

BARD SPELLS

1st-Level Bard Spells

Share Talents: Subjects gain +2 bonus on skill checks.
Stay the Hand: Change subject creature's attitude to helpful for 1 round.

2nd-Level Bard Spells

Blade Brothers: Use higher saving throw result between two creatures, but both suffer effects if the saves fail.
Celerity, Lesser: Take a move action immediately, but be dazed for a round.
Crown of Veils: Gain +2 to Disguise and Hide, discharge to gain +8.
Increase Virulence: Poison's DC increases by 2.
Insight of Good Fortune[M]**:** Subject rolls twice, takes best result.
Master's Touch: Subject gains immediate +4 bonus on a skill check.
Ray of the Python: Creature can only attack once per round, cannot make attacks of opportunity,–10 ft. penalty to speed.
Stretch Weapon: Melee weapon gains 5 ft. of reach for one attack.
Vertigo: Subject creature must succeed on a DC 10 Balance check to move each round.

3rd-Level Bard Spells

Alter Fortune[X]**:** Cause one creature to reroll any die roll.
Halt: Subject's feet become stuck to ground.
Hesitate: Force subject to lose actions.
Phantom Battle: Illusion of battle flanks creatures and denies attacks of opportunity.
Sonic Shield: +4 deflection bonus to AC; 1d8 sonic damage and push back creatures that hit you in melee.

4th-Level Bard Spells

Baleful Blink: Subject has 50% chance of failure on attacks and spells.
Celerity: Take a standard action immediately, but be dazed for a round.
Healing Spirit: Ball of light heals 1d8/round.
Mirror Image, Greater: As *mirror image*, but gain an additional image each round.
Thunder Field: Creatures in area take 1d8 sonic damage/round, knocked prone.

5th-Level Bard Spells

Dance of Blades: A weapon attacks on its own.
Friend to Foe: Make subject creature believe its allies are its enemies.
Incite Riot: Subjects attack nearest creature.
Magic Convalescence: Spells cast nearby heal you 1 hp/spell level.
Renewed Vigor: Remove fatigue and +2 bonus to Constitution for 1 round/level.

BEGUILER SPELLS

1st-Level Beguiler Spells
Rouse: Awakens creatures in area.
Whelm: Deal 1d6 nonlethal damage +1d6/2 levels above 1st (max 5d6).

2nd-Level Beguiler Spells
Blinding Color Surge: Blind subject for 1 round, gain *invisibility.*
Stay the Hand: Change subject creature's attitude to helpful for 1 round.
Vertigo: Subject creature must succeed on a DC 10 Balance check to move each round.
Whelming Blast: 15-foot cone deals 1d6 nonlethal damage/2 levels (max 5d6).

3rd-Level Beguiler Spells
Crown of Veils: Gain +2 to Disguise and Hide, discharge to gain +8.
Halt: Subject's feet become stuck to ground.
Hesitate: Force subject to lose actions.
Inevitable Defeat: Subject takes 3d6 nonlethal damage/round.
Legion of Sentinels: Ghostly swordsmen threaten a 10-foot radius, deal 1d8 damage +1/3 levels (max +5).
Vertigo Field: Creatures have 20% miss chance and possibly become nauseated.

4th-Level Beguiler Spells
Mirror Image, Greater: As *mirror image,* but gain an additional image each round.
Phantom Battle: Illusion of battle flanks creatures and denies attacks of opportunity.
Whelm, Mass: 1d6 nonlethal damage/level (max 10d6) to 1 creature/level.

5th-Level Beguiler Spells
Etherealness, Swift: Subject momentarily becomes ethereal.
Friend to Foe: Make subject creature believe its allies are its enemies.
Incite Riot: Subjects attack nearest creature.

6th-Level Beguiler Spell
Overwhelm: Nonlethal damage knocks out subject.

BLACKGUARD SPELLS

1st-Level Blackguard Spell
Blade of Blood: Weapon deals +1d6 damage, or +3d6 if you take 5 points of damage.

2nd-Level Blackguard Spell
Increase Virulence: Poison's DC increases by 2.

CLERIC SPELLS

1st-Level Cleric Spells
Blade of Blood: Weapon deals +1d6 damage, or +3d6 if you take 5 points of damage.
Invest Light Protection: Heal 1d4 damage + 1/2 levels, grant DR 1/evil.

2nd-Level Cleric Spells
Animalistic Power: Subject gains +2 bonus to Str, Dex, and Con.
Black Karma Curse: Subject damages self with melee attack.
Blade Brothers: Use higher saving throw result between two creatures, but both suffer effects if the saves fail.
Cloud of Knives: Release one knife/round, 1d6 damage +1/3 levels (max +5).
Insight of Good Fortune[M]**:** Subject rolls twice, takes best result.
Mark of Judgment: Creatures that attack subject heal 2 points of damage each successful hit.
Master's Touch: Subject gains immediate +4 bonus on a skill check.
Share Talents: Subjects gain +2 bonus on skill checks.
Stay the Hand: Change subject creature's attitude to helpful for 1 round.
Stretch Weapon: Melee weapon gains 5 ft. of reach for one attack.

3rd-Level Cleric Spells
Alter Fortune[X]**:** Cause one creature to reroll any die roll.
Channeled Divine Shield: Gain DR, amount based on casting time.
Crown of the Grave: Command undead, discharge to gain +4 on turn or rebuke.
Crown of Might: Gain +2 Strength, discharge to gain +8 bonus for 1 round.
Crown of Protection: +1 deflection bonus to AC, +1 resistance bonus on saves; discharge to gain +4 for 1 round.
Crown of Smiting[F]**:** +2 damage bonus, discharge to gain +8 damage on single attack.
Curse of Arrow Attraction: Subject takes −5 penalty to AC against ranged attacks.
Divine Retaliation: Weapon appears and strikes those who attack you.
Energy Aegis: Subject gains resistance 20 against one energy type for one attack.
Energy Vulnerability: Subjects gain vulnerability to the specified energy.
Hesitate: Force subject to lose actions.
Invest Moderate Protection: Heal 3d4 damage + 1/2 levels, grant DR 3/evil.
Mark of Doom: Subject takes 1d6 damage for each hostile action.

4th-Level Cleric Spells
Bleakness: 1d6 damage/round to living creatures, grants undead turn resistance and fast healing.

Blessing of the Righteous: Weapons deal +1d6 holy damage and become good-aligned.

Channeled Divine Health: Heal a creature, amount and range based on casting time.

Healing Spirit: Ball of light heals 1d8/round.

Mystic Aegis: You gain SR 12 + caster level against one spell.

Stifle Spell: Subject must concentrate or botch spell.

5th-Level Cleric Spells

Condemnation: Lowers subject outsider's SR and stuns for 1 round.

Etherealness, Swift: Subject momentarily becomes ethereal.

Invest Heavy Protection: Heal 5d4 damage + 1/2 levels, grant DR 5/evil.

Magic Convalescence: Spells cast nearby heal you 1 hp/spell level.

Mana Flux: Magic in area has 20% failure chance.

Meteoric Strike: Melee attack deals an extra 1d6 damage + 1d6/4 levels; adjacent creatures take half damage.

Radiance: Creates *daylight* that dazzles undead.

Renewed Vigor: Remove fatigue and +2 bonus to Constitution for 1 round/level.

6th-Level Cleric Spell

Chasing Perfection[M]: Subject gains +4 to all abilities.

7th-Level Cleric Spells

Animalistic Power, Mass: As *animalistic power*, but multiple subjects.

Plague: One creature/level contracts quickly terminal disease.

Pulse of Hate: Nearby enemies take 2d6 damage/round.

Righteous Burst[M]: Allies healed, enemies damaged 1d8 damage +1/level (max +35).

8th-Level Cleric Spells

Chain Dispel: Dispel multiple magical effects in multiple creatures.

Visions of the Future: +2 sacred bonus on saves, +2 dodge bonus to AC; discharge spell to gain bonus equal to half caster level.

9th-Level Cleric Spell

Summon Golem: Summon a clay, flesh, iron, or stone golem from a small amount of like material.

DRUID SPELLS

2nd-Level Druid Spells

Animalistic Power: Subject gains +2 bonus to Str, Dex, and Con.

Drifts of the Shalm: Create difficult terrain made of snow, leaves, or ash.

Linked Perception: Allies gain +2 bonus/ally in spell area on Listen and Spot checks.

3rd-Level Druid Spells

Alter Fortune[X]: Cause one creature to reroll any die roll.

Crown of Clarity: +2 to Listen and Spot, discharge spell to gain +8.

Evard's Menacing Tentacles: Grow two tentacles with 10-ft. reach that deal 1d8 damage each.

4th-Level Druid Spells

Call of Stone: Slowly turn subject to stone.

Healing Spirit: Ball of light heals 1d8/round.

Meteoric Strike: Melee attack deals an extra 1d6 damage + 1d6/4 levels; adjacent creatures take half damage.

Renewed Vigor: Remove fatigue and +2 bonus to Constitution for 1 round/level.

5th-Level Druid Spells

Blood Creepers: Vines deal 1/level damage for multiple rounds and entangle one creature.

Longstrider. Mass: Allies within 60 ft. gain +10 ft. bonus to speed.

Magic Convalescence: Spells cast nearby heal you 1 hp/spell level.

Radiance: Creates *daylight* that dazzles undead.

6th-Level Druid Spells

Bones of the Earth: Create pillars of stone.

Chasing Perfection[M]: Subject gains +4 to all abilities.

Thunder Field: Creatures in area take 1d8 sonic damage/round, knocked prone.

7th-Level Druid Spells

Animalistic Power, Mass: As *animalistic power*, but multiple subjects.

As the Frost: Transform into a creature of cold.

Plague: One creature/level contracts quickly terminal disease.

Wrack Earth: Deals 1d6 damage/level (max 15d6) to creatures in a line and creates a wall of rubble.

DUSKBLADE SPELLS

1st-Level Duskblade Spells

Bigby's Tripping Hand: Hand trips subject.

Blade of Blood: Weapon deals +1d6 damage, or +3d6 if you take 5 points of damage.

Deflect, Lesser: Gain a deflection bonus of +1/3 levels (max +5) against one attack.

Kelgore's Fire Bolt: 1d6 fire damage/level (max 5d6), partially ignore SR.

Rouse: Awakens creatures in area.

Stand: Subject stands up from prone.

2nd-Level Duskblade Spells

Animalistic Power: Subject gains +2 bonus to Str, Dex, and Con.

Bigby's Striking Fist: Hand deals 1d6 nonlethal damage/2 levels (max 5d6) and knocks subject back.

Deflect: Gain bonus to AC for one attack.

Dimension Hop: Teleport subject short distance.

Seeking Ray: Ray deals 4d6 electricity damage, ignores concealment and cover; you gain +4 on attacks with rays against the subject.

Stretch Weapon: Melee weapon gains 5 ft. of reach for one attack.

Sure Strike: Gain +1 bonus/3 levels on next attack.

3rd-Level Duskblade Spells

Crown of Might: Gain +2 Strength, discharge to gain +8 bonus for 1 round.

Crown of Protection: +1 deflection bonus to AC, +1 resistance bonus on saves; discharge to gain +4 for 1 round.

Dispelling Touch: Dispel one magical effect on touched subject.

Doom Scarabs: Scarab swarm deals 1d6/2 levels, gives you temporary hit points.

Energy Aegis: Subject gains resistance 20 against one energy type for one attack.

Energy Surge: As *lesser energy surge*, but 2d6 damage.

Halt: Subject's feet become stuck to ground.

Regroup: Teleports nearby allies to your side.

4th-Level Duskblade Spells

Channeled Pyroburst: Deal fire damage, amount and radius based on casting time.

Toxic Weapon: Coats weapon with poison.

5th-Level Duskblade Spells

Slashing Dispel: As *dispel magic*, but creatures take damage for spells dispelled.

Sonic Shield: +4 deflection bonus to AC; 1d8 sonic damage and push back creatures that hit you in melee.

PALADIN SPELLS

2nd-Level Paladin Spells

Crown of Smiting[F]: +2 damage bonus, discharge to gain +8 damage on single attack.

Mark of Doom: Subject takes 1d6 damage for each hostile action.

3rd-Level Paladin Spell

Healing Spirit: Ball of light heals 1d8/round.

4th-Level Paladin Spells

Blessing of the Righteous: Weapons deal +1d6 holy damage and become good-aligned.

Divine Retaliation: Weapon appears and strikes those who attack you.

Meteoric Strike: Melee attack deals an extra 1d6 damage + 1d6/4 levels; adjacent creatures take half damage.

RANGER SPELLS

1st-Level Ranger Spell

Linked Perception: Allies gain +2 bonus/ally in spell area on Listen and Spot checks.

2nd-Level Ranger Spells

Animalistic Power: Subject gains +2 bonus to Str, Dex, and Con.

Crown of Clarity: +2 to Listen and Spot, discharge spell to gain +8.

Curse of Arrow Attraction: Subject takes −5 penalty to AC against ranged attacks.

Hunter's Eye: Gain +1d6 sneak attack damage/3 caster levels for 1 round.

Share Talents: Subjects gain +2 bonus on skill checks.

4th-Level Ranger Spell

Longstrider, Mass: Allies within 60 ft. gain +10 ft. bonus to speed.

SORCERER/WIZARD SPELLS

1st-Level Sorcerer/Wizard Spells

Abjur **Deflect, Lesser:** Gain a deflection bonus of +1/3 levels (max +5) against one attack.

Conj **Stand:** Subject stands up from prone.

Kelgore's Fire Bolt: 1d6 fire damage/level (max 5d6), partially ignore SR.

Ench **Rouse:** Awakens creatures in area.

Whelm: Deal 1d6 nonlethal damage +1d6/2 levels above 1st (max 5d6).

Evoc **Bigby's Tripping Hand:** Hand trips subject.

Kelgore's Fire Bolt: 1d6 fire damage/level (max 5d6), partially ignore SR.

Necro **Blade of Blood:** Weapon deals +1d6 damage, or +3d6 if you take 5 points of damage.

Trans **Burning Rage:** Subject takes 4 points of damage/round, gains attack bonus and DR.

2nd-Level Sorcerer/Wizard Spells

Abjur **Deflect:** Gain bonus to AC for one attack.

Dispelling Touch: Dispel one magical effect on touched subject.

Conj **Cloud of Knives:** Release one knife/round, 1d6 damage +1/3 levels (max +5).

Dimension Hop: Teleport subject short distance.

Kelgore's Grave Mist: 1d6 cold damage/level, cause fatigue, partially ignore SR.

Div **Insight of Good Fortune**[M]: Subject rolls twice, takes best result.

Master's Touch: Subject gains immediate +4 bonus on a skill check.

Sure Strike: Gain +1 bonus/3 levels on next attack.

Ench **Black Karma Curse:** Subject damages self with melee attack.

Stay the Hand: Change subject creature's attitude to helpful for 1 round.

Whelming Blast: 15-foot cone deals 1d6 nonlethal damage/2 levels (max 5d6).

Evoc **Bigby's Striking Fist:** Hand deals 1d6 nonlethal damage/2 levels (max 5d6) and knocks subject back.

Bigby's Warding Hand: Hand of force slows opponent.

Electric Vengeance: 2d8 damage +1/level (max +10) to opponent who damages you in melee.

Seeking Ray: Ray deals 4d6 electricity damage, ignores concealment and cover; you gain +4 on attacks with rays against the subject.

Illus **Blinding Color Surge:** Blind subject for 1 round, gain *invisibility*.

Vertigo: Subject creature must succeed on a DC 10 Balance check to move each round.

Necro **Kelgore's Grave Mist:** 1d6 cold damage/level, cause fatigue, partially ignore SR.

Trans **Animalistic Power:** Subject gains +2 bonus to Str, Dex, and Con.

Celerity, Lesser: Take a move action immediately, but be dazed for 1 round.

Energy Surge, Lesser: One attack deals an extra 1d6 energy damage.

Increase Virulence: Poison's DC increases by 2.

Share Talents: Subjects gain +2 bonus on skill checks.

Stretch Weapon: Melee weapon gains 5 ft. of reach for one attack.

3rd-Level Sorcerer/Wizard Spells

Abjur **Energy Aegis:** Subject gains resistance 20 against one energy type for one attack.

Energy Vulnerability: Subjects gain vulnerability to the specified energy.

Conj **Dimension Step:** Allies can immediately teleport a distance equal to their speed.

Luminous Assassin, Lesser: Summons an assassin to attack the subject.

Melf's Unicorn Arrow[F]: 1d8+8 damage and bull rush; +1 unicorn arrow/3 levels beyond 5th.

Regroup: Teleports nearby allies to your side.

Scattering Trap: Imbue one 5-ft. square/2 levels with *teleport* trap.

Div **Alter Fortune**[X]: Cause one creature to reroll any die roll.

Crown of Clarity: +2 to Listen and Spot, discharge spell to gain +8.

Ench **Hesitate:** Force subject to lose actions.

Inevitable Defeat: Subject takes 3d6 nonlethal damage/round.

Evoc **Bigby's Disrupting Hand:** Hand disrupts opponent's spellcasting.

Prismatic Mist: Multicolored mist has random effect.

Ray of the Python: Creature can only attack once per round, cannot make attacks of opportunity, –10 ft. penalty to speed.

Illus **Legion of Sentinels:** Ghostly swordsmen threaten a 10-foot radius, deal 1d8 damage +1/3 levels (max +5).

Vertigo Field: Creatures have 20% miss chance and possibly become nauseated.

Necro **Crown of the Grave:** Command undead, discharge to gain +4 on turn or rebuke.

Trans **Crown of Might:** Gain +2 Strength, discharge to gain +8 bonus for 1 round.

Crown of Protection: +1 deflection bonus to AC, +1 resistance bonus on saves; discharge to gain +4 for 1 round.

Curse of Arrow Attraction: Subject takes –5 penalty to AC against ranged attacks.

Energy Surge: As *lesser energy surge*, but 2d6 damage.

Evard's Menacing Tentacles: Grow two tentacles with 10-ft. reach that deal 1d8 damage each.

Halt: Subject's feet become stuck to ground.

4th-Level Sorcerer/Wizard Spells

Abjur **Condemnation:** Lowers subject outsider's SR and stuns for 1 round.

Slashing Dispel: As *dispel magic*, but creatures take damage for spells dispelled.

Stifle Spell: Subject must concentrate or botch spell.

Conj **Bright Worms:** Fiery worms damage enemies within 20-ft. spread.

Doom Scarabs: Scarab swarm deals 1d6/2 levels, gives you temporary hit points.

Explosive Rune FieldM: Area is covered with runes that explode on contact with creatures.

Ench **Whelm, Mass:** 1d6 nonlethal damage/level (max 10d6) to 1 creature/level.

Evoc **Bleakness:** 1d6 damage/round to living creatures, grants undead turn resistance and fast healing.

Channeled Pyroburst: Deal fire damage, amount and radius based on casting time.

Crushing Grip: Subject takes –2 on attacks, checks, saves, and AC and –20 ft. penalty to speed, might be paralyzed.

Slashing Dispel: As *dispel magic*, but creatures take damage for spells dispelled.

Illus **Crown of Veils:** Gain +2 to Disguise and Hide, discharge to gain +8.

Mirror Image, Greater: As *mirror image*, but gain an additional image each round.

Phantom Battle: Illusion of battle flanks creatures and denies attacks of opportunity.

Necro **Doom Scarabs:** Scarab swarm deals 1d6/2 levels, gives you temporary hit points.

Trans **Baleful Blink:** Subject has 50% chance of failure on attacks and spells.

Call of Stone: Slowly turn subject to stone.

Celerity: Take a standard action immediately, but be dazed for a round.

Trollshape: You take on the form and abilities of a troll.

Univ **Mystic Surge:** Ally's spell gains +2 DC and +1 caster level.

5th-Level Sorcerer/Wizard Spells

Abjur **Field of Resistance:** Zone provides SR 11 + caster level.

Mana Flux: Magic in area has 20% failure chance.

Conj **Dimension Shuffle:** Teleport multiple creatures short distances within line of sight.
Luminous Assassin: As *lesser luminous assassin*, but the assassin is more powerful.
Toxic Weapon: Coats weapon with poison.

Ench **Incite Riot:** Subjects attack nearest creature.

Evoc **Electric Vengeance, Greater:** As *electric vengeance*, but 5d8 damage +1/level (max +15) and daze subject.
Radiance: Creates *daylight* that dazzles undead.
Sonic Shield: +4 deflection bonus to AC; 1d8 sonic damage and push back creatures that hit you in melee.

Illus **Friend to Foe:** Make subject creature believe its allies are its enemies.

Trans **Dance of Blades:** A weapon attacks on its own.
Etherealness, Swift: Subject momentarily becomes ethereal.

6th-Level Sorcerer/Wizard Spells

Ench **Overwhelm:** Nonlethal damage knocks out subject.

Evoc **Thunder Field:** Creatures in area take 1d8 sonic damage/round, knocked prone.

Trans **Chasing Perfection**[M]**:** Subject gains +4 to all abilities.
Energy Surge, Greater: As *energy surge*, but 3d6 damage.

7th-Level Sorcerer/Wizard Spells

Conj **Luminous Assassin, Greater:** As *luminous assassin*, but the assassin is more powerful.

Necro **Pulse of Hate:** Nearby enemies take 2d6 damage/round.

Trans **Animalistic Power, Mass:** As *animalistic power*, but multiple subjects.
As the Frost: Transform into a creature of cold.

8th-Level Sorcerer/Wizard Spells

Abjur **Chain Dispel:** Dispel multiple magical effects in multiple creatures.

Necro **Plague:** One creature/level contracts quickly terminal disease.

Trans **Celerity, Greater:** Take a full-round action immediately, but be dazed for a round.

9th-Level Sorcerer/Wizard Spells

Conj **Summon Golem:** Summon a clay, flesh, iron, or stone golem from a small amount of like material.

Evoc **Detonate:** Slays subject and creates 20-ft.-radius explosion that deals 1d6 damage/level (max 20d6).

Trans **Dragonshape:** You take on the form and abilities of a Huge red dragon.

Alter Fortune
Divination
Level: Bard 3, cleric 3, druid 3, sorcerer/wizard 3
Components: V, X
Casting Time: 1 immediate action
Range: Close (25 ft. + 5 ft./2 levels)
Target: One creature
Duration: Instantaneous
Saving Throw: None
Spell Resistance: No

With a single utterance, you create a momentary distortion that engulfs and confounds your foe.

You change the flow of chance, causing the subject to immediately reroll any die roll it just made. It must abide by the second roll.
   XP Cost: 200 XP.

Animalistic Power
Transmutation
Level: Cleric 2, druid 2, duskblade 2, ranger 2, sorcerer/wizard 2
Components: V, S, M
Casting Time: 1 standard action
Range: Touch
Target: Creature touched
Duration: 1 minute/level
Saving Throw: Will negates (harmless)

Spell Resistance: Yes (harmless)

A sparkling nimbus of green light appears around the creature. As the light fades, the creature seems a shade larger and assumes a more animalistic, even feral countenance.

You imbue the subject with an aspect of the natural world. The subject gains a +2 enhancement bonus to Strength, Dexterity, and Constitution.
   Material Component: A bit of animal fur, feathers, or skin.

Animalistic Power, Mass
Transmutation
Level: Cleric 7, druid 7, sorcerer/wizard 7
Range: Close (25 ft. + 5 ft./2 levels)
Targets: One creature/level, no two of which are more than 30 ft. apart

This spell functions like *animalistic power*, except that it affects multiple creature.

As the Frost
Transmutation [Cold]
Level: Druid 7, sorcerer/wizard 7
Components: V, S, M
Casting Time: 1 standard action

Range: Personal
Target: You
Duration: 1 round/level

With a crystalline tinkling, your body transforms into a figure of ice and cold, your equipment melding into your new form. Your skin becomes brilliant blue and transparent, with glimpses of liquid beneath. Frost forms across your hands and arms, dripping down to form knife-like icicles. Your breath hisses white in the bitterly cold air surrounding you. Snow swirls about you as your presence freezes the air's moisture. Ice crystals spread from your footprints.

Your creature type changes to outsider. Unlike other outsiders, you can be brought back to life if you die in this form.
   You gain the following qualities and abilities:
- Immunity to cold.
- Damage reduction 10/magic and piercing.
- At the beginning of your action, creatures within 15 feet of you take 2d6 points of cold damage per round. A creature that takes damage from this effect must make a Fortitude save (DC 17 + your key ability modifier)

or be *slowed*, as the *slow* spell, for the remaining duration of *as the frost*. Spell resistance applies to this effect.

Material Component: A chunk of ice or crystal.

Baleful Blink

Transmutation

Level: Bard 4, sorcerer/wizard 4

Components: V

Casting Time: 1 standard action

Range: Close (25 ft. + 5 ft./2 levels)

Target: One creature

Duration: 1 round/level

Saving Throw: Fortitude negates

Spell Resistance: No

You cause the creature to wink in and out of existence erratically, much to its chagrin.

You curse one creature to a frustrating existence on the edge of the Ethereal Plane. The subject shimmers between the Ethereal Plane and the Material Plane, has a 50% miss chance on any melee or ranged attacks (as if the target of the attack had total concealment), and there is a 50% chance that any spell she casts does not have an effect on the desired plane while she blinks between the planes.

Because the magic of the spell only causes the subject to blink when attacking or casting, attackers have no miss chance against her, and spells cast against her affect her normally. Because the blinking is so rapid, she cannot attempt to blink through walls or move in the Ethereal Plane.

The subject of a *baleful blink* spell can cast spells on itself with impunity; in this case, it has no miss chance because the target of its spell (itself) travels along with the spell. The subject can also target creatures on the Ethereal Plane, but still has a 50% chance of failure on attacks and spells. Spells with the force descriptor are unaffected by the effect of *baleful blink*.

Bigby's Disrupting Hand

Evocation [Force]

Level: Sorcerer/wizard 3

As the frost turns Mialee into an outsider with cold intentions

Components: V, S, F

Casting Time: 1 standard action

Range: Medium (100 ft. + 10 ft./level)

Effect: One hand of force

Duration: 1 minute (D)

Saving Throw: None

Spell Resistance: Yes

A small, spectral human hand springs into existence before your target. It hovers in the air, ready to deliver a backhanded blow.

Like *Bigby's interposing hand*, this spell creates a magical construct in the form of a human hand. The hand targets a single opponent of your choice within range. You choose this opponent as you cast the spell. You can target a different opponent with this spell by taking a move action to do so.

When the subject of *Bigby's disrupting hand* attempts to cast a spell, the hand punches him. This attack causes no damage, but it forces the subject to make a Concentration check with a DC equal to this spell's save DC. If the subject fails the check, the hand's blow ruins his casting attempt.

The hand is about 1 foot long. It has hit points equal to half your full normal hit points, and its AC is 20 (+4 size, +6 natural). It makes saving throws using your total save bonuses and takes damage from spells and attacks as normal.

Focus: A soft glove.

Bigby's Helpful Hand

Evocation [Force]

Level: Sorcerer/wizard 1

Components: V, S, F

Casting Time: 1 standard action

Range: 0 ft.

Effect: One hand of force

Duration: 1 hour/level (D)

Saving Throw: None

Spell Resistance: No

A magical construct in the shape of a hand appears next to you. Its fingers open toward you, waiting for you to hand it an item.

This spell creates a hand of magical force that holds items for you, helps you complete long, involved tasks, and otherwise aids you. The spell grants you a +2 competence bonus on Craft, Disable Device, and Open Lock checks for the duration of the spell. It can hold a single object weighing up to 20 pounds. You can grasp the object that the hand carries or place an object in its grasp as a swift action. The hand remains in your square at all times. It matches your speed, and you can bring the hand and the object along with you if you use *dimension door, teleport,* and similar spells. You cannot order the hand to move away from you. If you are separated from the hand, the spell immediately ends.

The hand is about 1 foot long. It has hit points equal to half your full normal hit points, and its AC is 20 (+4 size, +6 natural). It makes saving throws using your total save bonuses and takes damage from spells and attacks as normal.

Focus: A soft glove.

Bigby's Striking Fist
Evocation [Force]
Level: Duskblade 2, sorcerer/wizard 2
Components: V, S, M
Casting Time: 1 standard action
Range: Medium (100 ft. + 10 ft./level)
Target: One creature
Duration: Instantaneous
Saving Throw: Reflex partial
Spell Resistance: Yes

A large glowing fist, the size of a human torso, appears in front of the creature and slams into it with great force.

The attack bonus of this *striking fist* equals your caster level + your key ability modifier + 2 for the hand's Strength score (14). The fist deals 1d6 points of nonlethal damage per two caster levels (maximum 5d6) and attempts a bull rush (PH 154). The fist has a bonus of +4 plus +1 per two caster levels on the bull rush attempt, and if successful it knocks the subject back in a direction of your choice. This movement does not provoke attacks of opportunity. A subject that succeeds on its Reflex save takes half damage and is not subject to the bull rush attempt.
Material Components: Three glass beads.

Bigby's Tripping Hand
Evocation [Force]
Level: Duskblade 1, sorcerer/wizard 1
Components: V, S, M
Casting Time: 1 standard action
Range: Medium (100 ft. + 10 ft./level)
Target: One creature
Duration: Instantaneous
Saving Throw: Reflex negates
Spell Resistance: Yes

A large glowing hand, the size of a human torso, appears in front of the creature and sweeps at its legs.

The large hand sweeps at the target creature's legs in a tripping maneuver (PH 158). This trip attempt does not provoke attacks of opportunity. Its attack bonus equals your caster level + your key ability modifier + 2 for the hand's Strength score (14). The hand has a bonus of +1 on the trip attempt for every three caster levels, to a maximum of +5 at 15th level.

Material Components: Three glass beads.

Bigby's Warding Hand
Evocation [Force]
Level: Sorcerer/wizard 2
Components: V, S, F
Casting Time: 1 standard action
Range: Medium (100 ft. + 10 ft./level)
Effect: One hand of force
Duration: 1 round/level (D)
Saving Throw: None
Spell Resistance: Yes

A spectral human hand springs into existence. It pushes into the target, forcing him back as he attempts to move.

This spell creates a hand of pure force that hinders the subject's ability to move. You designate a target when casting this spell. You can change the spell's target by taking a move action to do so. This spell has no effect on Huge or larger creatures.
If the target of the spell attempts to move, it must make a Strength check (DC 12 + your key ability modifier). If this check fails, the creature moves at half speed. The target must make a new check each round to overcome the hand's hindering force.
The hand is about 1 foot long. It has hit points equal to half your full normal hit points, and its AC is 20 (+4 size, +6 natural). It makes saving throws using your total save bonuses and takes damage from spells and attacks as normal.
Focus: A soft glove.

Black Karma Curse
Enchantment (Compulsion) [Mind-Affecting]
Level: Cleric 2, sorcerer/wizard 2
Components: V, S
Casting Time: 1 standard action
Range: Close (25 ft. + 5 ft./2 levels)
Target: One creature
Duration: Instantaneous
Saving Throw: Will negates
Spell Resistance: Yes

With a word and a gesture, you compel the bewildered creature to attack itself.

If the target creature's saving throw fails, it immediately takes damage as if it had hit itself with its currently wielded weapon (or natural weapon). If the creature has more than one eligible attack form, it uses the one that deals the most damage.

Blade of Blood
Necromancy
Level: Assassin 1, blackguard 1, cleric 1, duskblade 1, sorcerer/wizard 1
Components: V, S
Casting Time: 1 swift action
Range: Touch
Target: Weapon touched
Duration: 1 round/level or until discharged
Saving Throw: None
Spell Resistance: No

Red blood erupts along the weapon's blade, bludgeon, or point. The blood drips to spatter in thick, viscous drops upon the ground.

This spell infuses the weapon touched with baleful energy. The next time this weapon strikes a living creature, *blade of blood* discharges. The spell deals an extra 1d6 points of damage against the target of the attack. You can voluntarily take 5 hit points of damage to empower the weapon to deal an extra 2d6 points of damage (for a total of 3d6 points of extra damage).
The weapon loses this property if its wielder drops it or otherwise loses contact with it.

Blade Brothers
Abjuration
Level: Bard 2, cleric 2
Components: V, S
Casting Time: 1 standard action
Range: Touch
Targets: Two willing creatures
Duration: 1 minute/level or until discharged
Saving Throw: Will negates (harmless)
Spell Resistance: Yes (harmless)

You reach out and touch two creatures, and a sparkling tether of multicolored light briefly forms between them.

One time during the duration of this spell, when one subject of the spell attempts a saving throw, both recipients can roll and apply the more favorable result. When rolling, each subject uses his own save bonus and save modifiers. If both saving throws fail, both creatures suffer the consequences of a failed save, even if the effect that prompted the saving throw only affected one of the subjects. If the affected creatures move more than 120 feet away from each other after the spell is cast, the effect ends.

Bleakness

Evocation [Darkness, Evil]
Level: Cleric 4, sorcerer/wizard 4
Components: V, S, DF
Casting Time: 1 standard action
Range: Close (25 ft. + 5 ft./2 levels)
Area: 20-ft.-radius emanation centered on a point in space
Duration: 1 round/level (D)
Saving Throw: None
Spell Resistance: No

A pulsing darkness bleeds from your body.

You conjure up a cloud of inky darkness laced with life-sucking energy from the Negative Energy Plane. Living creatures in the area take 1d6 points of damage each round, starting in the round when they enter the area and at the beginning of their turns each round they remain in the area. The damage can be prevented by any effect that protects against negative energy, such as *death ward*.

In addition, undead gain turn resistance +4 and fast healing 3 for as long as they remain in the area of the spell.

Bleakness counters or dispels any light spell of equal or lower level.

Blessing of the Righteous

Evocation [Good]
Level: Cleric 4, paladin 4
Components: V, S, DF
Casting Time: 1 standard action
Range: 40 ft.
Area: All allies in a 40-ft.-radius burst centered on you
Duration: 1 round/level
Saving Throw: Will negates (harmless)
Spell Resistance: Yes (harmless)

A sudden burst of warm, radiant light engulfs you and your allies. The light fades quickly but lingers on the weapons of those affected.

You bless yourself and your allies. You and your allies' melee and ranged attacks deal an extra 1d6 points of holy damage and are considered good-aligned for the purpose of overcoming damage reduction.

Blinding Color Surge

Illusion (Glamer)
Level: Beguiler 2, sorcerer/wizard 2
Components: V, S, F
Casting Time: 1 standard action
Range: Medium (100 ft. + 10 ft./level)
Targets: You and one creature
Duration: 1 round/level
Saving Throw: Will negates
Spell Resistance: Yes

You point at the target of this spell. The colors of your clothing, skin, and hair shine for a brief moment before they surge away from you, forming a multicolored ray that strikes your target. You disappear as the colors of your body and items leap from you into the beam. The target clutches his eyes and staggers.

You strip the color from your body and gear, turn it into a lance of energy, and hurl it at a target. When you cast this spell, you target a creature with the colors stripped from your form. The target must make a Will save or be blinded for 1 round.

You also gain the benefit of *invisibility,* for the duration of this spell, even if the target creature succeeds on its save or if its spell resistance protects it.

Focus: A small prism.

Blood Creepers

Conjuration (Creation)
Level: Druid 5
Components: V, S, DF
Casting Time: 1 standard action
Range: Medium (100 ft. + 10 ft./level)
Target: One creature
Duration: 1 round/level
Saving Throw: Fortitude negates
Spell Resistance: Yes

Thorny vines burst from the creature's body, punching through bone, flesh, and skin to enwrap its arms and legs and tether it to the ground.

The subject takes 1 point of piercing damage per caster level (maximum

15) as the creepers rip apart its body. In addition, the creepers entwine securely around it, trapping its legs and arms. The subject is immobilized (unable to move from its current location) and entangled.

Each round, the subject takes an extra 1 point of piercing damage per caster level (maximum 15) unless it is able to escape. A trapped creature can attempt to break free with a DC 20 Strength check or wriggle free with a DC 25 Escape Artist check, either of which ends the spell if successful. Other creatures can use the aid another action as normal on these checks. They can make attacks against these vines as if they were wooden objects with a thickness of 3 inches (see Smashing an Object, PH 185).

Despite its name, *blood creepers* is equally effective on living and non-living creatures.

Bones of the Earth

Conjuration (Creation) [Earth]
Level: Druid 6
Components: V, S, DF
Casting Time: 1 standard action
Range: 60 ft.
Effect: One 5-ft.-diameter pillar of stone per round
Duration: 1 round/2 levels (D)
Saving Throw: Reflex negates
Spell Resistance: No

A pillar of rock explodes upward from the ground.

Each round as a standard action, you conjure a pillar of rock that bursts from a stone or earthen surface anywhere within the spell's range. Each pillar fills a 5-foot square and grows to a height of 20 feet or until it hits a barrier such as a ceiling or wall. A Large or smaller creature in a square where a pillar erupts must succeed on a Reflex save or be carried upward by the force of the pillar. If a pillar is created in a room with a ceiling height of 20 feet or less, the rock slams into the ceiling, dealing 4d6 points of damage to any creature atop it.

In a location with a ceiling height of more than 20 feet, a creature carried up by a pillar must succeed on a DC 20 Balance check or fall from the top of the pillar when it reaches its maximum height. On a failed check, the creature plummets to the ground, taking 2d6 points of damage from the fall.

You can also cause a pillar to erupt from a vertical surface, in which case any creatures in the pillar's path must succeed on their Reflex saves or take 2d6 points of damage and be knocked prone.

The pillar created is permanent and has AC 3, hardness 8, and 900 hit points. A pillar can be climbed with a DC 20 Climb check.

Bright Worms

Conjuration (Creation) [Fire]
Level: Sorcerer/wizard 4
Components: V, S
Casting Time: 1 standard action
Range: Medium (100 ft. + 10 ft./level)
Area: 20-ft.-radius spread
Duration: 1 round/level (D)
Saving Throw: Reflex half
Spell Resistance: No

With a loud pop, a nest of writhing worms of multicolored light appears in the air.

You create a knot of living light with wormlike tendrils extending out from the mass. The worms hang in the air as if suspended. The worms drift away from the paths of your allies, but they attack enemies that enter the area, lashing out with lightning speed and combusting creatures that they touch.

When you cast the spell, and in each later round at the beginning of your turn, the flaming worms deal 2d6 points of fire damage to any of your enemies in the area. The fire damage increases as you gain levels, to 3d6 per round for an 11th-level caster and 4d6 per round for a 15th-level caster.

Any area spell that deals cold damage eliminates the *bright worms* from its area.

Burning Rage

Transmutation
Level: Sorcerer/wizard 1
Components: V, S
Casting Time: 1 standard action
Range: Close (25 ft. + 5 ft./2 levels)
Target: One creature
Duration: 1 round/level (D)

Saving Throw: Will negates
Spell Resistance: Yes

As you imbue an ally with this spell, a nimbus of shimmering blue flame surrounds him. He winces in pain as the flames scorch his flesh, but when the eldritch power flows into him, his muscles surge with might.

This spell imbues a creature with burning magical energy that enhances the subject's strength and endurance. The searing energy also burns and injures the subject.

The subject of this spell gains a +1 bonus on attack rolls, a +2 bonus on damage rolls, and damage reduction 2/magic. This spell's burning energy deals 4 points of fire damage to the subject at the start of each of its turns until the spell's duration expires or you dismiss the effect.

Call of Stone

Transmutation
Level: Druid 4, sorcerer/wizard 4
Component: V, S
Casting Time: 1 standard action
Range: Medium (100 ft. + 10 ft./level)
Target: One creature
Duration: 1 round/2 levels
Saving Throw: Fortitude partial
Spell Resistance: Yes

A beam of sickly gray energy strikes the target of this spell. He acquires an ashen tone to his skin. With each passing moment, the grayish tone becomes deeper in color as the target transforms into a stone statue.

This spell slowly transforms a creature into an inanimate stone statue. The target must make a Fortitude save each round for the duration of spell at the start of its turn or take a cumulative 10-foot penalty to speed and a –2 penalty to Dexterity. If the target's speed drops to 0 feet, it cannot move. If the target fails four or more saves, it permanently transforms into a statue as if affected by *flesh to stone*. Any effect or spell that reverses *flesh to stone* also cures this condition.

Celerity

Transmutation
Level: Bard 4, sorcerer/wizard 4

This spell works like *lesser celerity*, except that you pull even more time into the present. When you cast this spell, you can immediately take a standard action, as if you had readied an action. You can even interrupt another creature's turn when you cast this spell. However, after you take the standard action granted by this spell, you are dazed until the end of your next turn.

Celerity, Greater

Transmutation
Level: Sorcerer/wizard 8

This spell works like *celerity*, except upon casting this spell you can immediately take a full-round action (or a standard action plus a move action, or two move actions). After performing this action, you are dazed until the end of your next turn.

Celerity, Lesser

Transmutation
Level: Bard 2, sorcerer/wizard 2
Components: V
Casting Time: 1 immediate action
Range: Personal
Target: You
Duration: Instantaneous

You borrow a slice of time from the future, pulling it into the present so that you can act.

Upon casting this spell, you can immediately take a move action. After performing this action, you are dazed until the end of your next turn.

Chain Dispel

Abjuration
Level: Cleric 8, sorcerer/wizard 8
Components: V, S, M/DF
Casting Time: 1 standard action
Range: Close (25 ft. + 5 ft./2 levels)
Targets: One or more creatures, no two of which are more than 30 ft. apart
Duration: Instantaneous
Saving Throw: None
Spell Resistance: No

A coruscating bolt rips through the air, humming with power as it strikes each targeted creature.

Each creature struck by this spell is affected as if by a targeted *dispel magic*, except that you can add your caster level to the dispel check, up to a maximum of 25.

Material Component: A pair of bronze nails, each no less than 6 inches in length.

Channeled Divine Health

Conjuration (Healing)
Level: Cleric 4
Components: V, S
Casting Time: See text
Range: See text
Target: One creature
Duration: Instantaneous
Saving Throw: Will negates (harmless)
Spell Resistance: Yes (harmless)

You bring forth a sphere of pure healing energy. You pour divine power into it, slowly building the energy it holds, until it is ready to mend an ally's wounds.

This spell allows you to heal an ally, or damage an undead creature, at a range greater than touch. When you cast this spell, you channel energy into it. You can choose how long to spend casting this spell.

If you cast this spell as a swift action, it has a range of touch, and you heal a single touched creature of 1d8 points of damage. An undead creature you touch takes this amount of damage instead of being healed.

If you cast this spell as a standard action, it has a range of close, and you heal a single creature within range of damage equal to 1d8 points + your caster level (maximum +10). An undead creature you designate within range takes this amount of damage instead of being healed.

If you cast this spell as a full-round casting this spell, it has a range of medium, and you heal a single creature within range of damage equal to 2d8 points + your caster level (maximum +15). An undead creature you designate within range takes this amount of damage instead of being healed.

If you spend 2 full rounds casting this spell, it has a range of long, and you heal a single creature within range of damage equal to 4d8 points + your caster level (maximum +20). An undead

creature you designate within range takes this amount of damage instead of being healed.

You do not need to declare ahead of time how long you want to spend casting the spell. When you begin casting this spell, you decide that you are finished casting after the appropriate time has passed.

Channeled Divine Shield

Abjuration
Level: Cleric 3
Components: V, S
Casting Time: See text
Range: Personal
Target: You
Duration: 1 round/level

As you complete this spell, a shield crafted from divine energy appears before you. As you channel energy into the shield, it grows stronger and stronger.

This spell improves your defenses. The magnitude of this improvement depends on the amount of time you spend casting the spell.

If you cast this spell as a swift action, you gain damage reduction 2/evil for the duration of this spell.

If you cast this spell as a standard action, you gain damage reduction 5/evil.

If you cast this spell as a full-round action, you gain damage reduction 8/evil.

If you spend 2 rounds casting this spell, you gain damage reduction 10/evil.

The spell's duration does not begin until you finish casting the spell. You do not need to declare ahead of time how long you want to spend casting the spell. When you begin casting this spell, you decide that you are finished casting after the appropriate time has passed.

Channeled Pyroburst

Evocation [Fire]
Level: Duskblade 4, sorcerer/wizard 4
Components: V, S
Casting Time: See text
Range: Medium (100 ft. + 10 ft./level)
Area: See text
Duration: Instantaneous
Saving Throw: Reflex half

Spell Resistance: Yes

A sphere of fiery energy comes into being before you. You channel energy into it, causing it to bubble and seethe with power. When you have poured enough energy into the sphere, you send it flying into your foes.

This spell creates a bolt of fiery energy that blasts your enemies. The spell's strength depends on the amount of time you spend channeling energy into it.

If you cast this spell as a swift action, it deals 1d4 points of fire damage per two caster levels (maximum 10d4) against a single target of your choice.

If you cast this spell as a standard action, it deals 1d6 points of fire damage per caster level (maximum 10d6) to all creatures in a 10-foot-radius spread.

If you cast this spell as a full-round action, it deals 1d8 points of fire damage per caster level (maximum 10d8) to all creatures in a 15-foot-radius spread.

If you spend 2 rounds casting this spell, it deals 1d10 points of fire damage per caster level (maximum 10d10) to all creatures in a 20-foot-radius spread.

You do not need to declare ahead of time how long you want to spend casting the spell. When you begin casting this spell, you decide that you are finished casting after the appropriate time has passed.

Chasing Perfection

Transmutation
Level: Cleric 6, druid 6, sorcerer/ wizard 6
Components: V, S, M
Casting Time: 1 standard action
Range: Touch
Target: Creature touched
Duration: 1 minute/level
Saving Throw: Will negates (harmless)
Spell Resistance: Yes (harmless)

Energy courses through the creature touched. Its muscles grow and become more defined, it starts to move with greater alacrity and grace, and its bearing increases.

The subject improves in all ways. It gains a +4 enhancement bonus to each of its ability scores.

Material Component: A statuette of a celestial or fiend worth 50 gp.

Cloud of Knives

Conjuration
Level: Cleric 2, sorcerer/wizard 2
Components: V, S, M
Casting Time: 1 standard action
Range: Personal
Target: You
Duration: 1 round/level

You conjure a cloud of sharp knives around you. The knives float in the air around your upper body, pointing in the direction you look.

Each round as a free action at the beginning of your turn, you can release one of these knives at any target within 30 feet that you can see. This is a ranged attack that uses an attack bonus equal to your caster level + your key ability modifier. Each successful hit deals 1d6 points of damage +1 per three caster levels (maximum +5) and threatens a critical hit on a roll of 19–20.

Damage reduction applies to knife attacks from this spell. The knives are treated as magic for the purpose of overcoming damage reduction.

Material Component: A knife.

Optional Material Component: Using a silvered dagger (22 gp) in the casting of this spell allows the knives to overcome damage reduction as if they were both magic and silver, but the knives deal 1 less point of damage.

Condemnation

Abjuration
Level: Cleric 5, sorcerer/wizard 4
Components: V
Casting Time: 1 standard action
Range: Close (25 ft. + 5 ft./2 levels)
Target: One outsider
Duration: 1 round
Saving Throw: Will negates
Spell Resistance: Yes

Cloud of knives makes a caster into a ranged weapon threat

You speak words of power, forcing the entity to shrink with horror.

The outsider targeted by this spell must succeed on a Will save or be stunned for 1 round and have its spell resistance reduced by 10.

Crown of Clarity

Divination
Level: Druid 3, ranger 2, sorcerer/wizard 3
Components: V, S, F
Casting Time: 1 standard action
Range: Touch
Target: Creature touched
Duration: 1 hour/level (D) or until discharged
Saving Throw: Will negates (harmless)
Spell Resistance: Yes (harmless)

A crown of magical energy appears upon your head. For a moment, your vision blurs and a slight buzz fills your ears. These distractions pass, leaving you with sharpened senses.

You create an arcane crown that grants the wearer a +2 competence bonus on Listen and Spot checks.

As an immediate action, the creature wearing a *crown of clarity* can discharge its magic to gain a +8 bonus on a single Spot or Listen check. The spell ends after the wearer uses the crown in this manner.

The crown occupies space on the body as a headband, hat, or helm. If the crown is removed, the spell immediately ends.

Focus: A pewter hoop 6 inches in diameter.

Crown of the Grave

Necromancy
Level: Cleric 3, sorcerer/wizard 3
Components: V, S, M, F
Casting Time: 1 standard action
Range: Touch
Target: Creature touched
Duration: 1 hour/level (D) or until discharged
Saving Throw: Will negates (harmless)
Spell Resistance: Yes (harmless)

A ring of ghostly fog surrounds the target's head. With a swirl, the fog dissipates, leaving behind a crown made of human bones.

This spell creates a magic crown that grants its wearer the power to command undead. Once per minute, the crown's wearer can issue a one-word order to an undead creature, as per the *command* spell. The undead creature must make a Will save to resist this effect. Even though *command* is normally a mind-affecting spell, the crown channels holy or unholy energy (depending on your alignment; neutral casters choose one or the other) to compel obedience. In addition, a cleric who wears the crown can expend a use of his turn or rebuke undead ability to increase this ability's save DC by 4.

As an immediate action, the creature wearing a *crown of the grave* can discharge its magic to gain a +4 bonus on a single turn or rebuke undead attempt. The spell ends after the wearer uses the crown in this manner.

The crown occupies space on the body as a headband, hat, or helm. If the crown is removed, the spell immediately ends.

Material Component: A pinch of grave dirt.

Focus: A wooden hoop 6 inches in diameter.

Crown of Might
Transmutation
Level: Cleric 3, duskblade 3, sorcerer/wizard 3
Components: V, S, F
Casting Time: 1 standard action
Range: Touch
Target: Creature touched
Duration: 1 hour/level (D) or until discharged
Saving Throw: Will negates (harmless)
Spell Resistance: Yes (harmless)

A crown of plain copper appears upon the recipient's head. The crown has a front piece fashioned to resemble a bull's head.

This spell creates a crown of magical energy that grants the spell's recipient a +2 enhancement bonus to Strength.

As an immediate action, the creature wearing a *crown of might* can discharge its magic to gain a +8 enhancement bonus to Strength for 1 round. The spell ends after the wearer uses the *crown* in this manner.

The crown occupies space on the body as a headband, hat, or helm. If the crown is removed, the spell immediately ends.

Focus: A copper hoop 6 inches in diameter.

Crown of Protection
Transmutation
Level: Cleric 3, duskblade 3, sorcerer/wizard 3
Components: V, S, F
Casting Time: 1 standard action
Range: Touch
Target: Creature touched
Duration: 1 hour/level (D) or until discharged
Saving Throw: Will negates (harmless)
Spell Resistance: Yes (harmless)

A shimmering crown of force appears upon the recipient's head. A barely visible shield of force projects forward from it, warding off attacks aimed at its wearer.

This spell creates a crown of magical energy that grants the spell's recipient a +1 deflection bonus to AC and a +1 resistance bonus on all saves.

As an immediate action, the creature wearing a *crown of protection* can discharge its magic to gain a +4 deflection bonus to AC or a +4 resistance bonus on saves for 1 round. The spell ends after the wearer uses the crown in this manner.

The crown occupies space on the body as a headband, hat, or helm. If the crown is removed, the spell immediately ends.

Focus: An iron hoop 6 inches in diameter.

Crown of Smiting
Evocation
Level: Cleric 3, paladin 2
Components: V, S, F
Casting Time: 1 standard action
Range: Touch
Target: Creature touched
Duration: 1 hour/level (D) or until discharged
Saving Throw: Will negates (harmless)
Spell Resistance: Yes (harmless)

A crown of divine energy appears upon the target's brow. The holy symbol of the caster's faith is set at the front of the crown.

You create a magic crown infused with divine energy harmful to enemies of your faith. Choose a single alignment (chaotic, evil, good, or lawful) when you cast this spell. Once per minute, the crown's wearer gains a +2 divine bonus on damage rolls on his next melee or ranged attack if his target has the designated alignment. The crown's wearer must decide to use this extra damage before making his attack. If he misses, the extra damage is lost.

As an immediate action, the creature wearing a *crown of smiting* can discharge its magic to gain a +8 divine bonus on damage on a single attack. The spell ends after the wearer uses the crown in this manner.

The crown occupies space on the body as a headband, hat, or helm. If the crown is removed, the spell immediately ends.

Focus: A silver hoop 6 inches in diameter costing 25 gp.

Crown of Veils
Illusion (Figment)
Level: Bard 2, beguiler 3, sorcerer/wizard 3
Components: V, S, F
Casting Time: 1 standard action
Range: Touch
Target: Creature touched
Duration: 1 hour/level (D) or until discharged
Saving Throw: Will negates (harmless)
Spell Resistance: Yes (harmless)

A shimmering halo of energy surrounds the target's head like a crown. It flashes a spectrum of colors before fading away.

This spell creates a magic crown infused with illusion magic. The spell's recipient gains a +2 competence bonus on Disguise and Hide checks.

As an immediate action, the creature wearing the crown of veils can discharge its magic to gain a +8 competence bonus on a single Disguise or Hide check. The spell ends after the wearer uses the crown in this manner.

The crown occupies space on the body as a headband, hat, or helm. If the crown is removed, the spell immediately ends.

Focus: A brass hoop 6 inches in diameter.

Crushing Grip
Evocation
Level: Sorcerer/wizard 4
Components: V, S
Casting Time: 1 round
Range: Close (25 ft. + 5 ft./2 levels)
Target: One creature
Duration: 3 rounds
Saving Throw: Fortitude negates; see text
Spell Resistance: Yes

You conjure a band of energy that slowly squeezes your opponent. As the band tightens, it restricts his movement and eventually holds him in place, rigid with paralysis.

This spell has one effect on an opponent when you begin casting it. At the beginning of your next turn, when you finish casting the spell, it has a second effect. When you start casting this spell, your target takes a –2 penalty on attacks, checks, saves, and AC. He also takes a 20-foot penalty to speed. This effect does not allow a saving throw, but spell resistance applies. If you fail to overcome the target's spell resistance, you immediately stop casting the spell, and the secondary effect does not take place.

When you complete the casting of this spell, your target must make a Fortitude saving throw or be paralyzed. Even if the target makes this saving throw, this spell's initial effect continues to affect him for the spell's duration.

This spell's duration begins after you have completed casting it.

Curse of Arrow Attraction
Transmutation
Level: Cleric 3, ranger 2, sorcerer/wizard 3
Components: V, S, M
Casting Time: 1 standard action
Range: Medium (100 ft. + 10 ft./level)
Target: One creature
Duration: 1 round/level
Saving Throw: Will negates
Spell Resistance: Yes

You surround a creature in a nimbus of emerald light that seems to draw missiles toward it.

The subject is cursed so that missile weapons veer toward him and strike with extreme force. The subject takes a –5 penalty to Armor Class against any ranged attack, including projectile weapons, thrown weapons, and ranged touch attacks. In addition, any critical threats on such attacks are automatically confirmed.

Dancing Blade
Transmutation
Level: Bard 5, sorcerer/wizard 5
Components: V, S, F
Casting Time: 1 standard action
Range: Touch
Target: Weapon touched
Duration: 1 round/level
Saving Throw: None
Spell Resistance: No

With a word and a gesture, the sword in your hand leaps to life with a swooping salute.

This spell animates a melee weapon currently in your possession, causing it to fight your foes as you direct it. Once each round as a free action, you can direct the blade to attack an adjacent foe (a weapon with reach can attack a foe 10 feet away). The weapon's bonus on attack rolls is equal to your caster level + your key ability modifier, plus any enhancement bonus the weapon might have. It deals damage equal to the normal damage of the weapon, plus your key ability modifier and any enhancement bonus or other bonus on damage inherent in the weapon. The weapon attacks once per round. Despite the spell's name, it works on any melee weapon (not just blades).

While your weapon is dancing, it cannot make attacks of opportunity, and you are not considered armed with the weapon. It remains in your space and accompanies you everywhere, whether you move by physical or magical means. The weapon cannot be disarmed.

Focus: The melee weapon that serves as the target of the spell.

Deflect
Abjuration [Force]
Level: Duskblade 2, sorcerer/wizard 2

This spell functions like *lesser deflect,* except that you gain a shield bonus to AC equal to 1/2 your caster level (round down) against the next attack made against you before the end of your next turn.

Deflect, Lesser
Abjuration [Force]
Level: Duskblade 1, sorcerer/wizard 1
Components: V
Casting Time: 1 immediate action
Range: Personal
Target: You
Duration: 1 round or until discharged

With a word, you evoke a barrier of invisible force.

You project a field of invisible force, creating a short-lived protective barrier. You gain a deflection bonus to your AC against a single attack; this bonus is equal to +1 per three caster levels (maximum +5).

You can cast this spell even when it's not your turn; however, you must cast it before your opponent makes his attack roll to gain the benefit.

Detonate
Evocation [Death, Fire]
Level: Sorcerer/wizard 9
Components: V, S, M
Casting Time: 1 standard action
Range: Medium (100 ft. + 10 ft./level)
Target: One creature
Duration: Instantaneous
Saving Throw: Fortitude partial; see text
Spell Resistance: Yes

The creature you point at explodes in a massive spray of fire.

If the target fails its saving throw, this spell slays the creature, and the explosion extends out to a 20-foot-radius burst around it. Creatures in this area take 1d6 points of fire damage per caster level (maximum 20d6), though they can attempt Reflex saves for half damage. The exploded creature's remains are scattered and vaporized, leaving nothing but dry ash.

If the target succeeds on its saving throw, it is wracked by a series of small explosions and takes 7d6 points of fire damage. If this damage kills the creature, it explodes as described above.

Detonate has no effect on creatures that have immunity to fire.

Material Component: A tindertwig and a piece of string.

Dimension Hop

Conjuration (Teleportation)
Level: Duskblade 2, sorcerer/wizard 2
Components: V
Casting Time: 1 standard action
Range: Touch
Target: Creature touched
Duration: Instantaneous
Saving Throw: Will negates
Spell Resistance: Yes

Pale motes of light dance and swirl about your fingertips. When you touch the creature, it disappears, leaves a cloud of motes in its wake, and reappears somewhere nearby.

You instantly teleport the subject creature a distance of 5 feet per two caster levels. The destination must be an unoccupied space within line of sight.

Dimension Shuffle

Conjuration (Teleportation)
Level: Sorcerer/wizard 5
Components: V
Casting Time: 1 standard action
Range: Close (25 ft. + 5 ft./2 levels)
Targets: One creature/level, no two of which are more than 30 ft. apart
Duration: Instantaneous
Saving Throw: Will negates; see text
Spell Resistance: Yes

With a slight blue shimmer of energy and an audible pop, a number of creatures around you disappear and reappear in new positions.

You instantly transfer any subject creature from its current location to any other spot within 30 feet. You must have line of sight to its new location. An unwilling creature can make a Will saving throw to negate this effect. The creature must be placed on solid ground capable of supporting its weight. If you attempt to place a creature within a solid object or into a space where it cannot fit, the spell fails.

Dimension Step

Conjuration (Teleportation)
Level: Sorcerer/wizard 3
Component: V, S
Casting Time: 1 standard action
Range: Close (25 ft. + 5 ft./2 levels)
Targets: One willing creature/3 levels, no two of which are more than 30 ft. apart
Duration: Instantaneous
Saving Throw: Fortitude negates (harmless)
Spell Resistance: Yes (harmless)

All the creatures you target with this spell gain a dark, shimmering pattern of runes on their shoes and feet. The runes blaze with arcane light for a moment. Less than a second later, the targets have shifted position on the battlefield.

This spell allows your allies to make a short teleport. All creatures targeted by this spell can teleport a distance equal to their base land speed. A target can teleport to any square within its line of sight. This movement does not provoke attacks of opportunity. A creature can teleport up to a ledge, down to the base of a flight of stairs, and so forth as long as it observes the restrictions and limits given above.

Dispelling Touch

Abjuration
Level: Duskblade 3, sorcerer/wizard 2
Components: V, S
Casting Time: 1 standard action
Range: Touch
Target: One touched creature, object, or spell effect
Duration: Instantaneous
Saving Throw: None
Spell Resistance: No

Your touch causes one spell to rip free of its source and dissipate into nothingness.

You can use *dispelling touch* to end an ongoing spell that has been cast on a creature or object, or a spell that has a noticeable ongoing effect. You make a dispel check (1d20 + your caster level, maximum +10) against the spell effect with the highest caster level. If that check fails, you make dispel checks against progressively weaker spells until you dispel one spell or until you fail all your checks. Magic items carried by a creature are not affected.

Divine Retaliation

Evocation [Force]
Level: Cleric 3, paladin 4
Component: V, S, DF
Casting Time: 1 swift action
Range: 0 ft.
Effect: Magic weapon of force
Duration: 1 round
Saving Throw: None
Spell Resistance: No

A spectral weapon composed of pure force energy springs into existence next to you. Each time a foe strikes you, the weapon springs into action, chopping into your foe and dealing a grievous wound.

This spell creates a divine weapon that mimics your deity's favored weapon. Any time you are struck for damage by a melee attack, this weapon strikes at your foe. It has a base attack bonus equal to your caster level + your Str modifier or Wis modifier (your choice). It deals damage as per your deity's favored weapon, and is of a size equal to your current size. The weapon gains a bonus on damage rolls equal to 1-1/2 times your Str modifier or Wis modifier (your choice).

There is no limit to the number of attacks that this weapon can make. If a hydra bites at and hits you six times, this weapon in turn strikes at the hydra six times. The weapon has reach or range appropriate to its type. It shares a space with you. If you are Large or larger, it counts as occupying each square of the space you fill.

Doom Scarabs

Conjuration/Necromancy
Level: Duskblade 3, sorcerer/wizard 4
Components: V, S
Casting Time: 1 standard action
Range: 60 ft.
Area: Cone-shaped burst
Duration: Instantaneous
Saving Throw: Will half
Spell Resistance: See text

A swarm of scarabs surges from your outstretched hand. These insects rip and bite at all living creatures in the area, then return to you with life essence stolen from their victims.

This spell has two effects. It deals 1d6 points of damage per two caster levels (maximum 10d6) to all creatures in the area. Spell resistance does not apply to this damage. However, spell resistance does apply to the spell's secondary effect. If you overcome a creature's spell resistance, you gain 1d4 temporary hit points as the scarabs feast on the creature's arcane energy and bleed it back into you. You gain these temporary hit points for each creature whose spell resistance you overcome. You never gain temporary hit points from creatures that do not have spell resistance.

The temporary hit points gained from this spell last for up to 1 hour.

Dragonshape

Transmutation (Polymorph)
Level: Sorcerer/wizard 9
Components: V, S
Casting Time: 1 swift action
Range: Personal
Target: You
Duration: 1 round/level (D)

You feel a fire burning deep within you. Crimson scales quickly grow over your body, a pair of great wings sprouts from your shoulders, and your body expands in size until you stand as tall as a house!

You take on the form and abilities of a mature adult red dragon (see below for your new statistics). You gain 150 temporary hit points, which disappear at the end of the spell's duration. You do not gain the normal spellcasting ability of your new form. See the description of the new polymorph subschool on page 95 for more details.

MATURE ADULT RED DRAGON
Init +0; **Senses** blindsense 60 ft., darkvision 120 ft., quadruple-strength low-light vision; Listen +32, Spot +32
Languages as normal form

AC 32, touch 8, flat-footed 32
hp as normal form (+150 temporary hp); **DR** 10/magic
Resist SR 23
Immune fire

Fort +20, **Ref** +14, **Will** +18
Weakness vulnerability to cold

Speed 40 ft., fly 150 ft. (poor); Flyby Attack
Melee bite +34 (2d8+11/19–20) and 2 claws +32 (2d6+5/19–20) and 2 wings +32 (1d8+5/19–20) and tail slap +32 (2d6+16/19–20)
Space 15 ft.
Reach 10 ft. (15 ft. with bite)
Base Atk +25; **Grp** +44
Atk Options Cleave, Power Attack
Special Actions breath weapon, crush
Spell-Like Abilities (CL 9th): 7/day— *locate object*

Abilities Str 33, Dex 10, Con 23, Int 18, Wis 19, Cha 18
Feats Cleave, Combat Reflexes, Flyby Attack, Improved Critical (bite, claw, tail slap, wing), Multiattack, Power Attack
Skills Appraise +32, Bluff +32, Concentration +34, Diplomacy +34, Intimidate +34, Jump +39, Knowledge (arcana) +32, Listen +32, Search +32, Spot +32

Breath Weapon (Su) 50-ft. cone, 14d10 fire, Reflex DC 30 half.
Crush (Ex) Area 15 ft. by 15 ft.; Small or smaller opponents take 2d8+16 points of bludgeoning damage, and must succeed on a DC 28 Reflex save or be pinned.

Drifts of the Shalm

Evocation
Level: Druid 2
Components: V, S
Casting Time: 1 standard action
Range: Medium (100 ft. + 10 ft./level)
Area: One 5-ft. square/level (S)
Duration: 1 round/level
Saving Throw: None
Spell Resistance: No

You call upon the power of Obad-Hai and conjure forth a great drift of snow, leaves, or smoldering ash.

Druids of Obad-Hai routinely evoke the drifts of their lord to delay their enemies, to buy themselves time in the face of a sudden threat, and simply to decorate their groves.

You create drifts of snow, leaves, or ash 3 feet thick. It costs 2 squares of movement to enter a drift-covered square. Additional effects apply based on the type of drift.

A snow drift ripples with freezing energy. Anyone moving through or located in a snow drift takes 3 points of cold damage each round.

If any part of a leaf drift comes in contact with fire (anything from a torch to a *fireball* will do), the whole drift instantly ignites. The heat from the burning leaves deals 2d6 points of fire damage to anyone in the inferno.

An ash drift smolders with dying embers. Anyone moving through or located in an ash drift takes 3 points of fire damage each round.

Electric Vengeance

Evocation [Electricity]
Level: Sorcerer/wizard 2
Components: V, S
Casting Time: 1 immediate action
Range: 5 ft.
Target: One creature
Duration: Instantaneous
Saving Throw: None
Spell Resistance: Yes

As the creature strikes you, an arc of lightning springs from your body and blasts the creature in return.

You can cast this spell only when another creature has just dealt hit point damage to you with a melee attack. When you cast *electric vengeance*, a blast of lightning arcs from your body into the subject's; the arc deals 2d8 points of electricity damage +1 point per caster level (maximum +10).

Electric Vengeance, Greater

Evocation [Electricity]
Level: Sorcerer/wizard 5
Saving Throw: Fortitude partial

This spell functions like *electric vengeance*, except as noted here.

This spell deals 5d8 points of damage +1 per caster level (maximum +15), and the target of the spell must succeed on a Fortitude save or be dazed until the end of your next turn.

Energy Aegis

Abjuration
Level: Cleric 3, duskblade 3, sorcerer/wizard 3
Components: V, DF
Casting Time: 1 immediate action
Range: Close (25 ft. + 5 ft./2 levels)
Target: One creature

Duration: 1 round
Saving Throw: Will negates (harmless)
Spell Resistance: Yes (harmless)

A nigh-invisible ripple of magical energy courses through the creature touched, granting it resistance against one type of energy specified by you during the casting the spell.

When you cast *energy aegis*, specify an energy type (acid, cold, electricity, fire, or sonic). Against the next attack using this energy type that targets the subject, it gains resistance 20.

Energy Surge

Transmutation [see text for *lesser energy surge*]
Level: Duskblade 3, sorcerer/wizard 3

This spell functions like *lesser energy surge*, except that the attack deals an extra 2d6 points of energy damage.

Energy Surge, Greater

Transmutation [see text for *lesser energy surge*]

Level: Sorcerer/wizard 6

This spell functions like *lesser energy surge*, except that the attack deals an extra 3d6 points of energy damage.

Energy Surge, Lesser

Transmutation [see text]
Level: Sorcerer/wizard 2
Components: V
Casting Time: 1 swift action
Range: Close (25 ft. + 5 ft./2 levels)
Target: One weapon
Duration: 1 round
Saving Throw: Will negates (harmless)
Spell Resistance: Yes (harmless)

With a single utterance, you sheath the weapon in elemental energy—dripping acid, vaporous ice, crackling electricity, smoking flame, or thunderous air.

You temporarily imbue a weapon with elemental energy. When you cast this spell, specify an energy type (acid, cold, electricity, fire, or sonic). This spell is a spell of that type, and the target weapon is sheathed in that energy. If

the attack is successful, it deals an extra 1d6 points of damage of the specified energy type.

Energy Vulnerability

Abjuration
Level: Cleric 3, sorcerer/wizard 3
Components: V, S, M/DF
Casting Time: 1 standard action
Range: Medium (100 ft. + 10 ft./level)
Targets: One or more creatures within a 10-ft.-radius burst
Duration: 1 round/level
Saving Throw: Will negates
Spell Resistance: Yes

Silvery tendrils erupt from your outstretched arms and strike the creatures you choose. A lingering silvery aura engulfs them thereafter.

Energy vulnerability can affect a number of creatures with total Hit Dice equal to twice your caster level or lower. You select which creatures are affected.

When you cast this spell, specify an energy type (acid, cold, electricity, fire,

Hennet strikes down a gnoll with the electric vengeance spell

or sonic). The affected creatures gain vulnerability to that energy type (they take +50% damage from that energy, even on a successful save).

Arcane Material Component: A tiny wooden shield, which the caster snaps in half.

Etherealness, Swift
Transmutation
Level: Beguiler 5, cleric 5, sorcerer/wizard 5
Components: V, S
Casting Time: 1 swift action
Range: Close (25 ft. + 5 ft./2 levels)
Target: One willing creature
Duration: 1 round
Saving Throw: Will negates
Spell Resistance: Yes

With a single word and a quick wave of your hand, the creature disappears.

The subject becomes ethereal until the end of its next turn. If, at the end of the spell's duration, the subject creature rematerializes within a solid object or in an occupied space, it is shunted off to the nearest open space and takes 1d6 points of damage per 5 feet so traveled.

Evard's Menacing Tentacles
Transmutation
Level: Druid 3, sorcerer/wizard 3
Components: V, S, M
Casting Time: 1 standard action
Range: Personal
Target: You
Duration: 1 round/level

Two black tentacles sprout from your shoulder blades and arch over your shoulders.

The tentacles have 10-foot reach and are animate. Each round as a free action, starting on the turn when you cast the spell, you can direct each tentacle to attack one opponent within reach. The tentacles use your base attack bonus and Strength score, and each deals bludgeoning damage equal to 1d8 points + your Str modifier. The tentacles threaten the area within their reach, and each can make one attack of opportunity per round.

The tentacles also grant you a +4 bonus on Climb checks.

A dwarf wizard uses explosive rune field to ward an area against intrusion

Illus. by M. Sehley

Material Component: A piece of octopus, squid, or carrion crawler tentacle.

Explosive Rune Field
Conjuration (Fire)
Level: Sorcerer/wizard 4
Components: V, S, M
Casting Time: 1 standard action
Range: Medium (100 ft. + 10 ft./level)
Area: 20-ft.-radius burst
Duration: 1 round/level
Saving Throw: Reflex negates
Spell Resistance: No

You infuse an area with arcane patterns that shift and slide along the ground. They seethe with arcane energy, and an occasional bolt of energy surges from them with a bright flash.

This spell creates a hazardous field of energy similar to that created by an *explosive runes* spell. Unlike that spell, the runes created by this spell detonate when they come into contact with a living creature other than the caster. Any creature that begins its turn in the spell's area must attempt a Reflex save. On a failed save, the creature takes 4d6 points of fire damage.

Moving through the spell's area is hazardous at best. Creatures that move at their normal speed must succeed on Reflex saves to avoid the spell's explosive effects. Creatures that move at half speed through the spell's area can avoid the damage just as if they had succeeded on their saves.

Material Component: A piece of parchment scribed with runes. The runes must be drawn with silver-flecked ink (25 gp).

Field of Resistance
Abjuration
Level: Sorcerer/wizard 5
Component: V, S
Casting Time: 1 standard action
Range: Medium (100 ft. + 10 ft./level)
Area: 20-ft.-radius emanation centered on a point in space
Duration: 1 round/level (D)
Saving Throw: None
Spell Resistance: No

The air in this spell's effect shimmers with arcane energy. A buzzing sound echoes in your mind as the flow of magic into the affected area chokes off and ends.

This spell creates a zone that impedes the flow of magic. The energy of this zone clings to creatures and objects, granting them a shield against spells. All creatures in the spell's area gain spell resistance of 11 + caster level for as long as they remain in the area. If a creature already has spell resistance higher than this amount, this spell does not affect it. Unlike personal spell resistance, this spell resistance cannot be voluntarily lowered. A creature loses this spell resistance when it leaves the spell's area, and gains it again if it returns.

Friend to Foe

Illusion (Phantasm) [Mind-Affecting]
Level: Bard 5, beguiler 5, sorcerer/wizard 5
Components: V, S, M
Casting Time: 1 standard action
Range: Medium (100 ft. + 10 ft./level)
Targets: One living creature/level, none of which are more than 30 ft. apart
Duration: 1 round/level (D); see text
Saving Throw: Will negates
Spell Resistance: Yes

Your enemies transform into what they each hate the most, suddenly turning against each other.

You overlay phantasmal images over your enemies, making them appear to each other as loathsome and despicable, implanting an urge to kill and destroy the object of their ire. Orcs might see each other as elves or dwarves, demons might see angels, and so on. All subjects receive a Will save to see through the phantasm. Each individual failing its save turns on the closest ally and attacks until the first time it deals damage, which causes the spell to end for that attacker.

Material Component: A swatch of white silk.

Halt

Transmutation
Level: Bard 3, beguiler 3, duskblade 3, sorcerer/wizard 3
Components: V
Casting Time: 1 immediate action
Range: Close (25 ft. + 5 ft./2 levels)
Target: One creature
Duration: 1 round

Saving Throw: Will negates
Spell Resistance: Yes

You utter the word "Halt!" and, in that instant, the creature's feet stick to the floor.

The subject creature's feet (or whatever pass for its feet) become momentarily stuck to the floor. The creature must stop moving, and cannot move farther in its current turn. This spell has no effect on creatures that are not touching the ground (such as flying creatures), and the subject can still use a standard action (if it has one available in this round) to move by means of teleportation magic.

You can cast this spell even when it's not your turn; however, you must cast it before your opponent finishes its movement on its current turn to gain the benefit.

Healing Spirit

Conjuration (Healing)
Level: Bard 4, cleric 4, druid 4, paladin 3
Components: V, S
Casting Time: 1 standard action
Range: Close (25 ft. + 5 ft./2 levels)
Effect: One conjured healing spirit
Duration: 1 round/2 levels
Saving Throw: Will half (harmless); see text
Spell Resistance: Yes (harmless); see text

A 1-foot-diamater ball of light appears and moves by your command, healing those it touches.

You conjure an incorporeal object of magical energy that appears in any square within range. This *healing spirit* resembles a 1-foot-diameter ball of light. It sheds bright illumination in a 10-foot radius and shadowy illumination for another 20 feet. A *healing spirit* cannot be affected by attacks or spells.

A *healing spirit* flies at a speed of 30 feet with perfect maneuverability. In the round you cast the spell and at the start of your turn once per round thereafter, you can direct the *healing spirit* to move and touch a creature by entering its space. The spirit's touch carries positive energy, healing a living creature of 1d8 points of damage.

Since undead are powered by negative energy, a *healing spirit* damages them instead of healing them. The spirit can affect an unwilling target (such as an undead) by succeeding on an incorporeal touch attack, using your base attack bonus and a Strength bonus of +0. An undead creature hit by such an attack can use spell resistance against the effect and is allowed a Will save for half damage.

If a *healing spirit* travels farther from you than the spell's range, it winks out of existence and the spell ends.

Hesitate

Enchantment (Compulsion) [Mind-Affecting]
Level: Bard 3, beguiler 3, cleric 3, sorcerer/wizard 3
Components: V, S
Casting Time: 1 immediate action
Range: Close (25 ft. + 5 ft./2 levels)
Target: One living creature
Duration: 1 round/level (D); see text
Saving Throw: Will negates; see text
Spell Resistance: Yes

In the eyes of your enemy, you seem large, powerful, and indomitable.

You fill a subject with doubts and misgivings, making it believe it is inferior to you. On a failed save, the subject can take no action other than a move action on its current turn. *Hesitate* confers no special bonuses for attackers attempting to hit the subject; the subject still defends itself. If you attack the affected creature, the spell ends immediately.

Each round, as a swift action at the start of its turn, the subject can attempt a new saving throw to end the effect. If the save succeeds, the subject can then act normally.

You can cast this spell even when it's not your turn; however, you must cast it at the start of your opponent's turn to gain the benefit.

Hunter's Eye

Divination
Level: Ranger 2
Components: V, S
Casting Time: 1 swift action
Range: Personal
Target: You
Duration: 1 round

Your vision blurs for a moment. When it clears, you can see through your enemies' skin to spot their arteries, organs, and other vulnerable points.

Your slice into a foe with uncanny precision, allowing you to strike a foe's vulnerable points and deal extra damage. This spell grants you the sneak attack ability. You deal an extra 1d6 points of damage per three caster levels. If you already have the sneak attack ability, this damage stacks with it.

Incite Riot
Enchantment [Mind-Affecting]
Level: Bard 5, beguiler 5, sorcerer/ wizard 5
Components: V
Casting Time: 1 standard action
Range: Close (25 ft. + 5 ft./2 levels)
Targets: One creature/level, no two of which are more than 30 ft. apart
Duration: 1 round
Saving Throw: Will negates
Spell Resistance: Yes

You sow discord among your enemies, spurring them to physical violence.

Each creature that fails its saving throw attacks the nearest creature on its next turn, whether friend or foe. An affected creature attacks with whatever weapon is in hand, or with natural weapons. An unarmed creature attacks with an unarmed strike. An affected creature not already adjacent to another creature will move or (if possible) charge the nearest creature; if the nearest creature is not within range of a charge, the subject moves toward the nearest creature along the most efficient route.

Increase Virulence
Transmutation
Level: Assassin 2, bard 2, blackguard 2, sorcerer/wizard 2
Components: V, S, M
Casting Time: 1 minute
Range: Touch
Target: Vial of poison or creature touched
Duration: 1 minute/level
Saving Throw: None
Spell Resistance: No

Ribbons of green and black energy engulf your hand and pass into the vial or creature you touch.

You make the poison in a vial or a creature more lethal. The DCs for all saving throws against the poison increase by 2.
Material Component: Licorice root.

Inevitable Defeat
Enchantment (Compulsion) [Mind-Affecting]
Level: Beguiler 3, sorcerer/wizard 3
Components: V, S
Casting Time: 1 standard action
Range: Touch
Target: One creature
Duration: 1 round/level
Saving Throw: None and Will negates; see text
Spell Resistance: Yes

You touch the creature with your hand, and it teeters on the edge of unconsciousness.

You draw a cloud over the subject's mind, dealing 3d6 points of nonlethal damage. No saving throw is allowed against this effect. Each round on its turn, the subject must succeed on a Will save or take another 3d6 points of nonlethal damage. If the saving throw is successful, the damage for that round is negated and the spell ends.

Insight of Good Fortune
Divination
Level: Bard 2, cleric 2, sorcerer/ wizard 2
Components: V, S, M
Casting Time: 1 standard action
Range: Close (25 ft. + 5 ft./2 levels)
Target: One creature
Duration: 1 minute/level or until discharged
Saving Throw: Will negates (harmless)
Spell Resistance: Yes (harmless)

You toss a small golden die. It rolls toward the creature you choose, then disappears in a tiny golden flash of light.

The subject of the spell becomes unusually lucky. Once during the spell's duration, when he makes an attack roll, skill check, saving throw, or ability check, he rolls twice and takes the better result. He must choose to use this ability before the check is attempted, and the spell expires once the second die is rolled.
Material Component: A gold die (worth 20 gp).

Invest Heavy Protection
Conjuration (Healing)
Level: Cleric 5

This spell functions like *invest light protection*, except that it cures 5d4 points of damage +1 per two caster levels (maximum +12) and grants damage reduction 5/evil. Undead creatures take an extra 5 points of damage from any weapon or physical attack capable of overcoming good damage reduction.

Invest Light Protection
Conjuration (Healing)
Level: Cleric 1
Components: V, S
Casting Time: 1 standard action
Range: Touch
Target: Creature touched
Duration: Instantaneous; see text
Saving Throw: Will half (harmless); see text
Spell Resistance: Yes (harmless); see text

You invest the target with an infusion of divine energy. His wounds knit shut, while the power you grant to him helps ward off future injuries.

You heal a living creature you touch of 1d4 points of damage +1 per two caster levels (maximum +3). In addition, the creature touched gains damage reduction 1/evil for 1 minute.
    Like *cure light wounds*, this spell deals damage to undead creatures instead of curing them. In addition, on a failed save undead creatures take an extra 1 point of damage from any weapon or physical attack capable of overcoming good damage reduction for 1 minute.

Invest Moderate Protection
Conjuration (Healing)
Level: Cleric 3

This spell functions like *invest light protection*, except that it cures 3d4 points of damage +1 per two caster levels (maximum +6) and grants damage reduction 3/evil. Undead creatures take an extra 3 points of damage from any weapon or physical attack capable of overcoming good damage reduction.

Kelgore's Fire Bolt

Conjuration/Evocation [Fire]
Level: Duskblade 1, sorcerer/wizard 1
Components: V, S, M
Casting Time: 1 standard action
Range: Medium (100 ft. + 10 ft./level)
Target: One creature
Duration: Instantaneous
Saving Throw: Reflex half
Spell Resistance: See text

You conjure a shard of red-hot rock and hurl it toward an opponent. As it streaks through the air, a nimbus of arcane energy crackles around it.

This spell conjures a small orb of rock and sheathes it in arcane energy. This spell deals 1d6 points of fire damage per caster level (maximum 5d6). If you fail to overcome the target's spell resistance, the spell still deals 1d6 points of fire damage from the heat and force of the conjured orb's impact.

Material Component: A handful of ashes.

Kelgore's Grave Mist

Conjuration/Necromancy [Cold]
Level: Sorcerer/wizard 2
Components: V, S, M
Casting Time: 1 standard action
Range: Medium (100 ft. + 10 ft./level)
Area: 20-ft. radius spread, 20 ft. high
Duration: 1 round/level
Saving Throw: None
Spell Resistance: See text

With a gesture, you create a cloud of clammy, thin mist. The light in the area seems to dim as the mist appears, and a slight wind washes over the area, sending a chill down your spine.

This spell creates a thin mist within the spell's area. The mist is too thin to have any effect on vision, but the necromantic energy infused within it hampers the living. All living creatures within the mist become fatigued and take 1d6

points of cold damage per round. If the spell fails to overcome a creature's spell resistance, the subject takes the cold damage but ignores the fatigue.

Material Component: A handful of dirt taken from a graveyard or tomb.

Legion of Sentinels

Illusion (Shadow)
Level: Beguiler 3, sorcerer/wizard 3
Components: V, S, M
Casting Time: 1 standard action
Range: Close (25 ft. + 5 ft./2 levels)
Area: 10-ft.-radius emanation centered on a point in space
Duration: 1 round/level
Saving Throw: None
Spell Resistance: No

A phalanx of spectral swordfighters appears. Their blades are drawn, and they stand ready to strike.

A ghostly, incorporeal swordfighter appears in each square covered by this spell's area. A swordfighter can share a space with another creature or object. Each swordfighter

A group of hobgoblins succumbs to Kelgore's grave mist

threatens the squares adjacent to it and can make one attack of opportunity per round. The swordfighters do not hinder movement, block terrain, or block line of effect. They can flank an opponent with each other and with your allies.

Each swordfighter has hit points equal to twice your caster level and an Armor Class of 25. It makes saving throws or checks with a bonus equal to your caster level.

Material Component: A pewter swordfighter miniature figure.

Linked Perception

Divination
Level: Druid 2, ranger 1
Components: V, DF
Casting Time: 1 standard action
Range: 20 ft.
Area: 20-ft.-radius emanation centered on you
Duration: 1 minute/level (D)
Saving Throw: Will negates (harmless)
Spell Resistance: Yes (harmless)

Your senses are muddied for a moment, but when they clear, your sight and hearing are improved.

This spell imparts to all allies in its area a shared awareness of their surroundings. Each ally in the area (including yourself) gains a +2 bonus on Spot and Listen checks per each ally in the area. For example, if you and three allies are in the area, each of you gains a +6 bonus.

Longstrider, Mass

Transmutation
Level: Druid 5, ranger 4
Components: V
Casting Time: 1 swift action
Range: 60 ft.
Area: 60-ft.-radius emanation centered on you
Duration: 1 hour/level (D)
Saving Throw: Fortitude negates (harmless)
Spell Resistance: Yes (harmless)

Reality bends at your behest, speeding up your allies.

All allies in the area gain a +10-foot enhancement bonus to their speed scores.

Luminous Assassin

Conjuration (Summoning)
Level: Sorcerer/wizard 5

This spell functions like *lesser luminous assassin,* except that the assassin has the statistics provided below.

LUMINOUS ASSASSIN   CR 3

Male human rogue 3
N Medium humanoid (human, extraplanar)
Init +6; **Senses** Listen +6, Spot +6
Languages Common, Dwarven, Elven

AC 16, touch 12, flat-footed 14; Dodge, Mobility
(+2 Dex, +3 armor, +1 shield)
hp 16 (3 HD)
Resist evasion
Fort +3, **Ref** +6, **Will** +2

Speed 30 ft. (6 squares)
Melee mwk rapier +4 (1d6+1/18–20)
Ranged mwk shortbow +5 (1d6+1/×3)
Base Atk +2; **Grp** +3
Atk Options sneak attack +2d6
Combat Gear *potion of cure moderate wounds, potion of darkvision*

Abilities Str 12, Dex 15, Con 13, Int 14, Wis 10, Cha 8
Feats Dodge, Improved Initiative, Mobility
Skills Appraise +8, Balance +8, Disable Device +8, Escape Artist +8, Hide +8, Listen +6, Move Silently +8, Open Lock +8, Search +8, Spot +6, Tumble +8
Possessions combat gear plus masterwork studded leather armor, masterwork rapier, masterwork buckler, cloak of resistance +1, masterwork shortbow, 200 gp

Luminous Assassin, Greater

Conjuration (Summoning)
Level: Sorcerer/wizard 7

This spell functions like *luminous assassin,* except that the assassin has the statistics provided below.

LUMINOUS ASSASSIN   CR 5

Male human rogue 5
N Medium humanoid (human, extraplanar)
Init +7; **Senses** Listen +8, Spot +8
Languages Common, Dwarven, Elven

AC 17, touch 13, flat-footed 14; Dodge, Mobility, uncanny dodge
(+3 Dex, +3 armor, +1 shield)
hp 25 (5 HD)
Resist evasion
Fort +3, **Ref** +8, **Will** +2

Speed 30 ft. (6 squares)
Melee mwk rapier +5 (1d6+1/18–20)
Ranged +1 shortbow +7 (1d6+1/×3)
Base Atk +3; **Grp** +4
Atk Options sneak attack +3d6
Combat Gear *potion of cure serious wounds, potion of darkvision*

Abilities Str 12, Dex 16, Con 13, Int 14, Wis 10, Cha 8
SQ trap sense +1
Feats Dodge, Improved Initiative, Mobility
Skills Appraise +10, Balance +11, Disable Device +10, Escape Artist +11, Hide +11, Listen +8, Move Silently +11, Open Lock +11, Search +10, Spot +8, Tumble +11
Possessions combat gear plus masterwork studded leather armor, masterwork rapier, masterwork buckler, *cloak of resistance +1, +1 shortbow,* 200 gp

Luminous Assassin, Lesser

Conjuration (Summoning)
Level: Sorcerer/wizard 3
Components: V, S, F
Casting Time: 1 standard action
Range: Medium (100 ft. + 10 ft./level)
Effect: One summoned assassin
Duration: 1 round/level
Saving Throw: None
Spell Resistance: No

You conjure a vaguely humanoid being composed of yellow light. It wields a radiant blade and moves with unearthly grace.

A *lesser luminous assassin* appears above one creature within range and drops onto it, slashing and stabbing. The assassin attacks as it falls, and the target creature is considered flat-footed against this initial attack. Place the assassin in any square adjacent to the creature that can hold the assassin. The assassin's statistics are provided below.

After its initial attack, a *luminous assassin* attacks its target every round, taking its turn after your turn is completed. It fights intelligently and does not need to be directed by you. If the creature flees, the assassin pursues it to the best of its ability. If the creature dies or escapes, the assassin waits for you to direct it to another creature (a free action). You cannot command the assassin to do anything except attack creatures or wait (do nothing but defend itself), nor can you direct

it to attack another creature if the originally targeted creature still lives and is within the spell's range.

The assassin and all its possessions vanish when the spell's duration expires.

Focus: A serrated dagger.

LUMINOUS ASSASSIN   CR 1

Male human rogue 1

N Medium humanoid (human, extraplanar)

Init +6; **Senses** Listen +4, Spot +4

Languages Common, Dwarven, Elven

AC 15, touch 12, flat-footed 13; Dodge (+2 Dex, +3 armor)

hp 7 (1 HD)

Fort +1, **Ref** +4, **Will** +0

Speed 30 ft. (6 squares)

Melee mwk rapier +2 (1d6+1/18–20)

Ranged mwk shortbow +4 (1d6/×3)

Base Atk +0; **Grp** +1

Atk Options sneak attack +1d6

Combat Gear *potion of* cure light wounds

Abilities Str 12, Dex 15, Con 13, Int 14, Wis 10, Cha 8

Feats Dodge, Improved Initiative

Skills Appraise +6, Balance +6, Disable Device +6, Escape Artist +6, Hide +6, Listen +4, Move Silently +6, Open Lock +6, Search +6, Spot +4, Tumble +6

Possessions combat gear plus masterwork studded leather armor, masterwork rapier, masterwork shortbow, 50 gp

Magic Convalescence

Conjuration (Healing)

Level: Bard 5, cleric 5, druid 5

Components: V, S, M

Casting Time: 1 standard action

Range: 20 ft.

Area: 20-ft.-radius emanation centered on you

Duration: 1 round/level

Saving Throw: None

Spell Resistance: No

You alter the flow of magic about your body so that spells heal you.

Whenever a creature, including you, casts a spell within the area of this spell, you heal 1 hit point per level of the spell cast. The effect of each spell cast is resolved prior to your receiving the healing.

Material Component: A specially prepared, scented ointment.

Illus. by C. Frank

A luminous assassin prepares to dispatch its target

Mana Flux

Abjuration
Level: Cleric 5, sorcerer/wizard 5
Components: V, S
Casting Time: 1 standard action
Range: Medium (100 ft. + 10 ft./level)
Area: 20-ft.-radius emanation centered on a point in space
Duration: 1 round/level
Saving Throw: None
Spell Resistance: No

The air crackles and warps as you flood the area with unstable, disrupting magical energy. The light shed by a continual flame torch flutters wildly, while your magic items hum and vibrate.

This spell creates a field of unstable magical energy. Any creature trying to cast a spell, use a spell-like ability, activate a supernatural ability, or manifest a psionic power in the spell's area has a 20% chance of failure. Spell completion items, such as scrolls, also have this failure chance. If a creature within the spell's area has a spell failure chance due to some other source, such as wearing armor, check each source of spell failure chance separately. Feats and abilities that reduce the chance of spell failure due to armor have no effect on this field.

A failed spell uses up a spell slot or other resources as appropriate. Magic items do not have a chance of failure, since the power invested in them is too ingrained to be disrupted by this spell.

Mark of Doom

Necromancy
Level: Cleric 3, paladin 2
Component: V, S, DF
Casting Time: 1 standard action
Range: Medium (100 ft. + 10 ft./level)
Target: One creature
Duration: 1 round/level
Saving Throw: None
Spell Resistance: No

With a mighty invocation to your deity, you mark a creature as a target of your holy judgment. The ground shakes, the air grows still, and all wild animals in the air become suddenly quiet and fearful as your deity passes judgment upon the target.

This spell marks an opponent as an enemy of your faith, one who must pay for his transgressions. As long as the subject insists on fighting, it suffers divine punishment from your deity. The subject of this spell takes 1d6 points of damage each time it casts a spell that causes damage or disables a creature, makes a melee or ranged attack, or uses spell-like or supernatural abilities to harm other creatures.

The subject of this spell must have an alignment that opposes yours on at least one axis—evil if you are good, lawful if you are chaotic, and so on. For example, a chaotic good cleric can place a *mark of doom* upon a lawful good, lawful evil, or neutral evil opponent. A neutral caster can use this spell against any good, evil, lawful, or chaotic foe.

Mark of Judgment

Necromancy
Level: Cleric 2
Component: V, S, DF
Casting Time: 1 standard action
Range: Medium (100 ft. + 10 ft./level)
Targets: One creature/3 levels, no two of which are more than 30 ft. apart
Duration: 1 round/level
Saving Throw: Will negates
Spell Resistance: Yes

You call upon your deity to mark your foes as enemies of the faith. Divine energy surges through the area, and for a brief moment a holy symbol of your deity shines from the forehead of each targeted creature.

You and your allies see the *mark of judgment* on a creature and know to strike it in preference over other unmarked targets. Whenever a creature succeeds on a melee or ranged attack against any subject of a *mark of judgment* spell, that attacker heals 2 points of damage.

The targets of this spell must have an alignment that opposes yours on at least one axis—evil if you are good, lawful if you are chaotic, and so on. For example, a lawful good cleric can place a *mark of judgment* upon a chaotic good, chaotic neutral, lawful evil, neutral evil, or chaotic evil opponent. A neutral caster can use this spell against any good, evil, lawful, or chaotic foe.

Master's Touch

Divination
Level: Bard 2, cleric 2, sorcerer/wizard 2
Components: V
Casting Time: 1 immediate action
Range: Close (25 ft. + 5 ft./2 levels)
Target: One creature
Duration: Instantaneous
Saving Throw: Will negates (harmless)
Spell Resistance: Yes (harmless)

With a mere utterance, you grant the creature special insight into how best to complete a task at hand.

You cast this spell immediately before the target makes a skill check. The subject envisions how a master might accomplish the same task, gaining a +4 insight bonus on its skill check. *Master's touch* has no effect on skill checks that represent effort over more than 1 round of time (Craft checks, for example).

Melf's Unicorn Arrow

Conjuration
Level: Sorcerer/wizard 3
Components: V, S, F
Casting Time: 1 standard action
Range: Medium (100 ft. + 10 ft./level)
Target or Targets: One creature or up to five creatures, no two of which are more than 15 ft. apart
Duration: Instantaneous
Saving Throw: None
Spell Resistance: No

The shimmering, transparent form of a unicorn flies forward, its corporeal horn lowered in a charge at its enemy.

A translucent unicorn shape appears in midair and speeds toward the target of this spell. If you succeed on a ranged touch attack, the horn slams into the target and deals 1d8+8 points of damage. In addition, the target is subject to a bull rush, and must make a Strength check (with appropriate modifiers for a bull rush) against a DC of 21. If the check is failed, the subject is pushed back 5 feet, plus 5 feet for every 5 points by which it failed the check.

You can conjure an additional *unicorn arrow* for every three caster levels beyond 5th, up to five at 17th level. You can have them strike a single creature or several creatures, but each horn can strike only one creature. You must designate targets before you make your attack rolls. A creature struck by more than one horn is only required to make one Strength check to avoid the bull rush, but the DC of the check increases by 2 for each horn beyond the first that strikes it.

Focus: An ivory replica of a unicorn (25 gp).

Meteoric Strike

Transmutation [Fire]
Level: Cleric 5, druid 4, paladin 4
Components: V, S
Casting Time: 1 swift action
Range: 0 ft.
Target: Your melee weapon
Duration: 1 round or until discharged
Saving Throw: None or Reflex half; see text
Spell Resistance: See text

Your melee weapon bursts into orange, red, and gold flames, and shining sparks trail in its wake.

Your next successful melee attack deals extra fire damage equal to 1d6 points + 1d6 points per four caster levels. In addition, the flames splash into all squares adjacent to the target. Any creatures standing in these squares take half damage from the explosion, with a Reflex save allowed to halve this again. If a creature has spell resistance, it applies to this splash effect.

You are not harmed by your own *meteoric strike.*

You can cast *meteoric strike* before you make an unarmed attack. If you do, your unarmed attack is considered armed.

Mirror Image, Greater

Illusion (Figment)
Level: Bard 4, beguiler 4, sorcerer/
wizard 4
Components: V, S
Casting Time: 1 immediate action
Range: Personal; see text for *mirror image* (PH 254)
Target: You
Duration: 1 minute/level (D)

Several illusory duplicates of you pop into being.

This spell functions like *mirror image,* except that an additional image is created in each round after the first, up to a maximum of eight concurrent images. If all images are destroyed, the spell ends.

This spell also differs from *mirror image* in that you can cast this spell even when it's not your turn.

Mystic Aegis

Abjuration
Level: Cleric 4
Components: V, DF
Casting Time: 1 immediate action
Range: Personal
Target: You
Duration: Instantaneous

A mantle of scintillating, multicolored light appears around you to block the spell, then fades away.

You cast *mystic aegis* immediately when you are targeted by a hostile spell. You gain spell resistance equal to 12 + your caster level against that spell.

Mystic Surge

Universal
Level: Sorcerer/wizard 4
Components: V
Casting Time: 1 standard action
Range: Close (25 ft. + 5 ft./2 levels)
Target: One creature
Duration: 1 round
Saving Throw: Will negates (harmless)
Spell Resistance: Yes (harmless)

You utter a phrase, and magical power begins to swell within you.

The subject of *mystic surge* is able to channel a greater amount of magical energy into the next spell it casts before this spell's duration expires. That spell's save DC increases by 2, and its effective caster level increases by 1.

Overwhelm

Enchantment (Compulsion) [Mind-Affecting]
Level: Beguiler 6, sorcerer/wizard 6
Components: V, S
Casting Time: 1 standard action
Range: Touch
Target: One creature
Duration: Instantaneous

Saving Throw: Will negates
Spell Resistance: Yes

You grip the creature's head, and a surge of magical energy overwhelms its senses.

With a touch, you deal nonlethal damage to the subject equal to the creature's current hit point total.

Phantom Battle

Illusion (Figment)
Level: Bard 3, beguiler 4, sorcerer/
wizard 4
Components: V, S
Casting Time: 1 standard action
Range: Medium (100 ft. + 10 ft./level)
Area: 20-ft.-radius spread
Duration: 1 round/level
Saving Throw: Will negates
Spell Resistance: Yes

You create an illusory horde of snarling ogres, fierce orcs, and proud knights in armor, all locked in battle. Creatures in the area move cautiously as they are caught up in the phantom melee.

This spell creates the illusion of a fierce battle. Your enemies move cautiously and pass up the opportunity to strike their foes, since the roar and confusion of the battle distracts them.

All creatures within the area of the spell that fail their saving throws cannot make attacks of opportunity. In addition, all creatures within the area are considered flanked. A creature ignores these effects when it leaves the spell's area. If a creature reenters the spell's area after leaving it, the creature can attempt another save to resist the spell if its initial save failed. A creature that enters the area for the first time after the spell is cast must also make a saving throw to resist the effect.

A *phantom battle* spell produces noise appropriate to a mob of creatures locked in battle. Anyone in the battle can plainly see that the conjured fighters are no threat, since they strike solely at other phantom warriors, but the din, tumult, and confusion make it difficult to focus on the true foes at hand. A creature that succeeds on its save can still see the spectral outline of the illusion, but is able to block out the distraction and fight as normal.

When you cast this spell, you can choose for it not to affect a number of allies you designate less than or equal to your caster level.

Plague

Necromancy [Evil]
Level: Cleric 7, druid 7, sorcerer/wizard 8
Components: V, S
Casting Time: 1 standard action
Range: Close (25 ft. + 5 ft./2 levels)
Targets: One living creature/level, no two of which are more than 30 ft. apart
Duration: 1 round/level
Saving Throw: Fortitude negates
Spell Resistance: Yes

Your skin crawls as you utter the words and complete the gestures of this spell. Suddenly, one or more of the target creatures seem overcome by a dreadful malady.

The subjects contract a disease selected from the table below, which strikes immediately (no incubation period). The disease progresses rapidly; the subjects must attempt additional saves each round, instead of each day. Use *plague's* DC for all saves. See page 292 of the *Dungeon Master's Guide* for more information on these diseases.

Disease	Damage
Blinding sickness	1d4 Str*
Cackle fever	1d6 Wis
Filth fever	1d3 Dex, 1d3 Con
Mindfire	1d4 Int
Red ache	1d6 Str
Shakes	1d8 Dex
Slimy doom	1d4 Con

*Each time a victim takes 2 or more points of Strength damage from blinding sickness, he or she must make another Fortitude save (using the *plague* spell's save DC) or be permanently blinded.

Prismatic Mist

Evocation
Level: Sorcerer/wizard 3
Components: V
Casting Time: 1 standard action
Range: Medium (100 ft. + 10 ft./level)
Area: 30-ft.-radius spread
Duration: 1 minute/level
Saving Throw: See text
Spell Resistance: No

You call forth a thin, multihued mist that fills the area. Small incandescent lights, no brighter than candles, drift lazily throughout the mist.

The mist is too thin to obscure vision or provide concealmen, but walking through it is hazardous. Each round, a creature that begins its turn in the area of the spell, or that enters the mist during its turn, is subject to one or more of the following effects

Illus. by E. Widermann

Gimble and Lidda sneak through a phantom battle

based on the (randomly determined) color of the mist in the area around the creature.

Consult the table below to determine the color of the mist and its effect.

d8	Color	Effect
1	Red	1d4 points fire damage
2	Orange	1d6 points acid damage
3	Yellow	1d8 points electricity damage
4	Green	Poison; 1d4 points Str damage (Fort negates)
5	Blue	*Slowed* for 1 round (Will negates)
6	Indigo	*Lesser confusion* for 1 round (Will negates, mind-affecting)
7	Violet	*Dazed* for 1 round (Will negates)
8		At the junction of two colors; roll twice more, ignoring any "8" results

Pulse of Hate

Necromancy [Evil]
Level: Cleric 7, sorcerer/wizard 7
Components: V, S, M/DF
Casting Time: 1 standard action
Range: 20 ft.
Area: 20-ft.-radius emanation centered on you
Duration: 1 round/level
Saving Throw: Will half
Spell Resistance: Yes

A red light pulses at your feet, sending malign waves of energy through the area that damage your enemies.

Starting in the round you cast it, *pulse of hate* deals 2d6 points of unholy damage per round, on your turn, to all enemies in the area.

Arcane Material Component: A heart-shaped locket and a pin.

Radiance

Evocation [Good, Light]
Level: Cleric 5, druid 5, sorcerer/wizard 5
Components: V, S, DF
Casting Time: 1 standard action
Range: 60 ft.
Area: 60-ft.-radius emanation centered on you
Duration: 1 round/level (D); see text
Saving Throw: None
Spell Resistance: No

A bright, scintillating light shines from your body.

For the duration of this spell, you emanate a bright light that undead find uncomfortable. The illumination within the area is bright, the equivalent of a *daylight* spell. Undead in the area are dazzled for as long as they remain in the radius and for 1d6 rounds thereafter.

Radiance counters or dispels any darkness spell of equal or lower level.

Ray of the Python

Evocation
Level: Bard 2, sorcerer/wizard 3
Components: V, S
Casting Time: 1 standard action
Range: Close (25 ft. + 5 ft./2 levels)
Target: One creature
Duration: 1 minute
Saving Throw: Reflex negates; see below
Spell Resistance: Yes

A ray of pulsing yellow light springs from your hand. It strikes your target and wraps around him like a snake, hampering his ability to move and attack.

This spell creates a ropey strand of arcane energy that restricts a creature's movements. A creature struck by this ray can only make one attack per round and cannot make attacks of opportunity. In addition, the creature's speed is reduced by 10 feet.

After the spell has been in effect for 1 round, at the start of its turn in each round thereafter, the subject is allowed a Reflex save to resist the spell's effects. If the save succeeds, the creature ignores the spell's effects for that round. It must make a new save each round, regardless of the result of a previous save.

Regroup

Conjuration (Teleportation)
Level: Duskblade 3, sorcerer/wizard 3
Components: V, S
Casting Time: 1 standard action
Range: Close (25 ft. + 5 ft./2 levels)
Targets: One willing creature/level
Duration: Instantaneous
Saving Throw: None
Spell Resistance: No

You teleport your companions to your side.

A bugbear stares warily at an area filled with prismatic mist

Each subject of this spell teleports to a square adjacent to you. If those squares are occupied or cannot support the teleported creatures, the creatures appear as close to you as possible, on a surface that can support them, in an unoccupied square.

Renewed Vigor

Transmutation
Level: Bard 5, cleric 4, druid 4
Components: V, S
Casting Time: 1 standard action
Range: 30 ft.
Effect: 30-ft.-radius burst centered on you
Duration: Instantaneous; see text
Saving Throw: Fortitude negates (harmless)
Spell Resistance: Yes (harmless)

With a word and a gesture, you suffuse an area with a soft golden light, bestowing a second wind to creatures within.

When you cast this spell, you remove the fatigued condition from any creature in the area and cause exhausted creatures to become fatigued. In addition, affected creatures gain a +2 bonus to Constitution for 1 round per caster level.

Righteous Burst

Evocation [Good]
Level: Cleric 7
Components: V, S, M, DF
Casting Time: 1 standard action
Range: 30 ft.
Area: 30-ft.-radius burst centered on you
Duration: Instantaneous
Saving Throw: None or Will half; see text
Spell Resistance: Yes

Holy light blasts from your upraised fist.

This spell heals every ally in the area of 1d8 points of damage +1 per caster level (maximum +35). Every enemy in the area takes 1d8 points of damage +1 per caster level (maximum +35).

Enemies are allowed Will saves to halve the damage.
Material Component: A handful of silver dust (worth 15 gp).

Rouse

Enchantment (Compulsion) [Mind-Affecting]
Level: Beguiler 1, duskblade 1, sorcerer/wizard 1
Components: V, S
Casting Time: 1 standard action
Range: Close (25 ft. + 5 ft./2 levels)
Area: 10-ft.-radius burst
Duration: Instantaneous
Saving Throw: None
Spell Resistance: No

With a loud snap of your fingers, you cause any sleeping creatures in the spell's area to awaken.

This spell has no effect on creatures that are unconscious due to being reduced to negative hit points, or that have taken nonlethal damage in excess of their current hit points.

Scattering Trap

Conjuration (Teleportation)
Level: Sorcerer/wizard 3
Components: V, S, M

Illus. by D. Hudnut

Mialee uses a regroup spell to gather her friends

Casting Time: 1 standard action
Range: Close (25 ft. + 5 ft./2 levels)
Area: One 5-ft. square/2 levels
Duration: 1 round/level
Saving Throw: Reflex negates
Spell Resistance: Yes

Areas you designate on the floor flare dimly.

This spell imbues a number of 5-foot squares you designate with a teleportation trap. A creatures moving through one of these squares and failing its saving throw is teleported 1d6 squares in a random direction (use the Missing with a Thrown Weapon diagram, PH 158). If reaching the destination involves teleporting the subject into a solid space such as within a wall, the subject is forcibly shunted into the nearest open space and takes 1d6 points of damage.

When you cast this spell, the 5-foot squares you designate do not have to be adjacent but must all be within 30 feet of one another.

Material Component: A pinch of dandelion seeds.

Illus. by J. Nelson

Seeking Ray

Evocation
Level: Duskblade 2, sorcerer/wizard 2
Components: V, S
Casting Time: 1 standard action
Range: Medium (100 ft. + 10 ft./level)
Effect: Ray
Duration: Instantaneous; see text
Saving Throw: None
Spell Resistance: Yes

A ray of electricity springs from your hand. It snakes around obstacles, cover, and other impediments on its way toward your target.

You create a ray that deals 4d6 points of electricity damage if it strikes your target. While this ray requires a ranged touch attack to strike an opponent, it ignores concealment and cover (but not total concealment or total cover), and it does not take the standard penalty for firing into melee.

In addition to the damage it deals, the ray creates a link of energy between you and the subject. If this ray struck the target and dealt damage, you gain a +4 bonus on attacks you make with ray spells (including another casting of this one, if desired) against the subject for 1 round per caster level. If you cast *seeking ray* a second time on a creature that is still linked to you from a previous casting, the duration of the new link overlaps (does not stack with) the remaining duration of the previous one.

Share Talents

Transmutation
Level: Bard 1, cleric 2, ranger 2, sorcerer/wizard 2
Components: V, S, M
Casting Time: 1 round
Range: Touch
Targets: Two willing creatures touched
Duration: 10 minutes/level
Saving Throw: Will negates (harmless)
Spell Resistance: Yes (harmless)

Mialee uses a scattering trap spell . . .

Illus. by J. Nelson

. . . to get rid of an unwelcome guest

You touch two allies, and for a moment their features change so that they seem to blend their appearances into one new creature.

When you cast this spell on two subjects, you create a mystical link between them. For the duration of the spell, the subjects gain a +2 bonus on any skill checks they make, as long as at least one of the characters has 1 rank or more in the skill. In addition, if either character has ranks in a skill that is not normally usable by untrained characters (such as Tumble), the other character can make untrained checks using that skill.

Material Component: A knotted rope.

Slashing Dispel

Abjuration/Evocation
Level: Duskblade 5, sorcerer/wizard 4
Components: V, S
Casting Time: 1 standard action
Range: Medium (100 ft. + 10 ft./level)
Target or Area: One creature or 20-ft.-radius burst
Duration: Instantaneous
Saving Throw: None
Spell Resistance: No

You rip away the spell energy infused within a creature, turning it into a harmful burst of energy that burns into the creature before dissipating.

This spell functions like *dispel magic* (PH 223), except as noted here. Any creature that has a spell effect removed from it takes 2 points of damage per level of the dispelled effect. If a creature loses the effects of multiple spells, it takes damage for each one.

Sonic Shield

Evocation
Level: Bard 3, duskblade 5, sorcerer/wizard 5
Components: V, S
Casting Time: 1 standard action
Range: Personal
Target: You
Duration: 1 round/level

The air around you shifts and shimmers as a field of pure sonic energy forms before you. This shield repels all attacks with a blast of energy that sends the attacker stumbling backward.

This spell grants you a +4 deflection bonus to AC. In addition, anyone who successfully hits you with a melee attack takes 1d8 points of sonic damage and must make a Fortitude saving throw or be knocked 5 feet away from you into an unoccupied space of your choice. If no space of sufficient size is available for it to enter, it instead takes an extra 1d8 points of sonic damage.

Stand

Conjuration (Teleportation)
Level: Duskblade 1, sorcerer/wizard 1
Components: V, S
Casting Time: 1 immediate action
Range: Close (25 ft. + 5 ft./2 levels)
Target: One willing prone creature
Duration: Instantaneous
Saving Throw: Will negates (harmless)
Spell Resistance: Yes (harmless)

With a swift upward gesture of your arms and a single clarion command ("Stand!"), you enable the prone creature to safely rise to its feet.

The subject creature immediately stands, without provoking attacks of opportunity.

Stay the Hand

Enchantment (Charm) [Mind-Affecting]

Level: Bard 1, beguiler 2, cleric 2, sorcerer/wizard 2

Components: V

Casting Time: 1 immediate action

Range: Medium (100 ft. + 10 ft./level)

Target: One humanoid

Duration: Instantaneous

Saving Throw: Will negates

Spell Resistance: Yes

Your words invoke compassion and mercy in the merciless.

If the target creature fails its save against *stay the hand*, it refrains from attacking you or targeting you with spells for the remainder of the current round.

You can cast this spell during an opponent's turn after the opponent announces its intention to attack you or target you with a spell. If the opponent becomes subject to this spell, it can choose a new target to attack, but it takes a –4 circumstance penalty on its attack roll due to the sudden change of intentions at the last second. Likewise, the subject of this spell can redirect a spell that had been targeted on you, but it must succeed on a Concentration check (DC 15 + the spell's level) or the spell is wasted.

Stifle Spell

Abjuration

Level: Cleric 4, sorcerer/wizard 4

Components: V

Casting Time: 1 immediate action

Range: Close (25 ft. + 5 ft./2 levels)

Target: One creature casting a spell

Duration: Instantaneous

Saving Throw: See text

Spell Resistance: Yes

As the creature casts a spell, you utter a simple magical phrase that momentarily confounds it.

You cast this spell to distract another creature as it attempts to cast a spell. The target must succeed on a Concentration check (DC equal to 14 + your key ability modifier + the level of the spell being cast) to ignore the distraction, or else it loses the spell.

Stretch Weapon

Transmutation

Level: Bard 2, cleric 2, duskblade 2, sorcerer/wizard 2

Components: V

Casting Time: 1 swift action

Range: 0 ft.

Target: Melee weapon wielded

Duration: One attack

Saving Throw: Will negates (harmless, object)

Spell Resistance: Yes (harmless, object)

With a single utterance, the weapon in your hand elongates without becoming awkward or weighty.

The affected weapon stretches, extending toward its target, though it can be wielded normally. The spell adds an additional 5 feet of reach to a melee weapon for a single attack.

Summon Golem

Conjuration (Summoning)

Level: Cleric 9, sorcerer/wizard 9

Components: V, S, F

Casting Time: 1 round

Range: Close (25 ft. + 5 ft./2 levels)

Effect: One summoned golem

Duration: 1 minute/level

Saving Throw: None

Spell Resistance: No

You wave your hand over a lump of flesh, clay, stone, or iron while chanting a lengthy incantation. Moments later, a golem of similar substance appears in a flash of light to serve you.

You summon a flesh, clay, stone, or iron golem. The golem begins acting at the start of your next turn and follows your simple commands.

The golem disappears when it is destroyed or when the spell's duration expires.

Focus: A small lump of preserved flesh, dried clay, unworked stone, or iron ore.

Sure Strike

Divination

Level: Duskblade 2, sorcerer/wizard 2

Components: V

Casting Time: 1 swift action

Range: Personal

Target: You

Duration: 1 round or until discharged

You gain a fleeting glimpse into the future, enough to guide your impending attack.

You cast this spell immediately before you make an attack roll. You can see into the future for that attack, granting you a +1 insight bonus per three caster levels on your next attack roll.

Thunder Field

Evocation

Level: Bard 4, druid 6, sorcerer/wizard 6

Components: V, S

Casting Time: 1 standard action

Range: Medium (100 ft. + 10 ft./level)

Area: 20-ft.-radius spread

Duration: 1 round/level

Saving Throw: See text

Spell Resistance: Yes

The air around you crackles with the distant boom of thunder. A dome of translucent golden energy surrounds the spell's area. The dome shakes and rattles, while the muffled sounds of explosive blasts echoes from it. Any creature within the dome is knocked into the air by the powerful, ear-splitting blasts.

This spell creates an area of turbulent, sonic energy. For the duration of the spell, any creature that starts its turn in the spell's area must make a Fortitude save or take 1d8 points of sonic damage. In addition, affected creatures must make a Reflex save or be knocked prone. If a creature is already prone, failing this save has no effect on it.

Toxic Weapon

Conjuration (Creation)

Level: Duskblade 4, sorcerer/wizard 5

Components: V, S

Casting Time: 1 standard action

Range: Touch

Target: Piercing or slashing weapon touched

Duration: 1 hour or until discharged

Saving Throw: Fortitude negates; see text

Spell Resistance: No

You touch the weapon, and an oily liquid appears on its surface.

When you cast this spell, you coat the target weapon with poison. The next successful melee attack with that weapon delivers the poison. The poison deals 1d10 points of Constitution damage immediately and another 1d10 points of Constitution damage 1 minute later. Each instance of damage can be negated by a Fortitude save (DC equal to this spell's save DC).

If the weapon has not scored a successful hit after 1 hour, the poison becomes inert and evaporates.

Trollshape

Transmutation (Polymorph)
Level: Sorcerer/wizard 4
Components: V, S
Casting Time: 1 swift action
Range: Personal
Target: You
Duration: 1 round/level (D)

Your muscles ripple, and you hear bones crackling underneath your now mottled green skin as your form reshapes to that of a horrid troll.

You take on the form and abilities of a troll (MM 247). You gain 30 temporary hit points, which disappear at the end of the spell's duration. See the description of the new polymorph subschool on page 95 for more details.

Vertigo

Illusion (Phantasm) [Fear, Mind-Affecting]
Level: Bard 2, beguiler 2, sorcerer/ wizard 2
Components: V, S
Casting Time: 1 standard action
Range: Close (25 ft. + 5 ft./2 levels)
Target: One living creature
Duration: 1 round/level (D)
Saving Throw: Will disbelief
Spell Resistance: No

You cripple a target with sensations of falling.

The subject of this spell becomes dizzy as the ground seems to drop away beneath its feet. The subject must succeed on a DC 10 Balance check at the start of each turn to take a move action.

Illus. by R. Spencer

Jozan summons an iron golem

If it fails, it cannot move. If it fails the check by 5 or more, it falls prone. While affected, the subject also takes a –2 penalty on attack rolls and saving throws. Airborne creatures receive a +4 bonus on saves against this spell and do not need to make the Balance checks.

Vertigo Field
Illusion (Pattern)
Level: Beguiler 3, sorcerer/wizard 3
Components: V, S
Casting Time: 1 standard action
Range: Medium (100 ft. + 10 ft./level)
Area: 20-ft.-radius spread
Duration: 1 round/level
Saving Throw: Fortitude partial; see text
Spell Resistance: Yes

You create a field of swirling patterns of color, light, and motion. Creatures in the area stagger as the barrage of sensations overloads their senses and leaves them overcome with vertigo.

This spell creates a field of illusory magic that hampers the movement and senses of any creature that enters it. The area within the field counts as difficult terrain. Attacks made through or from inside the field have a 20% miss chance. A creature that begins its turn inside the field must make a Fortitude save or become nauseated for 1 round. Once a creature fails this save, it does not need to make another save against this effect.

When you cast this spell, you can choose for this nauseating effect not to apply to a number of allies you designate less than or equal to your caster level. Those allies still treat the *vertigo field* as difficult terrain and have the 20% miss chance on attacks.

Visions of the Future
Divination
Level: Cleric 8
Components: V, S
Casting Time: 10 minutes
Range: Personal
Target: You
Duration: 1 hour/level or until discharged

You view events slightly before they happen, gaining time to react to them.

You gain a +2 sacred bonus on all saving throws and +2 dodge bonus to Armor Class. Once during the spell's duration, as an immediate action, you can choose to discharge the spell to gain a greater bonus. When you discharge the spell in this manner, you gain a sacred bonus on all saving throws and a dodge bonus to your Armor Class equal to 1/2 your caster level (maximum +25). This bonus lasts until the beginning of your next turn.

Whelm
Enchantment (Compulsion) [Mind-Affecting]
Level: Beguiler 1, sorcerer/wizard 1
Components: V, S
Casting Time: 1 standard action
Range: Close (25 ft. + 5 ft./2 levels)
Target: One living creature
Duration: Instantaneous
Saving Throw: Will negates
Spell Resistance: Yes

You thrust one arm forward toward your foe, palm open and fingers splayed. The creature reels as an invisible surge of power invades its mind.

You launch a magical assault that wears at the target's mind, dealing 1d6 points of nonlethal damage if it fails its saving throw.

For every two caster levels beyond 1st, you deal an extra 1d6 points of nonlethal damage to the subject, to a maximum of 5d6 at 9th level.

Whelm, Mass
Enchantment (Compulsion) [Mind-Affecting]
Level: Beguiler 4, sorcerer/wizard 4
Components: V, S
Casting Time: 1 standard action
Range: Close (25 ft. + 5 ft./2 levels)
Targets: One living creature/level
Duration: Instantaneous
Saving Throw: Will negates
Spell Resistance: Yes

With a sweep of your arm, creatures reel as an invisible surge of magical power invades their minds.

This spell functions like *whelm*, except that it affects multiple targets and it deals 1d6 points of nonlethal damage per caster level to each subject, to a maximum of 10d6 at 10th level.

Whelming Blast
Enchantment (Compulsion) [Mind-Affecting]
Level: Beguiler 2, sorcerer/wizard 2
Components: V, S
Casting Time: 1 standard action
Range: 30 ft.
Area: Cone-shaped burst
Duration: Instantaneous
Saving Throw: Will negates
Spell Resistance: Yes

You stretch your arms before you, spread your hands wide, and unleash an invisible cone of magical power that assails the minds of the creatures within it.

You assail the mental faculties of creatures in the area, dealing 1d6 points of nonlethal damage per two caster levels (maximum 5d6 at 10th level) to each creature that fails its save.

Wrack Earth
Evocation [Earth]
Level: Druid 7
Components: V, S, DF
Casting Time: 1 standard action
Range: 30 ft.
Area: 30-ft. line
Duration: Instantaneous
Saving Throw: Reflex half; see text
Spell Resistance: No

You stomp your foot, causing a shockwave to shoot out from you.

When you cast this spell, earth and stone blast upward along a 30-foot line, smashing creatures and knocking them out of the way. This spell deals 1d6 points of bludgeoning damage per caster level (maximum 15d6) to every creature it contacts and creates a 5-foot-wide mound of stone and rubble along the path of the line. Creatures within the area that fail their Reflex saves are moved to a random side of the rubble. The rubble created is difficult terrain that requires 2 squares of movement to enter. Creatures that succeed on their saving throws take half damage and are not moved by the mound of rubble.

Illus. by R. Horsley

Your character is more than just a race, class, and level stapled together. At their best, D&D® characters are on par with characters in the best movies and novels, almost as complex as real people. You have many options at your disposal when crafting your character's personality. You could invent an intriguing history for your character and allow his or her personality to follow naturally from that. You could imitate characters (or aspects of characters) from books you have read, movies you have seen, or real people you know. With some attention on your part to his or her background, personality type, and significant traits, your character can possess realistic depth and motivation. This chapter offers tools to create well-rounded characters with memorable personalities, as well as advice on being a good player at the table.

CHARACTER BACKGROUND

Your character has a place in the fictional world of the D&D game. Whether you grew up on a farm, struggled for scraps of bread in an alleyway, or were raised by a pack of magical wolves, you had a life before you started walking the road to adventure. The following backgrounds can serve as inspiration for what your character's childhood and youth were like.

Each background includes several headers that describe how you can apply it to different parts of your character's life.

Youth: This section describes the typical experiences of a character who grew up in this background. It describes how that background shaped your early life.

Transition: Your background represents your past. This section offers two or three ideas on how you left your old life behind and became an adventurer.

At the Table: Your background shapes your outlook and your actions. This section discusses how your background might manifest when you roleplay your character.

ARTISAN

Apprenticed to a promising artisan, you worked hard throughout your childhood to develop the skills necessary to master your craft and make a good living in the world. Hours spent working in the shop alongside your master watching, assisting, practicing, and slowly gaining expertise in all aspects of your chosen craft allow you to truly appreciate the artistry that goes into every facet of the job. From conceptualization to gathering supplies to working the materials into the desired form and finally to the cleanup at the end of each project, you are proud to have the skills of a true artisan.

Youth: Working in your master's shop was no day at the carnival. Early on, you spent most of your time sweeping and scrubbing floors, cleaning tools, carrying supplies, and preparing simple meals so your master could spend his time working on his current project.

129

Each time he gave you a task that seemed meaningless to the actual job at hand, more often than not it proved necessary to achieving his goal. As you completed these tasks, you would quietly watch your master, learning all you could from observation before he gave your next task.

Transition: What drove you from the comforting grip of the workshop to the world of adventure? Your motivation could come from within, or events beyond your control might have cast you into the role of an adventurer.

Perhaps the toil of the workshop grew tiresome. You always preferred tales of heroes, monsters, and ancient treasures to your master's long lectures on responsibility, technique, and craftsmanship. As soon as you had enough money saved, you left your master and took up training in your current class. Your master might still hold a grudge for your desertion; if he is powerful in his community or guild, you can expect trouble from him in the future.

If your master was cruel, life on the road could have been a better option than another year of slaving away in his shop. Underfed, beaten for the smallest infraction, and worked to the point of exhaustion, you didn't so much leave your craft as escape from it. Alone in the world and penniless, you learned enough to survive and eventually became an adventurer. Perhaps a kindly new master took you in, or you were drafted into military or religious service.

Artisans need peace and stability to make a living. A war, plague, or other calamity could have forced you onto the adventurer's path. If orcs sacked your home city and burned it to the ground, you could have become an adventurer out of necessity rather than any desire for glory. Perhaps you thirst for vengeance against the cruel tyrant who slew your master and smashed your dreams of becoming a respected artisan with a shop of your own.

At the Table: Comment on the craftsmanship of weapons and armor you find. A dwarf craftsman might take the time to wonder at the beautiful carvings on an ancient, abandoned stronghold's walls. An elf artisan might be arrogant toward human goods. While other members of the party are excited at the magical properties of a sword, you find the excellent quality of its blade and the fine detailed work in its pommel worthy of comment. To you, a dungeon can also be a museum of an ancient civilization's artwork and craftsmanship.

ASCETIC

Sequestered in a convent, monastery, library, or school, you spent your youth in study, contemplation, and reflection. Through meditation, academic study, or prayer, you honed your passion for knowledge in the fire of your will. Through discipline and perseverance, you still constantly drive yourself to unlock lore, whether it is hidden in ancient texts or religious scripture or revealed through constant meditative practice.

Youth: As a child you spent hours retrieving and cataloging tomes and scrolls for older scholars who left you to your own devices once they had the materials they sought. Spending these hours with little supervision, you learned the location of nearly every work stored in the library of the mountain abbey you called home. While at that age you couldn't fathom the mysteries stored within, you kept a mental tally of those that

interested you most. From time to time you would be sent to the kitchen for food, or to wash dishes, or to run any number of errands. Each such excursion away from the library that you had come to call home felt like a test—of your resolve to learn, of your desire to spend time only in the library, or simply of your youthful patience.

Transition: A scholar can only learn so much in a library surrounded by books. Your masters ordered you out into the world to experience its wonders firsthand. Having learned everything your masters can teach, you can never return home until your magic or *ki* is strong enough, or until you have surpassed your masters, or you have achieved enlightenment or ultimate arcane or divine power.

Alternatively, a rivalry or power struggle among your masters might have forced you out into the world. Your tutor or sponsor fell into disgrace or disappeared under mysterious circumstances. Without your master around, there was no longer a place for you. You still seek him, or at least to avenge him.

Perhaps rather than simply leaving your order, you were expelled. Scholarship demands innovation and forward thought, but your thoughts were too radical for your elders. Your ideas were deemed dangerous or subversive or heretical, forcing your exile. Maybe you delved into lore too dangerous for mere apprentices, such as spells to summon forgotten gods or bind demons. Perhaps a rival student framed you.

At the Table: You know a lot, and you aren't afraid to show it off. While others might refer to creatures by common names such as "kobold," "troglodyte," and "bugbear," you know the proper classification of each in Old Draconic. If you find an ancient library, a collection of scrolls, or even ancient murals and frescoes that depict myths and prehistorical events, you happily lose yourself in studying them even in the midst of a dungeon.

If you trained as a monk or cleric, the habits, beliefs, and ethos instilled in you by your upbringing play a major role in your life. For example, you might be a vegetarian if your sect forbids the eating of meat, and you aren't afraid to tell others of the superiority of your diet. You have an old saying or a bit of wisdom for every occasion. When faced with a tough decision, you turn to a religious book or similar manual for guidance. You quote scripture or your master's sayings to support your arguments and decisions.

DRIFTER

Home? What's that? You spent your entire life on the road, moving from town to town. You get by taking odd jobs, some less savory than others, or performing for a night's bed and food. People are your stock in trade; your keen understanding of their attitudes, behaviors, and desires keeps you employed and alive. When things go bad, it's time for you and yours to move on to the next town. Survival has always been your first priority, and you have become quite good at it.

Youth: As a child, you spent the majority of your days either on the road or performing odd jobs and running errands for your elders. You put any talents you had to work for you just to get by and perhaps earn a little food or a few spare coins. You might have turned to crime when things became desperate, or you might have resisted all temptation no matter how bad things got.

You could have ended up on the road due to a number of reasons. You might have been separated from your family at a young age due to war or some other disaster. A plague could have left you a sole survivor and driven you from your hometown. Perhaps you grew up in an orphanage and ran away as soon as you were able. Your parents could have been wanderers themselves, so that you never knew any other life, at first being carried on your mother's back and then later walking beside her.

Transition: Moving from the life of a scrounging drifter to that of an adventurer was easy for you. The skills you learned on the roads or in the alleys and taprooms of the world prove useful to any adventurer. Perhaps you managed a heist that scored you enough money to buy you thieves' tools, a weapon, and some armor. That single windfall was enough to transform you from just another wanderer to a skilled, armed adventurer.

You might have stumbled into the adventurer's life by accident. Seeking shelter from a storm, you entered a cave that turned out to be a monster's lair. You managed to slay the beast and afterward helped yourself to its treasure. Your first taste of adventure was frightening and exhilarating (and profitable), and you developed a liking for the activity.

Adventure finds you as often as you find it. Perhaps monsters threaten the area you are traveling through, leaving you with a simple choice: fight, flee, or die. Maybe you've always tried to help others as you were passing through an area. Now that you're older, stronger, and more skilled, you can take a more active role in protecting the common folk and helping out where you can.

At the Table: You've done it all before, and your experience makes you calm in a crisis. When a sudden thunderstorm rolls in, you know how to find shelter. When it comes to surviving in the wilds or making your way through a city, you are a treasure trove of folktales, traveler's lore, and common sense. Worldly for your age, you aren't afraid to show off that knowledge in front of others. Sheltered people, those who grew up in far easier circumstances than you, earn your disdain if they can't keep up with you. You didn't grow up with much, but you learned to take care of yourself.

FARM HAND

Born and raised on the farm, you developed a keen understanding of agrarian life, as well as a strong work ethic. Accustomed to being up at dawn and asleep by dusk, you can track the seasons by touch and smell. You know the satisfaction of cultivating the earth on which you live, and you relish the responsibility of taking care of the animals that you depend on for food, clothing, and companionship. Some might consider this a simple life, but those who have that attitude know very little about how to work with the land or understand the respect necessary to coax it to bear fruit.

Youth: As a child, you hung upon the apron strings of those working in the home and hearth. You learned to clean the dwelling in which you lived, as well as cook for those who lived there with you. As you grew older, your daily chores became more complicated and laborious. From splitting and hauling firewood, feeding and cleaning up after the animals, and working the earth to produce the crops you need to live on, you learned

every aspect of farm life and grew to appreciate the hard work that was required just to put enough food on the table. In your free time you learned to fish and hunt, supplementing your daily diet with game from the nearby wood or stream.

Transition: Shifting from the humdrum life of a farmer to the exciting, deadly path of an adventurer was no easy change for you. You left behind generations of tradition to seek the adventuring life. Whether you were pushed into this decision or happily left your family's fields behind you, you know that you can never go back to that life again.

Life on the farm is never easy, and a cruel, demanding ruler only makes things worse. A distant war, a monarch obsessed with building monuments or enjoying the pleasures of the court, or a few years of insufficient rain and harsh winters: All these factors can drive a farmer to seek a better life. Perhaps the peasants and yeomen rose up in rebellion. You were one of the lucky ones who managed to escape when the king's men razed your village. You learned to handle a weapon in the uprising, and a slain mercenary raider's weapons and armor became your first set of adventuring gear. Maybe one day you'll return to avenge your family and friends, but until then you hone your skills.

Alternatively, you might have left the farm of your own free will. Maybe you weren't in line to inherit any of your father's land, leaving you with little choice but to seek another option. Too ambitious to stay on the farm, at the first opportunity you headed for a life of adventure. Your family still lives in your old hometown, and maybe you visit from time to time or send them a few coins now and then to help out when the harvest is bad and times are tight.

At the Table: You are accustomed to hard work and have little patience for those who are lazy, negligent, or irresponsible. You have toiled for hours under a hot sun to feed your family, and you have no time for those who aren't willing to put out a similar effort.

When you and your companions enter a rural community, you're the best choice to serve as your group's spokesperson. You might not be the most elegant figure in the party, but you know how to talk with ordinary people. Despite the armor you wear, the weapons you carry, or the magic you command, at heart you're still one of them. Any threat to the common folk is likely to draw a sharp reaction from you.

GLADIATOR

Born a slave, you trained from an early age to fight with weapons or magic. Experts were brought in from all over the world to train you and your fellows in various forms of attack and defense, imparting to you a respect for cultures outside your own, as well as their methods of combat. Even as a young child, you were forced to fight in the arena against other children as well as animals not considered a threat to older, more experienced gladiators. Given your innate sense of dramatic flair, you have come to enjoy the adulation of the crowd, as well as the respect of your peers.

Youth: Your daily routine began with a strict regimen of calisthenics followed by training in the pits. Every hour you trained with a different master, each focusing on different methods of fighting and teaching you ways to present yourself

Illus. by M. May

with a distinct theatrical air. After a noon meal, you were set to sparring in the arena, focusing on different tactics and scenarios—some meant for the individual and some done in pairs, each gladiator working in tandem with another.

Transition: A gladiator revolt allowed you to break free of your masters. In a single night of carefully planned violence, you turned the tables on your captors and made a daring escape. You were one of the lucky ones who made it out alive, but your former masters placed a price on your head. You have run far away, but who knows when a cunning bounty hunter or a vengeful tracker might find you? Thus, you keep to the road. You prefer never to talk about your past, and you make an active effort to disguise your true identity. Anyone who shows an unusual interest in you could be a threat.

Alternatively, perhaps you earned your freedom through your success in the arena. Even so, your past haunts you. Old rivals from your fighting days, relatives of opponents you killed, and cocky young brawlers seeking to make a name for themselves all seek you out with bloody intent. Your fame is an unwelcome burden, just as likely to cause trouble as earn favors.

Once you entered the wide world, you had few skills aside from those you learned in the arena and under the tutelage of the pit masters. Mercenary work didn't appeal to you, since you've already had your fill of demanding masters. As an adventurer, you can risk your life as you choose and for your own profit. Life is much better this way.

At the Table: You are an expert on weapons, armor, and fighting styles. When you size up others, you look at them in terms of their fighting ability. You collect trophies from fallen enemies, both to respect the talent they displayed in standing against you and to commemorate your

victories. When you face a problem, violence is your preferred solution (soft words and subtle methods never served you well in the arena). Politics are beyond you. There's no obstacle that can't be overcome with a swift blow to the head. When it comes time to make plans, you argue for a direct and violent solution.

Your weapons, armor, and other tools of combat are your wards against defeat. You spend time each morning caring for your weapons and gear. A warrior who doesn't take care of his gear risks losing his next fight, and you always plan to win.

GUTTERSNIPE

Born into poverty, you grew up on the streets. When other children went home to their parents, you slept in back alleys and dilapidated abandoned buildings, getting food where you could and making friends and family out of those in similar straits. Those with roofs over their heads and doors to close against the night looked down upon you, calling you a worthless, no-good street urchin. They didn't understand the kind of skills you possessed, skills that allowed you to find what you needed to survive, whether that was food, drinkable water, or a safe place to sleep.

Youth: Living on the streets was tough—dodging bullies and gangs, scrounging for food or standing in line for a daily bowl of soup at the temple, avoiding the heavy hand of the local constables. You were always hungry, but you had the freedom to do as you pleased, and from time to time a generous passerby might give you a few coppers to run a quick errand or deliver a message. You spent a great deal of time dodging a gang of

Guttersnipes grow up on the street, taking whatever they can get

toughs who only seemed interested in making you steal on their behalf. You made up your mind that if you were going to be the one stealing, then you would be the one to pick the time and place, determine what was and wasn't an acceptable level of risk, and reap the benefit if you pulled it off.

Transition: You couldn't dodge the gang and the constables forever. Perhaps you bit off more than you could chew in a daring robbery. After that your choice was simple: leave town until the heat died down or die at the hands of the gang's brutal enforcers. You took to the road and found that your skills worked just as well in other cities as in your own. Adventuring offered you the chance to make a fortune and set something aside for the long term.

Perhaps your burgeoning talents came to the attention of a small band of adventurers who needed an item liberated from a certain wizard's bedchamber. While they distracted the old mage, you climbed the wall of his tower and plucked an amulet from his armoire. You made a lot of money on that job, and you decided this was the life for you. The victimized wizard might seek you out (whether you are aware of that or not) to avenge his loss. If your past catches up to you, you had best hope that your adventuring companions can help bail you out.

At the Table: Old habits die hard. You're accustomed to scrounging for basic necessities, so you tend to keep extra supplies on hand—you never want to go to sleep hungry again. When you have spending money, you have trouble holding on to it. A few nights in a sumptuous inn, seven-course meals, and other luxuries leave you ready to strap on your equipment and head back into the world for another adventure. You live for the day and cast aside worries, long-term plans, and the like. That doesn't mean that you are foolish or reckless, just that you appreciate the finer things in life. To you, it's obvious that you should put off hard work till tomorrow when there's strong drink and good food to enjoy today.

MARINER

With a salty breeze in your hair and a hardwood deck underfoot, you spent your life in a constant search for whatever lay over the endless horizon of the sea. You loved the sea and all the dangers that life aboard a sailing vessel offered. Above all, you enjoyed the freedom that you had on such a ship: freedom to travel the world, and freedom from the laws that govern the people living on land.

Youth: As a young sailor aboard a ship, your life was filled with work. Cleaning and repairing the ship took up the majority of your time. You also spent a fair amount of time on watch, keeping a lookout for other ships that could have hostile intent. In rare moments when you were not working, you were free to enjoy the passing sea, to sing songs and learn an instrument from another crew member, or to take lessons in navigation from the captain or first mate whenever they had time to give them. You spent time fishing, working in the galley with the ship's cook to prepare meals, or even practicing swordplay with the master of arms in case another ship attacked yours.

Transition: Life as a mariner is almost the same as life as an adventurer. You must face terrible monsters, venture into unknown territories, and stand ready to fight for your life at a moment's notice.

Perhaps a terrible storm capsized your ship. You were lucky enough to make it to shore in a strange land, but you have no idea what happened to the rest of the crew. To make ends meet, you put your skill with weapons or spells to good use. For now, you adventure to earn enough coin to survive (and, if you strike it rich, someday buy your own ship). You want to discover what happened to your shipmates. Perhaps the storm had a sinister origin, and even now an unknown enemy plots against you.

A run-in with pirates might have sent you on the path to adventure. You were captured and separated from your crewmates. You managed to escape, and now you have sworn to find and free your comrades. Perhaps your family owned the ship you served upon, and now you must rescue your brothers and sisters, parents and cousins. You have no idea where to begin your search, but you hope that over the course of your adventures you can find some clue to their location.

At the Table: You use nautical terms in everyday conversation. Your weapon is a cutlass rather than a scimitar. You drink rum rather than ale. You know a lot about ships and boats, refer to others as landlubbers or scalawags, and never turn down the chance to take a sea voyage. You've been to dozens of ports around the world, and you love to talk about your exploits in each one. You have amassed a wealth of knowledge, tall tales, and stories. If your group fights a medusa, you might recall legends about a similar creature that haunts the waves. When you enter a port city, you prefer to stay near the docks and visit taverns where you can find other sailors and ask them for news from across the seas.

NOBLE SCION

Born with a silver spoon in your mouth, you knew very little about living a common life. No matter what your interests, you had the best instructors. You had servants and soldiers who jumped to do your bidding and ensure your safety. The only higher authority you had to answer to was your family—particularly your parents, who were so busy with the administration of your birthright that they left your education and upbringing to trusted servants.

Youth: You toured the countryside from the back of a pillow-laden carriage, sipping freshly squeezed fruit juice from an ice-chilled carafe. You spent entire days taking lessons in the warmth and comfort of your personal chambers. When you were not pursuing your own education, you diverted yourself with games, music, theater, and flirtations. You attended elegant parties dressed all in silk, with properly coifed hair and manicured nails. Above all, you spent countless hours at the court, observing your parents preside over those who served them, settle disputes, pass edicts, and hand down judgments. Some would say that you were blessed from birth, but you believed that the simple fact of your presence bestowed a blessing on others.

Transition: Leaving behind an easy life of costume balls, servants, and rolling estates, you took up life as an adventurer. After all, the luxuriant life of a noble depends on one thing: money. If your family managed to lose its fortune (perhaps through a rival's machinations, perhaps through simple mismanagement), you must now fend for yourself in the world.

If you took up the study of magic, or spent long hours working under the tutelage of a swordmaster, you already have the skills needed to become an adventurer. What once served as an amusing diversion became the primary skill you need to return your family to prominence.

Your family's fall from grace could be more sinister in nature. Your father might have betrayed his liege or sold out to a foreign power. When his scheme was uncovered, your family was stripped of its title, wealth, and land. You must travel in secret or venture far from home, because the mere mention of your name is enough to incite a hostile response in your countrymen. Perhaps your father was innocent and an enemy engineered his fall. The real villains managed to disgrace and destroy a force for justice; you adventure to restore your family's good name and avenge your losses.

Illus. by H. Lyon

Alternatively, perhaps you were the youngest in your family, and therefore you were not in line to inherit your family's fortune. You were expected to join the clergy or follow some other respectable vocation. Horrified at the prospect of a life of boredom, you rebelled and set out on your own. Your family might have agents searching for you, so you must travel incognito. You care nothing for your family's money and now see your old life as a suffocating burden. You only want to wander the road, defying the politics and the social responsibilities of the station that demands your return.

At the Table: You are used to fine food and comfortable accommodations. While you fancy yourself tough enough to live an adventurer's life, you miss the comforts of home. When on the road, you would rather spend a night in an inn with a hot bath and a warm meal than rough it under the stars. You can't help but complain about the poor food, the sour wine, and other minor indignities that you must endure. It's beneath your dignity to whine, but sometimes you let others know that their best falls short of your expectations. You admire those whose accomplishments earn them the right for you to consider them your peers, but the sense of entitlement and

The noble born are guaranteed a life of luxury, but some individuals crave more than that

arrogance that has been ingrained in you since childhood sometimes bubbles to the surface.

SOLDIER

From the earliest age you can remember, you were a servant in the army of your lord. You drilled to march, you drilled to fight, and you even drilled to bathe and eat. Every waking moment was utilized to its maximum potential, and you kept moving with one purpose or another as long as daylight lasted. Learning to fight, cleaning weapons and armor, and taking care of the cavalry's steeds were only a few of the tasks that greeted you each day. No task assigned was meaningless or trivial, and all of them could be accomplished with a sense of honor and pride in knowing that you served an organization whose purpose was much larger than yourself.

Youth: As a child you spent your days cleaning. Everything needed to be cleaned twice a day, from pots and pans to the horses' bridles to your quarters and sleeping mat. Everything was checked and rechecked to make sure it was tended properly. As you grew older, your responsibilities also grew. You were set to repairing practice dummies, patching uniforms, and (when fortune favored you) exercising the horses. Additionally, as you continued to grow older and taller, you began to train with various weapons, becoming skilled in their use through almost constant repetition and practice.

Transition: A soldier's life is an ideal training ground for adventuring. Your knowledge in weapons, armor, and tactics serves you well. Perhaps the prospect of another year of taking orders, cleaning stables, marching in formation, and obeying your officers grew tiresome; as an adventurer, you can do what you want, when you want. Perhaps you defied an unjust order and deserted rather than commit a war crime. Now you must dodge press gangs, bounty hunters, and old comrades if you want to keep your freedom.

Your old military unit might have been destroyed in battle, leaving you aimless and alone. Common labor or some other peaceful trade proved too boring and mundane for you.

Since you only know how to fight, an adventurer's life was the best fit for you. Although you enjoy your new life, your past still haunts you. Your unit's old enemies still seek you. Your surviving comrades might (wrongfully) blame you for their defeat. Perhaps your unit's destruction was no accident of war. Instead, someone wants you and your old comrades dead, and that individual has the ways and means to hunt you down one by one.

At the Table: You have a story about a battle you took part in for almost every occasion. You can't help but argue from an expert's point of view, and at times you are too dismissive of those who lack experience in your eyes. You cry out orders in battle, shouting advice and encouragement to your comrades. Part of you thinks that you simply know better than everyone else when it comes to combat, but you also feel a strong attachment and a sense of camaraderie with those who fight alongside you. You want to do everything in your power to keep your fellow adventurers safe.

TRIBAL ORIGIN

Born among the people, you were raised by the members of your extended family, all of whom participated in your upbringing to one extent or another. Your mother taught you to gather food and cook, your father taught you to hunt and fish. Your grandfather taught you to treat hide and make weapons, and your grandmother taught you the history of your people. Everyone had his or her place at home, and you experienced times of both joy and sorrow with all your kin.

Youth: As a child, your activities changed each day based on the needs of your people. Some days you gathered food with your mother, and others you stalked through the underbrush in pursuit of prey with your father. Your tasks depended on what was needed at the time, and you were productive for at least a few hours each day. You also spent a good deal of time in play—swimming with and running races against your siblings and cousins, practicing the use of weapons for hunting and defense from your enemies, and playing elaborate games meant to sharpen your senses and strengthen your body. From time to time you were even asked to stand watch and keep an eye out for the goblins that liked to attack your encampment without warning.

Transition: The road from your tribe's home territory to the heart of civilization was a long and arduous one. Perhaps you took to it freely, when the lure of cities and towns proved too strong. Perhaps the transition was violent and sudden, when a slave trader, raiding party, or other force from the outside world swooped in and plucked you from your home.

If you willingly left home, you could have felt a strong sense of wanderlust from an early age. You always wanted to know what lay over the mountains. The outside world seemed

Illus. by E. Fiegenschuh

Those of tribal origin band together for the good of all

so much more interesting than your humdrum existence, especially when the tribal elders told you stories of the great cities that stood beyond the horizon. Perhaps an old adventurer of the tribe, a warrior who had ventured into the world and returned years later with great treasure and renown, stoked your imagination with the tales of her adventures. As soon as you were old enough, you hired on with a passing caravan and ventured into the world.

Events could have forced you from home. While you were out hunting one day, a gang of slavers captured you and sold you into the service of a rich merchant. After years of toil, you escaped and now run free. While part of you wants to return home, civilization has proven too intriguing to leave behind. You remain one step ahead of the slave lord's bounty hunters, and by improving your skills in weapons and magic you hope one day to foil their pursuit once and for all. Perhaps the slave lords destroyed your village and you have no home to return to. You remain in civilization to grow in power until you can avenge your people one day. Once you have slain the slave lords and burned their fortress to the ground, you can found a new village peopled by those you free from their chains.

At the Table: You always compare the character of civilization to that of your people and find it wanting. You are fond of quoting your grandmother's sayings to drive home this point. Civilized folk lie, cheat, and steal from each other, actions that would doom a tribe in the wild. You see civilized folk as soft and complacent. Few of them have stalked a beast in the wild, and fewer still have fought off a dire wolf or displacer beast attack. Your origin sets you apart, but it makes you stronger, tougher, and more cunning than the soft-bellied folk of the cities. While you might be ignorant of civilization and its customs, you are by no means a fool.

PERSONALITY ARCHETYPES

Each of the following personality archetypes includes a quote (something a character corresponding to that archetype might say), a description, and a list of classes and of traits that are especially appropriate to that archetype. You are not limited to these classes and traits; they simply represent good combinations for D&D characters.

AGENT

"It shall be as you command."

An agent adventures not for herself but for an organization or society, whether a thieves guild sends her to gather information, she explores new territory for an emperor, or she carries the name of her deity into new lands. An agent might be loyal to her organization, or she might resent her role and look for a way to escape. An agent can create interesting dynamics in an adventuring party, especially when she must choose between her fellow PCs and her organization.

Classes: Bard, beguiler, cleric, druid, knight, monk, paladin, ranger, rogue, scout, warmage, wizard.

Traits: Ambitious, serious.

CHALLENGER

"I must fight him. Only by striving against those superior to myself can I achieve greatness."

A challenger adventures for personal growth. He cares about treasure and magic only if they can further this goal, and he cares about fame not at all. A challenger tries to reach the pinnacle of achievement in his chosen path, whether that path is defined by combat, magic, stealth, or some other ability. He does this by throwing himself against progressively greater challenges, reveling in those just on the edge of his ability to overcome. A challenger is a good character to have in an adventuring party, since he does not quail under duress and often allows other party members to take the best treasure. Indeed, some challengers see magic items as crutches, and they seek to attain perfection without them.

Classes: Barbarian, dragon shaman, duskblade, fighter, knight, marshal, monk, rogue, swashbuckler, warlock, warmage, wizard.

Traits: Bold, disciplined.

COMPANION

"Stand firm, Regdar. I am at your side."

A companion is the best ally anyone could ever hope for. He is loyal and dedicated, and he often shares a special kinship with a particular individual. A companion supports his allies in all they do and never abandons or betrays them. He doesn't lead, but he does offer cogent advice and support.

Classes: Cleric, duskblade, favored soul, fighter, knight, monk, paladin, sorcerer.

Traits: Connected, funny, loyal.

CRUSADER

"Crush the minotaurs and spread the word of Obad-Hai!"

A crusader serves a cause. The cause might be noble or heinous, universal or personal. She could belong to an organization that shares her cause, or she could act as her individual beliefs demand. Either way, a crusader adventures to further her cause. The normal motivations for adventuring—wealth, power, fame, personal betterment, excitement—hold scant appeal for a crusader; she is happiest when she is directly serving her cause. She keeps her party adventuring, since whenever her fellow PCs don't know what to do next, she is quick to suggest a course of action.

Classes: Cleric, druid, favored soul, knight, marshal, monk, paladin, wizard.

Traits: Bold, patriotic, religious.

DAREDEVIL

"You guys stay here. I'm going to scale the wall, sneak past the guards, swim the moat, have a look around, and come back."

A daredevil gets a rush from dangerous stunts. He is a risk-taker and a gambler, willing to put his money, his reputation, and his life at stake purely for exhilaration. He's the one who opens the door even though it's probably trapped, who enters the cave even though there's probably a dragon inside, and who puts on the necklace even though it's probably cursed. He's a valuable addition to a party, since he's always willing to take on the tasks no one else wants to do (and he often has the skills to succeed and even excel at them), but his recklessness can be his downfall—and that of his party.

Classes: Bard, beguiler, duskblade, hexblade, rogue, scout, sorcerer, swashbuckler, warlock.

Traits: Bold, energetic, flamboyant.

EXPLORER

"If we continue along this road, we'll come to the fallen country of Abu'nix."

An explorer is driven to find new places, interesting cultures, and fascinating objects. When she reads a map, she looks to the edges and wonders what's beyond. Her eyes fall first on the unknown areas: What's in the middle of that forest? On top of those mountains? Beneath that ocean? She is happiest when she discovers something new. She is driven to be the first person to look at a new land, battle a new creature, or discover a new item. An explorer keeps her party moving, and she guarantees constant adventure as she points her companions toward uncharted territory.

Classes: Barbarian, bard, druid, duskblade, ranger, rogue, scout.

Traits: Driven, exotic.

INNOCENT

"I've never done anything like that."

An innocent might have seen violence and brutality, but she did not participate. An innocent is blameless . . . so far. Other characters, particularly elder ones, find an innocent endearing because of this quality. An innocent might adventure to dispel her innocence, because she craves excitement, because she has no other choice, or for any of the other reasons characters adventure. An innocent is a blank slate, and seeing how she maintains or loses her innocence creates dynamic tension in the adventuring party. Seeing her triumph despite, or perhaps because of, her innocence is exhilarating.

Classes: Bard, cleric, druid, favored soul, monk, sorcerer, wizard.

Traits: Carefree, kind, naïve.

LEADER

"Onward, men! We have those orcs on the run!"

A leader leads. Others look to him for guidance, and he provides it. He might provide assurance and protection, or he might instill fear in his allies as well as his enemies. He speaks on his party's behalf and organizes his fellow PCs in combat, shouting strategies (preferably in languages his opponents can't understand). He drives the party forward outside of combat as well, keeping it moving toward a common goal, searching for adventure, and deciding which adventures to accept and which to decline. He might share leadership gracefully, or he might demand that power and position for himself. Leaders often, but not always, have high Charisma scores.

Classes: Cleric, dragon shaman, fighter, knight, marshal, paladin, warmage.

Traits: Ambitious, charming.

MARTYR

"My life for you."

A martyr willingly and even eagerly puts her life on the line for a greater purpose. This purpose might be a cause, an organization, a specific person, a group of people, or just about anything else. A martyr is willing to die to further this purpose, and in fact expects to do so. However, she refuses to die in vain—her death must have a greater meaning, and it must inspire others to greatness. A martyr's selflessness makes her a valuable addition to an adventuring party, since she is often willing to sacrifice herself for her companions. Her greater purpose provides motivation for adventures, but she can become self-righteous and reckless in her risk-taking.

Classes: Cleric, druid, favored soul, fighter, knight, monk, paladin.

Traits: Kind, merciful, reformed.

MERCENARY

"If there's gold involved, I'm in. Otherwise, count me out."

A mercenary cares about material things—chiefly gold, but also the goods and services that gold buys, such as equipment, magic items, good food, and good times. Concepts such as morality and loyalty matter little to a mercenary, or so she says. Circumstances and good friends might make her change her beliefs, but money still holds a special place in her soul. A mercenary is a good addition to an adventuring party because she is easy to motivate.

Classes: Barbarian, bard, beguiler, fighter, hexblade, marshal, rogue, sorcerer, wizard.

Traits: Boastful, greedy.

From an early age, crusaders train in anticipation of the day when they're called to action

Illus. by R. Spencer

ORPHAN

"I've been on my own my whole life. Always alone."

An orphan has no parents, at least not that he can remember, or parental figures in his life. He might have grown up in an orphanage or on the street, but in any case he spent his formative years fending for himself. This upbringing taught him self-reliance and confidence but also distrust of others. An orphan could be curious about his parentage and his lost past, and seeking answers to such questions can spark adventure. After he learns to trust his adventuring partners, he cleaves to them like the family he never had.

Classes: Barbarian, bard, beguiler, cleric, druid, fighter, hexblade, monk, ranger, rogue, scout, sorcerer, warlock.

Traits: Calm.

PROPHET

"I speak the word of Pelor."

A prophet sees herself as the voice of a deity in the world—which might or might not be true. She doesn't necessarily crusade or convert, but she does uphold her deity's values and believes that she embodies a piece of that deity in physical form. Other faithful worshipers gather about her, and priests of the faith welcome her. She prompts adventures that further her deity's ends and leads her party into adventures that she claims her deity instructed her to undertake.

Classes: Cleric, dragon shaman, druid, favored soul, monk, paladin.

Traits: Energetic, fatalistic, religious.

REBEL

"What has the kingdom done for us? They've rubbed our faces in the mud and expected us to be grateful!"

A rebel has a grudge against established authority. He might dislike all authority, or his feelings might be more focused on a single government (such as a kingdom), a small group (such as his family), or an individual (such as a baron, merchant prince, former employer, or parent). Highly individualistic, a rebel engages in activities in defiance of authority, and he might actively fight against that authority and all its manifestations. Whether bitter or idealistic, all rebels value their freedom highly. A rebel helps an adventuring party find adventure when he flees from his latest escapade or puts his next plan into motion.

Classes: Bard, fighter, hexblade, ranger, rogue, scout, swashbuckler.

Traits: Driven.

RENEGADE

"I can never return to my place of birth. My companions are my home now."

*Mialee the wizard
as a mercenary*

For some reason, a renegade cannot go home. He might be a wanted criminal on the run. He might have disgraced himself or be a member of a dishonored family. He might be a political exile or might hold beliefs counter to those currently in power. Perhaps his banishment will be lifted and he can return home after he accomplishes a specific task (atoning for a sin, recovering a lost artifact, capturing the real criminal), offering a motivation for him and his companions to adventure. Alternatively, he could be making his way in the world as best he can, now that his roots to home are severed.

Classes: Barbarian, bard, druid, duskblade, fighter, hexblade, ranger, rogue, scout, sorcerer, warlock, wizard.

Traits: Exotic, skilled, vengeful.

ROYALTY

"No, I'm not the princess. I just look like her."

This character might be a princess, a ruler's spouse, or a cousin of the royal family. For some reason, she is roughing it as an adventurer. Perhaps tales of adventure excite her, and she ran away from home to experience such events for herself. Perhaps her parents (or the court) were cruel or demanded unreasonable things of her, and she escaped. Perhaps she simply wished to experience life as an adventurer for personal or spiritual reasons (seeing firsthand what her people's lives are like, emulating her adventuring great-grandfather, or escaping a persistent suitor). Whatever the case, despite her exalted status she is largely unable to draw upon her wealth, fame, and power in the course of her adventures, and she and her companions could be forced to dodge agents from home seeking to bring her back. Still, her courtly experience provides valuable knowledge and insight, especially when her party deals with high-ranking government officials.

Classes: Bard, cleric, fighter, marshal, paladin, sorcerer, warmage, wizard.

Traits: Calm, charming, connected.

SAGE

"That is the rare and valuable Numhatch mushroom. You can grind it with other additives to make a deadly poison, smear its juice on your skin to reduce wrinkles, or stew it for a tasty meal."

A sage knows a lot about a lot, and he enjoys spreading his knowledge around. He might be self-righteous and condescending, or he could be humble and kind. Some sages possess spiritual knowledge and excel at explaining kinships, natural connections, one's purpose in life, and otherwise serving as spiritual guides. Others maintain a vast store of concrete, useful information. Many specialize, and some adventure to improve their knowledge in a given field through personal observation. When the PCs come across something unusual, they turn to a sage for advice.

Classes: Cleric, druid, sorcerer, wizard.

Traits: Calm, erudite.

SAVAGE

"I do not understand your ways, but I will fight for you."

A savage comes from a primitive culture, and the trappings of civilization that the other PCs take for granted—metalworking, architecture (stone buildings), distilled alcoholic drinks, and the like—are foreign to her. She greets new sights with wonder and excitement. Though her ways are primitive, she shares ties with the natural and spiritual worlds that others envy. She possesses a raw knowledge and wisdom that helps her and her allies out of difficult situations. She might face prejudice from others, but she is a stalwart friend to those who treat her well. Given enough time in this new culture, she can assimilate parts of it, creating a unique fusion of wild power and sophisticated knowledge.

Classes: Barbarian, dragon shaman, druid, ranger.

Traits: Brutal, exotic, naïve.

SEEKER

"Let us press on. The White Staff could be in that cave."

A seeker adventures because he is looking for something, often an object or an individual. The object of his quest might be specific (the *White Staff of the Grimalkin*) or general (a way to stop the disease in his home village). He grudgingly participates in adventures that do not pertain directly to his quest, but the object or individual he seeks gives him focus and provides motivation for further adventures. When his allies join him on his adventures, a seeker provides continued impetus for additional adventures.

Classes: Barbarian, cleric, dragon shaman, duskblade, favored soul, fighter, knight, monk, ranger, scout, sorcerer, wizard.

Traits: Angry, driven.

SIMPLE SOUL

"Ha ha! I like you, my friend!"

A simple soul enjoys the basic amenities of life: good food, good company, and good times. She also enjoys doing whatever she excels at, whether that's slaying monsters, casting spells, converting the faithless, or picking pockets. A simple soul sees adventuring as a job—an exciting and dangerous one, but a job. After a hard day in the dungeons, she takes pleasure in sitting by the fire, roasting mutton, and exchanging stories and gossip

Illus. by R. Spencer

Lidda the rogue as a savage

with her companions. A simple soul doesn't drive the party toward adventure, but she is a reliable and steadfast ally.

Classes: Barbarian, cleric, fighter, rogue, sorcerer.

Traits: Funny, skilled.

STRATEGIST

"If you wait here, and you wait there, and you distract the harpies over here while I cast my spells, we should take them with few difficulties."

A strategist likes to think things out. He is at his best when he's at a desk with a quill, planning. He plans for combat situations—even those he probably won't encounter—as well as other circumstances, such as the proper way to address the court at a victory feast, the right path to take to get to the dungeon, and the right spells to prepare before an encounter. He concerns himself with his party's well-being; if he knows what he's doing, he is a valuable asset.

Classes: Beguiler, duskblade, fighter, marshal, paladin, rogue, warlock, warmage, wizard.

Traits: Conservative, erudite, serious.

THEORIST

"Fascinating. And I wonder what happens if I cast stone shape in these circumstances?"

A theorist is equivalent to a scientist in the D&D world. She adventures to test her ideas and hypotheses and to see what happens under certain circumstances. Her interests could lie in magic, either in specific schools or in general ("What happens if I create illusions of demons in front of angels?"), strategy ("Try using your hammer against the vampire, and tell me what happens"), medicine ("Well, I guess this herb might help"), or anything else imaginable. A theorist adds energy and motivation to the adventuring party as she constantly seeks new ideas to understand and new circumstances under which to perform experiments. Her experiences often produce useful knowledge, which she and her party can apply to other adventures in the future.

Classes: Cleric, fighter, marshal, warlock, wizard.

Trait: Disciplined.

TRICKSTER

"You go in first, and cover your eyes. I have a surprise for you."

A trickster has a mind for pranks, bluffs, lies, and surprises. He likes to cause trouble and excels at misleading and fooling others. Sometimes he tricks others purely for enjoyment; other times his skills serve a useful purpose. He prefers subtlety and persuasion over combat. With his quick wits, a trickster often speaks for his party, especially when the conversation is difficult or dangerous.

Classes: Bard, beguiler, rogue, swashbuckler, warlock, wizard (illusionist).

Traits: Flamboyant, funny.

WANDERER

"I have no home. I have no family. I have no name."

A wanderer is a mysterious soul. She keeps her past to herself and doesn't talk much. Perhaps something horrible happened to her when she was younger. Perhaps she committed an unforgivable crime, or was accused of a crime she didn't commit.

Perhaps she simply got bored. Whatever the case, a wanderer left her home and has been drifting from place to place ever since. Her vague and intriguing past can be the impetus for interesting adventures and roleplaying experiences.

Classes: Barbarian, bard, beguiler, druid, duskblade, favored soul, hexblade, monk, ranger, rogue, scout, sorcerer, swashbuckler, warlock.

Traits: Peaceful.

PERSONALITY TRAITS

Described below are thirty personality traits, adjectives that others might use to describe your character. Select two to four of these and combine them to create a deep and believable character. Each trait description begins with a quote that epitomizes that trait.

Some traits lend themselves to certain archetypes, classes, or alignments. If you are looking for a challenge to stretch your roleplaying skills, try selecting traits that do not seem obvious matches for your character's alignment or archetype. Doing so makes for more interesting characters. An angry, fatalistic neutral good bard is more unusual, and thus more memorable, than a friendly, flamboyant neutral good bard.

AMBITIOUS

"I'll be the greatest wizard who ever lived."

You have big plans. You want to attain the highest heights and outdo all the rest. One day you'll take your place in the history books, become a legend, and perhaps even attain godhood.

At the Table: You speak of your plans and dreams. You make friends with powerful NPCs who might help you, even if you personally dislike them. The monetary reward for a successful adventure is nice, but the political favors and popularity the deed wins you are more important. You care little for money and gems. Instead, you always want the pick of magic items and artifacts the group finds. The Leadership feat is a great way to start your quest for empire or undying glory. You consider your eager followers to be among your most valued assets.

ANGRY

"You won't like me. Ever."

You're ticked off all the time. You enjoy taking out your anger on poor, unsuspecting monsters.

At the Table: You speak in curt sentences when angered. When it comes time to battle a monster, you use offensive spells or attacks that deal massive damage. Maximize your Power Attack feat, or prepare evocation spells that deal large amounts of damage. When you are angry, you seek to dish out tremendous punishment as quickly as possible to vent your temper.

BOASTFUL

"How do you like that, huh? Want some more?"

You're a showoff. You gloat about your accomplishments and disparage your enemies—calling them names, making rude gestures, and otherwise taunting them.

At the Table: You take mementos from defeated foes and show them off in public. When a foe or rival challenges your skill, you never back down. Each strike you deliver comes with a personal insult to match. When a foe pulls off an impressive maneuver, you make a big show of your disdain. You might make Intimidate checks to show off your skill while demoralizing others.

BOLD

"Come, let us crush the enemy where he stands!"

You are brave, eagerly risking your skin to come to grips with the enemy. Others might call this trait foolhardiness.

At the Table: You lead from the front. Unless a rogue or ranger scouts ahead, you want to be at the forefront of any attack. You charge the foe in battle to bring the fight to him. In your mind, the key to victory lies in seizing momentum. Feats such as Improved Initiative reflect your aggressive attitude.

BRUTAL

"He surrendered? Sorry, I didn't hear it; I was too busy chopping off his head."

You show little mercy to your enemies, preferring to hit them until they stop moving.

At the Table: Power Attack is your calling card if you are a fighter. A feat such as Spell Focus (evocation) captures the feel of this trait for spellcasters. Too much damage is never enough. The more destruction you can reap, the better. Unlike an angry character, you fight with a cold, calculating demeanor. An angry character with Power Attack might leap into the fray and convert her full base attack bonus into damage, while you play the odds and slowly but steadily increase your damage to deliver the maximum amount of punishment.

CALM

"Yes, I see the dragon. What's the big deal?"

You remain unfazed even in dire circumstances. You could be supremely confident, you could be otherworldly, or you could just be hard to impress.

At the Table: You are the eye at the center of the storm. You rely on reason and rationality despite the chaos that rages around you. While others shout and argue, you always speak in calm, measured tones. When you do lose your temper, your friends remember the event for years to come. The Iron Will feat reflects your indomitable spirit. Even an evil wizard's spells can't break your will.

CAREFREE

"Ah, it doesn't matter if we wake the wizard. What's the worst he can do, kill us?"

You have trouble taking things seriously. To you, adventuring is a big game.

At the Table: Nothing gets you down, regardless of how daunting a situation might be. You let the fates take you where they may. Your attitude can prove annoying to stuffy, lawful types, but in the face of grave danger your carefree ways lighten the mood and bring hope to the party. The bard class is a great match for this trait, since its musical abilities reflect your ability to bring hope to your allies.

CHARMING

"Let me hold that for you, my lady."

You go out of your way to observe social niceties. You might or might not have ulterior motives.

At the Table: Every word you speak is a tool calculated to help get you what you want. You are calm when the group needs a rational voice and smoothly effective when it's time to take down a monster. Like a master politician, you always work a room, seeking to win people over and make them like you. Put as many ranks as possible into Diplomacy to reflect your winning personality.

CONNECTED

"You'd better not be insulting my sister."

You have a historical connection with one of the other party members. You might be siblings, childhood friends, or fellow students of the same master. You might like each other, or you might not; it's also possible that one or both of you is unaware of your connection. Perhaps one of you was sent to protect the other or otherwise keep an eye on her.

At the Table: When the group faces a problem, you invariably find someone who can help you. When you enter a tavern, you strike up a conversation with the bartender, gossip with the locals, and otherwise fit right in. You swap stories, share news, and make friends even in a foreign land. The Gather Information skill is an excellent tool to showcase this trait. When the group needs to learn the latest news, you draw on your social network to hear what's out there.

CONSERVATIVE

"The old ways are the best ways."

You like order and stability. You believe that if the current system supports these qualities, you should work to ensure its longevity.

At the Table: You prefer tried and true methods over new ideas. If an old trick or tactic worked before, you'd rather try it again than work on a new plan that might or might not be as effective. You are slow and deliberate, believing that rash thought and quick actions are a good way to get yourself in trouble. During a battle, you hang back and wait for your foes to tip their hands. Rather than charge, you prefer to move forward slowly and ready an attack.

DISCIPLINED

"An hour of meditation and prayer before sleep."

You are rigorous and structured in your personal endeavors. This trait can manifest as constant combat training, time spend in meditation or prayer, monitoring the food you eat and the liquids you drink, and similar activities.

At the Table: You go through an exercise or meditation regimen each morning. If you miss it, you feel uneasy about the lapse in routine for the rest of the day. In your mind, your body is as much a tool as your sword, armor, or spellbook. It needs rest and proper care. You insist on getting a full night's sleep whenever possible, and you expect others to meet your standards. The Iron Will feat does a good job of reflecting your dedication.

DRIVEN

"I don't care how many vampires the inscription says are beyond this door. I'm going to get it open."

You are relentless in your pursuit of tasks. You might be driven only when you are involved in specific tasks (slaying demons, saving a friend), or you might be driven in everything you do.

At the Table: You never give up. Even in a hopeless situation, your impulse is to keep fighting. During the game, take 20 as often as possible—you're determined to keep trying until you succeed. You steadily overwhelm obstacles with your tireless devotion. The force of your will batters down your foes. The Great Fortitude feat allows you to display your indomitable nature.

ENERGETIC

"Okay, we've killed the trolls and grabbed the treasure and bypassed the traps—what's next?"

You brim with energy. Maybe you eat too much sugar or ingest too much caffeine, or maybe it's just in your nature, but for whatever reason, you're always ready to take on the next task, challenge, or mission.

At the Table: You never take 20. That activity requires patience and focus that you simply lack. In battle, you are always in motion. The Improved Initiative feat does a great job of reflecting your nature, as does the Tumble skill.

ERUDITE

"Our current plight derives directly from our dearth of aureate remuneration."

You are well schooled, and you like to show it off. You use big words just because you can.

At the Table: Purchase ranks in as many Knowledge skills as possible. Spread them around if your primary skills are maxed out. A broad range of knowledge allows you to answer almost any question. Make references to the campaign setting's past. An orc invasion might remind you of a previous humanoid incursion, and you speak of that attack at length to advise your allies. Work with the DM to gain access to more background and history of the campaign world that you can work into play.

EXOTIC

"Where I come from, this is normal."

You're different from most people of the region. You might be from an atypical culture or of a different race; you could belong to an unusual religion or organization. Others see you as strange and interesting, and they might be prejudiced against you or attracted to you.

At the Table: You find the local practices and traditions fascinating. You use a distinctive greeting, and you dress in your native land's garb. The Exotic Weapon Proficiency feat is a good choice to demonstrate your culture's unique aspects. Alternatively, you can fight with a trident or scythe or other weapon that PCs rarely use. If you are an arcane spellcaster, choose spells that a typical member of your class rarely employs (new spells out of this book would be a good start). If you are a divine spellcaster, work with your DM to find a suitable little-known deity.

FATALISTIC

"None of us is long for this world."

The end is coming. Maybe you'll help it get here faster.

At the Table: You fight with a fanatic's energy and conviction. You are a relentless foe and a great ally. Since the world is about to end, you do what you can to help your allies and smite your foes. Place ranks in Knowledge (religion) to reflect your mastery of dogma and prophecy. You study both your chosen faith and the religions of heretics, the better to fight them.

FLAMBOYANT

"With a twist of my sword, a couple of steps to the right, and . . . ha! The apple is sliced neatly in two!"

You do everything with flash and panache. You're never at a loss for words, and you don't mind standing out in a crowd. Your dress and fighting style are particularly distinctive.

At the Table: Weapon Finesse and Combat Expertise are a great combination for a fighter who prefers speed, agility, and grace over brute force. A flamboyant caster uses spells with dramatic visual effects, such as *lightning bolt*.

FUNNY

"What did the fighter say when asked if he liked mutton? 'Sword of.' Ha!"

You have a sense of humor. Others might or might not appreciate it. Many kinds of humor exist; yours might be quick-witted, slapstick, pun-heavy, anachronistic, vulgar, inappropriate, clever, dry, sarcastic, or some combination of these.

At the Table: The Perform (comedy) skill is perfect for you. When your group goes to a tavern, you make jokes and do you best to entertain everyone. Even if you have amassed a great fortune, you still love putting on a performance at the local watering hole for a few coins.

GREEDY

"Let's loot 'em!"

You love to amass money and other forms of materialistic rewards. Recognition means little to you in comparison to the thrill you feel when you stand over a defeated monster's treasure hoard.

At the Table: The Appraise skill is your favorite tool. When exploring a ruin, you take the time to check over anything that looks valuable. While everyone else gathers an ogre lord's coins and gems, you pull off his boots and armor to sell back in town.

KIND

"There, does that feel better?"

You go out of your way to help people, with no desire for a reward in return. Others see you as a nice person.

At the Table: You carry extra potions to heal your allies, along with ammunition, food, water, and other goods to keep the group going. When you have to choose between attacking a foe and using aid another to help an ally, you usually opt for the second choice.

LOYAL

"You can count on me."

You never let your allies down, abandon them, or betray them, and you stay by their sides even when it irritates them.

At the Table: Iron Will and other feats that improve your saving throws are right up your alley. Even a foe's spells cannot necessarily prevent you from helping your allies.

MERCIFUL

"He surrendered. Let's let him go."

You show leniency to defeated enemies. You might have ulterior motives for your generosity.

At the Table: When facing a badly injured foe, use a free action to offer it the option to surrender. Ready an attack to strike if it keeps fighting you.

NAÏVE

"Why is that person angry at me?"

You are inexperienced and perhaps led a sheltered existence before becoming an adventurer. You sometimes make mistakes because you don't know any better, but you mean well, and your naïveté lends you a certain charm.

At the Table: You make social gaffes due to your insular outlook. While others navigate situations with tact and aplomb, you stumble ahead like a bull in a china shop. Avoid placing ranks in Charisma-based skills, particular Gather Information and Intimidate. A poor Wisdom score, and the attendant low Will save, illustrates your naïve nature.

PATRIOTIC

"For the glory of the queen!"

You are devoted to your country, right or wrong.

At the Table: You prefer to fight in your homeland's traditional style. Your weapons, armor, and spells are more than simple tools—they are symbols of your homeland. Feats such as Weapon Focus and Spell Focus illustrate your tight bond with such symbols.

PEACEFUL

"Wait, this does not have to end in bloodshed!"

You dislike combat and killing, preferring to use diplomacy, subtlety, trickery, and other nonviolent means to solve your problems. However, when there is no other choice, you draw steel alongside your allies.

At the Table: The Diplomacy skill is your best asset, since you can use it to smooth out confrontations that might otherwise turn violent. Whenever you have a chance, step into a situation and use a few carefully considered words to defuse tensions.

REFORMED

"I used to kill people for money, but that was in another part of my life."

You have gone through a significant life change. Perhaps you're an ex-criminal turning over a new leaf or a new devotee of a religion. Perhaps you're a former nice guy who has decided that kindness doesn't pay.

At the Table: A few ranks in Hide and Move Silently betray your past. You might also invest skill points in Open Lock and Search, depending on the sorts of crimes you once took part in.

RELIGIOUS

"Kord grant me strength."

You revere a higher power. You might worship a single deity, or you might include all the gods in your prayers.

At the Table: Knowledge (religion) is more than a source of trivia and information for you. It provides you counsel and advice in almost any situation. When you argue with others, you cite scripture and religious teachings as important points of debate.

SERIOUS

"How can you think of dancing at a time like this?"

You take everything seriously and have little or no sense of humor.

At the Table: You grumble when others make jokes or venture off topic. During a planning session, you are the one who calls for order and keeps things organized. Invest a few ranks in Knowledge skills to give you the experience and insight needed to back up your demand for focus and careful planning.

SKILLED

"Spiced crab legs tonight!"

Before you were an adventurer, you were a skilled at some other trade. You might have been a blacksmith, a chef, a shepherd, a dancer, a sneak thief, or just about anything else.

At the Table: Invest ranks in Profession and Craft skills. Whenever you have the chance to use them, leap at the opportunity. Depending on the nature of your skills, you might carry a full set of tools even into a dangerous dungeon. For example, a skilled cook insists on carrying the group's food and preparing a nice meal each evening, while a skilled dancer looks for likely partners at the local tavern and accepts invitations to the local lord's ball as a matter of course.

VENGEFUL

"Giants? Wipe them out. All of them."

You have a grudge against a particular creature type, organization, country, or individual. Perhaps the offenders killed your family, burned your village, or kicked you when you were little.

At the Table: Take a level of ranger to gain the favored enemy class feature against your chosen foe. Make notes on each opponent you face and track the reasons you have to seek vengeance against them. The Power Attack feat, or spells that deal lots of explosive damage, are good choices to mete out punishment against your chosen foes.

BEING A GOOD PLAYER AT THE TABLE

This section offers some specific ideas on how to make each game session a more enjoyable experience for you and for everyone else at the table.

MANAGING THE PAPERWORK

Every D&D player uses a lot of paper. You have a character sheets that might be many pages in length. You might also have sheets that list the spells available to you, your equipment, pages of notes from adventures present and past, and your plans for the future. In addition, you probably have books like this one lying around the playing space.

The following bits of advice can help you manage this paperwork.

Write Everything in Pencil: This caveat is most important when it comes to your character sheet. Since the numbers and names that summarize your character's abilities will change over the course of your character's career, and even during specific adventures or rounds, you want to be able to mark the changes on your character sheet. Eventually, your character sheet will be smudged and torn from writing, erasing, and rewriting; feel free to treat yourself to a new sheet at this point.

Do Things the Same Way Your Friends Do: If you and the other players keep track of your characters' statistics in the same way, you save time and effort when one player can't show up and another has to take control of his character. How do you record hit points? Attack bonuses? Used spells? It helps to talk about these details and settle on a standard way of doing things. This way, you can spend less time trying to decipher a friend's code and more time playing the game.

Keep Track of Your Character Sheet: Losing your character sheet is bad. You then have to recreate the character as best you can or, in extreme circumstances, scrap it and start a new character. If you discover your sheet is missing at the beginning of a session, you delay the game and waste your fellow players' time. Make sure you store your character sheet properly and, if you cannot make it to a game session, send it along with one of your friends. Better yet, your DM could keep backup copies of all your group's character sheets, updated on a regular basis, so he can assign someone to play a character as an NPC in the event of that player's unexpected absence. Some DMs play custodian for all their players' character sheets, collecting them at the end of a session and passing them out again at the beginning of the next—thereby absolving you of all responsibility in the matter.

Use Page Notations: Inevitably, you'll have to flip through a rulebook at some point, perhaps to look up exactly how a feat, spell, or special ability functions. You can save time in this process by writing down page and book references on your character sheet for any complex or unusual feature. For example, if you select a spell from this book, next to it you might write "PH2 105," indicating the book and page number where the description is printed.

Know What Your Stuff Does: Even better than page notations, it's best if you simply know how your spells, feats, items, and special abilities function. When in doubt, quickly review them before a session.

Plan Your Combat Actions: When it's not your turn in combat, you should be thinking about what you're going to do when it is your turn. Flip through a rulebook and make sure you know the pertinent details about the spell you are going to cast. Then, when your turn comes up, the other players don't have to wait for you to figure out what you want to do. If possible, also have a backup plan in case things change suddenly before your turn (new foes enter the battle, the character you had planned to attack goes down, or the like).

Keep Track of Timed Effects: Many spells and other effects have durations measured in rounds. If you employ such a spell or ability, it's your responsibility to keep track of the duration (the DM has plenty of other things to worry about). One good way of keeping track of time is to make tally marks on a piece of scrap paper. Another technique is to use a die to keep track of the time—either count up for the total duration or count down for time remaining; at the start of your turn each round, turn the die to the next number. Be careful, though, that you don't accidentally roll this "duration die."

Rely on DM Arbitration: Playing the game is more important than looking up rules. Good Dungeon Masters don't like taking time away from the game to page through rulebooks, and so they often provide instant rulings on debated topics instead of suspending gameplay for a time-intensive rule search. Go along with the DM's arbitration, and then after the game or during a break you can look up the official rule and let your DM know; this information will be useful the next time that rule comes up.

Have All Pertinent Statistics on Hand: If your character has a familiar, animal companion, mount, cohort, or similar ally, make sure you have the proper statistics handy.

Use Electronic Aids: While they are by no means necessary, laptop computers and PDAs are valuable assets. They cut down on search time and on table clutter. You can keep an electronic character sheet and update it when you attain a new level or take poison damage. (Electronic character sheets also reduce the risk of losing a character sheet—and if you lose your laptop, you have bigger problems to worry about.) Numerous software programs that help you create D&D characters and use electronic character sheets are available. The System Reference Document is available for free on the Wizards of the Coast website, and it includes most of the spells and feats in the *Player's Handbook*. Typing "Ctrl-F, fireball" is much faster than paging through a book searching for the appropriate reference.

ROLLING CONVENTIONS

You roll a lot of dice in a typical D&D game. The following are common rolling conventions that you can use if you like; they accelerate gameplay and reduce ambiguity.

Decide What to Do if the Dice Land Cocked: You, your fellow players, and the DM should agree on what to do if a die lands on the floor or ends up cocked against a book (or a DM screen, or a can of soda, or a pizza box). Do you reroll the die? Take the result from the floor? Move the book and let the die fall naturally? Any of these options is fine, but you should decide before the start of a new campaign and be specific. The same rules should apply to all the players as well as the DM.

Supply Your Own Dice: Though everyone can share the same set of dice, play proceeds faster and smoother if every player has his or her own dice. You should have all the dice you think you need to play your character, so that you don't have to borrow dice from the other players. (D&D players are also infamous for having superstitions about other people touching their dice, and you don't want to come between a D&D player and her superstitions.)

Roll Attack and Damage Dice at One Time: If you're in a large group and combat is taking an inordinate amount of time at the table, consider streamlining your dice rolling. When making an attack, roll the d20 for your attack roll and the die or dice for your damage roll at the same time. (For example, if you are attacking with a +2 *flaming longsword*, roll a d20, a d8, and a d6 all at the same time.) If your attack roll is successful, you know how much damage you deal and thus save yourself a second roll. (Rolls don't take a long time, but you make so many of them that anything you can do to accelerate them is good for the game.) If your attack is unsuccessful, ignore the damage.

This technique encounters problems when it meets with abilities that allow you to alter your chance to hit after you make your attack roll. For example, action points (described in *Unearthed Arcana* and the *Eberron Campaign Setting*) allow you to add 1d6 to your attack roll's result after you roll the die, if you so choose. If you make your attack rolls and damage rolls simultaneously, you are more likely to spend that action point if your damage roll is high. To avoid these circumstances, roll the attack and damage dice separately if you have action points or a similar ability that can turn a miss into a hit.

Roll Multiple Attacks at One Time: If you have more than one attack, and you know you are going to use them all against the same target, regardless of how the first one turns out, roll all your attack dice at the same time. If you also roll damage simultaneously, as suggested above, you need some way to determine which damage dice belong to which attack. You might use color-coded dice (see below) or roll them with separate hands on opposite sides of a barrier (such as a book).

Use Color-Coded Dice: You can use dice of certain colors to designate specific attacks and damage types. For example, if you make two attacks and roll the attack and damage dice at the same time, using d20s of different colors and damage dice that match those colors avoids confusion. For example, when you are making two attacks in the same round that each deal 1d8 points of damage if successful, roll a yellow d20, a yellow d8, a red d20, and a red d8 all at the same time. You can also use color-coded dice to specify different damage types. When you shoot the demon with your +2 *holy flaming shock longbow*, roll two white d6s for the holy damage, a red d6 for the fire damage, and a yellow d6 for the electricity damage. This technique is helpful because some monsters are resistant or vulnerable to specific damage types.

Color-coded dice make rolling faster and easier

RESPECT THE SPOTLIGHT

Players take turns in a D&D game, and not just in combat. Characters always want to perform various activities, and the DM can focus on only one at a time. The spotlight consists of the DM's attention, and the game's current focus. Which character is active? Which player is telling the DM what he wants his character to do? That player has the spotlight.

The spotlight is a fun place to be. That's when you are active, when you are playing the game to its utmost potential. Because it's a good time, sometimes players are tempted to claim more than their fair share and remain in the spotlight for a disproportionate amount of time.

Players who hog the spotlight are bad for the game, because they decrease everyone else's involvement and therefore their fun. If you find yourself often demanding the DM's attention—if your character likes to do things such as head into town to pick pockets, rob houses, chat with the priestesses at the local temple, play music in inns to make a few gold pieces, and the like—be conscious of it. Some activities of this nature are fine, and they add depth and realism to your character and to the game world, but you don't want to take a great deal of time away from your fellow players. When another player gets her time in the spotlight, let her have it—as long as she doesn't abuse it.

A couple of spotlights deserve special mention.

The NPC-Interaction Spotlight: Roleplaying interactions with NPCs is one of the most enjoyable activities in a D&D game, and every player who wants to participate should have a chance to do so. Even if the party has a member who serves as its spokesperson—a charismatic bard or paladin, for example—a good DM supplies opportunities for other players to interact with NPCs. Perhaps the paladin is otherwise occupied, or maybe the party runs into a nefarious individual for whom the rogue would be a better choice to carry on discussions. Maybe an old acquaintance or relative of one of the other characters shows up. Whatever the case, be respectful of the NPC-interaction spotlight and of your fellow players. If they look bored, relinquish the spotlight in good grace.

The Dungeon Spotlight: Dungeons are big places with lots of doors and hallways. It is easy for a character, especially a stealthy one, to head out on his own and do a bit of exploring—and perhaps some combat and treasure-looting—away from the rest of the party. This strategy strains the game, because the DM must then split her attention and time between the solo character and the rest of the party. If you find yourself tempted to break away from the party, you might want to ask the other players first. ("What do you think about me scouting down this passageway?") If your character simply wanders off, forcing the DM to take time away from the other players, they might (rightly) resent you for it—so don't do it. You might make the claim, "But this is what my character would do!" If that's the case, rethink your character concept. The game is at its most enjoyable for everyone when the characters help each other and every player has a satisfying amount of time in the spotlight.

OTHER CONCERNS

The following pieces of advice are also helpful but do not involve rolling dice or managing paperwork.

Illus. by M. Sebley

Illus. by F. Vohwinkel

Gimble demands the spotlight

Avoid Distractions: D&D games often take place in areas surrounded by potential distractions: TVs, video games, books, and the like. Since you're spending time with your friends, another temptation is to chat and joke at the expense of the game. While some of this sort of activity is fun, and you play D&D to have fun, don't let the entire session pass in idle banter or witty repartee—especially if some players are not partaking in it.

In general, keep your attention focused on the game. Your fellow players might think you rude if you leave the table to surf the Internet or play video games, or if you distract other players with side conversations.

Help Your DM: The DM does a lot of work. If you clear off the table, get the pencils out, and otherwise prepare the playing space, he or she will appreciate it.

TALK ABOUT YOUR CHARACTER

D&D characters are at their best when they are more than just collections of numbers and words written on character sheets. This chapter discusses ways to add depth, motivation, and realism to your character, but these techniques are of limited use if you keep them to yourself. You should talk about your character.

Tell the other players about her. When the other characters first meet her, what impression do they get? How does she look? How does she move? Many players find fun and satisfaction in roleplaying their character's initial interactions with the other characters. The way she talks and the things she says

add enjoyment and verisimilitude for all involved. Even if your character is the silent, mysterious type, describe some of her actions. Do her eyes dart constantly about, examining the area for trouble? Does she stare morosely into her drink? Does she rub an old scar on her neck every so often? All these types of behavior make your character seem more like a real person.

Many D&D campaigns begin with strong player characters—they have interesting histories, developed personalities, and distinctive appearances. However, often these valuable details fade over the course of adventuring. Players are pretty good at remembering their own characters, but they sometimes forget the histories, appearances, names, or even gender of the other characters. Therefore, continued discussion about your character is important. Interact with one of the other PCs or an NPC to keep your character's personality fresh in everyone's mind. Mention how he walks or looks when he meets a new character or encounters a new challenge; describe how a new piece of equipment fits in with the rest of his appearance.

The best characters in movies and novels change as the story progresses, and the best characters in a D&D game are no different. How does your character evolve over the course of her adventures? What life-changing events have occurred to her? How are her beliefs, values, and views about the other characters different from what they were before?

Talking about your character and inserting characteristic details into the game make for a more fun and memorable time for everyone at the table.

CHAPTER SIX

Illus. by R. Horsley

very game has moments when particular characters shine. Players might tell and retell the story of the fighter taking out the ogre, or the rogue disabling the trap, or the wizard dispelling an enemy's magical defenses, or the cleric destroying the vampire. But such moments of glory are only part of what makes the D&D experience so exciting. The deeds of individual characters might be the stuff of game-table legends, but it's their teamwork that gets the job done in one adventure after another.

Team play is perhaps the most important aspect of the D&D game. Certainly solo play can be rewarding, but answering the call to adventure as a group is far more entertaining. In a group, the interplay between differing points of view brings both players and characters into conflict from time to time. When they learn to resolve their differences and pull together toward a common goal, they can achieve far greater results than any of them—no matter how powerful—could achieve alone.

This chapter examines what it means to be an adventuring party and how parties fit together within a campaign setting. It also offers advice for becoming a better team player and for making the most of your group, whatever its composition.

PARTY BACKGROUNDS

In many campaigns, the reasons why a particular group of adventurers came together in the first place are either glossed over or passed off as mere circumstance. At most, a couple of intrepid roleplayers might establish a relationship by making their characters siblings, childhood friends, or past lovers—or they could even concoct a shared event in their past, such as a debt that bound them together. But few groups extend this concept to the entire party.

Establishing a party's reason for existence can enhance the roleplaying experience, promote teamwork, and play a key role in keeping the group together in the face of the inevitable conflicts and disagreements. If the players know why the characters began working together in the first place, the ties between them immediately become stronger, and individual players are encouraged to work together as a team.

One way to build a strong group is to select a party background. Each of the backgrounds detailed below describes a shared event, commitment, or state of being that can help to hold a party together. These backgrounds can be used as written, or they can serve as guidelines for creating others.

CHARTER

The concept of a charter was first introduced in the FORGOTTEN REALMS campaign setting. Essentially, your characters form their own organization by becoming a group of adventurers for hire.

Establishing a charter takes a bit of work up front. To avoid conflicts later, everyone at the table should be

Illus. by F. Vohwinkel

involved in working out the ground rules for the group. The DM needs to be involved in the process as well, since the tone and nature of the charter will probably affect the overall flow of the campaign.

The first order of business is to define the purpose of your group and decide on its short-term and long-term goals. Next, determine what kinds of characters your group will accept as members. Choose an alignment and exclude characters who have alignments more than a step or two away from that one. For instance, if your charter demands that the group be committed to order and goodness, you probably wouldn't want to accept a chaotic evil character. You can also extend the restrictions to cover certain classes, races, and even house rules if desired, as long as those limitations can be framed in the context of the game world. You should also consider what functions are needed—does the group have a divine spellcaster, a person who can disable traps, a melee combatant and a ranged fighter, and so forth? Finally, consider the types of employers your characters are willing to work for and what kind of missions they will accept.

Once your charter is complete, write it out on paper. Doing so adds a measure of depth to the words, and having it prominently displayed during game sessions serves to remind everyone that the characters have bound themselves together for a purpose.

Not only does having a charter enhance roleplaying and deepen players' and characters' commitment to the party, but it also carries other benefits. Your group gains a reputation as a unit within the campaign world, which can make it easier to access services and even gain credit with merchants. Later in the campaign, when characters fall in combat or retire, it's easy to explain where replacements come from, since word of your group's heroics will have spread throughout the lands. Eventually, your party could even gain the same kind of prominence and notoriety that the Harpers enjoy in the FORGOTTEN REALMS setting.

CHILDHOOD FRIENDSHIP

Your group has been together since childhood. Perhaps the characters' parents, once adventurers themselves, were in the habit of entertaining their offspring with tales of fierce dragons, terrible sorcery, and vicious monsters. In such a situation, it would be only natural for the youngsters to follow in their parents' footsteps upon coming of age, and perhaps even try to surpass the achievements of their heroic forebears.

This background works especially well for a party whose members all belong to the same race, such as a group consisting solely of dwarves, elves, or halflings. Such a shared racial heritage can add yet another interesting dimension to your games. For instance, suppose you and the other players jointly decide that your dwarf characters all came from the same stronghold. Life changed for all of you when a horde of mind flayers and their minions boiled up out of the underground and overwhelmed your settlement. The dwarves who were not slain outright were enslaved and taken back to the cyclopean

Four young dwarves vow vengeance against those who destroyed their stronghold

depths of the mind flayer city, never to be seen again. Now your group, which was away on another mission at the time of the illithid attack, is all that's left of the clan. All the characters have taken a joint vow of vengeance against the denizens of the subterranean realm, and their goal is to free their enslaved people and restore the clan.

A group need not be racially homogeneous to have a shared childhood. Half-orcs, half-elves, humans, and halflings all reach maturity at around the same time, and dwarves and gnomes do so about 20 years later. Thus, the characters could easily have met as adolescents—perhaps when they all attended the same academy or neighboring institutions. Once all the characters graduated, they decided to stick together and strike out for a life of adventure. Characters in this model might be siblings, old flames, rivals, or just close friends.

CHOSEN

A popular motif for long-running campaigns is the concept of a shared destiny. Fate has decreed that one or more characters shall be in a certain place at a certain time, either to perform some great deed or to overcome a particularly nasty opponent. Perhaps the group's paladin has been chosen to wrest the *rod of Orcus* from the demon prince's grasp, or to save the Bastion of Souls. Or maybe the group as a whole will one day save the country, continent, or world from some terrible nemesis.

While the characters who are actually saddled with such a destiny are undoubtedly the center of the group, the other PCs play an equally important role—namely, ensuring that the prophesied event happens as it should. Without their assistance, the fated characters cannot hope to accomplish the task set before them. Alternatively, the characters might know that one of their number has been chosen to perform a given task, but not who it is. This arrangement ensures that the characters are motivated to work together while each one dreams that he will be the linchpin of some great future event. And even if the DM has already decided who should be the Chosen One, he can still change his mind if that character dies, or the player leaves the group.

Perhaps the ideal situation, though, is for fate to choose the entire party for the task. In this model, the avatar of a deity (or a powerful mage, noble, or prophet) hand-picks the characters and sets them on the path to greatness. The great and noble cause they champion (or the unbearable burden they bear) unites the party members and encourages them to believe that all must survive to fulfill the prophecy. This commitment to one another's survival in turn promotes party unity and teamwork, since each character must place a higher value on the lives and actions of his fellows than he otherwise would.

CIRCUMSTANCE

In some D&D campaigns, the adventuring party is formed when four heroes who have just met in a bar are hired for a dangerous mission by a shadowy individual in the corner. While this background is certainly the easiest to concoct, it does little to encourage teamwork and party unity. In fact, such a model relies on the relationships between players to keep the group together rather than those that evolve naturally among the characters.

Nevertheless, you can still use circumstance to advantage when building an adventuring party. The characters might be escaped slaves or fugitives who find a common purpose in escaping a shared enemy. Or a terrible calamity could befall the environment, and the characters could emerge as champions of the affected people. Or perhaps a band of reavers is plundering and destroying every settlement they come across, and the characters must band together to combat the common enemy.

A circumstance background relies heavily on the DM's intervention, since he must provide the catalyst that brings the group together. For example, the DM might open the campaign on a gruesome battlefield and reveal that the PCs are all survivors from the same squad. They knew little about one another before the battle; they were simply thrown into the same unit because of the way the orders fell. Alternatively, the DM might rule that the characters are all from the same region, but they hail from widely separated villages. After a plague swept through the land and emptied several communities, the survivors grouped together to seek a way to rebuild.

ORGANIZATION

One of the simplest methods for building an adventuring party is to base it on membership in the same organization. Characters who are loyal to a guild, order, or some other group should extend that loyalty to other members as a matter of course. For example, the Order of Illumination (see *Complete Adventurer*, page 179) exists to root out evil wherever it lurks and confront it directly. Since membership is open only to those who are pure of heart, the players are automatically encouraged to create characters of similar alignments.

While working on behalf of such an organization, the party is unlikely to run out of missions to perform. The characters receive their orders from the organization's leaders, and they gain experience points and treasure with every job they perform. In time, the characters can move up through the ranks of the organization, and perhaps one day even lead it.

The primary drawback to this model is the potential difficulty of getting everyone to agree on the organization. Some organizations are class-based or have strict membership requirements that might prevent certain characters from joining. But if everyone in your group likes this approach, have each player state his character interests first, then select an organization together, with the DM's assistance.

BUILDING THE PARTY

Choosing a background is just the first step in building a party. Ideally, an adventuring party should include a good mixture of classes and races, since each brings a particular set of useful abilities to the table. Abilities that no one else has not only make a character unique, but they also allow her a chance in the spotlight on a regular basis. When characters' abilities overlap, the chance for individuals to shine diminishes, and the party's ability to handle new threats lessens.

This section presents advice for working with your fellow players to build an effective adventuring party.

ADVENTURING PARTY BASICS

A typical adventuring party consists of four characters, each representing one of the iconic elements of fantasy roleplaying. The fighter, the wizard, the cleric, and the rogue form the classic group. The fighter relies on weapons to mete out damage and wears armor to avoid injury. The wizard uses spells to destroy enemies and to circumvent hazards. The cleric supports the other characters through healing spells and "buff" spells that enhance abilities, though he can also aid the fighter in combat. The rogue bypasses traps, assists the fighter and cleric on the battlefield, and brings to bear an impressive skill set that makes her the party's "go-to" person in just about any situation.

The D&D game offers many other classes, but the rest are variations on these core themes. The druid shares many of the cleric's spells but also has specialized abilities that allow her to thrive in wilderness environments. The ranger, an amalgam of both the druid and the fighter classes, has some of the druid's abilities plus bonus feats based on a chosen combat style. In like manner, the paladin blends the abilities of the cleric with those of the fighter. The monk is a fighting character who eschews armor to gain more mobility on the battlefield, and the bard blends the skills of the rogue with a smattering of magic from multiple classes. In short, almost every other class beyond the basic four is a combination, variation, or extension of the four basic themes.

Consider carefully how your character choice will interact with those of your fellow players in an adventuring party. If two people want to play rogues, and your group has only four players, the party might have to do without one of the four key elements unless someone else chooses a character whose abilities cover the missing theme. Even choosing characters similar to those in the ideal party can create problems. For example, choosing a druid or a paladin in place of a cleric, or a bard instead of a rogue can produce severe consequences for a party that cannot fill the gaps in expertise. The same problem exists with the new standard classes presented in recent publications. What must the other characters do to compensate when a party includes a warlock instead of a wizard, for instance?

Proper character class selection is vital to the long-term success of an adventuring party. The choices you make when building your team determine the group's ability to face off against the denizens of the dungeon as well as the horrors of the wilds. The following sections examine the four basic character roles—warrior, expert, arcane spellcaster, and divine spellcaster—as well as the implications of alternative class choices. Each section also provides some advice on how to compensate for deviations from the four iconic classes.

Warriors

The popularity of fighting characters is largely attributable to ease of play and overall satisfaction. The fighter's broad selection of feats, the ranger's array of abilities, the barbarian's raw destructive power, and the leadership potential of the paladin all offer exciting options for adventuring. Perhaps the biggest appeal of these classes, however, is that their primary abilities are never tapped out—they can always kill monsters.

As a warrior, your job is to stall the opponents with melee or ranged attacks long enough for the other party members to bring their special abilities to bear. You buy time for the arcane spellcaster to destroy the monster with a spell, or the cleric to turn the undead, or the rogue to eliminate tough opponents with sneak attacks. And if you happen to kill a bunch of goblins along the way, so much the better. When playing a warrior, it pays to think both offensively and defensively. You are consistently the heaviest hitter in the group, and you never run out of swings. However, you should also try to preserve yourself, since you are the last line of defense before the monsters reach the wizard and the cleric.

Fighter: The backbone of any adventuring group, the fighter is versatile, potent, and highly customizable because he can branch out into several feat trees that hone his skills in both melee and ranged combat. However, the best fighters are those whose abilities are broad enough to give them an edge over any kind of foe. Thus, when playing a fighter, you should resist the temptation to specialize in one feat path too exclusively. If possible, keep your ranged combat prowess as strong as your melee ability so that you can take on fliers and ground forces with equal proficiency.

Barbarian: A barbarian is primarily a melee combatant. His rage ability augments his Strength and Constitution—the two characteristics that are most valuable in face-to-face fighting. But the fact that Survival and Listen are among his class skills also makes him a great (albeit reckless) scout.

Unlike the fighter, the barbarian has only enough feat choices to develop one or maybe two feat paths. So if your barbarian is the party's primary melee warrior, the burden of ranged attack support falls on the party's spellcasters and experts. Thus, the arcane spellcasters should emphasize ranged spells that deal hit point damage. The party's experts also need to focus on developing their ranged attack prowess—particularly the rogue's ability to launch sneak attacks against targets up to 30 feet away.

Monk: Another great warrior choice, the monk is excellent at slipping past the ranks of lesser foes to focus her attacks on the leaders. Her great saving throws, evasion, and resistance to mind-affecting spells and abilities make her far and away the best warrior to throw at enemy spellcasters. But although she is never unarmed, the monk lacks the damage potential of fighters and barbarians, who can bring heavy weapons to bear against a foe. Furthermore, the monk must focus her feat selections on improving her Armor Class because she loses her best abilities if she wears armor.

If you're playing a monk as your party's lead warrior, the cleric must assume the role of heavy hitter in melee. Developing the Power Attack feat path can help a cleric in such a party dish out more damage than he otherwise could. The party's arcane spellcasters tend to fall back into a supporting role, using their spells to augment the team members' individual abilities, though they can fire off their deadly area spells without much worry of damaging you. Experts, who are often just as mobile as you are, can work with you to flank enemies and eliminate them quickly and efficiently.

Ranger: The ranger is a great character choice for nearly any adventuring party. Armed with spells, a few bonus feats,

Warrior types let it all hang out in combat

Illus. by J. Nelson

and great class features, the ranger can also work to improve his combat prowess against specific types of foes. However, he lacks the versatility of the standard fighter because he must focus on a single combat style. If you follow the archery combat path, the party's expert should support the cleric's necessarily broader role as a melee combatant. Conversely, if you follow the two-weapon path, both the arcane spellcaster and the expert need to build up their ranged arsenals.

In either case, the divine spellcaster must also support the ranger with buff spells (such as *cat's grace* and *magic vestment*) and keep plenty of spell slots available for *cure* spells to keep him on his feet. If possible, the arcane spellcaster in your party should summon additional monsters to distract enemies and spread damage around.

Don't neglect your ranger's Armor Class in your feat selection. When it's time to choose favored enemies, select the foes that your party is most likely to encounter and avoid the esoteric and unusual monsters that other team members can handle more efficiently.

Paladin: This virtuous knight not only makes a great spokesperson for the party, but she also serves as a support system for the cleric. The healing that the paladin can provide through her lay on hands ability leaves the cleric with more prepared spells that need not be converted to *cure* spells. Though a paladin isn't quite the equivalent of a fighter in terms of combat prowess, she more than makes up for this lack with turning abilities, a special mount, and the ability to smite evil. Like the barbarian, though, the paladin is starved for feats, so she can focus on only one or two feat paths. Most paladins

choose to develop the Mounted Combat path, which tends to reduce their effectiveness in certain common environments such as dungeons.

When you introduce a paladin into an adventuring party, the rest of the characters have to respect her code of conduct and alignment restrictions. The cleric and the rogue must play larger roles in combat—the former supplementing the paladin in melee and the latter offering ranged support. Also, the wizard should emphasize combat spells to make up for the lack of a reliable ranged attacker.

Other Classes: *Complete Warrior* offers three new warrior standard classes: the hexblade, the samurai, and the swashbuckler. All three of these are good choices, but each brings its own advantages and disadvantages to the group.

The hexblade gains a spell progression starting at 4th level, and he has a number of interesting abilities with which he can disrupt his opponents. However, he lacks the fighter's bonus feats, so he pretty much has to specialize in one combat technique.

The samurai is similar to the ranger in that his class features emphasize a particular style of fighting—a two-weapon style, in this case. But the samurai makes a poor ranged attacker, and his class features focus on fear effects, which are useful only against susceptible opponents.

The swashbuckler makes a great fighting companion for the rogue, but her Armor Class is low compared to most fighting characters, so she must use feats or other assets to compensate for it. Thus, she's unlikely to be the party's principal damage-dealer.

Adventure awaits just over that hill

Experts

An expert is a character who brings a broad skill selection and useful combat abilities to the table. The rogue is perhaps the best example of this category. Experts are invaluable members of any group because they can fill a variety of roles, from backup spellcaster to extra warrior.

When playing an expert, you depend heavily on your skills and class features. You have more skill points than any other character in the group, and you can generally get into and out of scrapes with a good skill check result.

Rogue: The rogue class offers three key advantages: sneak attacks, an excellent selection of class skills, and trapfinding. The sneak attack ability allows the rogue to support the party's key warrior by taking advantage of flanking opportunities and surprise attacks. The rogue's skill in breaking and entering allow the party to overcome obstacles such as locked doors and deadly traps. In addition, the rogue often scouts ahead to gain information about enemies. While the ranger, who sometimes serves as a rogue substitute, has a broad selection of skills and plenty of skill points to back them up, his talents make him more useful in wilderness environments than in dungeons, and he can't help his party bypass traps. On the other hand, he is more of a warrior than the rogue is, so he can hold his own next to fighters, paladins, and barbarians.

As a rogue, you are expected to fill in where needed. Don't ignore the Use Magic Device skill; it allows you to use a *wand of cure light wounds* to get the cleric back on his feet should he become disabled. Likewise, your ability to use a *wand of magic missile,* or even read a scroll, can make all the difference in combat. And perhaps most important, your sneak attack ability can help the party's main warrior bring down the tough opponents.

Bard: Heralded as the best fifth character in any adventuring party, the bard is the most often overlooked expert. The bard's best feature is his adaptability—he is a warrior, an expert, an arcane spellcaster, and a divine spellcaster rolled into one. Like the rogue, he has plenty of skill points and a wide selection of class skills. But while the rogue's class skills focus on scouting, sneaking, and subterfuge, the bard's allow him to play a strong role in supporting the other party members.

When you play a bard, you don't have the rogue's trapfinding ability, so the cleric must cover this aspect of the expert with his *find traps* spell—though you can help if you have the inspire competence ability. Likewise, you can use inspire greatness and inspire heroics to improve a warrior's combat abilities at higher levels. Furthermore, since you have access to spells, you can supplement both arcane and divine spellcasters, expanding the party's ability to circumvent minor threats and letting the more potent spellcasters reserve their spell slots for handling the really deadly enemies.

Other Classes: *Complete Adventurer* presents three new expert standard classes: the ninja, the scout, and the spellthief. All three have the trapfinding ability, plus special abilities such as sudden strike (which is similar to sneak attack) and great skill selections. Thus, playing one of these classes is just as good as having a rogue in the party.

Arcane Spellcasters

Wizards, sorcerers, and their ilk develop powerful spells in lieu of combat abilities. In fact, since they have the smallest Hit Die type of all the classes (d4 in most cases), they are more of a liability in melee than an asset. However, they make up for their poor combat skills with access to some of the most potent spells in the game.

As an arcane spellcaster, you must circumvent the gravest threats to the party. You can lob *fireballs* and *lightning bolts* at the party's opponents, conjure up terrible servants, and even transport your allies past obstructions and obstacles. Playing the party's arcane spellcaster is a big responsibility, but it can be both memorable and highly rewarding as well.

Wizard: The wizard's strength lies in the depth of her knowledge and her ability to cast a variety of different spells. In addition, she can modify those spells with metamagic feats and use them to create magic items that benefit not only herself but also the rest of the party.

Deciding which spells to prepare on a given day, however, requires a bit of strategy. A poorly prepared wizard all too often becomes meat for monsters. For instance, a 5th-level wizard who prepares *lightning bolt* before facing a creature that is immune to electricity now might lack access to a spell that could have overcome the opponent.

When you play an arcane spellcaster, resist the urge to prepare all offensive spells. A *charm person* spell can accomplish a lot more than a *magic missile* at times, and you shouldn't underestimate its value. By preparing a good mix of spells, you can be useful in situations ranging from diplomacy to divination to war.

Sorcerer: The sorcerer makes an excellent substitute for the wizard in an adventuring party. Although the number of different spells he can access is relatively small, he outstrips a wizard of equivalent level in the number of spells he can cast per day. If he chooses to specialize in offensive spells, he can be a formidable combat caster. However, most sorcerers can do little to supply their companions with magic items, and they typically don't have the same range of skills as their more learned counterparts. Worse still, using metamagic feats slows the sorcerer's casting time, turning this key spellcasting tool into a potential liability.

If your sorcerer is the party's key arcane spellcaster, it's best to focus on total offense. Let the cleric erect the magical defenses and the warrior block the hits. Your task is to bombard your enemies with a barrage of damaging spells. Make sure you learn spells of every energy type and take the Spell Penetration feat early to help you overcome spell resistance.

Other Classes: *Complete Arcane* presents three new arcane spellcasting classes: the warlock, the wu-jen, and the warmage. Each of these classes is a variation on the core arcane theme—one restricts the spell selection, another changes the fundamental methods of casting, and the third exchanges certain spellcasting elements for others. The warlock is a great alternative to the combat-oriented sorcerer, and he can offer ranged combat potential in a party with warriors who specialize in melee. On the other hand, if the group's warrior is an effective ranged combatant, the warmage can help the cleric and rogue cover the group's melee needs.

Illus. by M. Komarck

Divine Spellcasters

The divine spellcaster is the heart and soul of every adventuring party. Armed with good combat prowess, a broad range of buff spells, power over undead, and the always-in-demand *cure* spells, the cleric fills a vital role. In fact, a party without a cleric has a much harder time surviving than one that has clerical support from the start.

When you choose a divine spellcaster, you play an important support role in your party. You're the one everyone else relies on to supply healing spells, remove afflictions such as diseases and curses, and restore lost ability points. You can also bring extra support to the team with your *summon monster, summon nature's ally,* or *planar ally* spells. The more combatants you have on your side, the less damage your fellow characters have to take.

Cleric: The cleric is undoubtedly among the most effective characters in the game. With the right spells, he can rival even warriors in combat, and no character is more effective against undead. When you add unique domain abilities and the ability to heal others spontaneously, the cleric easily becomes one of the most important characters in the party.

Even so, playing a cleric can sometimes seem like a chore. Because your companions look to you to fix all their troubles, you might feel more like the party first-aid kit than a full-fledged member of the group. While it's true that no party would last long without your *cures*, you're far more than a simple healing factory. Your ability to fight and cast potent spells coupled with your access to abilities that no other character has ensure that you remain among the more powerful characters in the game.

Druid: The druid is a viable substitute for the cleric. While the druid lacks spontaneous healing ability, she can spontaneously summon creatures instead. Add the ability to change shape and a potent spell list that retains most of the *cure* spells, and the druid becomes an important addition to any adventuring party.

If you're playing a druid, you're more than likely the only character in the party with any ability to cast *cure* spells—unless your group also includes a bard or a higher-level paladin. So it pays to invest in disposable magic items such as *wands of cure light wounds* or *wands of cure moderate wounds* to free up your spell slots for more interesting spells. Don't be afraid to experiment with your spell selection; in a worst-case scenario, you can lose a prepared spell to cast a *summon nature's ally* spell of the same level.

Other Classes: *Complete Divine* offers three additional divine spellcasting classes: the favored soul, the shugenja, and the spirit shaman. Each brings a specialized set of abilities to the table, as well as a few disadvantages. The favored soul offers better combat potential, the shugenja a broader access to different kinds of spells, and the spirit shaman a set of unique abilities effective against specific kinds of creatures. All three however, cast spells like a sorcerer, so none has the same spell versatility as the cleric.

Missing Elements

Sometimes no one in the group wants to play a particular role, or the players don't want to be constrained by the four classic character roles. And some groups have only two or three players—none of whom might be interested in playing multiple characters.

While the absence of any one of the four classic character roles makes adventuring more difficult, it does not make it impossible. Individual characters can make extensive use of the multiclassing rules, invest in the Leadership feat to pick up cohorts, or even play two or more characters if the DM allows it. But when a party is just plain missing a crucial element, you can take a few specific actions to minimize the impact of that shortfall.

Missing Warrior: For most groups, the very idea of not having a front-line fighter is appalling. Yet this role is in some ways the most disposable. Clerics and druids are competent warriors in their own right, and with the right set of buff spells (such as *bull's strength, magic weapon,* and the like), they can be the equals of nearly any warrior-type character.

If your group lacks a warrior, consider adding a druid, whose wild shape ability and animal companion can make up for the missing component. A bard can also be an excellent choice, since the additional healing he can supply lets the cleric devote his spells to augmenting his own fighting abilities. The scout class from *Complete Adventurer* is another great choice. With ranger Hit Dice and the sudden strike ability, the scout not only has combat abilities that rival those of warriors, but she can also support the rogue as a secondary trap finder.

Ideal Four-Character Group: Cleric, druid, rogue, and sorcerer.

Ideal Three-Character Group: Cleric, rogue, and sorcerer.

Missing Expert: Not having an expert can make certain environments tricky—if not downright deadly. The lack of a character who can identify and disable traps means the party is at risk of springing nearly every trap in the dungeon.

When a party finds itself in this situation, it's up to the cleric to compensate. The Trickery domain offers some stealth skills and spells, and the *find traps* spell—though its use depletes the cleric's available spell slots—can make up for the missing rogue ability. A group that's missing a rogue can also consider filling the warrior's role with the paladin, since that class can help the cleric compensate for his expanded role. A ranger is also a good choice because he offers the party scouting abilities that would otherwise be lacking.

Ideal Four-Character Group: Cleric, paladin, ranger, and wizard.

Ideal Three-Character Group: Cleric, ranger, and wizard.

Missing Arcane Spellcaster: The lack of an arcane spellcaster can spell disaster for a party. Wizards and sorcerers provide the means to eliminate large numbers of foes, clearing the way for the principal warrior to hammer away at the key opponent. The arcane spellcaster also significantly improves a party's chances of overcoming particularly nasty opponents, such as dragons and magical beasts.

While having an arcane spellcaster is certainly preferable, a party can compensate for the lack of one. The best way is for the expert to keep pumping skill points into the Use Magic Device skill so that she can use items to produce the necessary magical effects. A bard, who can provide a small amount of arcane magic, is also extremely useful, as is an extra cleric, who can at least provide some damage-dealing divine magic. The hexblade, from *Complete Warrior*, makes a good backup as well.

Ideal Four-Character Group: Bard, cleric, fighter, and rogue.

Ideal Three-Character Group: Bard, cleric, and fighter.

Missing Divine Spellcaster: The divine spellcaster is the element most commonly missing from a party. Many players prefer to go for the spotlight with a fighter or wizard (or the equivalent) rather than playing what they see as a supporting character. But the lack of a divine spellcaster results in a considerable drain on party resources. Parties that lack this element soon discover that they must invest in multiple *wands of cure light wounds* just to compensate for the healing a cleric could have provided—fifty charges don't last as long as one might think. This healing deficit plus the loss of turning capability and the lack of strong divination spells (such as *augury* and *divination*) makes operating without a divine spellcaster quite expensive and more than a little dangerous. Still, a party that's missing this element can compensate with the bard and paladin classes, both of which have some healing abilities. The party rogue should maximize her ranks in Use Magic Device so that she can activate divine scrolls and wands.

Ideal Four-Character Group: Bard, paladin, rogue, and wizard.

Ideal Three-Character Group: Paladin, rogue, and wizard.

The Fifth Character

Groups with more than four players offer greater flexibility in class choices. The party doesn't suffer from having two wizards or two fighters, but the roles of the duplicate characters overlap, reducing the enjoyment for the two players who must share the spotlight. The best way to prevent role overlap is for players to branch out into different aspects of the same roles. Instead of two fighters, for example, consider a ranger or a barbarian for the second warrior. The ranger can provide the ranged attacks (assuming he has selected the archery combat style), while the barbarian serves as the melee menace. Likewise, instead of two wizards, try a wizard coupled with a bard or sorcerer. The wizard retains a diverse selection of spells, while the other arcane spellcaster helps to fill gaps in the party caused by casualties. The following sections offer recommendations for character choices in larger parties.

Two Warriors: Part of what makes the fighter a great class choice is his ability to develop several different combat techniques. When the party has the luxury of an extra warrior, both players have more flexibility, since they can take advantage of alternative techniques without diminishing the overall effectiveness of the party. For instance, a monk and a barbarian, though opposite in outlook, make a great team. They both move faster than normal for their races, so they can close with the enemy and reduce the need for warriors who specialize in ranged attacks. Likewise, a barbarian can handle melee combat with ease, while the second warrior, preferably a fighter or a ranger, can supply covering fire with a bow or crossbow, eliminating additional targets that are closing in on the barbarian. Substituting a paladin for a barbarian can give the same results, especially in a campaign that features undead, demons, or some equally evil nemesis as the dominant monster type.

Two Experts: At first glance, two rogues in a party looks like a winning combination, and in many ways it is. Multiple rogues can work together to flank enemies and dish out buckets of sneak attack damage. If they have ranks in Tumble, they can weave through their enemies and select the best targets for their attacks, while also supporting the party's primary warrior.

On the other hand, two rogues also overlap a great deal. The party really doesn't need more than one character to find traps, pick locks, and translate musty inscriptions on the wall. If the group does have a second translator, it's typically the wizard.

To prevent this kind of overlap, one of the players should consider playing a bard. Easily the most versatile kind of character, the bard offers a mix of abilities from all classes, including combat prowess, solid saving throws, and spellcasting ability. Better still, bardic music helps everyone, providing bonuses on certain tasks or in the heat of combat.

Other experts, such as the ninja and the scout, can help the rogue concentrate on developing the right skills and abilities to eliminate traps. Because these other characters are more combat-oriented, they excel at maneuvering through the battlefield to help the rogue flank enemies for sneak attacks, as well as to support the other warriors.

Two Arcane Spellcasters: Two wizards in the same party can effectively double the number of spells they ordinarily would have by sharing their spellbooks. And in heated combat, two *fireballs* from allied wizards are always better than one.

However, a better tactic for individualizing party roles is for one player to select a sorcerer. If that character focuses on combat spells, the wizard can take charge of the more utilitarian spells.

Multiple arcane spellcasters can help the party in other ways as well. If the party's primary warrior is not a fighter, a warmage can provide some great offensive spells, as well as some combat ability to shore up any shortcomings. A bard is also a great choice, since an extra character with access to healing spells is never bad.

Two Divine Spellcasters: Clerics are probably the best of all the classes to duplicate in a party. Sharing the burden of keeping the warrior on his feet gives each cleric more freedom to cast other spells. Multiple clerics can provide buff spells, such as *bull's strength* and *bear's endurance,* to boost the front line, as well as *eagle's splendor* to help the sorcerer cast more powerful combat spells. *Magic vestment, magic weapon, aid, bless,* and others used in combination can give the whole party a boost. If the primary cleric can do more than just function as the party's medic, his player is likely to enjoy the session more.

A druid is also a good addition to an adventuring party as a second divine caster. The druid's special abilities (wild shape and spontaneous casting of *summon nature's ally*) can add considerable power to the group. Furthermore, the druid has a useful selection of wilderness survival spells, and her animal companion can help other characters flank enemies.

Psionics: If your campaign includes psionics, the classes presented in *Expanded Psionics Handbook* offer the chance to play a unique and exotic character. A psychic warrior or soulknife works well as a secondary warrior, and psions and wilders are good replacements for arcane spellcasters.

BEING A TEAM PLAYER

Developing a shared background and carefully planning the group's character choices has little effect if the group doesn't act as a team. The story of one brave, bold hero overcoming

Hennet serves as party cartographer

adversity is fine for a fantasy novel, but what makes the D&D game great is the teamwork displayed by a group of such adventurers. Selfish thoughts and actions are the best way for your party to meet a terrible end. If your rogue sneaks off to claim the choicest bits of treasure before the rest of the group can arrive, the fighter might not have the right tool to defeat the next monster, and another ally might not have the right item to save your hide. And you aren't doing your companions any favors by pushing ahead to fight the next monster in the next room, because if you die, their chances for survival diminish considerably. Furthermore, a cleric who hoards his *cure* spells until someone is at death's door encourages his companions not to take risks and not to perform heroic acts, thereby reducing the fun for everyone involved.

Though roleplaying games technically do not have winners or losers, adventuring parties do—at least in a sense. Your team wins by achieving its objectives. If your party saves the town or clears the dungeon, all its members win. Therefore, in the most important sense, you win by working together.

Thinking as a Group

All encounter levels (ELs) are approximations based on a group of four reasonably healthy characters of the appropriate level. Thus, an EL 4 encounter is appropriate for a group of four 4th-level characters. If one or two of those characters dies, the encounter becomes more difficult. Thus, acting without regard for your companions is a surefire way to force everyone to make a new character and start over. So when working in a group, keep the following three points in mind.

First, your character is an integral part of the group, whether or not that fact is apparent to you. Every class and race provides a set of options and abilities that can help a party overcome an encounter. And even if you don't know what to do in a given round, you can always use the aid another action to help someone else.

Second, the party is always more important than the individual character. Always be aware of your comrades' positions and their ability to handle a particular threat. If the wizard is desperately battling five goblins, and you're playing the fighter, you'd better get over there and save the spellcaster's skin. Likewise, if you're playing the cleric, your primary job is to help the warriors stay on their feet, though you can also lend combat or spell support as necessary. So if the heavy hitter is disabled, cure him as fast as possible so he can continue to do his job. By staying cognizant of the battlefield and your fellow party members, you should be able to handle just about anything the DM throws at you.

Third, keep in mind that characters who hate each other don't generally work together for long. If your group includes a paladin, it's probably not a good idea to play a chaotic evil half-orc necromancer. Such contrasts, while they provide excellent opportunities for roleplaying, are never conducive to a good gaming experience. Playing a treacherous character diminishes or destroys the trust that is vital to party cohesiveness, and when you brave the depths of the underground, you want your friends to watch your back.

Team Roles

Well-defined party roles can help keep your group focused on teamwork. Each role represents a responsibility for a character, and the different roles ensure that each player has an opportunity to shine and gets a voice in the decision-making processes. Furthermore, team roles keep disagreements to a minimum and focus attention on the fun parts of gaming. The following sections provide some example roles other than the iconic ones discussed above.

Cartographer/Historian: The party cartographer is responsible for mapping, taking notes about certain rooms, and recording puzzles, riddles, and campaign notes. Though ideally this function should be a shared responsibility, some players are better at it than others. If another player shoulders the burden of keeping notes, pitch in whenever you can by helping to recall certain details.

Face: Your group should settle on one person in the group to be the default "front man." When your party needs a good negotiator to slip past some guards or to talk a dragon into letting everyone live, it falls to this character to do the convincing. So don't feel overshadowed when the "face" character speaks up; he's just doing his part. After all, a character who's good at talking is not always good at fighting.

General: A born strategist can look at the battle map, pick out the best paths for movement to avoid attacks of opportunity, place spells where they are most effective, and decide where everyone should be located to do well in combat situations. Such a player is an asset to the group because she can offer advice about where to attack, point out advantageous environmental conditions, and develop great strategies for the party. A general can also help other players make good combat decisions and show them how to maximize their resources in a fight.

Few people enjoy being bossed around, and a demanding player—even a well-intentioned one—can ruin the fun for everyone. Thus, the general must be receptive to others' opinions and sensitive to their feelings.

Judge: Inevitably, characters (and their players) come into conflict during the game. The dispute might be about who gets a certain piece of treasure, or it might be a disagreement over a proposed course of action. When such a conflict occurs, it's wise to put a time limit on the ensuing debate so that it cannot derail the game session. Furthermore, a disinterested character (or player) should listen to all sides of the argument and make a binding decision. This "judge" role can fall to different characters depending on who is involved in the debate, but someone who can make a quick decision and resolve the argument is invaluable for keeping the game on track.

Scout: Forewarned is forearmed, so just about every party recognizes the need for a scout. Ideally, the scout should be able to move forward quietly, inspect the scene ahead, and report back quickly to his comrades. A character with high Hide and Move Silently modifiers fits this role perfectly, so it often falls to the rogue.

The party scout can quickly overshadow the rest of the group if too much of the action falls on his shoulders. Thus, scouts should reserve their stealthy reconnaissance for when it's necessary. If the scout insists on inspecting every room, the game can quickly become all about him, with the rest of the characters as supporting cast.

Security: The character filling this party role is in charge of securing the area before the PCs enter a room or camp for the night. She might do a quick search for traps, make Listen checks, or examine the floor for recent tracks. She also determines the order of watches and is ultimately responsible for keeping the party safe from ambushes. If the security person feels that a particular location or action is too risky, the rest of the party should find an alternative solution.

Task Leader: Certain characters are just better at specific tasks than others. Thus, the character with the best Listen modifier should be listening at doors, not the fighter in full plate with the Wisdom score of 6. By the same token, the character with the trapfinding ability should be the party's authority on traps. Identify certain checks the group has to make frequently, and put the characters with the best modifiers in charge of them.

TEAMWORK BENEFITS

After a few adventures, the characters in an adventuring party tend to identify particular routines and tactics that work well for them. The wizard might select certain spells to complement the fighter's tactics, while the cleric and the rogue figure out where to stand in a fight so that they can lend support while still allowing the fighter to shield them from the worst of the enemy attacks. In this manner, the party can develop concrete teamwork benefits that evolve from the experience of working together.

WHAT IS A TEAMWORK BENEFIT?

Experienced players understand the value of specific tactics that depend on teamwork. However, teamwork also provides a more general benefit. Once characters have trained with specific comrades for a time, they become attuned to the nuances of how their companions fight, move, and communicate. Thus, characters who have spent time working as a team can derive a benefit simply from having their comrades nearby. This teamwork benefit can grant an expanded use of a skill, a bonus on certain checks, or a battlefield action otherwise unavailable to the team members.

To qualify for a teamwork benefit, PCs must meet two broad categories of requirements: training time and prerequisites.

First, the characters must jointly practice techniques relevant to the desired benefit for at least two weeks before acquiring it. This training period must be repeated whenever a new character joins the group, so that the newcomer can become accustomed to the operating procedures of the veteran team members.

Second, some teamwork benefits have prerequisites such as skill ranks, base attack bonus, or feats. A prerequisite can take one of two different forms.

Task Leader Prerequisites: These requirements must be met by at least one character on the team. If the only character who qualifies leaves the team, the group loses the teamwork benefit until that character returns or is replaced by another who meets the same prerequisites. Since prerequisites for teamwork benefits vary widely, the character who assumes the task leader position might differ depending on the specific benefit.

In addition to the indicated prerequisites, a task leader must have an Intelligence score of at least 8. (While he need not be a genius or have a strong personality, he must be at least reasonably capable of communicating his thoughts to others.)

Team Member Prerequisites: Every character on the team must meet these requirements. Any new character who joins the team must also meet them, or the team can no longer enjoy the benefit.

For example, the cunning ambush teamwork benefit has a task leader prerequisite of 8 ranks in both Hide and Listen, and a team member prerequisite of 1 rank in Hide. So, at least one character in the group must have 8 or more ranks in both Hide and Listen, and every other character on the team must have at least 1 rank in Hide. Thus, when the team is sneaking around, the task leader directs her less adept comrades in stealth techniques, covers any extra noise with environmental sounds, and so on.

A team (see The Team Roster, below) gets one teamwork benefit for every 4 Hit Dice the lowest-level member of the team has. If that character's level later drops below the required point (due to energy drain, for example), the team retains all its current teamwork benefits but can't gain a new one until that character regains his lost level(s), plus enough additional levels to qualify for an additional benefit.

Whenever a team gains a new teamwork benefit, it also has the option to swap out a benefit it previously had for a new one, as long as it meets the new prerequisites. In effect, the team can elect to lose one teamwork benefit to gain two others. Such swaps usually occur when the team roster has changed in such a way as to render a previously known teamwork benefit less useful than before.

Unless otherwise specified, each teamwork benefit can be taken only once. A teamwork benefit applies whenever the characters on the team can communicate with each other—be it verbally, through gestures, or by magical means.

THE TEAM ROSTER

Teamwork benefits are based on the notion that once characters have spent time training with their comrades, they can respond instinctively to subtle changes in body language and anticipate their teammates' likely moves. A group of PCs or

HANDLE ANIMAL (NEW TRICK: TEAMWORK)
Use this skill to train an animal as part of a team.

Check: Teaching an animal the teamwork trick requires a DC 20 Handle Animal check made as part of teamwork training. This trick allows the animal to be part of a team and thus benefit from any teamwork benefits enjoyed by that team. The animal must still meet any team member prerequisites required to gain the benefit.

NPCs must train together for at least two weeks before the group can gain any teamwork benefits. The PCs will undoubtedly occupy most of the positions on the team, but cohorts, animal companions, paladin mounts, familiars, and recurring NPC allies can also be members of a team.

A team must have at least two members and no more than eight. To join a team, a character must have an Intelligence score of 3 or higher. A creature with an Intelligence score of 1 or 2 can be included on a team only if it learns the teamwork trick through some character's use of the Handle Animal skill (see the sidebar). A creature without an Intelligence score can never be part of a team.

To maintain their teamwork benefits, the characters on a team must train together for at least four one-week periods per year. These training periods need not be consecutive and can happen at the same time when the characters are training to earn the new class features for a given level, so in most cases PCs don't have to spend additional time to keep their teamwork skills sharp.

Any new character added to a team after it has gained teamwork benefits must train with the other characters on the team for at least two weeks. During this time, she learns the team's standard operating procedures and the nuances of her comrades' behavior. This training can occur during the training time required to gain the benefits of a new level.

A character can join an adventuring party without joining the team that includes the other members of the group. In this case, the new character doesn't gain any teamwork benefits, but neither does her lack of prerequisites count against the team's qualification for those benefits.

A character can leave a team at her own option, or by consensus of the other team members. For more teamwork benefits, see *Dungeon Master's Guide II*, pages 190–194.

TEAMWORK BENEFIT DESCRIPTIONS

Below is the format for teamwork benefit descriptions.

BENEFIT NAME
Description of what the benefit does or represents.

Training: A brief discussion of the training procedure required to acquire the benefit. The task leader coordinates the training.

Task Leader Prerequisite: A base attack bonus, a feat or feats, a minimum number of ranks in one or more skills, a class feature, or some other requirement that at least one character on the team must have for the team to acquire this benefit. This entry is absent if a teamwork benefit has no task leader prerequisite. If a benefit has more than one task leader prerequisite, the same character must meet all of them for the team to gain that benefit.

Team Member Prerequisite: Every member of the team must meet this requirement for the team to acquire the benefit. This entry is absent if a teamwork benefit has no team member prerequisite. If a benefit has more than one team member prerequisite, every character on the team must meet all of them for the team to gain that benefit.

Benefit: What the teamwork benefit enables the team to do.

Tips: Advice for players and DMs about using this teamwork benefit.

AWARENESS

Your team knows where to look and what to listen for to anticipate ambushes.

Training: To train for this benefit, you and your teammates must run through scenarios in which half of you set up ambushes to snare the others. Through constant drilling, your team learns to listen for specific sounds and look for random visual clues. By regularly exploring dangerous locales, developing listening skills, and staying alert for the slightest movements, your team gradually develops a routine for examining an area to prevent enemies from getting the drop on the group.

Task Leader Prerequisite: Listen 12 ranks and Spot 12 ranks.

Team Member Prerequisite: Listen 2 ranks or Spot 2 ranks.

Benefit: Every member of the team gains a +2 circumstance bonus on Listen and Spot checks if any other team member is within 30 feet.

Tips: When moving into an area with poor lighting, or one that offers plenty of places for opponents to hide, it's best to spread out to the outer extent of this benefit's range. By doing so, your group presents a less attractive target to a hidden spellcaster. For example, if each character is exactly 30 feet (6 squares) away from the task leader, not everyone could be caught in a *fireball* or similar effect.

CAMP ROUTINE

The regular routine your group has established allows you to set up, watch, and break down camp quickly and efficiently.

Training: To develop a camp routine, the team must establish a regular schedule of tasks and responsibilities for each member. For example, one character might set up the tents while another starts the fire and a third prepares the evening meal. Your team must also set up a routine watch schedule so that everyone knows who goes on watch when, and for how long.

Task Leader Prerequisite: Survival 8 ranks or Self-Sufficient.

Team Member Prerequisite: Survival 1 rank.

Benefit: Your team can set up and break camp with an eye toward defensibility and efficiency. The team member on watch gains a +2 bonus on Spot and Listen checks, and each sleeping team member gains a +4 bonus on Listen checks to hear any sounds within 30 feet.

Tips: Be sure to put spellcasters on the first watch or last watch so that they can get enough uninterrupted rest to regain their spells. Your first priority when the party is attacked while you are on watch is to wake up your allies, so you should carry a signal whistle, bell, or similar item.

CIRCLE OF BLADES

The members of your team can combine their attacks to slice through the defenses of a foe they have surrounded.

Training: You and your teammates learn to anticipate each other's attacks and fighting maneuvers. By correctly timing your blows, you can strike at a foe's vulnerable points.

Task Leader Prerequisite: Weapon Specialization and base attack bonus +6.

Team Member Prerequisite: Sneak attack +1d6.

Benefit: Any team member who readies an action to attack when the task leader does gains a +2 bonus on damage rolls against the same target.

Tip: The circle of blades teamwork benefit works best against undead, oozes, and other monsters that have immunity to extra damage from sneak attacks.

CROWDED CHARGE

Because you and your allies know when to step out of each other's way, you can charge even when allies are blocking your path.

Training: The members of your team learn to step aside whenever one of them begins a charge.

Task Leader Prerequisite: Jump 8 ranks.

Team Member Prerequisite: Jump 1 rank.

Benefit: Other team members do not block movement for the purpose of determining whether a team member can charge. However, a charging team member must still end her movement in an unoccupied space.

Tips: This versatile benefit allows the party's rogue or ranger to scout ahead in a dungeon or other constrained terrain without worrying about blocking a fighter's or barbarian's charge. Furthermore, because the benefit also extends to mounted team members, a paladin can charge on horseback without worrying about trampling her comrades.

CUNNING AMBUSH

Your team can quickly take advantage of terrain to ambush opponents.

Training: The training for this benefit involves studying common environments, running through ambush scenarios, and devising strategies that take advantage of the terrain. Your team must spend a few days in the hills, then in the forest, and then—if possible—in the shifting sands of the desert.

Task Leader Prerequisite: Hide 8 ranks and Listen 8 ranks.

Team Member Prerequisite: Hide 1 rank.

Benefit: If the team members allow the task leader to prepare their hiding positions, he can make a special Hide check to camouflage them. This check is modified by each team member's armor check penalty and Dexterity rather than the task leader's, and the camouflage effect lasts until the team member moves. Hiding a team member in this manner requires 10 minutes of work.

Tips: The ambush teamwork benefit is a great way to play smart. Instead of always going after the monsters on their own turf, let them come to you. Try luring monsters into your trap with spells such as *dancing lights* or *major image*. Failing that, buff up the party scout with defensive spells to protect her while she acts as bait.

CUNNING AMBUSH, IMPROVED

When you are adequately prepared, your team can set a devastating ambush.

Training: Same as for cunning ambush.

Expert mountaineers gain the upper hand in a battle with harpies

+1 bonus on melee attacks). Alternatively, making ranged attacks from the other side of an area that features uncertain footing might discourage enemies from charging you.

EXPERT MOUNTAINEERS

Your team can work together to ascend difficult slopes and sheer surfaces with relative ease.

Training: Constant training with expert climbers has made your team comfortable with ascents and descents.

Task Leader Prerequisite: Climb 8 ranks and Use Rope 8 ranks.

Team Member Prerequisite: Climb 1 rank or Use Rope 1 rank.

Benefit: If a team member succeeds on a Climb check, every other team member adjacent to him gains a +2 circumstance bonus on Climb checks made to ascend the same surface. Furthermore, each team member can make an accelerated climb with only a –2 penalty on the Climb check. Finally, a team member can catch a falling comrade by succeeding on a Climb check against the wall's DC (not against the wall's DC + 10).

Tips: Using the appropriate climbing equipment makes Climb checks easier. So, to ensure success, invest in pitons to make your own handholds and footholds.

FOE HUNTING

Your team is especially good at tracking down and destroying specific types of creatures.

Training: The training for this benefit begins with intensive research on the specific creature type to be hunted. You and your teammates must drill on the various features

Task Leader Prerequisite: Hide 12 ranks and Listen 12 ranks.

Team Member Prerequisite: Hide 3 ranks and the cunning ambush teamwork benefit.

Benefit: During the surprise round, each team member who is not surprised and has been camouflaged (see Cunning Ambush, above) can take a full round's worth of actions.

Tips: As with cunning ambush, this benefit is best used to draw enemies into your trap. To maximize the benefit, try setting up ambushes in favorable terrain, such as forest (which grants a +2 bonus to AC and a +1 bonus on Reflex saves to any character standing in a space occupied by a tree) or a position of higher ground (which grants a and traits of the chosen creature until you learn its every idiosyncrasy. Finally, the team must stage mock combats so that each of you can learn to take advantage of the target creature's weaknesses.

Task Leader Prerequisite: Favored enemy (any one) +4.

Team Member Prerequisite: Survival 1 rank and base attack bonus +4.

Benefit: Each team member who assumes a flanking position with the task leader against his favored enemy gains a +2 bonus on damage rolls against that creature.

Tips: To make optimum use of this benefit, the task leader should wear light armor or use spells that improve his speed.

GROUP TRANCE

You and your teammates reduce your susceptibility to sleep by learning the ways of the elves.

Training: Your team members learn the secrets of elf trance and can slip into a trance state by establishing a physical link with the task leader. This trance state allows each member to gain the benefit of sleep by cleansing her mind and entering a deep meditative state.

Task Leader Prerequisite: Elf blood (elf or half-elf).

Team Member Prerequisite: Concentration 1 rank.

Benefit: When team members join hands, the task leader can create a trance link that allows each of them, regardless of race, to meditate in the same manner as elves do. Every team member gains the benefit of 8 hours of sleep after just 4 hours of meditation.

Tips: Let all the spellcasters in the group rest while the warriors stay on guard. If the group's elf trances with half the team at a time, your party can get by with two well-manned guard watches per night rather than several shorter shifts.

INDIRECT FIRE

Your team has a forward observer called a spotter, who locates enemies and reveals their positions.

Training: You and your teammates practice aiming at unseen targets using directions from allies. Eventually, you learn to fire accurately at targets that have cover based on the body language and gestures of the spotter.

Task Leader Prerequisite: Precise Shot and base attack bonus +6.

Team Member Prerequisite: Spot 3 ranks.

Benefit: This benefit denies opponents some of the protection normally granted by cover or concealment. If the spotter has an unobstructed line of sight to the covered or concealed target, she can, as a move action, use hand gestures, spoken directions, and body language to alert allies wielding ranged weapons to the target's position. If the target has cover, it gains only half the normal cover bonus to Armor Class against the team's ranged attacks. If the target has concealment, the attacker rolls the miss chance twice to determine whether his attack hits. A spotter who can see invisible targets can use this ability to allow a reroll on the miss chance to strike an invisible creature.

Tips: Team members with darkvision make the best spotters, since they can use their special sight to locate creatures that are taking advantage of shadowy or dark conditions.

LIKE A ROCK

Like dwarves, the members of your team are stable on their feet.

Training: Your team develops resilience against unbalancing attacks by working closely with a dwarf or some other sturdy member of the party. When the team stands together, its members are difficult to dislodge.

Task Leader Prerequisite: Stability (as dwarf racial trait).

Team Member Prerequisite: Balance 1 rank.

Benefit: The task leader's stability bonus against bull rush or trip attempts extends to all team members adjacent to her. This bonus stacks with that provided by stability.

Tips: This benefit requires the team to bunch up, so if the enemy has a number of area attacks, be sure to beef everyone up with spells and abilities that grant energy resistance. If you must spread out, don't move so far apart that you can't help an ally who is knocked prone.

MASSED CHARGE

When your team charges, it smashes into the foe as a single great, implacable mass.

Training: You and your teammates learn to charge as one. You line up in a tight formation and time your strides to move in tight synchronicity.

Task Leader Prerequisite: Balance 5 ranks.

Team Member Prerequisite: Balance 1 rank.

Benefit: The team can make a special charge attack. All team members move on the same initiative count, and each must charge and attack the same target. Each team member gains a bonus on his attack roll after the charge equal to the number of teammates participating.

Tips: This benefit works best against a single, large opponent. A smaller opponent presents too narrow a point of contact for you to maximize this ability.

MISSILE VOLLEY

Your team excels at firing as a group, unleashing a saturated wave of arrows and bolts. Each member places her shots so that the target cannot dodge them all.

Training: Your team practices by taking aim at a number of small targets clustered together (representing different spots on the body of a single enemy). Each of you can learn to place your shots so as to cover every part of a target with a single joint volley.

Task Leader Prerequisite: Far Shot and Precise Shot.

Team Member Prerequisite: Point Blank Shot.

Benefit: Every member of the team who readies an action to fire a missile weapon when the task leader does gains a bonus on the attack roll equal to the number of team members firing. The task leader also qualifies for the bonus, even though she did not ready an action. All these attacks must be made against the same target.

Tips: Since everyone except the task leader must ready an action to fire, the other team members lose their additional attacks. Thus, the team is trading a high number of attack rolls for a smaller number of attacks that are more likely to hit. This benefit works best when a single, skilled archer (the task leader) uses her teammates' help to improve her accuracy.

Illus. by D. Hudnut

STEADFAST RESOLVE

Your team members can use their camaraderie and shared experience to shrug off the effect of fear.

Training: Through long experience in dealing with adversity, you and your teammates develop the trust and support needed to bolster each other's minds when subjected to magical fear.

Task Leader Prerequisite: Concentration 8 ranks and Iron Will.

Team Member Prerequisite: Base Will save bonus +2.

Benefit: Any team member who must make a saving throw against a fear spell or effect gains a +2 circumstance bonus on the save if he can see or hear at least one team member.

Tips: Some fear-based spells affect areas. If you cast such a spell on an area that includes both allies and enemies, your teammates are likely to make the save while the foes run away.

SUPERIOR TEAM EFFORT

When your team works together on a task—whether it's battering down a door, talking a nervous innkeeper into allowing everyone to spend the night, or sneaking past a guard—everyone on the team does a better than average job of assisting each other's efforts.

Training: Your team focuses on improving a particular skill. Each team member watches the task leader and learns a few specific actions that can help her succeed.

Task Leader Prerequisite: 8 ranks in a skill and Skill Focus for the same skill.

Team Member Prerequisite: 1 rank in the skill to which the task leader's Skill Focus feat applies.

Special: This teamwork benefit applies only to checks made with the skill to which the task leader's Skill Focus feat applies.

Benefit: Any team member who attempts to aid another member's check with the relevant skill must make a DC 5 check to succeed rather than a DC 10 check.

TEAM MELEE TACTICS

Because your group fights as an effective team in melee, its members can use the aid another action with greater than normal efficiency.

Training: Your team studies each member's tactics, fighting style, and tendencies. These hours of focused observation allow each member to understand how best to help the rest of the team.

Task Leader Prerequisite: Combat Expertise and Dodge.

Team Member Prerequisite: Base attack bonus +6.

Benefit: Whenever a team member uses the aid another action to grant another member a bonus on attack rolls, that bonus increases by 1.

Tips: The aid another action allows an ally to strike with superior accuracy at the expense of the aiding character's own attacks. Thus, the ally who receives the assistance should be the best qualified team member to take down the foe—whether by virtue of damage reduction, high AC, or the ability to use Power Attack for extra damage.

TEAM RUSH

Your team travels faster than normal as a group. The efforts and assistance of the faster characters allow the slower ones to keep up.

Training: Your team must march for a week as a group, traveling across roads, dells, forests, and mountain passes. By so doing, each team member learns how best to help everyone move together.

Task Leader Prerequisite: Survival 8 ranks and Endurance.

Team Member Prerequisite: Survival 1 rank.

Benefit: When the entire team is traveling overland on foot, each team member moves at the task leader's speed. This benefit does not extend to combat and similar short-term movement situations, or to mounted characters.

Tips: A barbarian is the best task leader for this teamwork benefit. At the cost of a prerequisite feat, he allows his allies to travel much more quickly across the countryside. In campaigns that feature frequent wilderness or underground travel, the time saved might prove to be a major benefit.

TEAM SHIELD MANEUVER

When your team fights as a group, its members can close ranks to protect a badly injured ally.

Training: Your group learns to react quickly when an ally falls. You drill in pushing aside a wounded team member before he tumbles to the ground and moving him out of harm's way.

Task Leader Prerequisite: Shield Specialization (see page 82).

Team Member Prerequisite: Shield Proficiency.

Benefit: When a team member's hit points drop to –1 or lower, any teammate adjacent to him who carries a shield can use an immediate action to push him out of harm's way. The injured team member moves 10 feet before falling prone.

Tip: This tactic works best if one of the group's second-line characters has a potion or wand ready to heal the fallen character. In this case, even a character who isn't a member of the team can play a valuable role in making the most of this benefit.

WALL OF STEEL

By closing ranks and locking shields together, you and your teammates form an impenetrable barrier to shield a more vulnerable team member from enemies.

Training: Your group stands in a tight formation and locks shields while a hired mercenary or assistant pelts everyone with blunt arrows. Each bruising shot reminds you to improve your form and teamwork.

Task Leader Prerequisite: Tower Shield Proficiency and base attack bonus +8.

Team Member Prerequisite: Shield Proficiency and base attack bonus +2.

Benefit: As a swift action, any member of the team can lose his shield bonus to AC and grant it to a single adjacent team member instead. This bonus stacks with the recipient's existing shield bonus, if any.

Tip: Any arcane spellcasters who are frequently exposed to missile fire might want to take the Shield Proficiency feat to gain this teamwork benefit.

Illus. by R. Horsley

From the Knights of the Round Table to the Circle of Eight, from the Vestal Virgins to the Knights Templar, fantasy, myth, and medieval romance have always been filled with affiliations. Where would Robin Hood be without his band of Merry Men? For that matter, what challenge would the Sheriff of Nottingham present without his tax men and the support of the usurper King John? Could Frodo have survived without the Fellowship?

An affiliation can be large or small. Its armies could thunder like the wrath of a just god across continents and planes to change the face of the multiverse. It could quietly toil in an outlying village keeping the children asleep at night while a vampire is bound safely in the secret cellar under Old Man Hart's feed barn. An affiliation might be centuries old, or it might have begun only last fall with the discovery of a dryad's severed arm in the alley behind the tavern. An affiliation might be good or evil. It could solicit funds to build mithral-domed temples to Heironeous where crusading clergy heal the sick and rest after patrolling the night trade roads. It could subtly undermine the faith of the paladin king, inspiring him to kill his wife in a jealous rage and rise again as a blackguard to bring a dark age to the kingdom.

An affiliation can be almost any group of people, limited only by their imagination and their ability to form common goals. An ancient cabal of liches, the strict ecclesiastical Wee Jasian hierarchy, the king's bodyguards, the thieves' guild, the old apothecary and the three daughters that help to run his shop—all these and more are affiliations.

BROADENING YOUR GAME

Affiliations add another level to the D&D experience. They pull the focus back a step, broadening it from the adventure–loot–sell cycle that makes up some player characters' activities. With affiliations, the community comes to the fore. Conspiracies, kingmaking, war, piracy, famine, revolution, business, plague, or the founding of an empire take center stage for a time. When the tarrasque appears, an entire kingdom mobilizes (while the neighboring kingdom promises aid but sends assassins, hoping to advance on a weakened foe after planting season). When a new prophet preaches in the West and gathers followers, repercussions ripple through churches far and wide, tithes decrease, and the old rites are threatened. When kingdoms clash and food is scarce, when churches excommunicate the best among them and beatify the worst, when comets blaze forth the deaths of princes and revolution grips the land in a paroxysm of metamorphosis—that is when affiliations come to the fore to play out their grand drama.

This is not to disparage an individual's focus. Indeed, affiliations highlight individuals in the same way that a background serves to define the figure of a portrait. You need not be interested in world-spanning politics to find value in affiliations. Has your character ever recovered the poison sack from a monstrous scorpion, or a kuo-toa's idol of Blibdoolpoolp, or yet another masterwork sword from a bandit chief? Affiliations give you a ready place to liquidate such treasures. Has your character ever been drained by a shadow, ridden by a night hag, or victimized by an ethereal filcher? Hire an affiliation member to restore your strength, exorcise your demons, or track down the planar pickpocket while you concentrate on your main quest. Advancing in your affiliation can be almost as important to your character's development as attaining new levels.

Affiliations also allow your character to do things that she otherwise would not be able to do. Ever wanted to open your own tavern? Start your own smithy or weapon shop? Preach to a congregation of thousands? Clear Stirge Ridge, raise a curtain wall and a donjon, and assume the responsibility of nobility? Affiliations allow you to do this and more.

THE TWO CATEGORIES OF AFFILIATIONS

Like-minded individuals might gather in an affiliation for any number of reasons, but at the fundamental level there are two basic categories of affiliations: social and racial.

Social Affiliations

A social affiliation is formed when individuals with a common interest come together to promote or protect that cause. It's that common interest, rather than any physical or professional similarity (such as race or class), that binds the members.

The most energetic or accomplished people among the membership have the best chance of rising to a high rank within the group. Conversely, members who fail to advance the cause can see their status drop drastically—sometimes so drastically that they are forced to leave the affiliation.

Racial Affiliations

As the name implies, a racial affiliation is only open to individuals of the race in question. It's conceivable that, in the context of a given campaign, a human might perform an amazing deed that causes a group of dwarves to offer him a place in their affiliation, but such occurrences should be exceedingly rare.

Racial affiliations differ from social affiliations in a number of ways. It's usually easier for a member of a racial affiliation to maintain his status even if he fails in an endeavor, because racial affiliations don't typically penalize their members in such cases. Also, members of racial affiliations usually gain some tangible (that is, game-related) benefit from their membership at a lower level of status than is the case in social affiliations.

WHY JOIN AN AFFILIATION?

Affiliations can be viewed as another type of treasure. The coffer of rubies might have fallen into the acid swamp and melted, but the Brotherhood of Bahamut holds you in high esteem for slaying the young black dragon. Your standing in the Brotherhood goes up, and next time, instead of tithing a church to grow back your shield arm or emptying your gem pouch to book passage on a shady captain's barkentine, the Brothers will cast *regenerate* or *wind walk* for you, free of charge. In this way, an affiliation serves you, the same way that your sword, your spellbook, and your gold benefit you.

You can also consider affiliations as an additional class feature. The Skill Focus (Gather Information) feat provides a bonus on Gather Information checks, but so too does sufficient status in an affiliation of thieves. Join an affiliation of sages to gain bonuses on Knowledge checks. As you increase in status, you gain more affiliation benefits and greater personal power (as well as face greater risks and enemies).

Your affiliation brings rich potential to role-playing. The group can create many opportunities, including adding foils for your PC, rivals vying for your rank, and steadfast allies that can provide aid or request it of you. Affiliations also help drive your character's motivations; when considering your character's background, you should understand how his affiliations fit in.

From the Dungeon Master's point of view, affiliations can be used to spur adventures, to lend the world verisimilitude, to introduce NPCs, to act as treasure and reward, and even to explain the occasional *deus ex machina* (even the best campaigns can benefit from such a device from time to time!). You should work with your DM to determine what affiliations are available to your character. Perhaps your Dungeon Master will allow you to create your own affiliation and join it (or found it). You should also discuss possible NPC and enemy affiliations in the campaign. Affiliations with goals inimical to your own can serve as challenges that highlight your character and his allies—the Sun Fane of Pelor is opposed to the Reviled of Laogzed, while the King's Navy scours the seas through storm and swell to harry the *Thunder Sail Argosy* pirate fleet.

Also, while the affairs of some affiliations might be fixed in the campaign world firmament, unchanging outside of DM fiat, others can be more dynamic. Evolving affiliations add another dimension to your game. Using the materials presented later in this chapter, you and your DM can make your affiliations change as the world does, even in response to your character's actions.

No matter how you interact with affiliations, keep in mind that the goal is to have fun. Whether your thieves guild is a static fixture whose future is unquestionably secure, or whether it is a ragtag band of merry companions constantly on the run from the city watch and in danger of extermination or gaol, you should enjoy affiliations as you wish.

MEMBERSHIP HAS ITS PRIVILEGES

You have a separate affiliation score for each affiliation, but need only track those important to you. Your affiliation score defines your status in that group. Rising in status can earn benefits such as an offer of membership, a monthly flow of gold and emeralds, or research time at a wizard college.

You can't get ahead in an affiliation without devoting some of your character's time and effort to the cause. You might have to bring treasure to dragons, behead rival chieftains, break your halfling comrades out of jail, or perform any number of other types of activities. Your affiliation will be willing to meet you halfway, but you've got to help the group out if you want the rewards.

Multiple Affiliations: You can be associated with multiple affiliations at one time. However, each subsequent affiliation is harder to maintain. The first affiliation that you have (your primary affiliation) imposes a –10 penalty on all other affiliation scores. Subsequent affiliations oppose an additional –5 penalty to each affiliation that you gain afterward. In other words, you can have one affiliation score with no penalty, a second at –10, a third at –15, a fourth at –20, and so on. High-level characters are usually able to maintain one or two affiliations of note but only minor associations with other organizations.

Some affiliations might not be compatible, and the DM has final say on such issues. For example, in a campaign where the human kingdom of Althar wars with the elven realm of Gaelian, the DM might rule that no character with an affiliation to the Knights of Althar can also have an affiliation with the Greenfold Rangers of Gaelian.

Multiple Affiliation Benefits: If you have multiple affiliations, you can only gain the benefits of one affiliation at a time. If you have a high enough affiliation score to gain benefits from more than one affiliation, choose which set of affiliation benefits affect you at the beginning of each day. You gain all the benefits for which you qualify from the chosen affiliation.

FEATURES OF AFFILIATIONS

Your affiliation has many features, some primarily of use in roleplaying and background. These aspects include such basic information as the affiliation's name and its background, goals, and dreams. Most affiliations have a symbol that enables members to identify one another. An affiliation's

The halflings of the Caravan of Shadows (see page 169) stay one step ahead of the authorities

description might include information about high-ranking members and how the group feels about members joining or leaving its ranks, as well as facts about the group's significant enemies or allies. If an affiliation has a secret that relates to the group's basic nature or how it operates, that information is provided.

Some of an affiliation's features come into play when you join it or advance in it. Still others can be used to affect your campaign world. The following features are common to all affiliations.

Type: An affiliation can be of one of the following ten types: business, cabal, college, druid circle, fighting company, government, spy ring, temple, thieves' guild, or tribe. An affiliation's type limits the kinds of executive powers wielded by its leaders, and whether it is better at fighting, spying, or negotiation. In the example affiliation descriptions that follow, a racial affiliation is identified by the word "racial" in parentheses after its type. All other example affiliations are social.

Scale: An affiliation's scale is a measure of its scope of influence. As affiliations grow in size and power, they increase the scale of their activities. The Bulette Rampant Mercenary Company could be as inconsequential as a cadre of men-at-arms with a rotting ballista or as mighty as an army for hire with half a dozen battalions and flying dragon support. An affiliation's scale can be from 1 to 20 and is also defined by a descriptive term that indicates the extent of its influence. Scale directly affects an affiliation's capital and its ability to project power. Table 7–1, on page 184.

Affiliation Score Criteria: Base requirements for membership, if any, are given here. An affiliation might have race, nationality, alignment, class, or some other baseline membership criteria. The table in this portion of an affiliation description lists a number of factors and how they impact your affiliation score in that group.

Titles, Benefits, and Duties: A title is a designation of rank within the affiliation's hierarchy. Characters with an affiliation score of 3 or lower are usually not considered members. In social affiliations, members with affiliation

Illus. by E. Widermann

scores from 4 to 10 are generally looked upon as probationary members. A character with an affiliation score of 30 or higher attains the most prestigious title.

Lower-rank benefits carry over to higher ranks, but normal stacking rules apply.

Even if you have founded your own affiliation (as opposed to positing the existence of one that you can join as a recruit), you still must increase your affiliation score normally before you can gain the benefits (and take on the duties) of a titled member of your affiliation. This represents the fact that you can't simply say, "I am founding an affiliation," and by virtue of that declaration become entitled to send an assassin after the duke or bring a plague to the eastern river tribes. Rather, you must establish your affiliation as a force in the world by satisfying affiliation score criteria, proving by virtue of your deeds that your affiliation is a force to be reckoned with and a player on the political stage.

Executive Powers: Executive powers are wielded by the affiliation's leadership, generally those members with an affiliation score of at least 30. If a PC achieves a higher affiliation score than a leader NPC, the NPC might quietly step aside in favor of the newcomer. Many affiliations, however, force the two contenders to duel or to match wits in some fashion.

Unless otherwise noted, an affiliation's leadership can use one executive power per month.

Details about executive powers are given starting on page 186.

MAKING AFFILIATIONS DYNAMIC

The noon air cooled, and a shadow drifted across the bright silver coins stacked in Tabark's scales. The moneychanger looked up from his table in the bazaar and saw the clouds darkening. Large black raindrops began to fall. When the first blue lizard thudded onto his table, upsetting the scales and sending the silver coins tinkling into the air, Tabark realized this was no summer squall. "The Reviled!" he screamed. "Laogzed's priests plague us!" He ran for the Sun Fane as the lizard deluge began in earnest, reptiles plummeting through awnings and crashing into fruit stands, each lizard's body wrapped with crackling lightning and frigid from its recent altitude.

When you play with affiliations, a new avenue for conflict resolution and storytelling opens. Plagues, the births of kingdoms, wars, naval blockades, arcane research breakthroughs, trade embargoes, and other factors become part of your campaign in new ways. Your character need no longer do everything from winning the Battle of Stirge Ridge to lifting the curse on the southern farmlands to negotiating peace with the Frost Cavern quaggoths. You and your DM can rely on your affiliation to accomplish some of these tasks while you spend the bulk of your time focusing on your PC's main quest.

Have you ever wondered who will watch your character's family, castle, or subjects when he is off adventuring? If your PC is part of the Bulette Rampant mercenary company, you can simply have a detachment from your battalion watch over your loved ones. If your DM determines that the Valx

Nine-Eyes criminal syndicate strikes at your family while you are adventuring underground, you can resolve the attempt by playing out the details (in the absence of your character) or, more simply, by using opposed violence checks for your mercenary company and the brute squad sent by the beholder. (Violence checks are described below.)

Have you ever picked up a powerful magic item, say a *+2 thundering dire flail*, that no one in the party could use? Campaign credulity is stretched by simply selling it to an anonymous buyer who just happens to have 36,500 gp ready to spend. Instead, you donate it to your affiliation and increase its capital—it is reasonable to assume that a sizable affiliation includes a member who knows (or now wants desperately to learn) how to use a dire flail.

Have you ever heard yourself utter the lines that famously fill a DM's heart with annoyance, frustration, and uncertainty? Namely, "Can I buy magic items?" When you use affiliations, businesses and colleges have the trade executive power, which allows some wondrous items to come up for sale in the campaign—if a character has the right connections.

The following rules help guide a dynamic approach to affiliations.

Capital: An affiliation starts play with capital equal to its scale. Capital represents different types of assets for different affiliation types. A fighting company has its capital invested in soldiers, armor, weapons, and transport, while a cabal has its capital invested in wondrous items, spellbooks, bound demon servants, and political secrets.

In wartime and in months of hardship, your affiliation's capital might go down; in peacetime when trade prospers, your affiliation's capital might go up. An affiliation's minimum capital is 0; its maximum capital is twice its scale. If your affiliation does nothing for two consecutive months, normal daily processes increase its capital by 1. A good way to increase your affiliation's capital is to donate treasure. For every 1,000 gp × your affiliation's scale that you donate each month, its capital increases by 1. Thus, you must donate 5,000 gp during the course of a month to increase a scale 5 affiliation's capital by 1. For an affiliation that has a scale greater than 10, you must donate treasure in the amount of 10,000 gp × the scale to increase capital in this way. Such organizations have increased their scope to such an extent that they need not only gold, but vast tracts of real estate, arcane secrets, favors of the emperor, the name of the duke's bastard son, and other nonmonetary items to increase their stature and power.

An affiliation whose capital falls to –1 is disbanded and cannot be refounded for a period of 1d4 months.

An affiliation whose capital remains at its maximum for a number of consecutive months equal to twice its scale improves one category in scale. For example, if a scale 4 business maintains a capital of 8 for eight consecutive months, it becomes a scale 5 business.

Violence Check: When an affiliation attempts to do something using bullyboys, bludgeons, or battles, a violence check (1d20 + violence bonus) is made. Fighting companies, governments, and tribes have violence bonuses equal to

1/2 their scale. All other types of affiliations have violence bonuses equal to 1/4 their scale.

Espionage Check: An affiliation's attempts to sneak around, gather information, and infiltrate opponents are all summed up using espionage checks (1d20 + espionage bonus). Cabals, spy rings, and thieves guilds have espionage bonuses equal to 1/2 their scale. All other types of affiliations have espionage bonuses equal to 1/4 their scale.

Negotiation Check: Convincing arguments, delicate engagements, and subtle (perhaps even magical) manipulation are the province of an affiliation's negotiation checks (1d20 + negotiation bonus). Businesses, colleges, druid circles, and temples have negotiation bonuses equal to 1/2 their scale. All other types of affiliations have negotiation bonuses equal to 1/4 their scale.

EXAMPLE AFFILIATIONS

The following affiliations are representative of the standard D&D world and adaptable for most campaigns. Don't be shy about renaming or revising any of the example affiliations described below. The more specific to your world that you make them, the more likely they are to come to life at your gaming table.

BLOODFIST TRIBE

Symbol: The members of the Bloodfist Tribe emblazon their shields and tents with a red upraised fist, and many dye their sword-arm gauntlets red as well.

Background, Goals, and Dreams: For centuries, the Bloodfist Tribe has wandered the wilderness of the north, following great herds of elk and bison. Half-orc youths who are outcasts from human or orc communities often find their way north and join the tribe, leaving their old lives behind.

While it's comforting to be among other half-orcs, life among the Bloodfists isn't easy. The tribe often makes war against rival tribes of full-blooded orcs and fends off reprisals from the human communities it sometimes raids for food and supplies. Like hunter-gatherers everywhere, the Bloodfists risk starvation whenever hunting goes poorly or game is scarce. In hard times, the Bloodfist Tribe shrinks from the attrition of war, starvation, and younger members head south to seek an easier life.

The Bloodfist Tribe leaders' primary concern is where next to march. Sometimes they make war on the orcs and giants of the northern mountains, sometimes they raid the human lands to the south, and sometimes they are content to follow the elk herds as they migrate. Leaders also spend a lot of time mediating disputes within the tribe. It's no easy task to be the arbiter in a dispute when either aggrieved party can fly into a bloodthirsty rage at a moment's notice.

Type: Tribe (racial).

Scale: 6 (city).

Affiliation Score Criteria: Only half-orcs are eligible to join the tribe. The Bloodfists have made war against orcs and humans too much to ever fully trust those not of mixed blood.

Criterion	Affiliation Score Modifier
Character level	+1/2 PC's level
Barbarian or shaman	+2
Druid or ranger	+1
Track feat	+1
Assist tribe in major battle	+1
Bring word of bountiful land (wilderness with plentiful game, frontier with poorly guarded villages)	+1
Bring head of enemy chief to Bloodfist chieftain	+2

Titles, Benefits, and Duties: The greatest reward of affiliation with the Bloodfist Tribe is simply becoming part of a welcoming community with a shared heritage—something all too rare for half-orcs. But there's an additional benefit: the Blood Lodge, where worthy half-orcs test their resistance to pain and the strength of their blood.

When the chieftain deems a Bloodfist member worthy, he directs the shamans to build an earthen lodge. The shamans then use flint knives to cause painful wounds to the half-orc the tribe is honoring. Then the bleeding half-orc is enclosed in the Blood Lodge and suffers pain and waking nightmares for a day and a night.

The Bloodfist Tribe wanders the world, searching in vain for an ideal home

Illus. by S. Ellis

When the lodge door opens, however, the ritual has served its purpose: The tribe member emerges tougher and more cunning than before.

Affiliation Score	Title: Benefits and Duties
3 or lower	Not affiliated or junior member with no benefits.
4–10	**Bloodfist Tribe Member:** +4 racial bonus on Survival checks.
11–15	**Lodge of the Bear:** +2 circumstance bonus on attempts to influence the attitude of Bloodfist half-orcs. If you are a barbarian, your rage lasts for an extra round.
16–22	**Lodge of the Dire Wolf:** +2 inherent bonus to your Charisma or Intelligence score, +2 racial bonus on Fortitude saves, and +4 circumstance bonus on attempts to influence the attitude of Bloodfist half-orcs.
23–29	**Lodge of the Thunder Eagle:** +8 racial bonus on Survival checks, +2 inherent bonus to whichever ability score you didn't raise while at the Lodge of the Dire Wolf rank, and +8 circumstance bonus on attempts to influence the attitude of Bloodfist half-orcs.
30 or higher	**Lodge of the White Wyrm:** Cold resistance 10. When you emerge from the lodge, the tribe offers you a +2 weapon as a gift.

Executive Powers: Plunder, raid, terrorize.

BRIGHTMANTLE WEAPON FORGE AND TRADING CONSORTIUM

Symbol: The symbol of the Brightmantle Consortium is a forge over water.

Background, Goals, and Dreams: When the trees were new, and the earth chafed while the mountains grew in like baby's teeth, legend goes that Durgan Brightmantle soothed the stone with gifts of ore and the sweet taste of gems. Countless eons later, a dwarf clan devoted to Durgan Brightmantle and the extraction of the earth's riches founded their business based on mining and smithing. Since then, the small weapons shop in Isher has grown into one of the most powerful trading enterprises in the known world, shipping goods across kingdoms and even overseas, hiring caravan guards and traveling casters and buying land for forges in a large number of new towns. Brightmantle has even created entire new towns at particularly promising sites.

Enemies and Allies: Of necessity, the Brightmantle Consortium maintains good relations with all the monarchs in its scope of influence. Its relations with fighting companies are often strained, for while the latter are paid to go to war, business is difficult in those times.

Members: Most members of the Consortium are dwarves, although all the common races are represented.

The Brightmantle Consortium works diligently to retain its members, not wishing to expend resources on training new ones. If one chooses to leave, however, the Consortium does not contest the decision, with one exception. If the guild member joins another business, and the Consortium feels that trade secrets have been compromised, then the Consortium lobbies whatever local law exists in an effort to have the turncoat's new business outlawed.

Type: Business.

Scale: 14 (continental/seafaring kingdom).

Criterion	Affiliation Score Modifier
Character level	+1/2 PC's level
5 or more ranks in Diplomacy or Appraise	+1 per 5 ranks in each skill
Can cast *charm person*	+1
Can cast *sending* or travel by any means more than 100 miles in a day	+2
Makes peaceful contact with a new town or potential customer base	+1 per contact (max 3/year)
Successfully guards a caravan	+1 per caravan guarded
Sells 1,000 gp of weapons or other goods	+1 per sale (max. 1/month)
Discovers new iron, gem, or precious metal deposit	+2 per discovery
Less than 5 ranks in Diplomacy or Appraise	–2 per skill
Fails to deliver a caravan or message on time	–1/day
Loses a shipment of goods	–3/5,000 gp lost
Does not account for at least 10,000 gp of business per year (whether in direct sales, guard duty, or prospecting for ore or customers)	–6

Titles, Benefits, and Duties: As you rise through the ranks of the Consortium, you learn to increase your negotiating skills, and you gain access to great wealth.

Affiliation Score	Title: Benefits and Duties
3 or lower	No affiliation.
4–10	**Freelancer:** The Consortium occasionally calls on you to help on specific jobs.
11–20	**Associate:** +1 competency bonus on Diplomacy checks when speaking about business matters.
21–29	**Subguild Head:** Placed in charge of one of the many subguilds and commanding the services of five 4th-level experts (allot skill points as you like, for you can choose from the many clerks in the Consortium). Once per month, your experts must each make a DC 20 Appraise check and a DC 15 Gather Information check. If three or more fail the Appraise check, business is bad, and you lose 1 point from your affiliation score. If all five fail the Gather Information check, you fail to anticipate and deter a kidnap and ransom attempt targeting you or your family, and an EL 10 band of rogues arrives to carry out the deed.
30 or higher	**Secretary of the Overguild:** Can borrow up to 30,000 gp in cash from guild coffers, but this debt must be repaid within one year.

Executive Powers: Craft, gift, trade.

CARAVAN OF SHADOWS

Symbol: Once affiliated, you receive a tattoo of a game token on the back of your left hand in a solemn ceremony. When other members see the tattoo, they're more likely to talk to you and believe what you say.

Background, Goals, and Dreams: On the surface, the Caravan of Shadows is a prosperous halfling clan. But as with many halfling affairs, there's more going on beneath the surface. Halfling characters with a connection to the Caravan of Shadows are part of a network of thieves, spies, and con artists that stretches across a wide swath of civilization.

The Caravan of Shadows travels from city to city in a long wagon train, staying at each major settlement for a few days. The caravan's bards, acrobats, and other entertainers hold a series of performances, and the clan's merchants buy and sell spices and other valuable but easily portable goods. Less savory members of the caravan pick the pockets of the larger folk, commit burglaries on a nightly basis, or fleece the naïve in games of chance or shady business deals.

Type: Business (racial).

Scale: 7 (city and outliers).

Affiliation Score Criteria: Only halflings are eligible to join the caravan. Nonhalflings are sometimes allowed to travel with them—especially on dangerous roads—but fellow travelers don't get a glimpse of the inner workings of the caravan.

Criterion	Affiliation Score Modifier
Character level	+1/2 PC's level
Rogue	+2
Bard	+1
10 or more ranks in Sleight of Hand	+2
10 or more ranks in Perform	+1
Help another caravan member elude law enforcement	+1
Steal or cheat others out of at least 10,000 gp, then donate proceeds to the caravan	+1

Titles, Benefits, and Duties: The reward for greater affiliation with the Caravan of Shadows is a keener talent for the skills that have the made the caravan so prosperous. And if the caravan is in town, you can sell the loot from your adventures to them at an advantageous rate.

Affiliation Score	Title: Benefits and Duties
3 or lower	Not affiliated or junior member with no benefits.
4–10	**Caravan Member:** +2 racial bonus on Bluff, Gather Information, and Sleight of Hand checks.
11–15	**Shadow Pawn:** Can sell jewelry, art, and magic items to the caravan masters for 60% of their purchase price. +2 circumstance bonus on attempts to influence the attitude of caravan members.
16–22	**Shadow Knight:** Additional +2 racial bonus on all saving throws. +4 racial bonus on Bluff, Gather Information, and Sleight of Hand checks. +4 circumstance bonus on attempts to influence the attitude of caravan members.

Affiliation Score	Title: Benefits and Duties
23–29	**Shadow Rook:** You can sell jewelry, art, and magic items to the caravan masters for 70% of their purchase price.
30 or higher	**Shadow Castle:** +6 racial bonus on Bluff, Gather Information, and Sleight of Hand checks. +8 circumstance bonus on attempts to influence the attitude of caravan members.

Executive Powers: Pariah, shadow war, trade.

CASTLE MAIRO

Symbol: The symbol of Castle Mairo is the battered breastplate of Herridek I. In more intricate heraldic designs, the broken flint hammers of troglodytes can be seen lying below the shield.

Background, Goals, and Dreams: Three centuries and one day after the Third Troglodytic Ruin razed the original Fort Mairo to the ground, Castle Mairo was raised in its place. Regdar had defeated Iathra, Pharaoh of the Reviled, and the oases on the edges of the desert were once again safe. Before leaving, Regdar helped his brother, Herridek II, to found a small keep on the border of the dunes.

Life in the oasis can be harsh when the sandstorms roll through, but the presence of copper, platinum, and mithral in the surrounding hills and even the bubbling oasis itself provides ample reason for the castle's continued existence.

Members: Herridek II rules the castle wisely, and he recruits all manner of citizens to his nascent barony: men-at-arms, certainly, but also wizards, bards, rangers, and skilled rogues. The castle is especially desperate for divine casters and healers.

Herridek II is a beneficent monarch and allows individuals to enter and leave his domain at their leisure. In times of crisis—if a new pharaoh were to rise in the lands of the Reviled, for instance—all those nearby are drawn inside the castle walls and expected to aid in its defense.

Type: Government.

Scale: 9 (regional/barony).

Criterion	Affiliation Score Modifier
Character level	+1/2 PC's level
Base attack bonus +5 or higher	+1
Base attack bonus +10 or higher*	+2
5 or more ranks in Survival	+1
Can cast *cure* spells 2nd level or higher	+4
Explored the shafts of the Raptor-Pharaohs	+1 for each tomb shaft fully explored
Slew Raptor-Pharaoh mummy	+1/4 Hit Dice of mummy
Knew Regdar or Herridek I	+4
Takes part in defense of the fort against raiders	+4
Is an outlaw	−2
Retreats in battle	−2
Commits a crime within the barony	−10
Is member of a thieves guild	−10

* Overlaps (does not stack with) the modifier for a base attack bonus of +5 or higher.

Titles, Benefits, and Duties: As you advance in the hierarchy of the barony, you gain access to its riches and begin to enjoy the benefits of nobility, while accepting the duties thereof.

Once you attain the rank of Knight Baronet, you are invested with authority in the castle. Herridek the Second often makes forays into the desert for weeks or months at a time, harassing the Reviled and making sure that they are not a threat to the Castle and its mines.

Affiliation Score	Title: Benefits and Duties
3 or lower	No affiliation.
4–10	**Free Citizen:** Are a citizen of the barony but gain no special status.
11–20	**Hero:** +2 circumstance bonus on Diplomacy checks involving other citizens of the barony.
21–29	**Knight:** Gain the patronage of Herridek II, which grants a +4 bonus on Diplomacy and Gather Information checks made within the barony.
30 or higher	**Knight Baronet:** Command the services of an honor guard consisting of twelve 1st-level fighters, two 5th-level fighters, one 5th-level wizard, and two 7th-level halfling rangers mounted on giant eagles.

Executive Powers: Law, raid, war.

THE CHALICE

Symbol: The symbol of the Chalice is a ruby chalice with crossed ivory lightning bolts on the cup.

Background, Goals, and Dreams: The Chalice is an armed company dedicated to stamping out the influence of devils, demons, yugoloths and other slavering fiends on the Material Plane. The paladin Arbinget Ivenay founded the Chalice a millennia ago with one goal: to recover the Chalice of Heironeous from Dispater's Iron City of Dis. Aside from the members of the group's Lightning Council, no one knows if the chalice was recovered or not, but regardless of the chalice's fate, in the intervening ages the affiliation's purpose has broadened to ending the influence of the Lower Planes in the world.

Members: Many members of the Chalice are paladins, priests, and fighters; many of these eventually take levels in the knight of the Chalice prestige class (see *Complete Warrior*). Mortality is high among the membership of this combative affiliation, and as such the Chalice is always looking to induct new members of sufficient piety.

The Chalice is not a vengeful organization, and freely allows members to leave its ranks. If a member departs due to falling from paladinhood, fiendish possession, or alignment change—or tries to covertly corrupt the Chalice from within after suffering one of these fates—the Lightning Council dispatches an EL 14 exorcism squad (typically a 13th-level paladin and a 13th-level cleric of Olidammara) that is more inclined to smite first and ask for repentance by means of *speak with dead* much later.

Secrets: When you attain the rank of Lightning Councilor, the other councilors lead you somberly to the Eyrie of Heironeous. There, among the lightning rods of the order, under a clouding sky, they inform you of the true nature of the Chalice of Heironeous. What was stolen from Heironeous millennia ago—not by Dis, but by Hextor, who attempted to shirk responsibility for his deed (and to better secure his prize) by loaning the chalice to the Iron Lord of the Second—was not a powerful magic item, nor even an artifact. As revealed to Arbinget Ivenay by the solar Tomal on the eve of St. Vorgan's Day 1,223 years ago, the Chalice of Heironeous is in fact the daughter of Heironeous, a young goddess-angel now held in durance vile deep in Dispater's Iron Tower. Every day, the Lightning Councilors dream of rescuing her; every day, they come no closer.

Type: Fighting company.

Scale: 12 (multiregional/kingdom).

Criterion	Affiliation Score Modifier
Character level	+1/2 PC's level
Base attack bonus +10 or higher	+1
Can cast divine spells	+1
Knight of the Chalice prestige class	+1 per two levels
Wields a *holy avenger*	+8
Has slain a fiend with more than 9 HD	+1 per fiend
Has written a treatise on slaying fiends	+2
Successful mission on behalf of the Chalice	+2 per mission
Successful mission on behalf of the Lightning Council	+4 per mission
Neutral alignment	–15
Evil alignment	–25
Defeated by a fiend	–4
Friends with a half-fiend, tiefling, or other tainted	–10

Titles, Benefits, and Duties: As you advance within the ranks of the Chalice, you learn demon-fighting techniques and how to resist the temptations of fiends.

Affiliation Score	Title: Benefits and Duties
3 or less	No affiliation.
4–10	**Initiate:** The Chalice recognizes you as a potential ally or enemy in the struggle to eliminate fiends from the Material Plane.
11–15	**Defender:** You are inducted into membership, and can requisition a *potion of protection from evil* 1/week.
16–20	**Thunderer:** Chalice priests cast up to 3rd-level *cure* spells for free (excluding component costs) when you visit their temple.
20–24	**Scion of Heironeous:** Chalice priests cast up to 4th-level spells for free (excluding component costs) when you visit their temple.
25–29	**Paragon of Heironeous:** By taking a –5 penalty to your affiliation score, you can gain a *raise dead* spell from a Chalice priest. Fiends can make a Knowledge (the planes) check (DC 30 minus your character level) to recognize you, and if they succeed, their frenzy grants them +2 on damage rolls when attacking you.
30 or higher	**Lightning Councilor:** Once per year, you can borrow for 1 week any magic weapon or armor with a value of 18,000 gp or less from the Chalice's armory. While you do so, the affiliation takes a –1 penalty to its capital.

Executive Powers: Crusade, inquisition, war.

DARKSPIRE COLLEGE OF THAUN

Symbol: The college's symbol is three black stalactites, one larger than the other two, on a gold field.

Background, Goals, and Dreams: The Darkspire College's campus is built into the sides of three enormous hanging stalactites tapering down from the vaulted ceiling of a colossal underground cavern. Piercer, the largest stalactite, extends more than 300 feet down from the ceiling and has a base with a radius of 150 feet. It houses laboratories and libraries for each school of arcane magic, a concert hall, thirteen summoning chambers, two gymnasiums, the Desmodu Dormitory, and lecture halls. Each of the Fangs, the other two stalactites, is roughly two-thirds the size of the Piercer. They contain classrooms, studies, artists' cupolae, and practice rooms. The northernmost Fang also features the Sunless Rose tavern and a warehouse. The warehouse stores goods in transit to and from the surface and other underground communities, and it sells surplus and goods gone unclaimed when a caravan doesn't return. The warehouse has a 25% chance to have any given *Player's Handbook* item in stock and available at 150% of the price. The Piercer and the Fangs are connected by a network of rope bridges.

Faculty and students attend Darkspire to increase their arcane knowledge, and that is the stated goal of the organization.

Enemies and Allies: The students, faculty, and administration maintain friendly relationships with most of the other peaceful residents of Thaun (the underground cavern that hosts the college's spires on a small part of its roof). These peaceful residents include svirfneblin, deep dwarves, two nomadic tribes of myconids, and a small community of exiled drow.

The college is harassed by most drow, by an aboleth that lives in Thaun Lake, and by Cherruk, a derro warlord who claims ownership of the caverns immediately above Thaun.

Members: The College holds no grudge against those who leave its faculty. Indeed, given the college's location, it counts on losing at least one faculty member per year to beasts, slavers, or an accidental fall from a rope bridge.

Type: College.

Scale: 5 (city).

Affiliation Score Criteria: Joining the Darkspire College is as simple as enrolling; however, to become a faculty member requires long study and arcane puissance.

The inverted towers of Thaun hide many secrets

Illus. by M. May

Criterion	Affiliation Score Modifier
Character level	+1/2 PC's level
Has darkvision	+2
10 or more ranks in Knowledge (arcana)	+2
Has the Arcane Thesis feat	+4 per feat
Can cast arcane spells 3rd level or higher	+2
Can cast arcane spells 5th level or higher	+4
Has a magic staff	+4
Is an archmage or has a *staff of power*	+8
Donates 1,000 gp (or more) magic item, to the Department of Crafting	+2 per item, max 3 items/year
Is drow, derro, duergar, or drider	−2
No ranks in Knowledge (arcana)	−10
Can cast divine spells	−2
Does not spend at least 1 month per year on campus	−20

Titles, Benefits, and Duties: As you advance in the college, you improve your Knowledge skills and gain access to magic items. You also earn a modest stipend for sharing your expertise with the college.

Affiliation Score	Title: Benefits and Duties
3 or lower	No affiliation.
4–10	**Correspondent Student:** You can regularly correspond with the college while adventuring.
11–20	**Adjunct Researcher:** +2 competence bonus on Knowledge skills while in the college's libraries.
21–29	**Professor:** When crafting a magic item, you can scavenge materials from the college—spend only 90% of the normal gp cost to craft an item. Drow slavers and derro kidnappers recognize your value—5% chance per month that an EL 12 team of subterranean mercenaries comes to claim your bounty.
30 or higher	**Regent:** Can requisition any arcane scroll of 750 gp or less from the college stores, up to three times per month. Must replace these scrolls with scrolls of equal value within one month of taking them.

Executive Powers: Craft, research, trade.

DRAGON ISLAND

Symbol: The symbol of Dragon Island is a purple rampant dragon. The elder dragons chose purple as a compromise; it doesn't correspond to any true dragon's real color and thus represents dragonkind as a whole.

Background, Goals, and Dreams: A few miles off a remote stretch of coastland is Dragon Island, where humans soar over skies on draconic steeds. In this insular society, dragons and humans live in concert, with dragons supplying ancient wisdom and humans providing industry and vitality.

Dragon Island can appear anywhere you like in your campaign world, and you can give it a more evocative name if you wish.

The nature of the dragons it houses (metallic or chromatic) is deliberately undefined. Depending on the dictates of your campaign, Dragon Island could be a bastion of hope or the nexus of a gathering evil.

Members: Affiliation members are human characters who grew up on Dragon Island, learning magic under the wing (literally) of draconic masters and even riding loyal dragons as steeds.

Type: Government (racial).

Scale: 12 (multiregional/kingdom).

Affiliation Score Criteria: Only humans qualify for this affiliation because Dragon Island is an insular place with no elves, dwarves or other humanoids. Most grew up here, but you could also establish an affiliation with Dragon Island if you spend years here as an adult.

Criterion	Affiliation Score Modifier
Character level	+1/2 PC's level
Speak Draconic	+2
Sorcerer	+2
10 or more ranks in Ride	+1
Donate 20,000 gp in treasure to the hoard of a Dragon Island dragon	+1

Titles, Benefits, and Duties: You'll learn from your draconic teachers, but the most thrilling reward of affiliation with Dragon Island is the chance to take wing with a friendly dragon as your flying steed. Doing so isn't easy; raising your affiliation score on Dragon Island is difficult.

There are many more humans than dragons on Dragon Island, and the dragons often have better things to

On Dragon Island, humans and dragons live together in harmony

do than fly around with humans on their backs. Those who become dragonspeakers imbibe a ritual draught containing dragon blood; this liquid lengthens the human life span and makes the dragons more likely to regard you as a suitable rider. But only the best dragonspeakers are offered the ritual that turns them into dragonriders, who are able to command a dragon for as long as it takes a moon to wax and then wane into nothingness. The greatest heroes of Dragon Island mystically bond with their mounts, creating an ongoing relationship between willing steed and rider.

Affiliation Score	Title: Benefits and Duties
3 or lower	Not affiliated or junior member with no benefits.
4–10	**Dragon Island Native:** +2 circumstance bonus on attempts to influence the attitude of Dragon Island residents. Your age categories (see page 109 of the *Player's Handbook*) become twice as long, although you don't revert to a younger age category.
11–15	**Dragonspeaker:** +4 bonus on saving throws against a dragon's frightful presence. +2 racial bonus on Knowledge (arcana) and Knowledge (history) checks.
15–22	**Dragonrider:** +4 racial bonus on Ride checks when riding a dragon.
23–29	**Dragonknight:** If you take the Leadership feat, you can have a dragon cohort.
30 or higher	**Dragonmaster:** +8 racial bonus on Ride checks when riding a dragon. +8 circumstance bonus on attempts to influence the attitude of Dragon Island residents. Immune to the frightful presence of dragons. Your age categories (see page 109 of the *Player's Handbook*) become four times as long, although you don't revert to a younger age category.

Executive Powers: Holiday, law, mint, war.

ELVES OF THE HIGH FOREST

Symbol: A cluster of acorns is the symbol of the Elves of the High Forest. Their jewelry often uses this motif, and they use the real thing—actual clusters of acorns—as subtle trail markers within the High Forest.

Background, Goals, and Dreams: The Elves of the High Forest live in a typical elf community: a series of treetop villages and small towns that together form a network to keep their forest safe and thriving.

Type: Tribe (racial).

Scale: 6 (city).

Affiliation Score Criteria: To gain affiliation with the Elves of the High Forest, you need only be an elf or half-elf. The elves have many non-elf friends in the forest, but only those with elf blood can partake in the privileged Hunt of the Full Moon. You don't need to grow up among the Elves of the High Forest; you can be from a far-off elf community, and you'll still gain affiliation with these elves normally.

The Elves of the High Forest have a semicommunal lifestyle, so they favor characters with skills or class abilites that make a woodland lifestyle easier. The fastest way to gain status within the Elves of the High Forest is to perform missions on their behalf. The elves particularly favor missions that protect the forest as a whole from interlopers—from human woodcutters to drow raiders.

Criterion	Affiliation Score Modifier
Character level	+1/2 PC's level
Druid or ranger	+1
10 or more ranks in Knowledge (nature) or Profession (herbalist)	+2
Each successful mission	+2
Each successful forest defense mission*	+4

* Overlaps (does not stack with) the "each successful mission" bonus.

Titles, Benefits, and Duties: The Elves of the High Forest offer specialized training in woodcraft for those they favor.

Those who reach a new level of status within the Elves of the High Forest attain the new benefits after attending the Hunt of the Full Moon—a combination night-hunt and ritual. The greatest hunters among the elves take you on an all-night hunt for elusive game. The target is traditionally a half-fey white stag, but sometimes the elves hunt more dangerous quarry by necessity or for variety. During the night, they teach you specialized techniques in perception, stealth, and moving through the wilderness. Some say the hunters leave the Material Plane entirely and wind up hunting mystical game among the fey of Arborea. You'll return in the morning exhausted, but with the sharper perceptions and peerless camouflage of the greatest elf hunters.

Illus. by H. Lyon

The Elves of the High Forest take part in the Hunt of the Full Moon

173

Affiliation Score	Title: Benefits and Duties
3 or lower	Not affiliated or junior member with no benefits.
4–10	**Friend of the High Forest:** +2 circumstance bonus on attempts to influence the attitude of High Forest elves.
11–15	**Guardian of the Branch:** +4 racial bonus on Listen, Search, and Spot checks.
16–22	**Guardian of the Trunk:** +4 racial bonus on Hide and Move Silently checks performed outdoors. +4 circumstance bonus on attempts to influence the attitude of High Forest elves.
23–29	**Guardian of the Root:** +8 racial bonus on Listen, Search, and Spot checks, and the woodland stride ability (*PH* 48). +8 circumstance bonus on attempts to influence the attitude of High Forest elves.
30 or higher	**Guardian of the Forest's Heart:** +2 effective caster level to all druid and ranger spells when casting spells within the boundaries of the High Forest.

Executive Powers: Craft, harvest, plague.

THE GOLDEN HELM GUILD

Symbol: A golden helm is the symbol of the guild, naturally. Working in their smithies and forges, the gnomes often wear yellow skullcaps to indicate their affiliation.

Background, Goals, and Dreams: The Golden Helm Guild is a network of expert master crafters that spans dozens of gnome communities, making fine armor, weapons, and other gear for the greatest heroes of the gnomes. But the Golden Helm is no mere blacksmithing guild. It focuses on creating rare items invested with potent magic, each one a testament to its maker's skill and power.

Missions on behalf of the Golden Helm Guild often involve securing rare ores or finding other special ingredients that the guild can use in its most potent creations.

The guild often commissions its most talented members to make magic weapons, armor, or other gear to sell or give to a gnome-allied war effort. Each item you make on the guild's behalf worth at least 10,000 gp earns you +1 to your affiliation score. You can earn this bonus multiple times, but only if the Golden Helm Guild commissions the items ahead of time.

Type: Business (racial).

Scale: 10 (regional/march).

Affiliation Score Criteria: Guild membership is open only to gnomes, but anyone who can swing a hammer is welcome to sign up for an apprenticeship. Unless you have some talent for crafting either mundane or magic items, you won't derive any benefit from your affiliation.

Criterion	Affiliation Score Modifier
Character level	+1/2 PC's level
10 or more ranks in at least one Craft skill	+2
10 or more ranks in a second Craft skill	+2
20 or more ranks in at least one Craft skill	+4
Per item creation feat*	+1
Each successful mission	+1
Per magic item worth at least 10,000 gp made for guild	+1

* Does not include the item creation feat gained by someone who becomes a Golden Helm Master (see below).

Titles, Benefits, and Duties: When you've earned enough affiliation to attain new benefits, you need only apply for a promotion at the nearest Golden Helm chapterhouse, which exists in any gnome community of large town size or larger. After a series of examinations, the guild will award you the new rank and hold a lavish feast in your honor.

Affiliation Score	Title: Benefits and Duties
3 or lower	Not affiliated or junior member with no benefits.
4–10	**Golden Helm Apprentice:** +2 racial bonus on Appraise checks relating to stone or metal objects. +4 racial bonus on any one Craft skill.
11–15	**Golden Helm Journeyman:** +6 racial bonus on Appraise checks relating to stone or metal objects. +6 racial bonus on the Craft skill you chose when you were a journeyman, and a +4 racial bonus on another Craft skill.
15–22	**Golden Helm Master:** Gain Craft Magic Arms and Armor as a bonus feat. You can craft magic arms and armor as if you had a caster level equal to 1/2 your Hit Dice. This ability does not allow you to meet any other prerequisites of crafting a magic item.
23–29	**Golden Helm Grandmaster:** Craft magic arms and armor as if you had a caster level equal to your Hit Dice.

The gnomes of the Golden Helm Guild make fine weapons and armor—and they're capable of using them

Affiliation Score	Title: Benefits and Duties
30 or higher	**Golden Helm Exalted:** Spend 10% fewer experience points than normal when crafting a magic item.

Executive Powers: Craft, gift, trade.

THE LAND OF HONOR

Symbol: The Land of Honor doesn't have a nationwide symbol. Each feudal lordship has its own colorful heraldry, most using abstract decorations rather than real-world symbols like animals or words.

Background, Goals, and Dreams: Humans from this land live in a society guided by feudal lords who often war against one another. But the wars are largely fought by a caste of noble soldiers who regard battle as an opportunity to demonstrate their bravery and adherence to a rigid code of honor. Rather than draw inspiration from medieval and Renaissance Europe, this land hearkens back to feudal Japan and the Age of Samurai.

In your own game, the Land of Honor might be its own nation-state, or perhaps it remains a vague and exotic place beyond the periphery of the campaign map. Give it whatever name you like.

Your human character can be a traveler or an exile from the Land of Honor. If you want to retain your unique cultural identity, consider an affiliation with others from your land. Perhaps colonies or communities of exiles exist beyond the borders of the Land of Honor, or perhaps travel back and forth is sufficiently easy that you can periodically return to the land of your birth.

If you're wielding executive powers, you're either one of the feudal lords or the power behind the lord's throne. Your concerns vary as widely as those of any real-world ruler; you might care about the welfare of your subjects, or you might care only about games of power or living a life of wealth and leisure.

Type: Government (racial).

Scale: 15 (continental/empire).

Affiliation Score Criteria: Unless one is human and born in the Land of Honor, a character is accepted in this affiliation only under extraordinary circumstances.

Criterion	Affiliation Score Modifier
Character level	+1/2 PC's level
Fighter or monk	+2
5 or more ranks in Diplomacy	+1
10 or more ranks in Diplomacy	+2
Defeat worthy foe in honorable duel	+1
Perform mission at lord's request	+2 (and −4 if you fail)

Titles, Benefits, and Duties: As you gain affiliation with the Land of Honor, your feudal lord will reward you with a ceremonial—but very functional—katana. A katana is statistically identical to a bastard sword. Your willingless to live and die by your honor code becomes increasingly apparent from your bearing, and many foes will shamefacedly avoid a duel with you.

Affiliation Score	Title: Benefits and Duties
3 or lower	Not affiliated or junior member with no benefits.
4–10	**Citizen of Land of Honor:** +2 circumstance bonus on attempts to influence the attitude of other citizens of the Land of Honor. Your lord gives you a masterwork katana.
11–15	**Fearless One:** +2 racial bonus on Intimidate checks. Gain Knowledge (nobility and royalty) as a class skill, regardless of your class.
16–22	**Honorable One:** +4 racial bonus on Intimidate checks. +4 circumstance bonus on attempts to influence the attitude of citizens of the Land of Honor. Gain Quick Draw feat when drawing your katana.
23–29	**Selfless One:** +6 racial bonus on Intimidate checks. +8 circumstance bonus on attempts to influence the attitude of citizens of the Land of Honor. +4 bonus on attack rolls made to confirm a critical hit with your katana.
30 or higher	**Perfected One:** Gain damage reduction 1/– when you wield your katana.

Executive Powers: Gift, law, war.

MERATA KON

Symbol: There is no symbol for the Merata Kon as a whole. Most travelers recognize a Merata clan by its krenshar-hide tents and the smoke puffs that rise on the horizon when a Merata scout or companion band signals.

Background, Goals, and Dreams: The Merata Kon is a network of barbarian clans, sweeping nomadically from the coastal plains to the high scrub forest, living off wandering herds, seasonal vegetation, and ransomed travelers. Some tribes of the Merata Kon allow themselves to be hired as mercenaries, making raids on borderland baileys, but many would-be patrons shy away from these tribes because both its savagery and geographical uncertainty make it somewhat unreliable. Nonetheless, the people of the Kon are a powerful force due to their numbers and ferocity.

In the spring of each year, all the Merata clans gather in one place for an Althing, where horses are traded, daughters are wed, and alliances are fixed. Occasionally, in times of need, a Chief of Chiefs is selected, but most years there is no higher authority than the chiefs of the individual clans.

Enemies and Allies: The clans are constantly in a state of tension with the civilized city-states and kingdoms whose frontier lands and territories they drift over seasonally, ignoring political borders like rain or wind or any other force of nature.

Members: The tribe consists mostly of half-orcs, humans, and disaffected half-elves who find much in common with the natural and alienated lifestyle of the tribe. There are known to be Merata clerics, but there are virtually no arcane casters outside of a few skald bard/barbarians.

The varied Merata clans have no political argument against former members, but most clan chiefs take desertion personally. In most cases, a Merata who leaves his clan is disowned and shunned forevermore.

Type: Tribe.

Scale: 13 (multiregional/kingdom and vassal states).

Criterion	Affiliation Score Modifier
Character level	+1/2 PC's level
Base attack bonus +5 or higher	+1
Base attack bonus +10 or higher*	+2
5 or more ranks in Survival	+1
10 or more ranks in Survival	+2
Trophy Hunter feat	+1
Can cast *control weather*	+3
Defeat animal or magical beast of your level or higher one-on-one	+1/4 creature's HD
Defeat a clan champion one-on-one	+2 per win
No ranks in Survival	−2
Has lived in city	−2
Does not accept a challenge to combat	−6, and cannot improve affiliation score until challenge is accepted
Member of a civilized affiliation	−4 per affiliation

* Overlaps (does not stack with) the modifier for a base attack bonus of +5 or higher.

Titles, Benefits, and Duties: As you learn the ways of the Merata, you learn to make these smoke signals yourself as you increase your survival skills and become closer to nature.

Affiliation Score	Title: Benefits and Duties
3 or lower	No affiliation.
4–10	**Lowborn:** The Merata Kon hold less contempt for you than for most.
11–20	**Setaf Kon:** +2 competence bonus on Diplomacy checks involving your clanmates and a +2 competency bonus on Survival checks made when traveling with clanmates.
21–29	**Trebor Kon:** Become a subchief and have a 3rd-level adept to assist you. By a system of bonfires and smoke, you can transmit signals 200 miles across the Stalking Plains in 1d2 days.
30 or higher	**Clan Chief:** You are accompanied by four chief's men (6th-level barbarians), and your counsel is a 4th-level cleric/4th-level bard.

Executive Powers: Harvest, raid, terrorize.

THE ONE AND THE FIVE

Symbol: The symbol of the One and the Five is six black, hooded figures on a violet starburst field.

Background, Goals, and Dreams: A secret ring of six wizards and sorcerers is at the heart of this cabal. Arcane casters vexed by a lack of resources find this group's support exceptionally useful for purchasing spellbooks, researching new spells, and perfecting metamagic techniques.

Enemies and Allies: The cabal has strained relations with most other organizations. Its secretive core, the six wizards and sorcerers known as the titular One and the Five, frustrate the attempts of spy rings and thieves guilds to penetrate and gather information, while their subsidization of spell books, research, and material components irks arcane colleges and many business guilds.

Members: Most of the members are human, but the One and the Five welcome all to their cabal, and in addition to half-orcs, dwarves, and gnomes, two centaurs and one gyno-sphinx are known to be associated with the affiliation.

No one knows what happens if you try to leave the One and the Five. For some reason, no one ever has—or at least, no one is talking about it.

Secrets: Once you reach an affiliation score of 30, you must defeat one of the current One and Five in a mortal spell duel. After killing your opponent, you are inducted into the heart of the cabal, where you learn that the order is devoted to Vecna, and that the One represents his Eye, and the Five represent the fingers of his severed hand.

You need not worry about converting to worship of Vecna at this point—when you first attained an affiliation score of 25 or higher and the subtle wooings of the inner cabal did not persuade you to convert to the service of the Maimed Lord, EL 14 assault squads of summoned monsters and golems are sent to kill you before you learn the cabal's secret.

Type: Cabal.

Scale: 10 (regional/march).

Criterion	Affiliation Score Modifier
Character level	+1/2 PC's level
5 or more ranks in Knowledge (arcana)	+1
Can prepare arcane spells	+1
Can cast arcane spells of 3rd level or higher	+1
Can cast divination spells of 5th level or higher	+2
Has over 2,500 gp in magic items	+1
Donates magic item valued at 1,000 gp or more to the cabal	+1 per item, max six/year
Shares 5th-level or higher-level spell with other wizards at cabal Grand Convocation, held twice/year	+2
Completes mission for the leaders of the cabal, the One and the Five	+2 per mission
Can cast divine spells	−6
Divulges identities of members or other secrets of the cabal	−4
Is known to investigate the identities or the nature of the One and the Five	−10, and an EL 12 coterie of sorcerer wraiths is sent to dissuade or dispose of you
Is a member of a spy ring	−6

Titles, Benefits, and Duties: As you advance in the cabal, your knowledge of the arcane increases. You also gain access to spells and discounted components, paraphernalia, and research.

Affiliation Score	Title: Benefits and Duties
3 or lower	No affiliation.
4–10	**Of the Many:** The cabal is aware of your presence and judging you.
11–20	**Of the Mind:** When you gain a wizard level, automatically learn three spells rather than two.
21–29	**Of the Body:** When you craft a magic item, pay only 90% the gp cost.
30 or higher	**Of the One and the Five:** Three times per year, you can borrow any wondrous item in the *Dungeon Master's Guide* of 10,000 gp value or less for up to 1 week. You may not borrow a charged item in this manner.

Executive Powers: Craft, research, shadow war.

Eyeless Errol listens to a suggestion for the Restenford Guild's next job

RESTENFORD GUILD OF INSURERS, SOLICITORS, AND BEGGARS

Symbol: The symbol of the guild is a hand placing a gold piece into a beggar's uplifted cup.

Background, Goals, and Dreams: The Guild of Insurers, Solicitors, and Beggars exists for the aggrandizement of its members. This legitimate businessman's guild is run by Eyeless Errol, a sightless dwarf who spends much of his time on a chair in the guildhouse listening to his subordinates report. Eyeless Errol dresses neatly, always matching the color of kerchief that winds around his eyeless sockets to the color of his pants, and he smiles with distant awareness.

Enemies and Allies: This affiliation enjoys comfortable relations with the Restenford Assassins Guild and the worker guilds of the city (including the Sewerworkers and the Chimney Sweeps), walking a fine line between respectability and ruthless underworld efficiency.

Members: Most members are rogues, fighters, or arcane casters, with a few priests of Olidammara rounding out the roster.

The guild is highly vengeful. An EL 12 hit squad (typically two 8th-level fighters and two 8th-level rogues) is dispatched to squelch any member who attempts to leave the guild without Errol's express permission.

Secrets: Behind the façade of an honest businessman and a dandified hands-off owner, Eyeless Errol runs his guild according to best practices, using double-entry accounting and double-team extortion, and he is very hands-on despite being eyes-off. Some whisper that he is, in fact, not blind at

all, but is simply a polymorphed dragon with blindsense; others claim he is a mindspy doppelganger who sees through the eyes of his victims, watching himself as he attacks. No one ever really expects to unseat Eyeless Errol, but many aspire to become the Insurance Boss, the Chief Solicitor, or the Beggarmaster.

After becoming Insurance Boss, Chief Solicitor, or Beggarmaster, you must deal with regular assassination attempts. Either an ambitious underling or Eyeless Errol himself, wary of your own ambition, attempts to rub you out. If you succeed on a DC 30 Gather Information check, you learn of the plot and do not have to face an assassination attempt that month. If you fail to uncover the plot, you must either succeed on a DC 15 Fortitude save, with failure indicating you have been assassinated, or play out the attack with your DM's help (the assassin typically has a CR of your level minus 3).

Type: Thieves guild.

Scale: 6 (city).

Affiliation Score Criteria: To join, you must be a probationary footpad for some months, while the guild surveys your work. If you are sufficiently skilled, the guild invites you to run its gauntlet, a maze of mechanical and magic traps (and, according to some, an otyugh assassin retained by the guild to challenge overconfident would-be initiates).

Criterion	Affiliation Score Modifier
Character level	+1/2 PC's level
10 or more ranks in Hide, Sleight of Hand, Forgery, Disguise, or Open Lock	+2 per skill
Sneak attack +3d6 or higher	+2
Runs the gauntlet in initiation	+4
Spends one day per week appraising for the guild (requires 10 ranks in Appraise)	+1
Performs a heist or swindle for the guild that nets 1,000 gp or more	+1
Spends time in the City Watch gaol	+1
Tips off the guild about incoming City Watch raid	+2
Has no ranks in Hide, Sleight of Hand, Forgery, Disguise, or Open Lock	–2 per skill
Participates in a nonguild job, first time	–8, and an EL 8 team of thugs is dispatched to rough you up
Participates in a nonguild job, second time	–15, and an EL 12 team of rogues is dispatched to maim or kill you
Steals from someone under the guild's protection	–6

Titles, Benefits, and Duties: As you advance through the guild's ranks, you improve your skills as a rogue and gain access to equipment that will help you perform cons, heists, rackets, and shakedowns for the guild. You also become the beneficiary of the guild's skill at procuring lucre.

Affiliation Score	Title: Benefits and Duties
3 or lower	No affiliation.
4–10	**Probationary Footpad:** Your jobs are sanctioned so you do not incur the affiliation score penalty for an out-of-guild job.

Illus. by S. Ellis

Affiliation Score	Title: Benefits and Duties
11–15	**Hood:** You must run the gauntlet and be initiated. If you survive, you gain an income of 200 gp/month. you must purchase equipment only from the guild, which maintains supply houses selling everything in the *Player's Handbook* and items of 1,000 gp value or less from the *Dungeon Master's Guide.*
16–22	**Bravo:** In the city, +4 insight bonus on Hide and Move Silently checks and +2 circumstance bonus on Sleight of Hand checks. The City Watch recognizes you if its Spot check beats your opposed Disguise check and attacks on sight.
23–29	**Made Man:** You can fence up to 3,000 gp of items for 90% market value each month. Income of 400 gp/month to spend at guild supply houses as above. Travel with impunity through the Sewerworkers Union's sewers and the Chimney Sweeps' rooftops.
30 or higher	**Insurance Boss, Chief Solicitor,** or **Beggarmaster:** +6 bonus on Gather Information and Intimidate checks in the city. You can borrow any one of the following from guild coffers for 1 week at a time: a *cloak of elvenkind, boots of elvenkind,* or any wand described in the *Dungeon Master's Guide.* The City Watch considers you untouchable and no longer attacks on sight. Must make a DC 20 Diplomacy check each week or be forced to pay 100 gp in bribes and kickbacks. Must fight off regular assassination attempts.

Executive Powers: Pariah, plunder, shadow war.

RESTENFORD SEWERWORKERS GUILD

Symbol: The symbol of the Sewerworkers Guild is a stylized image of the guildmaster: a square with a circle in it, representing Smiling Gordin and the head it contorts into a grinning rictus when communicating.

Background, Goals, and Dreams: Rat runners, ooze masters, subterranean tinkers, exterminators, conjurors and abjurers of filth—the members of the Sewerworkers Guild are unnoticed by most and unthanked by all. The guild is responsible for the operation of the city's vast subterranean tunnel network. Repair work and extermination occupy much of the guild members' time, but these menial tasks only serve to mask the guild's true nature.

The guild's leader is Smiling Gordin, a miraculously *awakened* gelatinous cube, originally brought into the sewers because of its ability to scour a passageway clean simply by oozing through it. The origin of Gordin's intelligence is unknown, but the quality of that intelligence is unquestioned. Communicating by gelatinous convulsions that manipulate the vocal cords of various heads absorbed into his body and not yet dissolved (the city is a violent place, and there is no shortage of heads for Gordin), Gordin has built the Sewerworkers Guild into one of the most powerful spy rings in the region.

Enemies and Allies: Utilizing their near-invisible status and all-city access to the fullest, Gordin and the sewerworkers maintain good relations with the aboveground Guild of Insurers, Solicitors, and Beggars (thieves guild) and often collaborate with that guild on missions.

Members: Not surprisingly, most members of the Sewerworkers are rogues, but a fair number are arcane casters, and some who appear to be ooze masters are whispered to be priests of Juiblex.

The Sewerworkers cannot allow anyone to leave their ranks. The knowledge gained by the spies is valuable, and the tunnel crawlers are loath to risk letting it get away for free, but the real threat is one of exposure. Smiling Gordin simply cannot allow anyone to learn of the spy ring's existence. Anyone leaving the ranks soon comes face to face with an EL 14 strike team lead by an otyugh assassin.

Secrets: By the time you become Guild Boss, you learn that Smiling Gordin has become fixated on learning why it was chosen for intelligence. While it pursues that goal (and toward that end it might ask you to complete adventures that it cannot), Gordin is content to become the Guild Grandfather, retaining ultimate veto power but relinquishing day-to-day control to you.

Type: Spy ring.

Scale: 6 (city).

Criterion	Affiliation Score Modifier
Character level	+1/2 PC's level
Is deformed or maimed	+1
5 or more ranks in Hide or Disguise	+1 per skill
Can cast divination spells of 3rd level or higher	+6
Sneak attack +2d6 or higher	+2
Brings back sample of ooze, mold, or slime to study	+1 per sample
Completes a mission for the guild	+4 per mission
Lives in sewers	+4
Is double agent with another spy ring	+6
Has no ranks in Hide, Disguise, Bluff, Spot, Listen, or Sense Motive	–2 per skill
Is followed by City Watch or a member of a rival affiliation into the tunnels	–2
Is visibly shocked by Smiling Gordin's appearance (one time only, DC 15 Bluff check on first meeting)	–4
Fails a mission for the Sewerworkers	–6

Titles, Benefits, and Duties: As you advance in the Sewerworkers' Guild, you improve your spying and information-gathering skills and learn to use the city tunnels to your advantage.

Affiliation Score	Title: Benefits and Duties
3 or lower	No affiliation.
4–10	**Squatter:** The Sewerworkers allow you to squat at night in the tunnels.
11–20	**Rat Runner:** +2 competence bonus on Gather Information checks in the city.
21–29	**Ooze Master:** +2 circumstance bonus on Hide or Move Silently checks in the sewers.
30 or higher	**Guild Father:** Reroll a failed Spot or Listen check 3/day. +1 resistance bonus on saves against disease.

Executive Powers: Assassinate, pariah, research.

SHARULHENSA, THE ALABASTER TOWERS

Symbol: Sharulhensa has no particular symbol, but many of the buildings within the neighborhood have fonts and fountains incorporated into their design—a architectural nod to the magic pools.

Background, Goals, and Dreams: Sharulhensa is a half-elf enclave built within the walls of a human metropolis. Raised on the ruins of an ancient elf empire, the enclave holds onto its magical heritage even as other cultures have supplanted elves as the dominant humanoids across the land. The half-elves of Sharulhensa remember the mighty magic of their forebears, and they pass along ancient traditions to the new generation in an effort to connect their dual heritage.

Secrets: Throughout the city of Sharulhensa are sacred pools believed to hold the spirits of departed half-elves in a quiescent state. When a half-elf drinks of these waters, he or she gains a measure of magical power and a sense of the eldritch tapestry that weaves together residents of Sharulhensa, no matter how far they roam. The enclave's elders keep the locations of the sacred pools a secret even from the ordinary residents of Sharulhensa, so the only way to get access to the pools is by garnering favor with Sharulhensa's elders—earning affiliation, in other words.

The movers and shakers within Sharulhensa have intense academic rivalries with each other as they vie to recapture more of their elven heritage.

Type: College (racial).

Scale: 2 (neighborhoods).

Affiliation Score Criteria: Only half-elves are eligible to join this affiliation. Sharulhensa residents regard full-blooded elves as lacking sufficient vitality and energy to guard the heritage of their ancient forebears.

Criterion	Affiliation Score Modifier
Character level	+1/2 PC's level
Wizard	+2
Other spellcaster	+1
10 or more ranks in Knowledge (arcana)	+2
Each successful mission	+1
Recovers a magic item worth 30,000 gp or more	+2
Recovers a spellbook with at least 7th-level spells	+1

Titles, Benefits, and Duties: Sharulhensa sometimes needs adventurers to undertake missions on its behalf. If you complete such an adventure successfully, you can increase your affiliation score with the half-elf enclave. But moreso than the standard "Stop the orc horde marching toward the city" mission, recovering the elves' ancient heritage earns favor with Sharulhensa's elders—even if you're recovering that heritage from the elves themselves. In particular, you can improve your status with Sharulhensa if you retrieve major magic items crafted by the elves long ago and grimoires with high-level arcane spells. Not any magic sword or spellbook will do, however—Sharulhensa is interested only in items steeped in elven history.

The reward of Sharulhensa affilation—access to the magic pools—is great, but earning affiliation with Sharulhensa is

The half-elves of Sharulhensa are dedicated to preserving ancient lore

more difficult than most other racial affiliations. Those who persevere find their ability to wield magic, especially the subtle enchantments of the elves, vastly improved.

Affiliation Score	Title: Benefits and Duties
3 or lower	Not affiliated or junior member with no benefits.
4–14	**Citizen of Sharulhensa:** +2 circumstance bonus on attempts to influence the attitude of Sharulhensa half-elves.
15–22	**Pool of the Inscrutable:** +1 to the DC of saving throws against your enchantment spells and spell-like abilities.
23–29	**Pool of Influence:** +8 circumstance bonus on attempts to influence the attitude of Sharulhensa half-elves.
30 or higher	**Pool of the Endless:** Gain *detect magic* as a spell-like ability usable at will (caster level equal to your Hit Dice).

Executive Powers: Gift, research, trade.

Illus. by C. Frank

SUN FANE

Symbol: The symbol of the Sun Fane is the same as that of Pelor: a shining sun.

Background, Goals, and Dreams: The Sun Fane is a powerful Pelorite temple. A cyclopean golden dome, representing the sun, rests atop colossal blue marble walls, representing the sky, and both are supported by golden flying buttresses, completing the tableau by representing the sun's rays shining down on the earth.

The goal of the temple is to witness for Pelor and spread the glory of its merciful diety. All members of the temple turn a stern eye on those who disparage Pelor as a "part-time god" who only works half the day.

The prelates, canons, and bishops of the Sun Fane are all ardent in their worship of Pelor, but this does not stop them from engaging in heated internal politics. The One Sun is the archcanon of the temple, and when a leader steps down or passes away into the sun's brilliant radiance, the infighting is fierce.

Members: Most of the Sun Fane's members are clerics, and only a cleric can rise to become the One Sun. Paladins, rogue scholars, and a few druids also climb the ecclesiastical ladder of the Sun Fane's hierarchy.

In keeping with its merciful teachings, the Sun Fane holds no grudge against those who leave its ranks. The temple is notoriously persistent, however, in trying to win back souls, and those who leave the Sun Fane hierarchy can expect many old friends to come calling with news of brilliant grace and blessed light.

Type: Temple.

Scale: 12 (kingdom).

Affiliation Score Criteria: The Sun Fane is open only to those of non-evil alignment.

Criterion	Affiliation Score Modifier
Character level	+1/2 PC's level
5 or more ranks in Heal	+1
Can cast divine spells of 3rd level or higher	+1
Can cast divine spells of 5th level or higher*	+2
Undertakes missionary voyage	+1 per voyage
Converts creature to Pelor's faith (convert must remain a believer)	+1 per convert
Raises or *resurrects* an innocent soul with own funds	+2
Donates 15% or more of treasure to Sun Fane	+2
Cannot cast divine spells	−2
Sells spells to neutral creature	−2
Sells spells to evil creature for nonevil purpose	−6
Acts against alignment	−10 ,and cannot improve affiliation score until undergoing *atonement*

* Overlaps (does not stack with) the bonus for casting divine spells of 3rd level or higher.

Titles, Benefits, and Duties: As you advance in the ranks of the Pelorite priesthood, you learn to win converts to your faith, to spread the healing light of your faith, and to scourge the undead (along with, some would say, rivals for the archbishopric).

Affiliation Score	Title: Benefits and Duties
3 or lower	No affiliation.
4–10	**Lay Worshiper:** The Sun Fane welcomes you as a faithful member of the congregation.
11–20	**Ordained:** +2 competence bonus on Knowledge (religion) checks when consulting the Sun Fane's library.
21–29	**Canon:** +1 competence bonus on Diplomacy checks.
30 or higher	**Archbishop:** The *Sun Fane brooch*, vestment of your office (does not take up space on the body) grants you a +2 bonus on turning checks.

Executive Powers: Crusade, excommunicate, holiday.

THE THUNDER SAIL ARGOSY

Symbol: The symbol of the Argosy is emblazoned on the sails of all three brigantines: a gold lightning bolt on sable.

Background, Goals, and Dreams: The gentle heaving of the deck underfoot slows, then stops. The gulls overhead quiet, and the only sound is the rhythmic lapping of the suddenly becalmed salt sea at the hull. A peal of thunder cracks over the horizon, and clouds come scudding across the sky only a few knots slower than the bolt-on-sable Thunder Sails.

Captain Jonas Jakes commands an outlaw fleet of three brigantines: the *Rain Hawk*, the *Red Lightning*, and the flagship *Maelstrom Aria*. Few of the current pirates in his fleet were with him when he started, and those few who have been in his quarters wonder about the strange crystal sphere kept there. Slightly larger than the glass buoys used by fisherfolk, the sphere contains a swirling turquoise mist, and it rests clutched near the captain's bedstand in a preserved and upended harpy's talon. During battle, Captain Jakes hauls the crystal sphere and harpy-leg monopod onto the aft deck, where he sits on a closed locker, hunches over the sphere, and strokes it possessively while barking orders to his mates and crew. He appears quite mad, but the Thunder Sail Argosy has survived, and the crew doesn't care whether that is due to cunning or luck as long as the gold is good and the grog is thick.

Members: Most members of the Argosy are fighter/rogues or swashbucklers, and many take levels in duelist. A few important officers are sorcerers or druids, and they function as artillery and environmental control. Finally, like every sailing ship, each Thunder Sail vessel has at least one bard, to sing shanties in time with the hauling of ropes and alleviate the thirsty, languorous days between plunderings.

The Argosy is not concerned about those who leave its ranks—and in fact it frequently asks men to leave the crew (often at the end of a plank after they have crossed the captain).

Secrets: When you rise to a captaincy, Captain Jakes informs you of the Thunder Sail Argosy's hidden power and purpose. Once a prominent plantation owner in a southern kingdom, Jonas Jakes saw his daughter, a powerful druid who helped him tend his crops, polymorphed into a green mist by a chaotic, mad archmage who rode his horse through town one day and casually sowed destruction in his wake. By some arcane accident, Jonas's daughter Ellyrese retained her intelligence and spellcasting ability. Jonas keeps her in the crystal sphere on the harpy-leg monopod in his quarters, and now she uses her druid magic to cast spells for him to turn the tide of a battle or to speed the Argosy on its way. Jonas is desperately searching for an island with a white alabaster cliff dwelling containing "no more than one eye, no less than five mouths," which a seer once told him would be the key to restoring his daughter.

Type: Fighting company.

Scale: 5 (city).

Criterion	Affiliation Score Modifier
Character level	+1/2 PC's level
Base attack bonus +5 or higher	+2
5 or more ranks in Profession (sailor)	+2
5 or more ranks in Perform (sing) or another Perform skill suitable for shipboard life	+2
Can cast *control weather* or similar effect	+10
Can summon water elementals, water natural allies to career ship without need to run it aground	+4
Is an outlaw	+2 (per outlawing kingdom)
Sails on a successful raid with the Argosy	+4 per raid
Has own ship to add to the Argosy	+6
Has no ranks in Profession (sailor), Climb, or Balance	−2 per skill
Has tattoo of Imperial Naval service or kills an albatross	−8
Disobeys captain	−10, and you are flogged
Causes ship to be scuttled	−50, and you are marooned

Titles, Benefits, and Duties: As you advance in the Argosy, you develop your seamanship, win plunder, and perhaps even rise to the captaincy.

Affiliation Score	Title: Benefits and Duties
3 or lower	No affiliation.
4–10	**Able-Bodied Seaman:** The affiliation does not recruit you, but does recognize your seamanship.
11–20	**Corsair:** +2 competence bonus on Profession (sailor), Balance, and Climb checks while on board one of the Argosy's ships.
21–29	**Ship's Officer:** Gain an average of 200 gp per month in plunder.
30 or higher	**Captain of the Rain Hawk or the Red Lightning:** You assume the captaincy of a pirate ship; you can command a group of ten pirates (eight 1st-level fighter/1st-level rogues, one 3rd-level fighter/4th-level rogue, and one 7th-level druid) on one mission per month.

Executive Powers: Plunder, raid, terrorize.

WINTERVEIN DWARVES

Symbol: The Wintervein symbol is a triangular mountain rent with cracks or veins.

Background, Goals, and Dreams: A collection of clans, the Wintervein Dwarves are a cross between a nomadic tribe and a crusading army, continually on the move against the goblinoids, aberrations, and other horrors of the deepest caverns. The Winterveins delve deeper into the earth than most other dwarves, seeking out new caverns and transforming them into

Illus. by M. May

The Thunder Sail Argosy approaches another stepping stone on Captain Jakes's quest

habitable communities. Winterveins typically secure a cavern complex deep underground, build a fortress-city there, then push deeper underground until they find a hospitable spot for their next city. They're the dwarves on their race's most important frontier: the one that extends below the feet of all other dwarves.

Type: Fighting company (racial).

Scale: 11 (multiregional/duchy).

Affiliation Score Criteria: The Winterveins function like a "super-clan," so every blood member is a dwarf. The group has a number of nondwarf allies, but only dwarves can earn affiliation.

The Winterveins often send clan members on scouting or raiding missions, either in the company of their clan comrades or with allies of other races (such as an adventuring party). But the deeds that earn the most respect among the Winterveins aren't the assaults on goblin forts or mind flayer strongholds—they're the successful defense of dwarven communities on the underground frontier when they are beset by invading drow, vengeful duergar, or other opponents.

Criterion	Affiliation Score Modifier
Character level	+1/2 PC's level
Cleric, fighter, or paladin	+1
Dwarven defender prestige class	+2
Per successful mission	+2
Per defense of besieged dwarf citadel	+4

Titles, Benefits, and Duties: The Wintervein dwarves are masters of both alchemy and genealogy, and they can create "ancestral infusions" that give the imbiber a measure of the fortitude and strength of their famous forebears. Those infusions are the mechanism that delivers your affiliation benefits.

The Winterveins delve deep into the darkest underground reaches

When you reach a leadership position among the Winterveins, you are the leader of a large extended family (with all the politics that entails), and you're the general of a dwarf army on the march. Over the course of a single council meeting, you might declare a crusade against a mind flayer city, hire adventurers to find the lost Hammer of Resounding Rings, and placate a dwarf elder who is having a hard time finding wives for his sons.

Affiliation Score	Title: Benefits and Duties
3 or lower	Not affiliated or junior member with no benefits.
4–14	**Defender of Wintervein:** +2 racial bonus on attack rolls against orcs and goblinoids.
15–22	**Hero of Wintervein:** As bonus feats, gain Weapon Focus (dwarven waraxe) and Weapon Focus (dwarven urgrosh). +6 racial bonus on attack rolls against orcs and goblinoids. Dodge bonus against giants improves to +6.
23–29	**Foehammer of Wintervein:** +4 racial bonus on attack rolls against orcs and goblinoids. Dodge bonus against giants improves to +8.
30 or higher	**Lord of Wintervein:** As bonus feats, gain Improved Critical (dwarven waraxe) and Improved Critical (dwarven urgrosh).

Executive Powers: Craft, crusade, raid.

CREATING YOUR OWN AFFILIATIONS

To create your own affiliation, follow these steps:

(1) Devise a concept, name, symbol (if desired), and background.

(1a) Create information (if desired) pertaining to members, enemies and allies, and secrets of the affiliation.

(2) Choose your affiliation's type and category.

(3) Choose its scale.

(4) Select the affiliation score criteria.

(5) Create the titles held by members and select the benefits and duties that accompany each title.

(6) Choose the executive powers available to the leader or leaders of the affiliation.

Keep in mind that creating your own affiliation is a bit like creating a new magic item and pricing it; tweaking is sometimes necessary. While these rules can be used like a cookbook to combine ingredients and make a decent product, there is always room for extra flavor. Astute readers will notice that the sample affiliations do not always follow this process in lockstep. You are encouraged to modify your affiliations as desired, and your DM is encouraged to allow for it, so that they fit your game and campaign world as well as possible.

As discussed, affiliations bring many new aspects to your game. As you're working through your creation ideas, don't forget that many of them can be enriched even further if other people at the table are doing the same with affiliations of their own. Friendly rivalries between affiliations can provide great motivation and background for adventure.

CONCEPT AND BACKGROUND

It is most helpful to devise a general concept for your affiliation at the outset. Will it openly rule in an area, or will it act behind the scenes? Are its members, assets, or abilities clandestine or hidden? Does it have a specific creed or objective? The answers to these questions help direct your creative efforts and make the affiliation more coherent and real.

Beyond a general concept, the extent of your affiliation's background is entirely up to you. Indeed, the extent of what's known about your affiliation is as broad as your imagination. The following topics can be considered when devising your affiliation. They might be set at the outset. Alternatively, you can move on to the other creation steps after only jotting down a few notes about your concept. Further details can be left for the end of the creation process, or for description and evolution during game sessions.

The example affiliations described earlier in this chapter make up a varied collection, yet they barely scratch the surface of what sorts of affiliations you can create for yourself. Each piece of information that can be part of an affiliation's description is discussed below.

Name: The name of your affiliation could be descriptive of its interests or concerns, or it could be a "false front" hiding its true agenda. It could be complex, legalistic, or long-winded, evincing an effort to impress or awe the general populace. Or it might be short or obscure, requiring a certain level of inside information to understand its true meaning.

Symbol: Design your affiliation's symbol (if you want it to have one), bring it to the table, and place it near your character sheet whenever affiliations are involved in play.

Motto: Perhaps everyone in your affiliation shares a battle cry, or perhaps they intone the same blessing before every sunset. (The example affiliations in this chapter have no mottoes, so you can come up with one you like if you want to use an affiliation "out of the box.")

Background, Goals, and Dreams: Just as your character is motivated by his past and driven to his future, so should your affiliation be. Did it start in the slaughterhouse of Bravik, only to become a powerful mercenary company scourging the hinterlands? Did it once rise to dominate the city's arcane society, only to be shattered by the demons it once commanded? Does your affiliation want to merge with another affiliation? Destroy one? Draft the king's niece into its ranks?

Enemies and Allies: You might choose one or two affiliations, races, regions, or creature types that your affiliation cannot abide. Perhaps your affiliation wants to expunge them from the earth, feels snubbed by them at court, or was almost exterminated by them after a mass immigration from another continent. In combat, members of the affiliation attack these

enemies preferentially, and in parley, they bait and insult them. The opposite applies to those creatures of individuals you choose as allies. They should be given aid and succor where possible, and you should expect similar treatment in return. Some information on how this relationship came about, what the degree of cooperation is, and how steadfast the relationship is would be useful as well.

Members: Name some of the other people in your affiliation. Identify the leader, his or her subordinates, and the rivals vying for position within the affiliation. You might consider, with the DM's permission, co-opting several previously existing NPCs from the campaign to be members of your affiliation. Think about how your affiliation treats ex-members (if it tolerates them at all).

Secrets: The byzantine politics of some affiliations afford them ample opportunity to gestate a tangled mass of secrets. If you like, choose one or two secrets for your affiliation. Share them with your DM, but only give hints about them within your party. Then, at an opportune time, unveil the secret. Perhaps your order is more ancient than anyone guesses, and under another name it founded the ruined castle you are now exploring—only your order's motto will activate the *magic mouth* on the nether cyst below the throne room. Perhaps you've been hinting at surprise allies, and when you reach the vampire's manse, you tap on the portcullis to summon the beast's apothecary, who is actually a spy for your guild.

TYPE

Choose your affiliation's type: business, cabal, college, druid circle, fighting company, government, spy ring, temple, thieves' guild, or tribe. This selection affects the executive powers available to the affiliation's leaders.

Some concepts might be difficult to define neatly. A group of related individuals (tribe) might be engaged in a profitable enterprise (business) selling illegal goods (thieves guild). However, for the purpose of executive powers, you'll need to set one type as the affiliation's primary focus.

CATEGORY

Decide whether your affiliation is a racial one or a social one, and include "(racial)" in the Type entry of the affiliation description if appropriate. (The concept you create could dictate which category the affiliation belongs in.)

SCALE

Choose your affiliation's scale in conjunction with your Dungeon Master. Table 7–1, below, provides guidelines.

As a general rule, the scale of an affiliation is an indication of how high up the ladder of influence it can rise. For instance, a scale 12 affiliation could obtain an audience with the king; a scale 8 affiliation probably has the count's ear; a scale 3 affiliation might get a hasty hearing by the local burgomaster on a slow day.

The exact meaning of scale could vary from affiliation to affiliation, however. For example, an affiliation does not necessarily need to be scale 19 to have influence on the Outer Planes. Take a cabal of scale 6—it has influence throughout a roughly city-sized area or population. This city might be the

City of Brass on the Elemental Plane of Fire, and the cabal's scale might be explained by the fact that it is extremely secretive and almost unheard by the general population on its home plane.

You must have the Leadership feat to found an affiliation. If you do so, it normally begins at scale 1. Campaign circumstances might dictate otherwise, however, so you should consult with your Dungeon Master.

Table 7–1: Affiliation Scale

Scale	Scope of Influence	Examples
1	Neighborhood	Bakery, druid hermit
2	Neighborhoods	Crossroads tavern
3	City quarter	Small abbey, small nomadic tribe
4	City quarter	Bank, slaughterhouse, barbarian trading post
5	City	Arena, pirate ship, githzerai rrakma
6	City	City watch, wild elf tree tribe
7	City and outliers	Large college, tyrant wizard in tower, death slaad commanding a populous gnoll tribe
8	City/county	Frontier fort, druid sect
9	Regional/barony	Small castle, established church
10	Regional/march	Minor nobility, powerful guild
11	Multiregional/duchy	Nobility, established knightly order, dread pirate fleet
12	Multiregional/kingdom	Standing army, orc hordes led by legendary chieftain
13	Multiregional/kingdom and vassal states	Vast army raised to fight off the tarrasque
14	Continental/seafaring kingdom	Centuries-old large kingdom, illithid underground nation
15	Continental/empire	Emperor and his legions, circle of archmages
16	Multicontinental/empire	Imperial legions with arcane and divine support
17	Global	Ancient order of epic-level knights
18	Astral Plane	Githyanki incursion force
19	Multiplanar	Armies in the Blood War between demons and devils
20	Cosmos	Epic-level affiliations, hero-deities

AFFILIATION SCORE CRITERIA

Affiliations measure a member's value by a number of factors. Some are baseline: If a character is not of the proper religion, nationality, race, alignment, class, or other nature, his affiliation score is irrelevant (absent special dispensation from the leadership). First, decide if your affiliation enforces any such prerequisites.

Other than baseline criteria, numerous other aspects of a character are considered when awarding benefits and status in a group. For your affiliation, choose up to thirteen of the criteria listed on Table 7–2.

A social affiliation can (and usually does) have some negative criteria—characteristics or accomplishments that reduce a character's affiliation score instead of increasing it. As a rule of thumb, select one negative criterion for every positive

criterion beyond the fifth one you choose (six positive and one negative, seven positive and two negative, eight positive and three negative, or nine positive and four negative).

For the most part, racial affiliations do not have negative criteria; once you're in a racial affiliation, you have to do something pretty outrageous to lower your status in the group—and such lowering is usually accomplished by simply kicking you out of the group.

Because it is easier to move up in the ranks of a smaller affiliation than a larger one, the base modifiers given on Table 7–2 must be adjusted according to the affiliation's scale. The base modifiers given are for affiliations with a scale of 1 to 7. For affiliations of scale 8 to 14, divide the modifiers given by 2. For affiliations of scale 15 to 20, divide the modifiers given by 4. The minimum impact of a criterion after modification is 1/2.

Table 7–2: Affiliation Score Criteria

Positive Criteria	Affiliation Score Modifier
Expertise and power	+1/2 character levels
Is a member of a favored race	+1
Charisma 13 or higher	+1
Base attack bonus of +5 or higher	+1
Base attack bonus of +10 or higher	+2
5 or more ranks in an appropriate skill	+1
10 or more ranks in an appropriate skill	+2
Has a feat that is significant to the affiliation	+1
Can cast arcane or divine spells	+1
Can cast 3rd- to 4th-level spells	+2
Can cast 5th- or higher-level spells	+3
Has/does not have a familiar	+2
Member of a prestige class important to the affiliation	+2
Possesses a magic item significant to the affiliation	+1/10,000 gp value
Wealth	+1/20,000 gp value
Landowner	+2
Noble title	+2
Lives in a favored region	+1
Parents or siblings in the affiliation	+2
Marries into a family whose head is an affiliation member	+2
Recruits a new member into the affiliation	+1
Spends ten or more years in the affiliation	+2
In the thrall of a member of the affiliation	+2
Recommendation of a member who has an affiliation score of 21 or higher	+2
Saves the life of a member who has an affiliation score of 21 or higher	+3
Adventures with a member of the affiliation	+1
Completes a mission assigned by the affiliation	+2
Makes a discovery important to the affiliation	+2
Humiliates an enemy of the affiliation	+2
Defeats a violent enemy of the affiliation in combat (the foe's CR must be equal to or or greater than the character's level)	+1/4 the creature's CR
Destroys an artifact anathema to the affiliation	+4
Razes a stronghold of one of the affiliation's enemies	+8
Makes a pilgrimage or journey important to the affiliation	+2
Donates money or magic items to the affiliation (a maximum per year might be set, after which donations accrue no additional bonus)	+1/1,000 gp donated

Negative Criteria	Affiliation Score Modifier
Is of unfavored race	–2
Associates with unfavored race	–2
Has been dead	–4
Has been undead	–6
Charisma 8 or lower	–2
Lacks base attack bonus of a certain level	–3
Lacks ranks in a certain skill	–2
Lacks a feat that is significant to the affiliation	–3
Lacks ability to cast a spell	–2
Has/does not have a familiar	–2
Is of opposed alignment	–4 to –20
Acts in a manner befitting opposed alignment	–4
Known to be friendly with opposing affiliation	–2 to –20
Known to be a member of opposing affiliation	–20
Face, hair, time and place of birth, birthmark, or other quality marks the character as undesirable	–20
Lives in unfavorable area	–2
Loses or destroys affiliation property	–1/1,000 gp value
Fails in combat	–2
Falls in combat with affiliation's hated foe or rival	–4
Steals from the affiliation	–10
Composes a song ridiculing the affiliation or a prominent member	–10
Has been/has never been to an Outer Plane	–2

TITLES, BENEFITS, AND DUTIES

Fill in titles as you wish for affiliation scores of 4 through 30. In general, each ranking covers a range of six points of affiliation score, but variances are common. Often it is easier to move through the lower ranks than the upper.

Choose three to five benefits from Table 7–3 for your affiliation. If you choose more than three benefits, it's a good idea to choose one duty (so that members don't get too many benefits without having to do something to earn them). If you choose four benefits, you should select one duty, and if you choose five benefits, you should select two duties.

Not all the benefits and duties detailed in the example affiliations appear in Table 7–3. You and your DM should feel free to devise your own benefits and duties, using the ones given here as guidance.

TABLE 7–3: AFFILIATION BENEFITS AND DUTIES
Benefits (affiliation score 11 or higher, or 4 or higher for racial affiliations)
+2 circumstance bonus on particular skill checks within a geographical region

+2 circumstance bonus on particular skill checks when working with other affiliation members or affiliation resources

100 gp/month income (or 200 gp for a business affiliation)

Ability to share spellbooks with one spellcaster of your level once per month

Personal valet or servant (CR 1 or lower)

Purchase spellcasting from your affiliation or an allied one at 3/4 standard price

Rent-free use of small flat in undesirable neighborhood

Requisition one 1st-level potion or scroll per month

Travel with impunity through an allied affiliation's territory

Benefits (affiliation score 21 or higher, or 15 or higher for racial affiliations)
+1 on attack rolls against members of an enemy affiliation

10% discount on experience or gp cost when crafting

Bard song—+1 bonus on Diplomacy checks in a tavern whose primary language matches that of the song

Call in favor—lower your affiliation score by 5 permanently to gain access to arcane or divine spell of 5th level or higher for 1/4 standard price

Claim audience with the king/emperor/theocrat within 1d6 days once per month

Communications network lets you use the Gather Information skill across the duchy, sea, or planes, depending on the scope of your affiliation, without requiring you to move from your hometown

Dreamwalker—if sleeping in affiliation headquarters and can prepare arcane spells, prepare one unknown spell per 8 hours sleep if it is known to another sleeper in the headquarters

Paper charm—when burned, *word of recall* (caster level equal to affiliation scale, minimum 11th) takes you and possibly allies back to your headquarters

Personal honor guard of 4–6 appropriate creatures (EL 8)

Purchase spellcasting from your affiliation or an allied one at 2/3 standard price

Benefits (affiliation score 30 or higher)
Personal hagiographer (6th-level gnome bard) shadows your every move with quill in hand, recording your deeds for the affiliation's records and the benefit of general posterity, strumming his lute and rhyming about your life when not engaged in his primary task

Borrow one item of up to 15,000 gp value from the affiliation's stores once per month for 2d4 days (30,000 gp value if the guild's scale is above 10); while the item is borrowed, the guild's capital is decreased by 1 if the item is valued at more than 10,000 gp

Monument—your affiliation, a grateful populace, or a coterie of rich, adoring sycophants erect an obelisk, a dolmen garden, or a statue in your honor, granting you a +2 bonus to your Leadership score and a +2 circumstance bonus on Diplomacy and Intimidate checks when dealing with people who have seen your monument

Personal honor guard of 4–12 appropriate creatures (EL 12)

Form friendship with head of allied affiliation (often a creature of CR 10 + 1/2 scale)

Ancient advisors—the spirits of the former affiliation heads are trapped within will-o'-wisplike glowing balls on the Wisp Crown, a symbol of your office; three times per day you can use the Wisp Crown's ancient advisors to grant you a +6 insight bonus on any Appraise, Decipher Script, Knowledge, Sense Motive, or Use Magic Device check

Claim audience with a rival (but not enemy) affiliation head within 1d4 weeks once every three months

Duties (affiliation score 11 or higher, or 4 or higher for racial affiliations)
Enemy affiliation's members gain +1 on damage rolls against you

Enemy affiliation's members have hostile reaction and impose –10 penalty on Diplomacy checks

Must destroy five items or creatures anathema to your affiliation in one month or reduce affiliation score by 1

Must donate 5% of treasure to affiliation

Must make pilgrimage or endure initiation ritual or dangerous journey

Duties (affiliation score 21 or higher, or 15 or higher for racial affiliations)

Good judgment—make DC 20 Appraise check once per month; failure indicates loss of 200 gp and affiliation score reduced by 1

Must recruit one new member per month or reduce affiliation score by 1

Must defeat a CR 9 creature in single combat

Must donate 10% of treasure to affiliation

Duties (affiliation score 30 or higher)

Assassination attempts—if you fail to uncover a plot each month with a DC 30 Gather Information check, then you must face a CR 12 assassin (can be simplified: make DC 15 Fort save or die)

Great judgment—make DC 20 Appraise check once per month; failure indicates affiliation loses 1 capital

Must defeat a CR 13 creature in single combat

Mutiny—succeed on DC 15 Diplomacy check once per month or face mob/challenger (EL 12)

EXECUTIVE POWERS

Affiliation leaders wield executive powers to accomplish many tasks on a grand scale. Generally, a leader must have an affiliation score of 30 or higher in order to gain the authority necessary to exercise these powers.

Choose three executive powers for your affiliation from among those described below. The executive power descriptions limit certain powers to certain affiliation types. This was done to balance out the value of the various types. You are free to ignore those restrictions if your campaign or storyline dictates otherwise.

Some of the abilities encompassed by executive powers are only used if you are playing with dynamic affiliations (using the rules for capital, violence checks, espionage checks, and negotiation checks).

Assassinate: Your affiliation can retain the services of an assassin (or send one of its own). The level of the assassin is equal to 1/2 the affiliation's scale (minimum 1; maximum 10 + 1/2 its scale). Because it takes time to prepare a strike, an assassin can be assigned one mission each three months. You could resolve the results of an assassin strike using normal D&D rules, or you might decide to resolve things "offstage." In the latter case, make an opposed espionage check against the victim's affiliation (or against the victim's Spot check, if he has no affiliation). If you succeed, the assassin penetrates your target's counterinfiltration measures and strikes. The victim must succeed on a Fortitude save against the normal DC for the assassin's death attack or perish.

Cabals, druid circles, governments, spy rings, temples, and thieves' guilds can retain assassins.

Beatify: The deeds of a saint are to those of an ordinary man as the clouds are to the earth. Serene, high, and aloof, the saints move through our world, and yet seem not wholly a part of it. Your affiliation has the power to declare someone a potential saint; someone who is beatified gains the title Blessed or Hallowed. A living creature who is beatified gains a +2 sacred bonus on Bluff, Diplomacy, and Intimidate checks when dealing with other members of her faith. When she casts a *cure* spell on a member of her own faith, she adds her

Wisdom bonus to the amount cured (maximum bonus equal to the spell's level).

Druid circles and temples can beatify a creature.

Craft: Hammers ring on anvils, saws hum through wood, and kraken-ink quills scratch on half-petrified calf vellum at your affiliation's headquarters. Your affiliation is adept at producing valuable items. It can craft any masterwork item or magic item from the *Dungeon Master's Guide* with a market price of up to 2,000 × the affiliation's scale. This item belongs to the affiliation, but you can borrow it according to the benefits of your title in the affiliation description. Mobilizing the affiliation in this way is a big job; to do so requires either an expenditure of 1 capital or a successful negotiation check (DC 15 + 1 per 2,000 gp value of the item) to bargain with supply and labor vendors. The process of crafting is not quick; you must wait 1–2 months to receive the item. During this time your affiliation is free to engage in other actions.

Businesses, cabals, druid circles, colleges, temples, and tribes can craft items.

Crusade: Your affiliation can declare a crusade. You designate an enemy and attempt a Diplomacy check (DC 20 + scale of target affiliation, or DC 20 + level of target creature). If you succeed, your followers martial their resources and travel any distance to attack the offending blasphemer. If the target is an affiliation, make opposing violence checks. If your affiliation is successful, an opposing affiliation loses 1 capital. If the target is an individual, he must make a Fortitude save (DC equal to your violence check result). If the target fails, he perishes under your affiliation's righteous onslaught.

If you wronged an enemy affiliation by prying out the ruby eyes of its sacred idol, selling the head of its demon guardian at auction, or rescuing a screaming sacrifice from its altar, your rival might retaliate by targeting your character with an unholy crusade. Your DM might set aside the normal Fortitude save and choose to play out an encounter. In that case, you will be set upon by creatures appropriate to the rival affiliation, with an EL equal to 10 + your opponent's violence bonus.

Each month that it crusades, an affiliation loses 2 capital due to the cost of the ongoing operations.

Fighting companies, temples, and tribes can crusade. A crusade can target an individual, business, college, fighting company, government, temple, or tribe. Spy rings, druid circles, cabals, and thieves' guilds are too elusive for such punishment.

Excommunicate: You might instruct your affiliation to shun an individual or an entire group. No cleric of your affiliation will help an excommunicated creature or a member of an excommunicated affiliation. If the excommunicated creature fails a Will save (DC 10 + the scale of your affiliation), your edict is so strong that for a period of 1 year, the subject cannot benefit from a divine spell cast by anyone with an alignment descriptor in common with those of your church. For example, if a lawful good church of Heironeous excommunicates a creature and it fails its save, the creature cannot benefit from divine spells from a caster who is either lawful or good.

Druid circles, temples, and tribes can excommunicate individuals.

Gift: Your affiliation might bestow a valuable gift when it matters most. After receiving a gift, the mercenary company sends extra troops, the temple sends its *staff of life* along with the bishop, and the thieves guild doesn't pickpocket your members on the way back from the tavern. When your affiliation sends a gift to someone, you or an agent of your affiliation receives a +4 competence bonus on your next Diplomacy check involving the recipient of the gift.

Alternatively, when your affiliation sends a gift to an appropriate organization, it secures a +2 competence bonus on its next violence, espionage, or negotiation check, provided the attempt is undertaken within 2 months of the gift. For example, a gift to a fighting company could secure a bonus on your next violence check.

Businesses, colleges, governments, and temples can send gifts.

Harvest: The wisdom or savvy of your affiliation's leader allows your members to work the land to your advantage, coaxing crops from grudging soil or teasing out precious metals from jealous rock. When your affiliation uses the Harvest power, make a DC 20 Appraise check. If your result is between 21 and 30, each member of the affiliation receives gold (your share is 50 gp × the affiliation's scale), and the affiliation itself enjoys a +1 circumstance bonus on all violence, espionage, and negotiation checks for the next 2 months. If your result was over 30, you can choose the above benefits, or your affiliation can gain 1 capital.

Businesses and tribes can harvest.

Holiday: Your affiliation has the power to declare holidays. These holidays can be perennial (Angels Day, Wyrm Waking Day, Feast of the Chapeaux of St. Cuthbert) or one-day events marking grand occasions (the dauphin's wedding day, the triumph over Snurre and the hill giants, the arrival of the Duke of Brass's ambassador). Any citizen in a land celebrating the holiday, and any member of an affiliation observing the holiday, gains a +1 morale bonus on all attacks, saves, and skill checks during the day. No more than one holiday per month can be declared.

Druid circles, governments, and temples can designate holidays.

Inquisition: With the ringing of the steeple bells, your holy organization declares a hunt for blasphemers. Designate one target affiliation. Throughout your area of influence, that affiliation falls under the shadow of suspicion.

On an individual level, members of the targeted affiliation are harassed by dedicated inquisitors. For each day they spend in the lands of the inquisition, they must succeed on a Fortitude save (DC 10 + your affiliation's scale) or be fatigued.

On an affiliation level, suspected groups are forced to curtail some activities and conceal others. The target of an inquisition must succeed on an opposed espionage check or be unable to use any executive power requiring a violence or negotiation check during the next month.

Maintaining an inquisition is expensive and interferes with day-to-day activities. Each month when you conduct an inquisition, you must succeed on an opposed negotiation check with the local government or lose 2 capital.

Druid circles and temples can press an inquisition. Individuals, businesses, colleges, fighting companies, governments, temples, and tribes can be targeted. Cabals, druid circles, spy rings, and thieves' guilds are too elusive for persecution.

Law: Your affiliation can write and enforce law throughout its domain. You might outlaw arcane or divine casting, concealed weapons, magic items, gnomes, or anything else you desire. If an object or practice is outlawed, anyone caught using it, engaging it, or being it is fined or jailed, as you decide. Penalties beyond a fine of 100 gp × your scale are rare.

An individual can attempt a Disguise check (DC equal to your espionage check result) to engage in an outlawed practice with impunity. If you outlaw an affiliation, it goes underground and takes a −2 penalty on all checks until it relocates or the ban is lifted. A banned affiliation has a maximum capital of 1.5 × its scale, and it is exterminated if its capital reaches 0.

Particularly outrageous laws could require your affiliation to present the plan persuasively to your countrymen; a Diplomacy check (DC 20 + scale) is required to accomplish this.

Your affiliation can also make a law requiring certain tasks of citizens in your area. If all citizens are required to undergo martial training, each adult militia member in your lands gains

EXCEPTIONS TO THE RULES

If your concept for a new affiliation doesn't mesh neatly with the guidelines for creating your own affiliation, don't let the guidelines keep you from doing what you want (within reason, of course).

In particular, several of the affiliations presented earlier in this chapter don't rigidly follow the guidelines concerning executive powers, so they can serve as examples of exceptions to the general rules.

The Caravan of Shadows is a business that has the executive powers pariah and shadow war, both of which are not normally available to businesses—but they work well in the context of this affiliation's concept.

The Chalice is a fighting company that has the inquisition executive power—a justifiable exception for a group of holy crusaders.

Dragon Island is a government affiliation that has four executive powers rather than the usual three, reflecting the overall power not only of the affiliation but of its highest-ranking members.

The leaders of the Wintervein Dwarves have access to the craft executive power, which is not normally available to a fighting company—but for a fighting company of dwarves, it makes perfect sense.

a +1 competence bonus on attack rolls, and your government as a whole gains a +1 competence bonus on violence checks. If you require all citizens to be literate, local civil servants are recruited from a more knowledgeable populace and your government gains a +1 competence bonus on negotiation checks. If you require all citizens to participate in a state religion or a state industry, every citizen gains at least 1 rank in Knowledge (religion) or Profession (relevant industry), and a +1 competence bonus on checks made using that skill. If you raise taxes to an extraordinary level, you have a 25% chance of gaining 1 capital each month. Other requirements and benefits are possible; consult with your Dungeon Master. Requirements demand a citizen's time and energy, however, and only one such requirement can be in place at a time (establishing a new requirement counts as the affiliation's use of executive power for that month). Requirements are also oppressive—your affiliation's leader must make a DC 30 Diplomacy check or reduce his affiliation score by 1 each month that the requirements are in place.

Normally, only governments can set laws. If there is no government in a region, druid circles or temples might enforce scripture as law.

Mint: Your affiliation stamps its leader's face on coins and issues them as currency. You gain a +2 circumstance bonus on Intimidate and Diplomacy checks with money-using creatures in lands where the coins circulate. The awe inspired by such a powerful act might shake your foes' resolve; anyone who confronts you in battle and has used your coins spends the first round of combat shaken (no save). You also receive free meals and free stays in inns or roadside houses with a DC 5 Diplomacy check.

Governments can mint coins, and if the government allows it, businesses can do so as well.

Pariah: Through rumor, propaganda, forgeries, and lies, you portray an individual as anathema to his affiliation. You spread tales of priests slaughtering innocents, of businessmen squandering riches on games of knucklebones, of soldiers plotting sedition. This causes the individual to be outcast from his affiliation. The target's affiliation score drops to 0 temporarily, during which time he has no access to any affiliation benefits, funds, items, or abilities.

Your affiliation must succeed on an espionage check or negotiation check opposed by the individual's Diplomacy check to make the rumors stick. If the individual exercises executive power within his affiliation, he can add his guild's negotiation bonus on his Diplomacy check as a competence bonus.

Each month, the pariah can attempt to clear his name by making the same opposed check. When he succeeds, the record is finally set straight, and the sheep-faced members of his affiliation welcome him back with his full affiliation score restored. A pariah who has cleared his name cannot be again outcast from his guild with the pariah power for 1 year plus 1d12 months.

Cabals, spy rings, and thieves guilds can declare a member to be a pariah.

Plague: Filth fever, centipede swarms, corn blight, a rain of shocker lizards—all these are examples of plague. When your affiliation plagues a land or another affiliation, each affected person must make a Will save (DC equal to your violence check result) each day of the month. Failure imposes a –1 penalty on all saving throws for that day. Any leader of a plagued affiliation must make a Diplomacy check (DC equal to your violence check result) with the members of his affiliation any time he wants to use an executive power; failure means that he is powerless in the face of the plague and his affiliation score decreases by 1.

Druid circles, temples, and tribes can bring a plague. Businesses, colleges, druid circles, fighting companies, governments, temples, and tribes can be targeted by a plague. Cabals, spy rings, and thieves' guild are too small and too diffuse to be affected by a plague.

Plunder: Treasure is the goal, and speed is the means. When your affiliation plunders an area, you are not attempting to damage it permanently only to add to your own wealth. When your affiliation launches a plundering attack, make an opposed violence check. If successful, you gain gold and gems; your share of the loot is 100 gp × your affiliation score. The enemy has a 1 in 6 chance of losing 1 capital as a result of your plundering; your affiliation has a separate 1 in 6 chance of gaining enough treasure to increase its capital by 1.

Fighting companies, governments, spy rings, thieves' guilds, and tribes can plunder. Only businesses, colleges, governments, and temples can be plundered.

Raid: A raiding party seeks to deal as much damage as possible and escape unscathed. Make an opposed violence check with the target affiliation. If your check is successful, the opposition suffers the loss of 1 capital. If unsuccessful, your raiding party has been trapped in the enemy's territory. Make opposed espionage or negotiation checks to either sneak or talk your way home. Failure indicates that the raiding party perishes and your affiliation loses 1 capital.

Cabals, druid circles, fighting companies, governments, spy rings, thieves' guilds, and tribes can stage raids.

Research: Gathering information is the raison d'etre for spy rings and colleges, but it is useful for other affiliations as well. When your affiliation conducts research, you can make an arcane discovery or unearth information about your enemies.

Your affiliation can research any arcane spell. The leader must pay the market price of a scroll of that spell in seed money for the research. In 1d4 months, your affiliation produces a scroll of the researched spell.

Your group can also research opponents. Against any NPC who has been researched, you and other members of your affiliation gain a +1 insight bonus on attack rolls in the first round of combat (after that, the NPC realizes you are anticipating his moves and switches tactics).

Finally, research can be conducted on an enemy affiliation. Your group gains a +2 insight bonus on its next violence, espionage, or negotiation check against that affiliation.

Cabals, colleges, and spy rings can conduct research.

Shadow War: Your affiliation stalks the alleys, the underpasses, the rooftops, and the dark copses on the edges of country lanes. From concealment you strike, and to concealment you return. When engaged in a shadow war, your affiliation makes an opposed espionage check against your target. If your check fails, your target exposes your affiliation before it can strike, and your affiliation takes a –2 penalty on negotiation checks for the next month. If your check succeeds, your shadow strike is true. If your successful check result was 10 or lower, your enemy affiliation's internal structure is disrupted, and it takes a –2 penalty on violence, espionage, and negotiation checks for the next month. If your successful check result was between 11 and 20, the opposition's command and control structure is paralyzed, preventing any affiliation member from using any benefits for the next month. If your successful check result was higher than 20, your opponent loses 1 capital.

Cabals, druid circles, spy rings, and thieves' guilds can start a shadow war.

Terrorize: Skull flags on the horizon, ominous drums along the mountains, illusions cast on pillows that cackle suddenly to life and screech out bloody warnings when the target lies down to bed—all these are techniques used by your affiliation to strike terror in the hearts of individuals and other groups.

Your affiliation can speak eloquently to the victim, threatening violence, or it can swing for the kneecaps and actually provide the violence. A terrorized individual must make two Will saves (DC equal to your violence or negotiation check result). If she succeeds on both, there is no effect. If she fails one, for the next month she is shaken in the first round of combat when fighting a member of your affiliation. If she fails both, for the next month, she is frightened of any member of your affiliation and flees at the first opportunity.

Your group can also attempt to terrorize an enemy affiliation. To do so, make an opposed negotiation or violence check (depending on how you would like to deliver the threat). If your affiliation wins, the opposing affiliation cannot use any executive powers during the next month.

Even the worst atrocities become commonplace if repeated too often. An individual or affiliation cannot be targeted for terrorism more than one month out of every four.

If your affiliation succeeds on an opposed espionage check before terrorizing another affiliation, the victim does not know who terrorized it.

Cabals, druid circles, fighting companies, governments, spy rings, thieves guilds, and tribes can terrorize. Cabals, druid circles, spy rings, and thieves guilds cannot be terrorized.

Trade: Commerce is the life blood of business, and it can provide a much-needed infusion of capital for other affiliations as well. When your group trades, choose one friendly affiliation. Each organization gains 1 capital. Make opposed negotiation checks; whoever wins has a 1 in 6 chance of gaining 1 additional capital.

Alternatively, your affiliation's trade connections can help an individual entrepreneur. If your affiliation's trading facilities are put at the disposal of an individual, he gains a +4 competence bonus on Appraise checks and a +2 competence bonus on any Diplomacy checks that involve trade for 1 month.

Lastly, a trading network can provide rumors of exotic items. Make a DC 20 negotiation check. If it succeeds, a seller has been located who possesses a wondrous item determined randomly from those described in the *Dungeon Master's Guide* (50% chance for a minor item, 30% chance for a medium item, 20% chance for a major item; roll on Table 7–27, 7–28, or 7–29 as appropriate). Because of your trading connections, you have a percentage discount equal to your affiliation's scale should you purchase the item. For example, if you belong to an affiliation with a scale of 12, you would receive a 12% discount on the purchase.

Only businesses and colleges can instigate trades, but any other type of affiliation can be the other partner in a transaction.

War: Fires sweep the rooftops, and the plains shake under the boots of marching troops. War means many different things depending on your campaign, but two results are constant. First, throughout your affiliation's sphere of influence, prices double. This price increase affects everything from adventuring equipment such as 10-foot poles and scrolls of *lesser restoration* to mundane items such as livestock and food. It applies both to purchases and to crafting expenses, including item creation costs.

Second, whenever a PC attempts to contact an NPC who resides in the area ravaged by war, the NPC must make a DC 12 Fortitude save. Failure means the NPC has perished in the war. Your DM might make this check once per month for other important NPCs she deems at risk, regardless of whether anyone attempts to contact them.

Every month that your affiliation is at war, the war effort decreases its capital and its enemy's capital by 1. Additionally, make opposed violence checks. The loser suffers an additional loss of 0–2 capital (roll 1d6; 1–2 = 0, 3–4 = 1, 5–6 = 2).

Your DM might have an NPC-controlled affiliation declare war. If two governments exist in the same territory, they must go to war until one perishes (even if war is not an executive power possessed chosen by either government). A wise affiliation keeps its warchest well stocked with ingots; poor affiliations are ripe targets for conquest.

Fighting companies, governments, and tribes can start a war. War can be waged against a college, fighting company, government, temple, or tribe. Cabals, druid circles, spy rings, and thieves guilds are too elusive. Businesses are mobile enough to avoid war, but can be outlawed by governments. If a business is outlawed, however, it simply turns to the black market (see the law executive power).

EXAMPLE OF PLAY

The players at the table include Leigh (Mialee the wizard), Wendy (Lidda the rogue), William (Regdar the fighter), and Matt (Jozan the cleric). Jody is the Dungeon Master.

William (Regdar): A 1! I leap back out of the way.

Wendy (Lidda): I was trying to open the—

Jody (DM): Lidda trips the wire and stone rumbles overhead. The crepuscular light fades. When you look up, you can see by Regdar's torch that a stone disk has rotated into place over the exit, trapping you at the bottom of this raptor-pharaoh shaft.

Matt (Jozan): How are we going to get back out? Mialee, what about Hanali's Circle?

Leigh (Mialee): No, don't you remember the shadow war with the Vecna cabal? They attacked in Avrillet last month and paralyzed a lot of our activities. So, no new *word of recall* charms for a while. We really do need to go after the One and the Five once we get out of here.

Wendy (Lidda): Right, Tall and Slender, your friends might be flinging acid arrows in the alleys up north, but my guild mates are right here guarding the codex. I bet they can let us out.

Lidda climbs to the top of the shaft and hangs from two pitons and a krenshar-hide saddle strap.

Wendy (Lidda): I shout for my guild mates to help while I am trying to pick the lock.

Jody (DM): It's unpickable from this side. In fact, there is no lock. However (makes a Listen check for Lidda), you do hear the sounds of shouts, then ringing steel on steel and the whoosh of fireballs.

William (Regdar): Blood of the emperor! It must be the Reviled vanguard. On open ground. Can your rogues take them?

Wendy (Lidda): I don't know . . .

Jody (DM): You specifically brought them for this mission, so I'm going to rule that they're not surprised by the Reviled, even though the light-adapted trogs belly-crawled through the sand from the direction of the sunset. Do you have individual stats for your guild force? [Lidda shakes her head.] Then give me a violence check.

Wendy (Lidda): I rolled a 14 and add my guild's +2 violence bonus. 16!

Jody rolls d20 adds the Reviled affiliation's violence bonus.

Jody (DM): 15. The Violet Ghosts win by one. A single surviving guild mate arm-drags himself through the reeking, bloodied sand to the top of the shaft. He scratches at the stone, and after a great deal of encouragement from you, he finally hits the mechanism to tilt the plug-disc. The stars are out by now, and the stench of the Reviled comes through the opened gap.

Later, after the party has set up watches:

Leigh (Mialee): If there's nothing going on during my watch, I'm going to read the codex for any clue on which shaft is Iathra's tomb, since our first guess obviously wasn't right.

Jody (DM): The stiff pages are filled with religious iconography and veiled allusions. Give me a Knowledge (religion) check.

Leigh rolls d20 and adds her Knowledge (religion) skill modifier plus another 1 because religious knowledge has permeated her homeland, the territories around Castle Mairo, ever since the baron made it the law for all citizens to participate in the Pelorite religion.

Leigh (Mialee): Let's see, with modifiers, I rolled a 15.

Jody (DM): Just made it!

Leigh (Mialee): Heh. Jozan, I might grumble, but apparently the mandatory worship of Pelor has its uses!

Jody (DM): You learn that the shafts of the raptor-pharaohs are laid out according to dynasty, and Iathra's shaft should be the one closest to where the sun sets on Wyrm Waking Day.

The next day, the party descends into the correct tomb.

Jody (DM): Jozan's boots bang down on the sandstone tomb and puff up a cloud of dust. All right, everybody that has been living in Castle Mairo, this is the start of the day's activities, so let's see the Will saves. These are to avoid the effects of the rain of shocker lizards that the Reviled plagued you with last new moon. They rolled a 14 on their violence check, so that's the DC.

Matt (Jozan): 17. Pelor has no respect for the Reviled.

William (Regdar): 13. Gah! –1 to all my saves today.

Leigh (Mialee) 21. I scoff at the darkness.

Jody (DM): Okay, as you're cursing the ape-frogs, Regdar, you become aware of a scurrying in the dust. A small spider is running out of the passage to the north, zipping past Jozan's feet.

Matt (Jozan): I squash the nasty thing with my mace!

Jody chuckles.

Jody (DM): It offers no resistance. Both you and Regdar hear something in the passageway behind the spider. Suddenly you see what the spider was running from—three troglodyte degenerates galloping on all fours straight toward you.

William (Regdar): Troglodytes! I charge and yell, "For Herridek!"

Jody (DM): A bloody battle brews, it would seem. Jozan, I need an espionage check for the Sun Fane. There are Reviled agents within; if you fail, they have infiltrated your hierarchy and knew that you were coming. In that case, they will have sent at least a few more tomb denizens to your little welcome party.

Matt (Jozan): Whoa. Espionage is not the Sun Fane's strong suit.

Wendy (Lidda): Can the Violet Ghosts assist?

Jody (DM): Sure, make an espionage check, DC 10. If you succeed, you add a +2 bonus on the Sun Fane's check.

Wendy rolls d20 and adds her affiliation's espionage bonus.

Wendy (Lidda): 23, no problem.

Matt rolls d20 and adds his affiliation's espionage bonus plus 2 for Wendy's help.

Matt (Jozan): Only an 11. Ouch!

Jody rolls d20 and adds the Reviled's espionage bonus.

Jody (DM): 16. The Reviled spies in the Sun Fane have compromised your agents and learned their plans. There are two additional carrion crawlers here to welcome you. I could have done this a while ago, of course, but I wanted you to see the rolls and have an opportunity to roll for your own affiliation.

Jody picks up two carrion crawler miniatures.

Matt (Jozan): Remind me to ask you about an inquisition when we get back! There are spies in the fort!

Jody (DM): The degenerates leap upon you, their familiar stench closing around your lungs like a dragon's claw. You can hear the wet sucking sounds of the crawlers' footpads as they blindly feel their way down the walls and ceiling of the passageway behind the troglodytes. It's that time, everyone—roll for initiative!

Illus. by R. Horsley

he DUNGEONS & DRAGONS game offers a great deal of flexibility in character creation and advancement. When you make a character, you can choose any race or class combination, select from a wide variety of feats, and buy ranks in any skills you wish. Once you've made these decisions, however, they cannot be changed. Most of the time those early decisions work out fine, but sometimes you might regret your previous choices. Maybe you didn't fully understand the ramifications of the choice you made. Or maybe you constructed a character around a great concept, but in play, the particular set of circumstances that would let your character shine never cropped up. And even if you built your character to perfection, each new supplement presents new classes, feats, spells, and special abilities, many of which might better serve the needs of your character or the campaign than those you previously selected.

It's true that part of the D&D game's challenge is making smart choices in creating or advancing your character. But a DM who forces someone to play a character he doesn't find enjoyable isn't making the game fun for that player or the others at the table. In such a situation, the player usually either throws away the character and rolls up a new one, or quits the game. If your campaign values character continuity (as many campaigns do), neither of those outcomes is especially attractive. Why force Mike to throw away the elf fighter he's been playing for three months just because he made a couple of bad feat choices, when allowing him to change those choices would be so much better for the storyline? If Mialee has been an integral part of the campaign since Day 1 but has regretted being an elf since Day 2, wouldn't it be better to let her become the halfling she would prefer to be by undergoing a dramatic transformation at the Necrotic Cradle (see page 203) than to abruptly replace her with Liamee the halfling wizard? The fact that Liamee the halfling coincidentally has the same spells, feats, skill ranks, and familiar as Mialee the elf did but has no connection to the campaign or the rest of the party is stretching credulity perhaps a bit too far.

This chapter presents rules for revising various aspects of your character during play. With this system, you can modify elements of your character to better fit your vision of who your character should be—both to meet the needs of the party and to face the threats presented during the course of an entire campaign. Though character revision does allow you to "rewrite" certain elements of your character, the rules presented here ensure that the changes remain within reason and do not upset the story that has already been created by each character's deeds in the campaign.

The two methods of character revision described below are retraining and rebuilding. Each description defines the scope of the allowed revisions and includes clear guidelines on how to adjudicate the changes.

Retraining involves small-scale changes to your character, such as reallocation of feat slots and skill ranks. Such changes are relatively simple to apply, and they don't usually lead to dramatic changes in the character's capabilities or party role.

Rebuilding, on the other hand, encompasses much broader alterations to your character's identity—up to and including such cornerstones of identity as class and race. For that reason, rebuilding can be achieved only by completing specific DM-chosen quests. Since such missions typically center on visiting some legendary location or overcoming a tremendous challenge, they should always be completed in cooperation with your DM so that they can be woven into the storyline of the campaign.

For players and DMs who are accustomed to treating character creation and advancement decisions as permanent, the idea of character revision can seem strange or daunting—and some might even think of it as a form of cheating. Such reactions are natural, but if you think about it, normal people "revise" their abilities all the time. Skills you learn early in life are forgotten as new talents supplant them. For example, a foreign language mastered in high school might be virtually forgotten only a few years later from disuse. Likewise, a college student might change her major halfway through her junior year, or an unexpected job transfer or layoff could result in a new position in a totally different field, requiring quick mastery of new skills. Viewed from that perspective, allowing D&D characters similar opportunities to reinvent themselves seems perfectly reasonable.

Maybe your group already uses some form of character revision, such as a house rule, or even a reliance on ad hoc decision-making by the DM. If your method works for your group, don't let this chapter stop you from playing the game your way. However, if you're looking for a coherent system that balances fun and playability with story and believability, this chapter might be just what the healer ordered.

After your character goes through the retraining or rebuilding process, you might notice that he doesn't quite match the specs of a similar character built up to the same level by the normal method. Maybe his skill points don't add up quite right, or his hit points are off a bit from the expected value. But the small variations that crop up in this process don't significantly impact play balance, and writing rules to eliminate them would complicate the process without really improving the quality of your game.

So if you'd like to change some aspect of your character, give the character revision rules a try. You'll be happier with your character in the long run and, more important, you'll have more fun playing the game.

The most basic level of character revision is retraining—that is, adjusting a decision you made earlier in your character's career by selecting a different legal option. This technique represents the character's practicing new talents in lieu of honing older ones. In a way, the process is similar to attaining a new level. In keeping with that concept, the retraining option can be chosen only during level advancement.

Six different character aspects (see Table 8–1) can be changed through retraining. Each time your character attains a new level, you can select one (and only one) of these options. For instance, you can't change a feat selection and your spells known at the same level. Since these options represent two different sessions of retraining, they must occur at different levels.

The decision to retrain must be implemented before any benefits of the newly attained level are applied. For example, if a 10th-level rogue wants to trade her improved evasion class feature for the opportunist class feature, she can do so immediately upon attaining 11th level, before she gains any of the benefits for that level (such as additional hit points, skill points, and so on).

TABLE 8–1: RETRAINING OPTIONS

Character Aspect	Effect
Class feature	Exchange one class feature option for another
Feat	Exchange one feat for another for which you qualify
Language	Exchange one language for another
Skill	Trade ranks between two skills
Spell	Exchange one spell known for another
Substitution level	Trade a class level for a substitution level

CLASS FEATURE RETRAINING

Some class features offer two or more different options, such as the choice of combat style a ranger must make at 2nd level. Class feature retraining allows you to swap out one such option for another. Maybe your ranger would prefer to be an archer instead of a melee fighter, or your cleric of Heironeous feels that the War domain would be a better option than the Law domain. The character remains basically the same, since his class levels haven't changed, but he's now highlighting a different aspect of his class.

The Process

Change one class feature option to another legal one. The new option must represent a choice that you could have made at the same level as you made the original choice. Also, the new choice can't make any of your later choices illegal—though it might automatically change class features acquired later if they are based on the initial choice.

Class features from the *Player's Handbook* that are subject to change in this manner are given on Table 8–2. Chapter 2 of this book provides class feature options for a variety of additional classes.

TABLE 8–2: CLASS FEATURE RETRAINING OPTIONS

Class	Option
Cleric*	Choice of domains (each domain counts as a separate choice)
Neutral cleric	Choice to turn or to rebuke undead (can be changed only if deity allows it)
Druid or ranger	Choice of animal companion
Fighter, monk, or wizard	Choice of bonus feat
Ranger	Choice of combat style
Rogue	Choice of special ability
Sorcerer or wizard	Choice of familiar
Wizard**	Choice of school specialization and prohibited schools

*A cleric's choice of deity can't be changed by class feature retraining. See the Divine Conversion sidebar for details on how to accomplish this change.

**School specialization and prohibited schools are treated as a single class feature. Thus, a character could change one, two, or even all three choices at the same time.

Example: Upon gaining a new level, a ranger could change the combat style class feature he gained at 2nd level from two-weapon fighting to archery. Thereafter, he would be treated as if he had the Rapid Shot feat instead of the Two-Weapon Fighting feat. If he had at least six levels of ranger before making this change, he would exchange both the Two-Weapon Fighting feat (gained at 2nd level) and the Improved Two-Weapon Fighting feat (gained at 6th level) for the appropriate archery feats, since both of these features are derived from the choice made at 2nd level. However, the ranger couldn't make this change if he had selected the Two-Weapon Defense feat in the interim, since losing Two-Weapon Fighting means he would no longer meet the prerequisites for that feat.

Example: Upon gaining a new level, a necromancer could change her school specialization to evocation, thus becoming an evoker. At the same time, she could also choose to change her prohibited schools from conjuration and illusion to abjuration and transmutation. Doing so would cause her to lose access to all spells from the newly designated prohibited schools. Even if her spellbook contains one or more such spells, she would lose the ability to prepare and cast them.

Example: Upon gaining a new level, a wizard could choose to specialize in the enchantment school, thereby becoming an enchanter. At the same time, she would have to select two prohibited schools, as normal for a specialist wizard.

Example: Upon gaining a new level, a conjurer could choose to become a wizard. By doing so, she would lose the benefits of specialization. But since she would also lose her prohibited schools, she could then learn spells from those schools as normal.

FEAT RETRAINING

Sometimes a feat choice looks great on paper, but it just doesn't work for your character in practice. Maybe an early feat choice reflected the character's personality and style, but a little experience changed his outlook. For instance, you might have selected Improved Initiative for your 1st-level character because you pictured him as ambitious and a little reckless. But after falling victim to a wight's touch because he just couldn't wait until the cleric turned the undead, he decides it's better to use a little more care in combat, causing you to regret your early feat choice. New supplements, with their wealth of exciting feat options, also provide plenty of reasons to reconsider your earlier feat selections.

The Process

You can exchange one of the feats you previously selected for another feat. If the new feat has prerequisites, not only must your character meet them in his current state, but you must also be able to show that he met them at the time you chose the previous feat.

Example: A 4th-level fighter/1st-level rogue couldn't trade the Mobility feat he chose at 3rd level for Improved Critical because he doesn't currently meet a prerequisite for the latter feat (base attack bonus +6). He also couldn't trade that Mobility feat for Weapon Specialization, even though he currently meets the prerequisite (fighter level 4th), because he could not have done so as a 3rd-level character.

DIVINE CONVERSION

As noted in the *Player's Handbook,* a cleric who grossly violates the code of conduct imposed by his deity loses all spells and class features and cannot attain any more levels as a cleric of that deity. All these penalties remain in effect until he atones. But what if he doesn't want to atone? What if a cleric of Hextor finds new meaning and purpose in serving Heironeous after a dramatic conversion experience? Such a character need not become a multiclass ex-cleric of Hextor/cleric of Heironeous. Instead, Heironeous can simply reinstate the character's cleric powers once he has proven his loyalty, talent, and ability.

A cleric who changes his patron deity must complete a quest to prove his devotion to his new patron. The nature of the quest depends on the deity, and it always clearly reflects the deity's alignment as well as his or her goals and beliefs. To start the process, the cleric must voluntarily accept a *geas/quest* spell cast by a higher-level cleric of his new deity. During the quest, the cleric has no access to spells or cleric class features—except his weapon and armor proficiencies, which he does not forfeit.

Upon completing the quest, the cleric receives the benefit of an *atonement* spell from a cleric of the new deity. The character then becomes a cleric of the new deity and is inducted into the clergy during an appropriate ceremony of the DM's choosing. After selecting two of the new deity's domains in lieu of his old ones, the character has all the powers and abilities of his previous cleric level, plus the granted powers of his new domains.

This method is the only one by which a cleric can change his deity. The retraining rules can't be used to accomplish this task—it is simply too substantial a change in the character's identity (not to mention his source of power) to chalk up to a bit of practice in his off hours.

LANGUAGE RETRAINING

It made a lot of sense to speak Goblin, Kobold, and Orc at 1st level, but now that you're mostly fighting giants, demons, and dragons, it would be nice to understand your new enemies.

The Process

Subtract one language from your list of known languages and add a new one to the list. It doesn't matter how your character earned the original language—it could have been an automatic language for her race, a bonus language gained from a high Intelligence score, or a language purchased with skill points.

SKILL RETRAINING

Some skills that are particularly valuable at lower levels become less useful later on, and vice versa. For example, when everyone in the party is carrying a bag full of antitoxins and *potions of cure light wounds*, the need for successful Heal checks drops dramatically. Whether your character has skill ranks that aren't as necessary as they once were, or you just want to adapt her to new challenges, skill retraining provides a simple method of adjusting your character's capabilities in a small but measurable way.

The Process

Subtract up to 4 skill ranks from one skill and add an equal number of ranks to any one other skill (not including Speak Language). The skill to which you add the ranks must be a class skill for one of your character's classes, including a class he is about to gain with his current level increase. It doesn't matter whether the lost ranks were purchased as class skills or as cross-class skills.

Example: You decide to give your 2nd-level ranger a level of the rogue class as his third character level. At this point, he could use the skill retraining option to lose 4 ranks in Handle Animal that he purchased with his ranger skill points and gain 4 ranks in any other ranger or rogue class skill (such as Survival or Disable Device). He couldn't gain ranks in any skill that isn't on either the ranger or the rogue class skill list (such as Spellcraft).

SPELL OR POWER RETRAINING

Much like feats, magic spells and psionic powers sometimes look better when you select them than they do after you've used them for a while. And when you're playing a character with a limited number of options (such as a sorcerer or a psychic warrior), every spell or power you choose represents a significant percentage of your character's overall options. You can't afford to have dead weight taking up valuable spell slots, so ditch that *sleep* spell now that the party isn't facing foes with low Hit Dice anymore and replace it with the niftier 1st-level spell you just found in a recent supplement.

The Process

Exchange up to two currently known spells or psionic powers for other spells or powers. Each new spell or power must be usable by the same class and of the same spell level or power level as the spell or power it replaces.

Special: Bards and sorcerers already have a limited ability to learn new spells in the place of older ones (see page 28 and page 54 of the *Player's Handbook*). This method of retraining allows exchanges over and above what their classes already permit.

Example: A sorcerer could change *lightning bolt* to *fly* or *dispel magic*, since all three are 3rd-level sorcerer/wizard spells, but he couldn't change it to *wall of ice* (a 4th-level spell) or to *cure serious wounds* (a cleric spell).

Example: A 5th-level sorcerer advancing to 6th level could use spell retraining to exchange up to two of his known spells (of any level he knows) for others of the same levels. Then he could exchange one 0-level or 1st-level spell for another just as any sorcerer could upon attaining 6th level.

SUBSTITUTION LEVEL RETRAINING

Substitution levels, as presented in *Planar Handbook* and the *Races* series of supplements, offer characters interesting ways to adjust the benefits granted by their classes. A wizard with elf wizard substitution levels, for example, seems a bit different from a traditional wizard, and that difference reinforces her racial identity. Since most substitution level options are offered for relatively low class levels (many at 1st level), you might already have missed one or more chances to add such flavor to your character. Revising a character to incorporate this feature amounts to a combination of retroactive continuity ("Of course I've always been a dwarf fighter!") and getting back to one's roots ("I can't believe I forgot/never learned that trick!").

RETRAINING COSTS

In general, retraining is assumed to be a background activity, just like normal level increases are. However, if your DM's campaign requires the PCs to spend time and/or money to improve their skills, gain feats, learn spells, or acquire class benefits (*DMG* 197), the DM can apply similar requirements when characters use the retraining rules presented in this chapter. The table below shows some suggested time and gp costs for the various retraining options. These costs are purely optional; the game works perfectly well without them, just as it works without requiring downtime in order to attain higher levels.

Retraining Option	Time	GP Cost
Class feature	1 week/2 levels[1]	500 gp/week
Feat	2 weeks	50 gp
Skill	1 week[2]	25 gp[2]
Spell	1 day	5 gp/spell level
Substitution level	1 week/2 levels[1]	500 gp/week

1 Based on the original level at which the class feature or substitution level is gained.
2 Per skill rank changed.

The Process

You can trade one of your character's current class levels for a substitution level, or exchange a substitution level she currently has for a normal class level. If the level to be gained has prerequisites, not only must the character meet them in her current state, but you must also be able to show that she met them when you could have chosen the level originally.

Since a substitution level is actually a collection of different mechanical elements, use the following guidelines to make the necessary changes to your character. In all cases, "current level" refers to the class level currently occupying that level slot (probably a normal class level), and "new level" refers to the class level the character is gaining through the retraining system (probably a substitution level).

Hit Points: If the new level does not use the same Hit Die as the current level, don't reroll your character's hit points. Just add or subtract 1 hit point from your character's current total per step of difference between the two die sizes (or 2 hit points per step if the new level is her first level in a class). For instance, if the current level has a d8 Hit Die, and the new level has a d10 Hit Die, your character would gain 1 hit point (or 2 hit points if the new level is her first level in a class). Alternatively, if the new level has a d4 Hit Die, she would lose 2 hit points (or 4 hit points if the new level is her first level in a class).

Skill List: If the new level doesn't offer any additional class skills over and above those on the current level's class skill list, make no changes to your character's existing skill ranks. If the new level offers any class skills that aren't on the class skill list of the current level, you can subtract up to 4 skill ranks from any skill in order to add the same number of ranks to any of the new level's class skills.

Example: The dwarf fighter racial substitution levels in *Races of Stone* offer Knowledge (dungeoneering) as an additional class skill. So if you choose to retrain your character's 1st level as a fighter and change it to 1st level as a dwarf fighter, you could subtract up to 4 ranks from any skill and add an equal number of ranks to Knowledge (dungeoneering), in addition to the other changes that substitution level retraining allows.

Skill Points: If the new level does not grant the same number of skill points as the current level, you must adjust your character's skill ranks appropriately. If the new level grants fewer skill

points than the current level, remove 1 rank from any skill per point of difference between the two levels. If the new level grants more skill points than the current level, you must immediately spend those skill points using the new level's class skill list. For example, if your character gained 2 skill points, you could buy 2 ranks in your new level's class skills or 1 rank in a cross-class skill. You must still abide by the skill rank limit for your character level in this process.

Spellcasting: If the new level changes some aspect of your character's spellcasting ability (for example, if she gains or loses spells known or spells per day), apply these changes as appropriate. If she must lose one or more spells known, you can select the spells lost from all the legal options.

Class Features: If the new level offers a different class feature in place of one from the current level, treat the situation as if you had used the class feature retraining option detailed above. If the new level simply alters one of your character's existing class features, just apply the alteration.

Illus. by D. Hudnut

Regdar undergoes retraining so he can learn how to wield a spiked chain

Illus. by S. Prescott

*Rebuilding a character opens up
countless possibilities for change*

REBUILDING

Retraining allows you to change a small aspect of your character, but rebuilding is a much more drastic step. This method of character revision allows you to change your character's ability scores, class levels, background, templates, or even race. You can change as many of these aspects at once as you wish, though such alterations require great effort—and often great sacrifice as well.

Since rebuilding constitutes such a major change in your character's identity, accomplishing it isn't simply a matter of erasing an entry on your character sheet and replacing it with new information. In essence, you are altering reality in order to rewrite your character's personal history. Therefore, to accomplish a character rebuild, your PC must complete a significant and challenging quest. Two such quests are detailed in this chapter, each one appropriate for a range of character levels. For instance, the Gates of Dawn quest is designed for characters of 6th to 8th level. Characters who are lower or higher in level gain no benefit from completing the quest and in fact should be actively discouraged from undertaking it.

The DM can design new character rebuild quests for your campaign by using the ones presented here as examples. Each should be appropriate for a small range of character levels (typically about three) and include guidelines on how to adjust the challenge for characters within that range.

Ideally, a character rebuild should be a relatively rare event. Unless your world is particularly unusual, constant character rebuilding tends to undermine the believability of both the campaign and its storyline. Therefore, the quest should represent a significant challenge for the characters involved. After all, if players consider a rebuild quest to be a cakewalk, they're likely to underestimate the value of the reward.

ABILITY SCORE REBUILDING

Sometimes the ability scores you roll aren't exactly the ones you'd like. And even if that 15 Intelligence seemed like a good idea at the time, perhaps it didn't pay off quite the way you'd hoped in actual play. In such cases, you might eventually come to the conclusion that your character would be better off with different ability scores.

When you rebuild ability scores, you can reduce one or more scores in order to increase others, though the exchange is not necessarily one-for-one. In effect, the process is similar to creating a character using the point-buy system detailed on page 169 of the *Dungeon Master's Guide*.

The system is intentionally designed to make improving high scores more costly than improving low ones, since improving an already high ability score usually gives a greater benefit than improving a low score. Also, reducing an ability score from an odd number to an even number isn't very costly to a character, since the reduction probably doesn't result in a significant change to his power.

The Process

Each time your character completes a rebuild quest, you can reduce one or more of his ability scores and then improve one or more different ability scores.

TABLE 8–3: REDUCING ABILITY SCORES

Old Score	New Score	Points Gained
30	29	9
29	28	7
28	27	8
27	26	6
26	25	7
25	24	5
24	23	6
23	22	4
22	21	5
21	20	3
20	19	4
19	18	2
18	17	3
17	16	1
16	15	2
15	14	1
14	13	1
13	12	1
12	11	1
11	10	1
10	9	1
9	8	1

TABLE 8–4: IMPROVING ABILITY SCORES

Old Score	New Score	Point Cost
30	31	10
29	30	9
28	29	9
27	28	8
26	27	8
25	26	7
24	25	7
23	24	6
22	23	6
21	22	5
20	21	5
19	20	4
18	19	4
17	18	3
16	17	3
15	16	2
14	15	2
13	14	1
12	13	1
11	12	1
10	11	1

Improving an ability score of less than 10 costs 1 point.

No ability score can be reduced below 8 in this fashion, and you can't reduce a score that is already below 8. Furthermore, you can't reduce any ability score so much that it makes one of your other choices (such as a feat) illegal. For example, if your character has Power Attack, you can't reduce his Strength to less than 13.

Determine the points for each reduction by consulting Table 8–3. For ability scores higher than 30, simply extend the table by continuing the progression. Add up the points gained in this process.

Next, spend the total points you gained through ability score reduction to improve one or more of your character's other ability scores. Consult Table 8–4 to determine the cost

of each desired improvement. Again, for ability scores higher than 30, extend the table by continuing the progression.

Be sure to adjust all other aspects of your character that depend on ability scores—including saving throws, skill modifiers, and the like—after you've rebuilt his ability scores. The one exception is skill ranks. A permanent Intelligence change doesn't retroactively increase or reduce the skill ranks your character has already gained from previous levels.

CLASS LEVEL REBUILDING

From the multiclass sorcerer who's tired of lagging behind in spell acquisition to the fighter who wishes he had taken a level of rogue so that he could more easily qualify for a desired prestige class, characters often come up short of their players' expectations. Even if you haven't made a "mistake" in choosing classes, it's entirely possible that a new class or prestige class might offer abilities that are more appropriate for your character. For instance, a player whose stealthy rogue considers herself a spy and assassin might decide that the ninja class (from *Complete Adventurer*) better describes that character. If ninja wasn't an available option when the player first created the character, it's not fair to say that she made a mistake in taking rogue levels. A more accurate assessment would be that the new class better describes what the character was always meant to be.

Your character's class levels are the most powerful tools for defining his role in the party, not to mention his place in the world. So, consider carefully any class level rebuilds that would dramatically alter the way your character functions in the game—if he's the only front-line fighter in the party, trading away a couple of paladin levels for sorcerer levels might not be the best decision.

You can also use this method to trade out (or add in) prestige class levels, though if you want to take levels in a prestige class that's new to your character, you must be able to demonstrate that he can still qualify for it using what he has gained from his remaining class levels. For example, a 7th-level dwarf fighter couldn't trade a fighter level for a dwarven defender level, since his remaining fighter levels wouldn't allow him to meet the +7 base attack bonus requirement for that prestige class.

If reallocating your character's class levels disqualifies him for a prestige class in which he already has one or more levels, he loses the benefit of any class features or other special abilities granted by that prestige class. He retains the hit points gained from advancing in that class, as well as any improvements to base attack bonus and base save bonuses that those levels provided. However, you can always use the class level rebuilding option to replace the now-useless prestige class levels as well—and you probably should, unless you're sure that the character will be able to meet the requirements again soon.

Some players might find it tempting to use this method of character rebuilding to create a bizarre but powerful amalgam of classes, or to drastically rewrite a character's history. As with any important character decisions, the DM and the player should work together to ensure that the player's new vision of his character still works in the game and fits in with the other characters in the party. As long as the changes don't significantly disrupt the game, though, players should play characters that they find enjoyable, and if swapping out a couple of class levels accomplishes that goal, then doing so is well worth the effort.

The Process

Each time your character completes a rebuild quest, you can change a number of levels equal to 1/5 his character level (rounded up) from one class to any other class (or classes). For example, a 5th-level sorcerer could trade a sorcerer level for a single level of any other class, while a 12th-level barbarian/4th-level fighter could trade up to four of his class levels (any combination of fighter and barbarian) for other class levels of his choice.

Since every class level is a composite of several different elements, use the following step-by-step process to adjust your character.

Base Attack and Base Save Bonuses: Adjust these bonuses to match your new array of class levels, just as if you had created a brand-new character with those classes.

Hit Points: If the new class level does not use the same Hit Die as the current level, don't reroll your character's hit points. Just add or subtract 1 hit point from your character's current total per step of difference between the two die sizes (or 2 hit points per step if the new level is his first level in a class). For instance, if you trade a fighter level (d10 Hit Die) to gain a barbarian level (d12 Hit Die), your character would gain 1 hit point (or 2 hit points if the new level is his first level of barbarian). If you traded that fighter level for a sorcerer level (d4 Hit Die), your character would lose 3 hit points (or 6 hit points if the new level is his first level of sorcerer).

Skill Points: If the new class level grants the same number of skill points as the current level does, you don't have to make any changes to your character's skill ranks. Even if the class skill lists are widely different, it's generally more work than it's worth to fiddle around with skill ranks in this manner. If you wish, you can also use the skill retraining option (see page 194) to adjust some of your skill ranks.

If the new level does not grant the same number of skill points as the current level, you must adjust your character's skill ranks appropriately. If the new level grants fewer skill points than the current level, remove 1 rank from any skill per point of difference between the two levels. If the new level grants more skill points than the current level, you must immediately spend those skill points using the new level's class skill list. For example, trading a fighter level to gain a barbarian level would grant 2 skill points to a character with Intelligence 10. With those extra points, you could buy 2 ranks of barbarian class skills or 1 rank of a barbarian cross-class skill. You must still abide by the skill rank limit for your character's level in this process.

Spells: If you added or subtracted any levels from a spell-casting class, adjust your character's spells per day and spells known appropriately. You can choose any spells the character must lose from his entire repertoire of the appropriate spell level. For example, a 5th-level sorcerer who becomes a 4th-level sorcerer/1st-level rogue must lose one 1st-level and one 2nd-level sorcerer spell, but you can choose these freely—they need not be the ones the character actually learned at 5th level.

Class Features: Eliminate any class features the character no longer possesses and add those he gains from his new levels.

RACE REBUILDING

Changing your character's race is a major decision, since it has probably affected many of the decisions he has made during his adventuring career. Still, the concept of major physical transformation isn't unknown in fantasy, so a character might well seek to recreate himself as an entirely different person. Perhaps you really want to try out a race featured in a new book, or you've finally reached a high enough level to play the monstrous character you've always wanted. Whatever your reason, the race rebuilding rules show you how to keep playing the same person in a new body.

This method of rebuilding can also be used to recreate characters brought back by *reincarnate* and similar effects that restore characters to life as members of different races.

The Process

Each time your character completes a rebuild quest, you can change his race. First, remove all racial traits (including ability score modifiers) granted by your character's original race. Then add all the racial traits and ability score modifiers from the new race. The character's known languages don't change unless you also choose the language retraining option (see page 194).

So far the process sounds simple, right? Unfortunately, it isn't always easy. Many potential complications can arise from this aspect of character rebuilding. The sections below demonstrate how to handle the various issues that might arise.

Feat: If a change of race means that your character no longer qualifies for a feat she already has, she loses access to the feat, as well as to any others for which it is a prerequisite. However, the feat still occupies a feat slot unless you also use the feat retraining option (see page 193).

Prestige Class: If a change of race disqualifies the character for a prestige class in which she already has one or more levels, she loses the benefit of any class features or other special abilities granted by that prestige class. She retains the hit points gained from advancing in that class, as well as any improvements to base attack bonus and base save bonuses that those levels provided. However, you can use the class level rebuilding option to replace the now-useless prestige class levels—and you probably should, unless you're sure that the character will be able to meet the requirements again soon.

Racial Substitution Level: Changing your character's race might well mean that any racial substitution levels (detailed in the *Races* series of supplements) she has are no longer appropriate. Treat this situation as if you were replacing one class level with another (see Class Level Rebuilding, page 197).

Level Adjustment: If your character's original race had a higher level adjustment than her new race does, you can replace any lost level adjustment "points" with the same number of new class levels of your choice.

If the new race has a higher level adjustment than the original race did, you must remove class levels until the character's effective character level is the same as it was before the rebuilding occurred. You can choose the levels lost from all those that the character has, regardless of the order in which they were gained.

Racial Hit Dice: Adding or subtracting racial Hit Dice is perhaps the most complicated part of character rebuilding. Work with your DM to ensure that he approves of this degree of change and that you're doing it correctly.

If your character's original race had any racial Hit Dice, you must remove all the benefits they granted. This process is similar to removing class levels (see Class Level Rebuilding, page 197). Next, replace these racial Hit Dice with class levels of your choice until the character's effective character level is the same as it was before the rebuilding occurred.

If your character's new race has any racial Hit Dice, you must subtract class levels until his effective character level is the same as it was before the rebuilding occurred. You can choose the lost levels from all those the character has, regardless of the order in which they were gained.

TEMPLATE REBUILDING

Admit it—when fighting lycanthropes, you've been tempted at least once to let your character get bitten, in hopes that the wound infects him. Such a desire is perfectly normal—it's hard to look at the hybrid form ability modifiers for, say, a werebear and not imagine the sheer devastation that your character could wreak if he had that template.

Lycanthropy isn't the easiest template to pick up during an adventuring career, but it's certainly not the only interesting option. Whether you've dreamed of playing a celestial dwarf, a half-dragon elf, or a vampire halfling (don't worry, we won't tell), templates offer the promise of a tantalizingly different character that can't be created from mere class levels.

Adding a template can represent a pretty big change for your character, so make sure your choice is acceptable to your DM before proceeding. After all, transforming your chaotic good elf wizard into a vampire might not be appropriate for the style of play the DM has in mind. On the other hand, "realizing" your character's celestial heritage by adding that template represents a much smaller overall shift in identity and would probably cause no problem at all.

To utilize this rebuild, your character must be able to adopt the template you want to gain. For example, a warforged fighter (a living construct from the EBERRON campaign setting) can't become a vampire, since that template can be applied only to humanoids and monstrous humanoids.

This rebuilding option also works reasonably well for a character who picks up a template during play (from a weretiger's bite, for example), if the DM wants the character's effective character level to remain consistent with the rest of the party. If a difference in effective character level isn't an issue, don't worry about these rules—just add the template and move on with your game.

The Process

Each time your character completes a rebuild quest, you can add, subtract, or replace one template. For example, a dwarf paladin could gain the celestial template, a half-dragon elf

fighter could lose the half-dragon template, or a celestial human rogue could replace his celestial template with the fiendish template.

Adding a template is a lot like changing your character's race, except that he usually doesn't lose many (if any) existing racial abilities. Follow the guidelines presented in the Race Rebuilding section above, paying special attention to the information on gaining or losing Hit Dice and level adjustment. If the character's Hit Die size changes (for instance, from transformation into a vampire), use the Hit Points entry in the Class Rebuilding section above to determine the new hit point total.

Removing an existing template, on the other hand, requires you to eliminate any of the template's effects and benefits, which might include special attacks, special qualities, skill modifiers, ability modifiers, bonus feats, and a variety of other bits and pieces. Use the guidelines in the Race Rebuilding and Class Rebuilding sections to rework your character's statistics.

REBUILD QUESTS

Note: This section addresses the DM and is intended primarily for his or her eyes.

A quest to rebuild a character should excite and frighten players. It's an adventure few characters would willingly embark upon and fewer still could survive. To make rebuilding an option at all levels of play, however, the degree of challenge must change according to the PCs' level.

The two example locations below outline ideas for rebuild quest objectives, each of which is suitable for a range of character levels. You can use them as described, modify them to suit your needs, or devise your own rebuild quest objectives.

Each objective represents the final encounter before a character can undergo rebuilding. The PCs might need to embark on a perilous overland journey or a long dungeon crawl to get to this encounter, or they might take a short break from an ongoing adventure to teleport there and have one or more encounters before returning. Set up the preliminary adventures in whatever way best fits your game and your players' desires.

REBUILD QUESTS IN THE GAME

The rebuild quest objectives described here are designed to allow any type of character rebuild, but in your game, each might allow only particular kinds of rebuilds. Creating different quests for different rebuilds not only makes each one seem more significant, but it also helps to curtail unplanned rebuilding by players who are largely satisfied with their characters. ("Well, as long as he's here, Gravar Orc-Killer is going to turn into a half-celestial umber hulk.") Below are some suggestions for making these locations serve particular needs that suit their ambiance.

The Gates of Dawn: Character rebuilds relating to divine magic and fey would be particularly appropriate for this location, as would any kind of rebuild that could be viewed as redemption (for example, exchanging rogue or ninja levels for fighter levels, changing fighter levels into paladin levels, or increasing Wisdom).

The Necrotic Cradle: Character rebuilds that relate to necromancy (both undeath and aspects of the physical body) seem particularly appropriate for the Necrotic Cradle. This location might allow any or all of the following rebuilds: return an undead character to life, exchange life for undeath at the cost of an appropriate number of character levels, change ability scores, or exchange class levels or prestige class levels for necromancy-themed class levels or prestige class levels.

THE GATES OF DAWN (LEVELS 6–8)

"Travel to the Lost Isle to become lost. Leave it to find yourself anew."
—The wizard Faldor Stardust, formerly a druid

Knowing oneself generally leads to a sense of belonging, but wishing to change one's essential being can bring about a sense of loss. At the Gates of Dawn, characters can lose and find themselves, and in that finding rediscover their true selves.

The Lost Isle floats in a hundred lonely lakes and in none of them. A place of mysterious magic, it appears out of the dawn mist on foggy days and then vanishes again when the sun burns the mist away. Tales told at fireside discourage the curious from visiting this fey place, warning that most of those who go there never return, and those who do always come back profoundly changed.

The Lost Isle might appear in a distant forest lake, or a crystal-clear pool high in the mountains, or a body of water within an area that some race considers sacrosanct. The journey to the island could be part of the adventure. Perhaps the PCs must give a great gift to the creatures that guard the lands around the lake, or sneak past them to avoid being slain on sight. Alternatively, the PCs might have to go to a lake where the island has appeared before and wait until conditions are right for it to come again, weathering assaults by the native creatures in the meantime.

Lore of the Lost Isle and the Gates of Dawn

Characters with ranks in Knowledge (arcana), Knowledge (local), Knowledge (nature), or Knowledge (religion) can research the Lost Isle and the Gates of Dawn to learn more about these places. When a character makes a skill check, read or paraphrase the appropriate information from one of the following tables, including the information from lower DCs.

If the PCs are just looking for a place to rebuild and want to know if they have heard about such a site, use the entire table. If they have heard of the Lost Isle specifically and want to see whether they know more about it, reveal information only for check results of 20 or higher.

After getting information from a Knowledge check, the characters should be able to learn more about the Lost Isle by consulting village elders who know the old tales, using divination magic, or trying to find individuals who were referenced in the information they have gained. Such resources can reveal the information for Knowledge DCs higher than the PCs' check results, or other any information about the Lost Isle that you'd like the characters to have.

Knowledge (arcana)

DC	Result
20	Certain places of power allow those with mettle to change themselves in strange and wondrous ways. In some such places, a person can change nearly any aspect of her being that she does not like, including race, weaknesses, abilities, and even personal history.

Knowledge (local)

DC	Result
15	Old stories tell of a place called the Lost Isle. These legends hold that people who return from this place are always profoundly changed.
20	The Lost Isle is a mist-shrouded island that sometimes appears in lakes and large ponds in various parts of the world. Most who visit it don't come back, and those who do are never the same again.
25	A fisherman disappeared while fishing one day, and everyone thought he had drowned. Two years later, a ranger came to his village claiming to be the fisherman, though he didn't resemble the lost man in the slightest. He said he had been to the Lost Isle and passed through the Gates of Dawn. The fisherman's wife had remarried and wanted nothing to do with the stranger, so he left.
30	The lost fisherman was named Brent Vostig, and his village was Milford. He disappeared while fishing in the nearby Misty Lake.
35	Beautiful music is often heard on the shores of the body of water in which the Lost Isle appears. Those who hear it should stop up their ears, because the melody calls them to death.

Knowledge (nature)

DC	Result
15	Those who visit a certain fey place called the Lost Isle either return profoundly changed or never return at all.
20	The Lost Isle appears in a lake or other body of water somewhere in the world at dawn each day. As soon as the sun and wind disperse the fog surrounding the misty island, it vanishes.
25	Rumor holds that a fey creature lives on the Lost Isle as its caretaker.

Knowledge (religion)

DC	Result
20	Certain places of power allow those with mettle to change themselves in strange and wondrous ways. Rumor holds that in some such places, a person can ignore the plans of the gods and even change his race.
25	The god Pelor created the Gates of Dawn as a place where the worthy might find a" new dawn" by changing themselves in some fundamental way. Eventually, however, he had to take the privilege away from mortals due to their misuse of it.
30	The Gates of Dawn exist on the Lost Isle, a place that appears only at sunrise in certain lakes. Only the most worthy of Pelor's followers have seen it, and the last reported sighting was at least a hundred years ago.
35	When Pelor hid the Gates of Dawn, he cursed some creature to remain on the island as its guardian. No church records of this ancient event remain, but legend has it that the curse was punishment for foul acts committed against Pelor's faithful.

Random Encounters

Characters traveling to the Lost Isle might encounter several dangerous threats before reaching it. You can either roll 1d4 times on the table below for encounters, or select a few that you prefer. Even if the journey to the Lost Isle is supposed to be only a brief detour from the current adventure, consider giving the PCs a few warmup encounters with the creatures that lair near the island before they reach the Gates of Dawn.

LOST ISLE ENCOUNTERS

d%	Encounter	EL
1–20	2 sea hags (*MM* 144)	6
21–40	Will-o'-wisp (*MM* 255)	6
41–60	2 trolls or scrags (*MM* 58)	7
61–80	Huge water elemental (*MM* 110)	7
81–90	Athach (*MM* 21)	8
91–100	Treant (*MM* 244)	8

The Isle

The Lost Isle appears in a mist-covered lake at dawn every morning. It remains for 1 hour, or until the sun and wind disperse the fog from the lake. At that point, the island and all its occupants are transferred to another lake elsewhere in the world—often hundreds of miles distant—where a foggy dawn is occurring. If no such lake is available, the island instead appears somewhere on Belierin, the third layer of Elysium (*DMG* 165), until a lake on the Material Plane has the proper conditions to host it.

Read or paraphrase the following text when the Lost Isle appears.

The fog coils thickly over the dark waters of the lake as the sky gradually brightens from night-blue to predawn gray. A faint pinkness on the horizon grows slowly into a blurry sliver of crimson as the sun rises, casting its warm glow through the mist. As the first light of dawn falls on the lake, a curling billow of fog rolls aside like a parted curtain, revealing the outline of a forested island floating in the mist-covered water. Moments later, the sweet notes of a distant pipe drift out over the lake. Sometimes lilting and happy, sometimes slow and sad, the distant melody seems to call to its listeners, cajoling them closer.

A satyr named Fauldwick who long ago committed a terrible transgression against Pelor's worshipers was cursed by the god to remain on the island forever as caretaker and guardian of the Gates of Dawn. The satyr is effectively immortal—he does not age, and if slain, he reappears alive and well on the Lost Isle the next time it appears. Fauldwick can leave the island, but when it reappears in another place, he goes with it, no matter how far he was from the lake when it vanished.

Fauldwick has lost track of how long he has lived on the Lost Isle. Over the centuries, loneliness has driven him quite

Fauldwick the satyr, trapped on the Lost Isle until the end of time

mad, despite the company of the blink dogs and the invisible stalkers that Pelor has placed there to serve him. Fauldwick's piping is the source of the music that the PCs hear.

The Clearing

When the characters arrive, an invisible stalker that was flying above the island to watch for visitors reports their whereabouts to Fauldwick, who then tries to lead them to the Gates of Dawn with his music. He stays in the woods where the PCs can't see him and moves slowly toward the gates while he plays. The invisible stalker (or stalkers; see Creatures, below) provides reconnaissance but flees from combat until Fauldwick commands it to fight.

If the PCs ignore Fauldwick's music, allow them to explore the Lost Isle as they wish, but they still have only an hour at most before the island vanishes. Describe the gradual clearing of the mist and the brightening of the sunlight through the trees at every opportunity. If they grow bored with their exploration, a random encounter with a will-o'-wisp or two might be appropriate.

Approaching the Gates: When the PCs near the Gates of Dawn, read or paraphrase the following text.

The sweet music seems to swell and grow louder. A quick glance through the trees reveals an immense, grassy field studded by shrubs. Dozens of man-sized, oblong hummocks dot the field, and objects jut up from the ground near many of them—a rusted sword here, a graying wooden oar there, a necklace of shells dangling from a stick over there. A well-trodden path wends through these grassy hills, ending at pair of rusted iron gates in the side of a huge, open-topped, circular structure made of a stone so light in color that it almost blends with the fog. The gates, which are at least 20 feet wide and nearly twice that tall, appear to be slightly ajar, and the music seems to be coming from somewhere beyond them.

Over the years, Fauldwick has trapped many individuals on the Lost Isle. Some died here of old age and others were murdered by Fauldwick when they attempted to leave. Fauldwick buries each such unfortunate aboveground in a makeshift graveyard outside the entrance to the building that holds the Gates of Dawn, placing an item the individual wore or carried at the head of the resulting hummock as a sort of grave marker.

When the PCs come close enough to enter the map, they can see into the building. Read or paraphrase the following text at that point.

Inside the structure stands a second set of gates the same size as the rusted iron ones. These inner gates are attached to a pair of thick pillars and seem to be made of brilliant gold. Other smaller pillars stand around this huge structure in a symmetrical arrangement.

In a moment, a humanlike creature with a ram's horns and legs dances into view, playing a set of pipes. A few dogs scamper up to him and excitedly jump and gambol about his legs. The creature stops playing and dancing for a moment and shouts, "Come and dance! Come and dance! Dance before the Gates of Dawn!" Then he goes back to playing and prancing with his dogs.

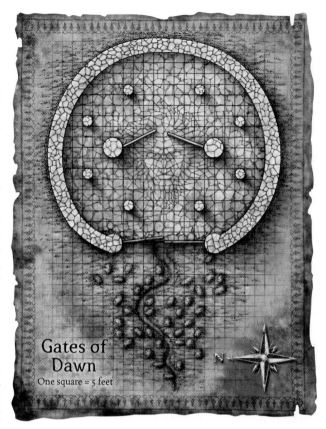

Gates of Dawn
One square = 5 feet

Fauldwick doesn't reply to any questions the PCs ask; he merely continues to play his pipes and wave the visitors closer. When at least one character has come through the rusted gates, he stops playing to greet that person.

Rusted Gates: The iron gates are rusted firmly in place. Medium and Small creatures must squeeze through the opening to get in.

Gates: 1 in. thick, hardness 10, hp 30, break DC 24, DC 30 Strength check to move.

Creatures: Creatures for three separate encounters are provided below. Choose a set that has an EL 3 higher than the average PC level of the party.

EL 9: One invisible stalker (*MM* 160), one satyr with pipes (*MM* 219), and four blink dogs (*MM* 28).

EL 10: Two invisible stalkers (*MM* 160), one satyr with pipes (*MM* 219), and four blink dogs (*MM* 28).

EL 11: Three invisible stalkers (*MM* 160), one satyr with pipes (*MM* 219), and four blink dogs (*MM* 28).

Tactics: After greeting the PCs, Fauldwick attempts to convince them to stay with him on the island using the *charm person* effect of his music. If any PC refuses or resists, Fauldwick orders his blink dogs and invisible stalkers to attack. The invisible stalkers concentrate on any airborne foes, while the blink dogs harry those on foot. Fauldwick remains in the rear, readying an action to attack with his shortbow whenever someone tries to cast a spell. If it seems useful, Fauldwick commands a blink dog to go through the Gates of Dawn, then shuts his eyes and hopes the PCs will be blinded (see below).

The Gates of Dawn

The Gates of Dawn are made of solid gold, and they swing open easily. Whenever any creature moves through them in either direction, the gates emit a blinding flash of light. At that point, every creature within the Gates of Dawn structure must make a DC 15 Fortitude save or be blinded for 1d4 rounds. Creatures that succeed on the save are dazzled for 1d4 rounds.

Any creature that passes through the Gates of Dawn immediately changes in the manner desired (that is, the planned rebuild instantly takes effect), but it also falls unconscious for 1 hour, even if it is a construct, undead, or other creature that does not need to sleep or is immune to sleep effects. Any attempt to damage the Gates of Dawn causes the perpetrator to fall unconscious in the same manner.

Development: If the PCs want to help Fauldwick break his curse, a *remove curse* spell isn't enough. Fauldwick must honestly repent his misdeeds, both those he committed in the distant past and those he has committed since he has been on the island. Thereafter, he must receive an *atonement* spell from a cleric of Pelor. After being trapped on the island for so long, however, Fauldwick no longer has any interest in apologizing for his actions.

Returning to the Lost Isle

If the PCs want to return to the Lost Isle for another rebuild, you have many options. Fauldwick is still there, and he might have new charmed or willing allies. Alternatively, some new creatures, such as fey or powerful outsiders, might also have moved in to help guard the Gates of Dawn.

If you don't want the PCs to use the same rebuild location a second time, the Lost Isle might never appear to them again. Or perhaps it does appear, but the Gates of Dawn have been destroyed by Fauldwick. For this greater transgression, Pelor has further punished the satyr by turning him into some much more more terrible creature.

THE NECROTIC CRADLE (LEVELS 13–15)

"You must journey through the lands of the dead to be reborn."
—The dwarf Taklinn Ungart, previously a human

Encountering death and the undead can spark a deep and full reevaluation of life. In the Necrotic Cradle, characters can face their own mortality and remake the threads of life that brought them to their current existence.

The Necrotic Cradle lies hidden in a place notorious for its connection to undead, but its exact location and the nature of the dangers it holds were lost with the lives of the creatures that now haunt the area as undead. Few living beings know about the Necrotic Cradle, and fewer still believe it actually exists. A few nearly lost legends, however, say that it is a place where birth, death, life, and undeath meet and become indistinguishable from one another.

The Necrotic Cradle might lie hidden beneath a city of the dead, or within an ancient burial ground that has served many races, or at the heart of a dark land haunted by undead creatures. The journey to this place could be part of the adventure. Perhaps the PCs need to talk to undead creatures they might ordinarily attack on sight, or maybe they have to help one undead creature in its struggle against another to learn the location of the Necrotic Cradle.

Lore of the Necrotic Cradle

Characters with ranks in Knowledge (arcana), Knowledge (local), or Knowledge (religion) can research the Nectoric Cradle to learn more about it. When a character makes a skill check, read or paraphrase the appropriate information from one of the following tables, including the information from lower DCs.

If the PCs are just looking for a place to rebuild and want to know if they have heard about such a site, use the entire table. If they have heard of the Nectoric Cradle specifically and want to see whether they know more about it, reveal information only for check results of 25 or higher.

Knowledge (arcana)

DC	Result
20	Certain places of power allow those with mettle to change themselves in strange and wondrous ways. In some such places, an individual can change nearly any aspect of his being that he does not like, including race, weaknesses, abilities, and even personal history.
25	The Necrotic Cradle is a place where an imbalance exists in the world's magic. Powerful individuals can use that imbalance to alter themselves.
30	The Necrotic Cradle is suffused with strange necromantic and transmutative energies that can break the boundaries of life and death. Such forces are likely to attract undead, but they might also attract outsiders and other strange beings. The Necrotic Cradle is located beneath the dead city of Drathmere (or under Tomb Tor in the Deathlands, or any other place you care to put it).
35	The Necrotic Cradle probably has a guardian, and that guardian might be an inevitable—a thinking construct that concerns itself with the laws of the universe. A place such as the Necrotic Cradle, which breaks universal laws, could certainly be perceived as a threat by such creatures.

Knowledge (local)

DC	Result
20	About 10 years ago, a fallen paladin sought a legendary place where he could redeem himself. Legend has it that he emerged from that place not only redeemed, but also reborn.
25	The paladin was a human who had been transformed into a vampire by the bite of one of those unholy creatures. The place in which he sought redemption was called the Necrotic Cradle.
30	A vampire paladin went to the Necrotic Cradle with several companions, but only he returned. Rumors say after he was restored to full-fledged life, he sought absolution for some crime at the church where he had received his training.
35	The paladin, whose name was Tanneth Silverwright, was refused atonement for his evil deeds as a vampire. Thereafter, he dropped into anonymity and became a drunkard.

Knowledge (religion)

DC	Result
20	Certain places of power allow those with mettle to change themselves in strange and wondrous ways. Rumor holds that in some such places, a person can ignore the plans of the gods and even change his race.
25	Because the Necrotic Cradle is a place where life and death meet and mix, great changes can be wrought there. A fallen paladin of Heironeous who became a vampire once went to the Necrotic Cradle with several companions seeking to restore himself to life.
30	The paladin succeeded in his quest, but afterward, he appeared at the Sliver House of Justice—the temple where he had been trained—and sought absolution for some crime. The Necrotic Cradle is located beneath the dead city of Drathmere (or under Tomb Tor in the Deathlands, or any other place you care to put it).
35	The former vampire was refused atonement because he would not return to the Necrotic Cradle and fight his old companions, who had refused rebirth after he had turned them into vampires. One of these vampires, a half-elf monk named Sashess, is rumored to haunt the lands around the Necrotic Cradle still.

After getting information from a Knowledge check, the characters should be able to learn more about the Necrotic Cradle by consulting sages, searching through a great library, using divination magic, or trying to find individuals who were referenced in the information they have gained. Such resources can reveal the information for Knowledge DCs higher than the PCs' check results, or other any information about the Necrotic Cradle that you'd like the characters to have.

Random Encounters

Characters traveling to the Necrotic Cradle might encounter several dangerous threats before reaching it. You can either roll 1d4 times on the table below for encounters, or select a few that you prefer. Even if the journey to the Necrotic Cradle is supposed to be only a brief detour from the current adventure, consider giving the PCs a few warmup encounters with the creatures drawn to the location by the necromantic energy of the place and its connection to both life and death.

NECROTIC CRADLE ENCOUNTERS

d%	Encounter	EL
01–10	Ice devil (*MM* 56)	13
11–30	2 kolyaruts (*MM* 159)	14
31–40	Nalfeshnee (*MM* 45)	14
41–60	4 devourers (*MM* 58)	15
61–80	4 dread wraiths (*MM* 258)	15
81–90	2 nightwings (*MM* 197)	16
91–100	Glabrezu (*MM* 166) and 10 Nessian warhounds (*MM* 151)	16

The Cradle Entrance Cavern

The transmutation magic that flows through the Necrotic Cradle redirects any attempts to teleport into or out of it. Thus, whether the PCs arrive by magic or on foot after traversing catacombs filled with undead, they first see the Necrotic Cradle from the cavern directly outside it.

Read or paraphrase the following text when the PCs arrive outside the cavern.

A sense of foreboding hangs almost palpably in the air within this cavern. Ahead, an opening in the rock wall admits a beam of brilliant light that silhouettes a titanic armored figure standing just before the aperture. Beyond it lies a yawning abyss of utter blackness, and beyond that is the source of the light—a bulbous hemisphere of stone projecting from the cavern wall on the other side of the abyss. This enormous rock formation looks anything but natural. Black cracks in the stone, like the veins in an eye, reach up from the abyss to surround a gaping hole in the center of the projecting rock. Through that aperture shines the light.

The silhouetted figure is a marut—an inevitable charged with guarding the Necrotic Cradle. Concerned with the unnatural blending of life and death in this place, it warns visitors away from the Necrotic Cradle and attempts to destroy any who persist in trying to bypass it.

The cavern is roughly 40 feet high, and the light beaming from the Necrotic Cradle provides bright illumination equivalent to that of daylight. Some areas of the cavern count as difficult terrain because of the rubble that has fallen from the ceiling.

Dark Abyss

The Dark Abyss on the map is actually a planar rupture that leads to the Plane of Negative Energy. Any creature that falls into it drops for 400 feet before crossing over into the Plane of Negative Energy. Once there, it has no means of return.

Necromancy spells cast within or over the Dark Abyss are function as if affected by the Heighten Spell (two levels) and Empower Spell feats, but *cure* spells and other spells that use positive energy automatically fail.

Creatures: Creatures for three separate encounters are provided below. Choose a set that corresponds to the average level of the party.

Party Level 13th: One marut (*MM* 159), two dread wraiths (*MM* 258), and four human vampire 5th-level fighters (*MM* 250).

Party Level 14th: As the Party Level 13th version, plus a half-elf vampire monk 9/shadowdancer 4 (*MM* 251). If you wish, this vampire could be Sashess, once the companion of Tanneth Silverwright.

Party Level 15th: Two maruts (*MM* 159) plus the vampire described in the Party Level 14th version.

Tactics: Regardless of which Encounter Level applies, the tactics for the marut (or maruts) remain the same. The marut periodically activates its *air walk* and *true seeing* abilities, and it has already done so when the PCs arrive. With *true seeing*, it should be able to spot the PCs, and with *air walk*, it can fight opponents who take to the air.

When the marut spots the PCs, it sets up a *wall of force* along the edge of the abyss to block access to the Necrotic Cradle, then delivers its only warning: "This place is forbidden. Leave now or be destroyed." If the PCs don't immediately leave, the marut uses *greater command* and orders them to flee. Those who remain or in any way persist in their efforts to reach the Necrotic Cradle must face the marut's *greater dispel magic*, *chain lightning*, and *circle of death* abilities, as well as its potent melee attacks. The marut also takes advantage of any opportunities to bull rush PCs into either the Dark Abyss behind it or the Brilliant Abyss within the Necrotic Cradle. If the marut believes it is losing the battle, it uses its *earthquake* ability in hopes of bringing the ceiling down on the PCs (and itself).

The vampires and dread wraiths are all that remain of Tanneth Silverwright's companions. They wish to enter the Necrotic Cradle to transform themselves into liches so that they need not fear sunlight, but they haven't yet been able to get past the guardian. They arrive 1d4 rounds into the PCs' combat with the marut (or maruts). Hoping that the PCs can distract the marut long enough to allow them entrance, they fly across the Dark Abyss during the battle. If the PCs appear to have the upper hand, the vampires and dread wraiths stop long enough to attack them until it looks like the marut has a fighting chance before proceeding on to the Necrotic Cradle.

The dark energies of the Necrotic Cradle can reshape life itself

The Necrotic Cradle

Read or paraphrase the following when a PC enters the Necrotic Cradle.

The interior of the bulbous protrusion is a largely spherical space with a huge rent in the floor that echoes the black abyss outside. This hole, however, is so filled with radiant light that it's difficult to look at. Shining white cracks in the stone extend away from the hole, just as night-dark cracks extend from the entrance. Where these cracks meet, they fragment into smaller crevices of light and darkness that swirl around one another in ever-tightening spirals but never actually meet. The largest of these formations lies in the center of the bowllike floor. Fully 15 feet across, this spiral pulsates with crackling white and black energy. In its center, the two types of cracks actually meet, and the two forces win and lose a thousand battles with each second that passes.

The light in the Necrotic Cradle causes all creatures inside to become dazzled (no save). Because of all the cracks in the interior, the entire floor is considered difficult terrain, and the Climb DC for the walls is 12. In addition, any living or undead creature touching the walls or floor inside the cradle must make a DC 20 Will save. Success indicates that the creature is struck by energy (positive energy if the creature is living, or negative energy if it is undead) that heals it of 2d8 points of damage. Failure indicates that the creature is struck by the opposite energy type and takes 2d8 points of damage. The only area that is safe from this effect is the central spiral of cracks.

Brilliant Abyss

The Brilliant Abyss is a planar rupture that leads to the Plane of Positive Energy. Any creature that falls into it drops for 200 feet before crossing over into the Plane of Positive Energy. Once there, it has no means of return.

Transmutation spells cast within or over the Brilliant Abyss function as if affected by the Heighten Spell (two levels) and Empower Spell feats, and *cure* spells and other spells that use positive energy are maximized.

Central Spiral

Any creature standing in the largest spiral of cracks can rebuild itself. Each round that it remains in contact with

Brilliant Abyss

Central Spiral

The Necrotic Cradle

One square = 5 feet

Side View

Dark Abyss

the spiral, the creature takes 10 points of damage from whichever type of energy (positive or negative) damages it. Any creature killed by this damage is torn apart by the warring energies and sucked—equipment and all—into the cracks of the spiral. Then the rebuilt creature comes into existence in the same place, with full hit points and all the equipment the previous creature possessed when it was destroyed. If the creature is killed by some means other than positive or negative energy while in contact with the central spiral, it dies and does not get the opportunity to rebuild. A creature that is not damaged by either negative energy or positive energy cannot use the Necrotic Cradle to rebuild.

Returning to the Necrotic Cradle

If the PCs want to return to the Necrotic Cradle for another rebuild, you have many options. More maruts or other inevitables might be guarding it. Alternatively, some new creatures, such as powerful undead or outsiders, might also have moved in to possess the site.

If you don't want the PCs to use the same rebuild location a second time, you could rule that the Necrotic Cradle works only once for any given creature. Or perhaps some creatures tried to repair the rifts in the plane and nullified the reforming properties of the Necrotic Cradle in the process. Alternatively, one of the two abysses might have won the energy battle, closing one side and opening a two-way gate to an energy plane.

OTHER REBUILD QUEST OBJECTIVES

Here are some other ideas for places the PCs might go to rebuild and the kinds of creatures they might encounter there.

Bastion of Unborn Souls: Somewhere on the Plane of Positive Energy floats this place of powerful magic from which all souls come and to which gods fear to go. Strange beings made of energy and soulstuff guard it from those who would abuse its power. This location is fully described in the *Bastion of Broken Souls* adventure.

Forge of Remaking: In this strange place, a character must confront himself and defeat his fears or die trying. By doing so, he can change his truename and thus change his being. This location is fully detailed in *Tome of Magic*.

Morpheus the Changer: The titan Morpheus has strange powers to reshape others through their dreams. Those who wish his aid must defeat the titan in single combat, because he uses this ability only on those who can best him.

Seldarine Pool: The magic waters of the Seldarine Pool are in a hidden shrine to the elf gods. Legend holds that washing in the waters of the Seldarine Pool can heal wounds and cure ills, but that drinking from it grants the imbiber the power to alter his being. A tribe of wild elves fiercely guards the pool, killing all who come to it—even other elves.

Shattershear Cliffs: The winds that rip at someone falling from the Shattershear Cliffs can actually tear a body to pieces and put it back together. Anyone who can make it there, win her way past the guardian beast, leap from the roc's nest, and somehow survive the fall, can remake herself.

Appendix: Quick PC and NPC Creation

This section presents quick and easy ways to create characters for both players and DMs. If you're a fast study and need a relatively low-level character, you can create one in 5 minutes with the system presented here.

For ready-to-play 1st-level characters, consult the starting packages presented in Chapters 1 and 2.

Creating a character always involves making certain decisions. Below are the ordered steps to create a character in an efficient manner.

1. CHOOSE A CLASS

Character class determines the types of feats you need to select, the magic items your character needs, and many other factors. So the first decision you need to make is what kind of character you want to create.

2. DETERMINE ABILITY SCORES

To speed up the process, use the elite ability score array from the *Dungeon Master's Guide*. You can either use the suggested ability arrangement for your chosen class or assign the scores as you wish. The elite array gives you scores of 15, 14, 13, 12, 10, and 8 to distribute as you wish.

Barbarian: Strength 15, Dexterity 13, Constitution 14, Intelligence 10, Wisdom 12, Charisma 8.

Bard: Strength 10, Dexterity 14, Constitution 13, Intelligence 12, Wisdom 8, Charisma 15.

Beguiler: Strength 8, Dexterity 14, Constitution 12, Intelligence 15, Wisdom 10, Charisma 13.

Cleric: Strength 12, Dexterity 8, Constitution 13, Intelligence 10, Wisdom 15, Charisma 14.

Dragon Shaman: Strength 15, Dexterity 12, Constitution 14, Intelligence 8, Wisdom 10, Charisma 13.

Druid: Strength 10, Dexterity 12, Constitution 14, Intelligence 8, Wisdom 15, Charisma 13.

Duskblade: Strength 15, Dexterity 13, Constitution 12, Intelligence 14, Wisdom 10, Charisma 8.

Favored Soul: Strength 14, Dexterity 10, Constitution 12, Intelligence 8, Wisdom 15, Charisma 13.

Fighter: Strength 15, Dexterity 13, Constitution 14, Intelligence 10, Wisdom 12, Charisma 8.

Hexblade: Strength 15, Dexterity 13, Constitution 12, Intelligence 10, Wisdom 8, Charisma 14.

Knight: Strength 15, Dexterity 12, Constitution 13, Intelligence 10, Wisdom 8, Charisma 14.

Marshal: Strength 14, Dexterity 13, Constitution 12, Intelligence 10, Wisdom 8, Charisma 15.

Monk: Strength 13, Dexterity 15, Constitution 12, Intelligence 10, Wisdom 14, Charisma 8.

Paladin: Strength 13, Dexterity 8, Constitution 14, Intelligence 10, Wisdom 12, Charisma 15.

Ranger: Strength 12, Dexterity 15, Constitution 14, Intelligence 10, Wisdom 12, Charisma 8.

Rogue: Strength 13, Dexterity 15, Constitution 12, Intelligence 14, Wisdom 10, Charisma 8.

Scout: Strength 14, Dexterity 15, Constitution 12, Intelligence 10, Wisdom 13, Charisma 8.

Sorcerer: Strength 8, Dexterity 13, Constitution 14, Intelligence 12, Wisdom 10, Charisma 15.

Swashbuckler: Strength 13, Dexterity 15, Constitution 10, Intelligence 14, Wisdom 8, Charisma 12.

Warlock: Strength 8, Dexterity 14, Constitution 13, Intelligence 12, Wisdom 10, Charisma 15.

Warmage: Strength 8, Dexterity 13, Constitution 12, Intelligence 14, Wisdom 10, Charisma 15.

Wizard: Strength 8, Dexterity 13, Constitution 14, Intelligence 15, Wisdom 12, Charisma 10.

If you are creating a character above 1st level, you might also have attribute bonuses to spend. Your character gains a 1-point bonus at 4th, 8th, 12th, 16th, and 20th level. Be sure to spend these points before moving on to the next step, if applicable.

3. PICK YOUR RACE

Like class, race is primarily a matter of taste or need. If you lack any real preference, choose the race that best matches your chosen character class from Table A–1: Preferred Races by Class. Some entries also mention a second race taken from another supplement; those races in italics have a level adjustment of +1 or higher and thus can't be used as 1st-level characters.

TABLE A–1: PREFERRED RACES BY CLASS

Class	Race
Barbarian	Half-orc (or *goliath*[1])
Bard	Gnome
Beguiler	Half-elf (or *changeling*[2])
Cleric	Human
Dragon shaman	Human (or *dragonborn human*[3])
Druid	Elf (or *killoren*[4])
Duskblade	Elf
Favored soul	Human
Fighter	Dwarf (or *warforged*[2])
Hexblade	Human
Knight	Human
Marshal	Human
Monk	Human (or *buomman*[5])
Paladin	Human (or *aasimar*)
Ranger	Elf (or *shifter*[2])
Rogue	Halfling (or *whisper gnome*[1])
Scout	Elf (or *raptoran*[4])
Sorcerer	Human (or *spellscale*[3])
Swashbuckler	Human (or *tiefling*)
Warlock	Human
Warmage	Human
Wizard	Elf (or *illumian*[6])

1 *Races of Stone*
2 *Races of Eberron*
3 *Races of the Dragon*
4 *Races of the Wild*
5 *Planar Handbook*
6 *Races of Destiny*

4. PICK YOUR SKILLS

Find your character class on Table A–2: Number of Skills by Class to determine how many skills your character can have.

TABLE A–2: NUMBER OF SKILLS BY CLASS

Class	Base Number of Skills
Barbarian	4 + Int mod
Bard	6 + Int mod
Beguiler	6 + Int mod
Cleric	2 + Int mod
Dragon shaman	2 + Int mod
Druid	4 + Int mod
Duskblade	2 + Int mod
Favored soul	2 + Int mod
Fighter	2 + Int mod
Hexblade	2 + Int mod
Knight	2 + Int mod
Marshal	4 + Int mod
Monk	4 + Int mod
Paladin	2 + Int mod
Ranger	6 + Int mod
Rogue	8 + Int mod
Scout	8 + Int mod
Sorcerer	2 + Int mod
Swashbuckler	4 + Int mod
Warlock	2 + Int mod
Warmage	2 + Int mod
Wizard	2 + Int mod

SKILL PRIORITY LISTS

Each of the entries below is a list of skills, rated in order from most important to least important for a typical member of the class. Start at the beginning of your class's skill list and count off the number of skills your character is entitled to based on the information in Table A–2. The character gains each of those skills at the maximum ranks allowed for his level. A human character gains one bonus skill at maximum ranks.

For example, if you're playing a half-orc barbarian with an Intelligence score of 8, you are entitled to 4 – 1 = 3 skills. Take the first three skills from the barbarian list (Survival, Listen, and Jump), and spend the maximum ranks allowed for each (character level + 3).

Barbarian: Survival (Wis), Listen (Wis), Jump (Str), Climb (Str), Swim (Str), Handle Animal (Cha), Ride (Dex).

Bard: Perform (Cha), Concentration (Con), Use Magic Device (Cha), Bluff (Cha), Diplomacy (Cha), Gather Information (Cha), Intimidate (Cha), Spellcraft (Int), Knowledge (local) (Int), Decipher Script (Int).

Beguiler: Hide (Dex), Move Silently (Dex), Spot (Wis), Search (Int), Disable Device (Int), Open Lock (Int), Concentration (Con), Bluff (Cha), Listen (Wis), Tumble (Dex).

Cleric: Concentration (Con), Heal (Wis), Knowledge (religion) (Int), Diplomacy (Cha), Spellcraft (Int), Knowledge (the planes) (Int).

Dragon Shaman: Three skills from totem dragon choice (see class), Climb (Str), Intimidate (Cha), Knowledge (nature) (Int).

Druid: Survival (Wis), Handle Animal (Cha), Spot (Wis), Listen (Wis), Knowledge (nature) (Int), Spellcraft (Int), Ride (Dex), Swim (Str).

Duskblade: Concentration (Con), Jump (Str), Spellcraft (Int), Climb (Str), Knowledge (arcana) (Int), Decipher Script (Int).

Favored Soul: Concentration (Con), Heal (Wis), Diplomacy (Cha), Sense Motive (Wis), Spellcraft (Int), Knowledge (arcana) (Int).

Fighter: Climb (Str), Jump (Str), Intimidate (Cha), Swim (Str), Ride (Dex), Handle Animal (Cha).

Hexblade: Concentration (Con), Intimidate (Cha), Bluff (Cha), Spellcraft (Int), Knowledge (arcana) (Int), Ride (Dex).

Knight: Intimidate (Cha), Ride (Dex), Handle Animal (Cha), Knowledge (nobility and royalty (Int), Jump (Str), Climb (Str).

Marshal: Diplomacy (Cha), Spot (Wis), Listen (Wis), Intimidate (Cha), Sense Motive (Wis), Knowledge (history) (Int), Swim (Str), Ride (Dex).

Monk: Tumble (Dex), Spot (Wis), Move Silently (Dex), Hide (Dex), Escape Artist (Dex), Climb (Str), Jump (Str), Balance (Dex).

Paladin: Diplomacy (Cha), Ride (Dex), Sense Motive (Wis), Heal (Wis), Concentration (Con), Knowledge (religion) (Int).

Ranger: Survival (Wis), Hide (Dex), Listen (Wis), Spot (Wis), Handle Animal (Cha), Move Silently (Dex), Knowledge (geography) (Int), Search (Int), Jump (Str), Swim (Str).

Rogue: Hide (Dex), Move Silently (Dex), Search (Int), Disable Device (Int), Open Locks (Dex), Sleight of Hand (Dex), Tumble (Dex), Spot (Wis), Listen (Wis), Bluff (Cha), Climb (Str), Escape Artist (Dex).

Scout: Hide (Dex), Move Silently (Dex), Spot (Wis), Search (Int), Disable Device (Int), Listen (Wis), Tumble (Dex), Survival (Wis), Climb (Str), Jump (Str), Knowledge (dungeoneering) (Int), Balance (Dex).

Sorcerer: Concentration (Con), Bluff (Cha), Knowledge (arcana) (Int), Spellcraft (Int), Craft (Int), Profession (Wis).

Swashbuckler: Tumble (Dex), Bluff (Cha), Jump (Str), Diplomacy (Cha), Balance (Dex), Escape Artist (Dex), Swim (Str), Sense Motive (Wis).

Warlock: Concentration (Con), Use Magic Device (Cha), Bluff (Cha), Spellcraft (Int), Intimidate (Cha), Knowledge (arcana) (Int).

Warmage: Concentration (Con), Spellcraft (Int), Intimidate (Cha), Knowledge (arcana) (Int), Knowledge (history) (Int), Craft (Int).

Wizard: Concentration (Con), Spellcraft (Int), Decipher Script (Int), Knowledge (arcana) (Int), Knowledge (the planes) (Int), Knowledge (dungeoneering) (Int).

5. PICK YOUR FEATS

In many ways, your character's feats define his basic abilities and talents. The following feat progressions map out appropriate selections from 1st to 20th level. The "H" entry in the tables represents a human's bonus feat, and the numbers represent the levels at which a character of that type would gain a feat in question.

TABLE A–3: FEAT PROGRESSIONS BY PARTY ROLE

BARBARIAN

	Destroyer	Hunter	Whirlwind
H	Power Attack	Track	Two-Weapon Fighting
1st	Cleave	Weapon Focus (any two-handed)	Weapon Focus (kukri)
3rd	Mad Foam Rager*	Trophy Collector*	Skill Focus (Tumble)
6th	Weapon Focus (greataxe)	Combat Focus*	Two-Weapon Pounce*
9th	Improved Critical (greataxe)	Blind-Fight	Improved Critical (kukri)
12th	Improved Sunder	Combat Vigor*	Improved Two-Weapon Fighting
15th	Defensive Sweep*	Combat Awareness*	Two-Weapon Rend*
18th	Overwhelming Assault*	Flay*	Greater Two-Weapon Fighting

BARD

	Controller	Problem Solver	Vanguard
H	Skill Focus (Perform)	Skill Focus (Use Magic Device)	Still Spell
1st	Negotiator	Arcane Flourish*	Combat Expertise
3rd	Wanderer's Diplomacy*	Magical Aptitude	Exotic Weapon Proficiency (spiked chain)
6th	Combat Panache*	Battle Dancer*	Improved Trip
9th	Master Manipulator*	Arcane Accompaniment*	Improved Disarm
12th	Spell Focus (enchantment)	Improved Initiative	Combat Reflexes
15th	Improved Feint	Combat Reflexes	Weapon Focus (spiked chain)
18th	Fade into Violence*	Vexing Flanker*	Power Attack

BEGUILER

	Controller	Investigator	Trickster
H	Spell Focus (enchantment)	Spell Focus (enchantment)	Spell Focus (illusion)
1st	Improved Initiative	Stealthy	Combat Expertise
3rd	Greater Spell Focus (enchantment)	Wanderer's Diplomacy*	Improved Feint
5th†	Silent Spell	Silent Spell	Silent Spell
6th	Arcane Thesis*	Quick Draw	Fade into Violence*
9th	Spell Penetration	Eschew Materials	Acrobatic Strike*
10th†	Still Spell	Still Spell	Still Spell
12th	Heighten Spell	Weapon Finesse	Shadow Striker*
15th	Scribe Scroll	Spell Penetration	Spell Penetration
18th	Greater Spell Penetration	Greater Spell Focus (enchantment)	Greater Spell Focus (illusion)

CLERIC

	Defender	Destroyer	Healer
H	Extra Turning	Extra Turning	Combat Casting
1st	Improved Turning	Divine Justice*	Sacred Healing*
3rd	Iron Will	Weapon Focus (any)	Divine Ward*
6th	Spell Focus (evocation)	Divine Armor*	Extra Turning
9th	Sacred Radiance*	Smiting Spell*	Brew Potion
12th	Combat Casting	Power Attack	Sacred Purification*
15th	Tower Shield Proficiency	Combat Casting	Quicken Spell
18th	Lunging Strike*	Armor Specialization* (heavy)	Extra Turning

To use this table, find the number of feats your character is entitled to, then start at the beginning of the chosen progression and take that number of feats. If your character is not human, you can still start with the feat labeled "H," but this often isn't necessary.

For example, a 7th-level half-orc barbarian has three feats. If you're using the destroyer progression, you would need to take the "H" feat, Power Attack, since that feat is a prerequisite for Cleave.

Some of the progressions require certain ability scores to meet their prerequisites. After you choose the feat progression you want, check the prerequisites and be sure to fulfill them, even if you have to go back and change your character's attributes to match the requirements. In some cases, you must also buy ranks in certain skills to qualify for a particular feat progression. In this case, make sure you purchased the relevant skills when you spent your character's skill ranks in step 4 (or go back and change your skill choices).

Most of the feats in these progressions are found in the *Player's Handbook* or in this book (those marked with an asterisk). Any class appearing in a book other than the *Player's Handbook* might mention some feats from another book (usually the supplement in which the class appeared).

DRAGON SHAMAN

	Defender	Destroyer	Second-Rank Warrior
H	Armor Proficiency (heavy)	Power Attack	Combat Reflexes
1st	Shield Specialization* (heavy)	Cleave	Power Attack
2nd†	Skill Focus	Skill Focus	Skill Focus
3rd	Shield Ward*	Weapon Focus (morningstar)	Weapon Focus (longspear)
6th	Active Shield Defense*	Ability Focus[1] (breath weapon)	Hindering Opportunist*
8th†	Skill Focus	Skill Focus	Skill Focus
9th	Improved Natural Armor[1]	Brutal Strike*	Short Haft*
12th	Weapon Focus (morningstar)	Improved Critical (morningstar)	Lunging Strike*
15th	Blind-Fight	Improved Sunder	Stalwart Defense*
16th†	Skill Focus	Skill Focus	Skill Focus
18th	Armor Specialization* (heavy)	Shield Specialization* (heavy)	Improved Critical (longspear)

† Bonus feat; see page 13 for options.
1 See *Monster Manual*, page 303.

DRUID

	Beastmaster	Feral Beast	Warden
H	Animal Affinity	Combat Casting	Spell Focus (conjuration)
1st	Companion Spellbond*	Alertness	Augment Summoning
3rd	Combat Casting	Keen-Eared Scout*	Shield Specialization* (heavy)
6th	Combat Reflexes	Natural Spell	Extend Spell
9th	Empower Spell	Improved Natural Attack (any)[1]	Imbued Summoning*
12th	Quicken Spell	Power Attack	Shield Ward*
15th	Vexing Flanker*	Flay*	Spell Penetration
18th	Extend Spell	Improved Bull Rush	Armor Specialization* (medium)

1 See *Monster Manual*, page 304.

DUSKBLADE

	Blaster	Defender	Skirmisher
H	Weapon Focus (ranged spell)	Toughness	Weapon Focus (any one-handed)
1st	Point Blank Shot	Combat Expertise	Dodge
2nd†	Combat Casting	Combat Casting	Combat Casting
3rd	Precise Shot	Arcane Toughness*	Mobility
6th	Empower Spell	Shield Specialization* (heavy)	Spring Attack
9th	Improved Critical (ranged spell)	Shield Ward*	Improved Critical (any one-handed)
12th	Improved Precise Shot	Armor Specialization* (medium)	Combat Tactician*
15th	Spell Penetration	Craft Magic Arms and Armor	Combat Expertise
18th	Greater Spell Penetration	Weapon Focus (longsword)	Whirlwind Attack

† Bonus feat.

FAVORED SOUL

	Defender	Healer	Vanguard
H	Armor Proficiency (heavy)	Spontaneous Healer[1]	Combat Focus*
1st	Shield Specialization* (heavy)	Augment Healing[1]	Combat Casting
3rd	Weapon Focus†	Weapon Focus†	Weapon Focus†
3rd	Shield Ward*	Combat Casting	Power Attack
6th	Combat Focus*	Brew Potion	Cleave
9th	Active Shield Defense*	Craft Wand	Craft Magic Arms and Armor
12th	Weapon Specialization†	Weapon Specialization†	Weapon Specialization†
12th	Combat Vigor*	Scribe Scroll	Combat Vigor*
15th	Blind-Fight	Reach Spell[1]	Improved Critical (deity's favored weapon)
18th	Combat Awareness*	Flyby Attack	Armor Specialization*

† Bonus feat; applies to deity's favored weapon.
1 See *Complete Divine*.

FIGHTER

	Archer	Defender	Destroyer
H	Point Blank Shot	Blind-Fight	Power Attack
1st	Precise Shot	Iron Will	Cleave
1st†	Weapon Focus (longbow)	Weapon Focus (longsword)	Weapon Focus (greatsword)
2nd†	Rapid Shot	Shield Specialization* (heavy)	Flay*
3rd	Dodge	Combat Reflexes	Improved Sunder
4th†	Weapon Specialization (longbow)	Weapon Specialization (longsword)	Weapon Specialization (greatsword)
6th	Mobility	Shield Ward*	Iron Will
6th†	Shot on the Run	Combat Expertise	Improved Bull Rush
8th†	Greater Weapon Focus (longbow)	Greater Weapon Focus (longsword)	Greater Weapon Focus (greatsword)
9th	Ranged Weapon Mastery* (piercing)	Melee Weapon Mastery* (slashing)	Melee Weapon Mastery* (slashing)
10th†	Manyshot	Improved Disarm	Improved Critical (greatsword)
12th	Armor Specialization* (medium)	Armor Specialization* (heavy)	Armor Specialization* (heavy)
12th†	Greater Weapon Specialization (longbow)	Greater Weapon Specialization (longsword)	Greater Weapon Specialization (greatsword)
14th†	Improved Precise Shot	Vexing Flanker*	Slashing Flurry*
15th	Improved Critical (longbow)	Defensive Sweep*	Overwhelming Assault*
16th†	Improved Initiative	Power Attack	Intimidating Strike
18th†	Quick Draw	Improved Initiative	Improved Initiative
18th	Weapon Supremacy* (longbow)	Weapon Supremacy* (longsword)	Weapon Supremacy* (greatsword)
20th†	Penetrating Shot*	Robilar's Gambit*	Cometary Collision*

† Bonus feat.

HEXBLADE

	Defender	Destroyer	Skirmisher
H	Ability Focus[1] (hexblade's curse)	Power Attack	Ability Focus[1] (hexblade's curse)
1st	Armor Proficiency (medium)	Cleave	Dodge
3rd	Battle Caster[2]	Weapon Focus (any two-handed)	Mobility
5th†	Spell Focus (necromancy)	Combat Casting	Spell Focus (enchantment)
6th	Combat Casting	Power Critical	Spring Attack
9th	Practiced Spellcaster[2]	Improved Critical (any two-handed weapon)	Dash[3]
10th†	Greater Spell Focus (necromancy)	Spell Focus (necromancy)	Greater Spell Focus (enchantment)
12th	Armor Specialization (medium)	Power Critical[3]	Bounding Assault*
15th	Extra Slot[2] (3rd)	Improved Toughness[3]	Elusive Target[3]
15th†	Spell Penetration	Greater Spell Focus (necromancy)	Spell Penetration
18th	Extra Spell[2] (3rd)	Defensive Sweep*	Rapid Blitz*
20th†	Greater Spell Penetration	Spell Penetration	Greater Spell Penetration

†Bonus feat.
1 See *Monster Manual*, page 303.
2 See *Complete Arcane*.
3 See *Complete Warrior*.

KNIGHT

	Cavalier	Defender	Destroyer
H	Skill Focus (Ride)	Shield Specialization* (heavy)	Power Attack
1st	Mounted Combat	Weapon Focus (any one-handed)	Cleave
2nd†	Weapon Focus (lance)	Mounted Combat	Mounted Combat
3rd	Shield Specialization* (heavy)	Shield Ward*	Improved Bull Rush
5th†	Ride-By Attack	Endurance	Endurance
6th	Short Haft*	Ability Focus[1] (test of mettle)	Weapon Focus (any one-handed)
9th	Improved Critical (lance)	Improved Critical (any one-handed weapon)	Cometary Collision*
10th†	Spirited Charge	Diehard	Diehard
12th	Armor Specialization* (heavy)	Armor Specialization* (heavy)	Ability Focus[1] (daunting challenge)
15th†	Trample	Iron Will	Great Fortitude
15th	Power Attack	Indomitable Soul*	Steadfast Determination*
18th	Lunging Strike*	Defensive Sweep*	Armor Specialization* (heavy)

† Bonus feat.
1 See *Monster Manual*, page 303.

MARSHAL

	Defender	Second-Rank Warrior	Vanguard
H	Shield Specialization* (heavy)	Combat Reflexes	Improved Initiative
1st	Shield Ward*	Deft Opportunist[1]	Battlefield Inspiration[1]
1st[2]	Skill Focus (Diplomacy)	Skill Focus (Diplomacy)	Skill Focus (Diplomacy)
3rd	Armor Proficiency (heavy)	Weapon Focus (reach weapon)	Weapon Focus (any)
6th	Goad[1]	Hindering Opportunist*	Intimidating Strike*
9th	Shieldmate[1]	Short Haft*	Endurance
12th	Blind-Fight	Distracting Attack[1]	Diehard
15th	Combat Expertise	Stalwart Defense*	Daunting Presence[1]
18th	Armor Specialization* (heavy)	Lunging Strike*	Overwhelming Assault*

1 From *Miniatures Handbook*.
2 Bonus feat.

MONK

	Defender	Destroyer	Skirmisher
H	Combat Focus*	Improved Natural Attack	Improved Initiative
1st†	Stunning Fist	Improved Grapple	Stunning Fist
1st	Dodge	Weapon Focus (unarmed strike)	Ability Focus[1] (stunning fist)
2nd†	Deflect Arrows	Combat Reflexes	Deflect Arrows
3rd	Versatile Unarmed Strike*	Power Attack	Dodge
6th†	Improved Trip	Improved Trip	Improved Disarm
6th	Leap of the Heavens*	Improved Bull Rush	Mobility
9th	Combat Defense*	Improved Overrun	Spring Attack
12th	Combat Vigor*	Cleave	Weapon Focus (unarmed strike)
15th	Fiery Fist*	Improved Sunder	Blind-Fight
18th	Fiery Ki Defense*	Great Cleave	Improved Critical (unarmed strike)

1 See *Monster Manual*, page 303.
† Bonus feat.

PALADIN

	Cavalier	Destroyer	Vanguard
H	Mounted Combat	Power Attack	Improved Initiative
1st	Ride-By Attack	Weapon Focus (any two-handed)	Shield Specialization* (heavy)
3rd	Mounted Archery	Extra Turning	Combat Focus*
6th	Spirited Charge	Divine Justice*	Ritual Blessing*
9th	Trample	Improved Critical (any two-handed weapon)	Combat Vigor*
12th	Power Attack	Divine Armor*	Sacred Purification*
15th	Improved Critical (lance)	Improved Sunder	Sacred Radiance*
18th	Shield Specialization* (heavy)	Divine Fortune*	Shield Ward*

RANGER

	Archer	Hunter	Skirmisher
H	Point Blank Shot	Blind-Fight	Dodge
1st	Precise Shot	Alertness	Mobility
1st†	Track	Track	Track
2nd†	Rapid Shot	Rapid Shot or Two-Weapon Fighting	Two-Weapon Fighting
3rd	Weapon Focus (longbow)	Keen-Eared Scout*	Combat Reflexes
6th	Dodge	Combat Focus*	Spring Attack
9th	Mobility	Combat Vigor*	Shadow Striker*
12th	Improved Initiative	Combat Awareness*	Two-Weapon Pounce*
15th	Shot on the Run	Weapon Focus (longbow)	Two-Weapon Rend*
18th	Far Shot	Combat Strike*	Improved Critical (short sword)

† Bonus feat.

ROGUE

	Archer	Duelist	Explorer
H	Point Blank Shot	Combat Expertise	Alertness
1st	Precise Shot	Improved Feint	Combat Reflexes
3rd	Rapid Reload	Weapon Finesse	Vexing Flanker*
6th	Deadeye Shot*	Tumbling Feint*	Adaptable Flanker*
9th	Rapid Shot	Improved Initiative	Acrobatic Strike*
12th	Crossbow Sniper*	Einhander*	Shadow Striker*
15th	Weapon Focus (light crossbow)	Dodge	Keen-Eared Scout*
18th	Improved Precise Shot	Combat Cloak Expert*	Spectral Skirmisher*

SCOUT

	Archer	Hunter	Skirmisher
H	Point Blank Shot	Track	Dodge
1st	Precise Shot	Alertness	Two-Weapon Fighting
3rd	Weapon Focus (shortbow)	Keen-Eared Scout*	Weapon Focus (short sword)
4th†	Dodge	Skill Focus (Survival)	Mobility
6th	Mobility	Point Blank Shot	Two-Weapon Defense
8th†	Shot on the Run	Brachiation[1]	Spring Attack
9th	Improved Initiative	Precise Shot	Two-Weapon Pounce*
12th†	Quick Draw	Improved Initiative	Quick Draw
12th	Improved Critical (shortbow)	Weapon Focus (shortbow)	Improved Two-Weapon Fighting
15th	Telling Blow*	Deadeye Shot*	Dual Strike[1]
16th†	Danger Sense[1]	Blind-Fight	Blind-Fight
18th	Improved Precise Shot	Improved Critical (shortbow)	Telling Blow*
20th†	Quick Reconnoiter[1]	Danger Sense	Improved Initiative

† Bonus feat.
1 See *Complete Adventurer*.

SORCERER

	Battle Mage	Blaster	Infernal Summoner
H	Toughness	Lightning Reflexes	Infernal Sorcerer Heritage*
1st	Bonded Familiar*	Spell Focus (evocation)	Infernal Sorcerer Howl*
3rd	Improved Counterspell	Greater Spell Focus (evocation)	Spell Focus (conjuration)
6th	Arcane Toughness*	Spell Penetration	Augment Summoning
9th	Spell-Linked Familiar*	Blistering Spell*	Imbued Summoning*
12th	Dampen Spell*	Greater Spell Penetration	Infernal Sorcerer Eyes*
15th	Combat Familiar*	Empower Spell	Infernal Sorcerer Resistance*
18th	Lurking Familiar*	Widen Spell	Extend Spell

SWASHBUCKLER

	Destroyer	Duelist	Skirmisher
H	Weapon Focus (short sword)	Weapon Focus (rapier)	Dodge
1st†	Weapon Finesse	Weapon Finesse	Weapon Finesse
1st	Two-Weapon Fighting	Combat Expertise	Mobility
3rd	Two-Weapon Defense	Improved Feint	Dash[1]
6th	Improved Two-Weapon Fighting	Dodge	Spring Attack
9th	Two-Weapon Pounce*	Melee Evasion*	Combat Acrobat*
12th	Improved Two-Weapon Defense[1]	Improved Disarm	Bounding Assault*
15th	Greater Two-Weapon Fighting	Tumbling Feint*	Combat Tactician*
18th	Two-Weapon Rend*	Combat Cloak Expert*	Rapid Blitz*

† Bonus feat.
1 See *Complete Warrior*.

TABLE A–3: FEAT PROGRESSIONS BY PARTY ROLE (CONT.)

WARLOCK

	Blaster	Controller	Problem Solver
H	Point Blank Shot	Necropolis Born[1]	Skill Focus (Use Magic Device)
1st	Precise Shot	Intimidating Strike*	Communicator[1]
3rd	Weapon Focus (ranged spell)	Ability Focus[2] (eldritch blast)	Spell Hand[1]
6th	Point Blank Shot	Sudden Extend[1]	Ranged Spell Specialization[1]
9th	Spell Penetration	Precise Shot	Extra Invocation[1] (least)
12th	Maximize Spell-Like Ability[1] (eldritch blast)	Extra Invocation[1] (lesser)	Extra Invocation[1] (lesser)
15th	Quicken Spell-Like Ability[2] (eldritch blast)	Quicken Spell-Like Ability[2] (eldritch blast)	Spell Penetration
18th	Ability Focus[2] (eldritch blast)	Extra Invocation[1] (greater)	Extra Invocation[1] (greater)

1 See *Complete Arcane*.
2 See *Monster Manual*, page 303.

WARMAGE

	Battle Mage	Blaster	Sharpshooter
H	Battle Caster[1]	Lightning Reflexes	Point Blank Shot
1st	Toughness	Spell Focus (evocation)	Precise Shot
3rd	Weapon Finesse	Greater Spell Focus (evocation)	Weapon Focus (ranged spell)
6th	Arcane Toughness*	Extra Edge[1]	Ranged Spell Specialization[1]
7th†	Sudden Empower[1]	Sudden Empower[1]	Sudden Empower[1]
9th	Armor Proficiency (heavy)	Spell Penetration	Spell Penetration
10th†	Sudden Enlarge[1]	Sudden Enlarge[1]	Sudden Enlarge[1]
12th	Extra Edge[1]	Greater Spell Penetration	Split Ray[1]
15th†	Sudden Widen[1]	Sudden Widen[1]	Sudden Widen[1]
15th	Lunging Strike*	Arcane Mastery[1]	Extra Slot[1] (6th)
18th	Twin Spell[1]	Repeat Spell[1]	Improved Critical (ranged spell)
20th†	Sudden Maximize[1]	Sudden Maximize[1]	Sudden Maximize[1]

1 See *Complete Arcane*.

WIZARD

	Blaster	Controller	Problem Solver
H	Combat Casting	Spell Focus (enchantment)	Combat Familiar*
1st†	Scribe Scroll	Scribe Scroll	Scribe Scroll
1st	Spell Focus (evocation)	Greater Spell Focus (enchantment)	Grenadier*
3rd	Spell Penetration	Spell Penetration	Mad Alchemist*
5th†	Craft Wand	Heighten Spell	Brew Potion
6th	Arcane Toughness*	Improved Counterspell	Craft Wondrous Item
9th	Precise Shot	Dampen Spell*	Spell-Linked Familiar*
10th†	Empower Spell	Silent Spell	Craft Wand
12th	Craft Staff	Spell Penetration	Eschew Materials
15th†	Maximize Spell	Craft Staff	Extend Spell
15th	Greater Spell Penetration	Improved Initiative	Elven Spell Lore*
18th	Arcane Thesis*	Greater Spell Penetration	Spell Penetration
20th†	Quicken Spell	Quicken Spell	Quicken Spell

† Bonus feat.

6. MISCELLANEOUS CHARACTERISTICS

Select your character's name, gender, age, height, weight, alignment, and personality. You can roll randomly for age, height, and weight, or just select the averages, as described in the *Player's Handbook* (see Vital Statistics, page 109). If you don't want to worry about which alignment to pick, make your character neutral good and she'll get along with most people.

If you have some ideas for your character's personality, this is the time to solidify them and perhaps jot down a few notes. You might determine her random personality traits by rolling on the tables on page 221.

If you have trouble choosing a name, the *Player's Handbook* offers examples for each race, and many random name generators exist online. You could also take the name of a character from a book or a movie and change a couple of letters or a syllable.

7. CHOOSE EQUIPMENT

Purchasing equipment can prove to be a long, involved task. To help you get started, this section presents sample equipment sets for NPCs from 1st to 20th level. Each set includes a basic weapon, armor, and other items appropriate for a particular character class, complete with their gold piece values. If you need to create an NPC, you can simply take the indicated gear and spend the excess gold on scrolls, wands, potions, and other consumable items. If you want to tinker with the equipment on the list, you can easily swap out individual items for others based on their gold piece values.

At most levels, PCs have much higher budgets for equipment than NPCs do. So when you make a player character, use the NPC equipment lists as a starting point. The NPC package provides the basic necessities your character needs to function. From there, you can expand your character's equipment to fit his specific needs, investing the excess money in better weapons or armor, or a variety of powerful, wondrous items. See Table A–5: PC Remaining Budget by Level to see how your PC's wealth compares to the gear available to an NPC of your level.

If you are in a rush, just purchase a few expensive items to supplement the NPC gear. For a fighter or similar character, buy a second weapon with the maximum enhancement bonus you can afford. Use it as your primary weapon if it is better than the one in the NPC package (perhaps trading in the weapon from the NPC package for another useful item).

Potions are useful to any character, and if you're playing a spellcaster, wands and scrolls can fill any gaps in your character's spell lists. *Knock*, *see invisibility*, and similar spells are useful in certain situations, but they lack the overall utility to make them worth preparing.

1st-Level Characters: Beginning characters are a special case because they don't have wealth comparable to 1st-level NPCs. To equip a 1st-level PC quickly, consult the starting packages for your class in Chapter 1 or 2.

Table A–4: PC and NPC Wealth by Level

Character Level	NPC Wealth	PC Wealth
1st	900 gp	Varies by class
2nd	2,000 gp	900 gp
3rd	2,500 gp	2,700 gp
4th	3,300 gp	5,400 gp
5th	4,300 gp	9,000 gp
6th	5,600 gp	13,000 gp
7th	7,200 gp	19,000 gp
8th	9,400 gp	27,000 gp
9th	12,000 gp	36,000 gp
10th	16,000 gp	49,000 gp
11th	21,000 gp	66,000 gp
12th	27,000 gp	88,000 gp
13th	35,000 gp	110,000 gp
14th	45,000 gp	150,000 gp
15th	59,000 gp	200,000 gp
16th	77,000 gp	260,000 gp
17th	100,000 gp	340,000 gp
18th	130,000 gp	440,000 gp
19th	170,000 gp	580,000 gp
20th	220,000 gp	760,000 gp

Table A–5: PC Remaining Budget by Level

Character Level	Budget
1st	—
2nd	Use 1st-level NPC*
3rd	200 gp
4th	2,100 gp
5th	4,700 gp
6th	7,400 gp
7th	11,800 gp
8th	17,600 gp
9th	24,000 gp
10th	33,000 gp
11th	45,000 gp
12th	61,000 gp
13th	75,000 gp
14th	105,000 gp
15th	141,000 gp
16th	183,000 gp
17th	240,000 gp
18th	310,000 gp
19th	410,000 gp
20th	540,000 gp

*1st-level NPCs and 2nd-level PCs have identical 900-gp budgets for gear.

A LA CARTE SHOPPING

If you prefer to start from scratch, or if you need guidance on how to spend your excess cash after acquiring an NPC gear package, the following steps can help you focus your search for cool items that will help your character survive. (The rapid character creation process described in this appendix uses this method.)

1. Buy standard adventuring necessities.

2. Buy the weapon you want (or two, if that fits your character).

3. Buy the best armor you can afford with your remaining gold.

4. Buy ability enhancers (low-level characters can skip this step).

5. Buy miscellaneous equipment (low-level characters can skip this step).

6. Save any money left over.

1. Every character should own the necessities of dungeon delving. The standard adventurer's kit costs 15 gp and includes a backpack, a belt pouch, a bedroll, flint and steel, two sunrods, ten days worth of trail rations, 50 feet of hempen rope, and a waterskin (the bedroll is free as part of the package deal). The individual prices of these items, along with a few others of use to certain character classes, are given in the table below. If you can't afford the whole adventurer's kit, you can simply drop items from it until it fits your budget. If you want any of the optional items, you must pay for those separately.

You need an additional piece of equipment if you're a cleric (a holy symbol for 1 gp); a beguiler, rogue, or scout (thieves' tools for 30 gp); or a wizard (spellbook for 15 gp, assuming it contains the minimum number of spells known). If you're a spellcaster of any kind, you probably want a spell component pouch (for 5 gp) as well.

Table A–6: Necessities

Standard Adventurer's Kit (15 gp)

Backpack	2 gp
Belt pouch	1 gp
Bedroll	1 sp
Flint and steel	1 gp
Hempen rope (50 ft.)	1 gp
Sunrods (2)	4 gp
Trail rations (10 days)	5 gp
Waterskin	1 gp

Optional Items

Holy symbol	1 gp
Spell component pouch	5 gp
Spellbook	15 gp
Thieves' tools	30 gp

2. Buy Weapon: Unless you're playing a sorcerer or wizard, spend about half of your wealth on the most expensive melee or ranged weapon available, depending on whether you prefer melee or ranged combat. First, choose which weapon you want to use—morningstar, bastard sword, longbow, or the like. (Use the suggestions above for equipment and starting packages if you wish.) Make it masterwork (+300 gp, or +300 gp per side if it's a double weapon). If the weapon is a longbow or shortbow, make it composite, adding a strength rating equal to your character's Strength bonus (+100 gp per plus). Next, make the weapon magic, giving it an enhancement bonus on attack and damage rolls. The applicable costs are summarized on Table A–7: Weapon Enhancement Bonuses.

Table A–7: Weapon Enhancement Bonuses

Enhancement Bonus	Cost
+1	2,000 gp
+2	8,000 gp
+3	18,000 gp
+4	32,000 gp
+5	50,000 gp
+6*	72,000 gp
+7*	98,000 gp
+8*	128,000 gp
+9*	162,000 gp
+10*	200,000 gp

*A weapon cannot have an enhancement bonus above +5 unless it is epic; instead, the weapon has one or more special properties. See *DMG* 223.

If you're playing a sorcerer or wizard, you'll want to spend a good chunk of money on a wand, staff, and/or ability-enhancing item (a *headband of intellect* or *cloak of Charisma*) instead of buying an expensive weapon. (See Buy Ability Enhancers, below, for more information.)

3. Buy Armor: If your character wears armor, spend a hefty portion (maybe three-quarters) of your remaining funds on armor. Include a shield if you use one.

You want the best armor with which the character is proficient—namely full plate armor if he can wear heavy armor (go with banded mail if you can't afford full plate armor), a breastplate if medium armor is the heaviest he can wear, or a chain shirt if he can wear only light armor. Buy the armor, then make it masterwork (+150 gp). Next, make

the armor magic, giving it an enhancement bonus to AC. The applicable costs are summarized on Table A–8: Armor Enhancement Bonuses.

Table A–8: Armor Enhancement Bonuses

Enhancement Bonus	Cost
+1	1,000 gp
+2	4,000 gp
+3	9,000 gp
+4	16,000 gp
+5	25,000 gp
+6*	36,000 gp
+7*	49,000 gp
+8*	64,000 gp
+9*	81,000 gp
+10*	100,000 gp

*A suit of armor or shield cannot have an enhancement bonus above +5 unless it is epic; instead, the armor has one or more special properties. See *DMG* 217.

If your character is a sorcerer, monk, wizard, or other character who doesn't wear armor, spend some gold on other defensive items instead. *Bracers of armor* are a good choice, and you might supplement these with a *ring of protection* and/or an *amulet of natural armor*. A *cloak of displacement* is an excellent choice if you can afford it, and a *ring of invisibility* is one of the best protection items around.

4. Buy Ability Enhancers: You should have about 25–30% of your starting gold left now. You have many options available for spending that cash—the *Dungeon Master's Guide* has a truly prodigious selection of magic items, and other books add even more to this list. For simplicity and speed, however, it's best to spend this gold on ability enhancers. Your options are *gauntlets of ogre power, belt of giant strength* (Strength), *gloves of Dexterity, amulet of health* (Constitution), *headband of intellect* (Intelligence), *periapt of Wisdom,* and *cloak of Charisma.*

Decide which ability scores are most important to you and buy items that provide enhancement bonuses to these abilities. Each item adds a +2 (for 4,000 gp), +4 (for 16,000 gp), or +6 (for 36,000 gp) enhancement bonus to the appropriate ability score. The only exceptions are *gauntlets of ogre power,* which offer only a +2 enhancement bonus to Strength, and the *belt of giant strength,* which gives a +4 or +6 enhancement bonus to Strength.

If you are creating an extremely high-level character, spend some cash on inherent ability bonuses (which you can get from *manuals of bodily health* and the like). Inherent bonuses cost 27,500 gp for each +1, and your character can have up to a +5 inherent bonus on any ability score.

5. Buy Miscellaneous Equipment: Spend the rest of your gold on some minor magic trinkets. A *cloak of resistance* provides a +1 resistance bonus on saving throws for 1,000 gp, +2 for 4,000 gp, +3 for 9,000 gp, +4 for 16,000 gp, or +5 for 25,000 gp. A few *potions of cure wounds* are also in order, since restoration of lost hit points is good for everyone. You can buy a *potion of cure light wounds* (restores 1d8+1 hit points) for 50 gp, a *potion of cure moderate wounds* (restores 2d8+3 hp) for 300 gp, and a *potion of cure serious wounds* (restores 3d8+5 hp) for 750 gp. If you're playing a spellcaster, pick up a few wands or scrolls of utilitarian spells, such as *knock* and *water breathing*.

EQUIPMENT BY LEVEL

The following tables detail appropriate NPC equipment for each level of the various classes. Each set of equipment also includes an adventurer's kit (see page 215) and any other items necessary for the character (such as a spellbook, spell component pouch, thieves' tools, or holy symbol).

Barbarian, Dragon Shaman, Druid[1], Duskblade[2], or Favored Soul

1st Level: Masterwork weapon, masterwork breastplate (or masterwork hide armor, 185 gp), heavy steel shield, 200 gp

2nd Level: Masterwork weapon, +1 breastplate (or masterwork dragonhide breastplate, 650 gp), heavy steel shield, 350 gp

3rd Level: Masterwork weapon, +1 breastplate (or masterwork dragonhide breastplate, 650 gp), heavy steel shield, 850 gp

4th Level: Masterwork weapon, +1 breastplate (or masterwork dragonhide breastplate, 650 gp), heavy steel shield, *cloak of resistance +1*, 650 gp

5th Level: +1 weapon, +1 breastplate (or masterwork dragonhide breastplate, 650 gp), heavy steel shield, 650 gp

6th Level: +1 weapon, +1 breastplate (or masterwork dragonhide breastplate, 650 gp), +1 heavy steel shield, 800 gp

7th Level: +1 weapon, +1 breastplate (or masterwork dragonhide breastplate, 650 gp), +1 heavy steel shield (or potion of barkskin +3, potion of shield of faith +4), *cloak of resistance +1*, 50 gp

8th Level: +1 weapon, +2 breastplate (or +1 dragonhide breastplate, ring of protection +1, 650 gp), +1 heavy steel shield (or potion of barkskin +3, potion of shield of faith +4), 250 gp

9th Level: +1 weapon, +2 breastplate (or +2 dragonhide breastplate, -350 gp), +1 heavy steel shield (or amulet of natural armor +1, potion of barkskin +3, potion of shield of faith +4), 850 gp

10th Level: +2 weapon, +2 breastplate (or +1 dragonhide breastplate, ring of protection +1, 650 gp), +1 heavy steel shield (or potion of barkskin +3, potion of shield of faith +4), 850 gp

11th Level: +2 weapon, +2 breastplate (or +2 dragonhide breastplate, -350 gp), +1 heavy steel shield (or potion of barkskin +3, potion of shield of faith +4), gauntlets of ogre power (or periapt of Wisdom +2), *cloak of resistance +1*, 850 gp

12th Level: +2 weapon, +3 breastplate (or +3 dragonhide breastplate, -350 gp), +1 heavy steel shield (or potion of barkskin +3, potion of shield of faith +4), gauntlets of ogre power (or periapt of Wisdom +2), *cloak of resistance +1*, brooch of shielding, 350 gp

13th Level: +3 weapon, +3 breastplate (or +3 dragonhide breastplate, -350 gp), +1 heavy steel shield (or potion of barkskin +3, potion of shield of faith +4), gauntlets of ogre power (or periapt of Wisdom +2), 850 gp

14th Level: +3 weapon, +4 breastplate (or +4 dragonhide breastplate, -350 gp), +2 heavy steel shield (or amulet of natural armor +1, ring of protection +1, 200 gp), gauntlets of ogre power (or periapt of Wisdom +2), *cloak of resistance +1*, 850 gp

15th Level: +4 weapon, +4 breastplate (or +4 dragonhide breastplate, -350 gp), +2 heavy steel shield (or amulet of natural

armor +1, ring of protection +1, 200 gp), gauntlets of ogre power (or periapt of Wisdom +2), cloak of resistance +1, 850 gp

16th Level: +4 weapon, +4 breastplate (or +4 dragonhide breastplate, -350 gp), +2 heavy steel shield (or amulet of natural armor +1, ring of protection +1, 200 gp), belt of giant strength +4 (or periapt of Wisdom +4), cloak of resistance +2, dust of disappearance, 350 gp

17th Level: +5 weapon, +4 breastplate (or +4 dragonhide breastplate, -350 gp), +2 heavy steel shield (or amulet of natural armor +1, ring of protection +1, 200 gp), belt of giant strength +4 (or periapt of Wisdom +4), cloak of resistance +3, dust of disappearance, 350 gp

18th Level: +5 weapon, +5 breastplate (or +5 dragonhide breastplate, -350 gp), +3 heavy steel shield (or amulet of natural armor +1, gloves of Dexterity +2, ring of protection +1, 1,200 gp), belt of giant strength +4 (or periapt of Wisdom +4), cloak of resistance +3, dust of disappearance, winged boots, 350 gp

19th Level: +6 weapon, +6 breastplate (or +6 dragonhide breastplate, -350 gp), +4 heavy steel shield (or amulet of natural armor +2, gloves of Dexterity +2, ring of protection +1, 2,200 gp), belt of giant strength +4 (or periapt of Wisdom +4), cloak of resistance +3, dust of disappearance, winged boots, 350 gp

20th Level: +7 weapon, +6 breastplate (or +6 dragonhide breastplate, -350 gp), +6 heavy steel shield (or amulet of natural armor +3, gloves of Dexterity +2, ioun stone (dusty rose), ring of protection +2, 1,200 gp), belt of giant strength +4 (or periapt of Wisdom +4), cloak of resistance +3, dust of disappearance, winged boots, 4,350 gp

1 Druid characters should replace heavy steel shield with heavy wooden shield, 13 gp.

2 Duskblade characters below 4th level should replace breastplate with chain shirt, 100 gp; duskblades below 7th level should replace heavy steel shield with light steel shield, 11 gp.

Bard, Hexblade, Ranger, Rogue, Scout, or Swashbuckler

1st Level: Masterwork weapon, masterwork studded leather, *elixir of hiding*, 50 gp

2nd Level: Masterwork weapon, mithral shirt, masterwork secondary weapon, *elixir of hiding*, 50 gp

3rd Level: Masterwork weapon, mithral shirt, masterwork secondary weapon, *elixir of hiding*, *elixir of sneaking*, 300 gp

4th Level: Masterwork weapon, mithral shirt, masterwork secondary weapon, goggles of minute seeing, 350 gp

5th Level: +1 weapon, mithral shirt, masterwork secondary weapon, *elixir of hiding*, 350 gp

6th Level: +1 weapon, +1 mithral shirt, masterwork secondary weapon, *elixir of hiding*, 650 gp

7th Level: +1 weapon, +1 mithral shirt, +1 secondary weapon, *elixir of hiding*, 250 gp

8th Level: +1 weapon, +1 mithral shirt, +1 secondary weapon, cloak of elvenkind, 200 gp

9th Level: +1 weapon, +1 mithral shirt, +1 secondary weapon, boots of elvenkind, cloak of elvenkind, 300 gp

10th Level: +1 weapon, +1 mithral shirt, +1 secondary weapon, boots of elvenkind, cloak of elvenkind, gloves of Dexterity +2, 400 gp

11th Level: +2 weapon, +1 mithral shirt, masterwork secondary weapon, *boots of elvenkind, cloak of elvenkind, gloves of Dexterity +2,* 1,300 gp

12th Level: +2 weapon, +2 mithral shirt, +1 secondary weapon, *boots of elvenkind, cloak of elvenkind, gloves of Dexterity +2, ring of protection +1,* 300 gp

13th Level: +2 weapon, +2 mithral shirt, +1 secondary weapon, *boots of elvenkind, cape of the mountebank, gloves of Dexterity +2, ring of protection +1,* 200 gp

14th Level: +3 weapon, +2 mithral shirt, +1 secondary weapon, *boots of elvenkind, cape of the mountebank, gloves of Dexterity +2, ring of protection +1,* 800 gp

15th Level: +3 weapon, +3 mithral shirt, +2 secondary weapon, *boots of elvenkind, cape of the mountebank, gloves of Dexterity +2, chime of opening, ring of protection +1,* 800 gp

16th Level: +4 weapon, +4 mithral shirt, +2 secondary weapon, *boots of elvenkind, cape of the mountebank, gloves of Dexterity +2, ring of protection +1,* 800 gp

17th Level: +4 weapon, +5 mithral shirt, +2 secondary weapon, *cape of the mountebank, gloves of Dexterity +2, ring of protection +1, winged boots,* 1,300 gp

18th Level: +5 weapon, +5 mithral shirt, +3 secondary weapon, *cape of the mountebank, gloves of Dexterity +2, ring of protection +1, winged boots,* 3,300 gp

19th Level: +6 weapon, +5 mithral shirt, +4 secondary weapon, *gloves of Dexterity +4, ring of protection +1, winged boots, ioun stone (dusty rose),* 300 gp

20th Level: +6 weapon, +6 mithral shirt, +3 secondary weapon, *amulet of natural armor +1, cape of the mountebank, gloves of Dexterity +4, ring of protection +2, winged boots, ioun stone (dusty rose),* 3,300 gp

Beguiler, Sorcerer, Warmage, or Wizard

1st Level: Masterwork weapon, masterwork chain shirt (or 250 gp), 350 gp

2nd Level: Masterwork weapon, +1 chain shirt (or *bracers of armor +1,* 250 gp), 450 gp.

3rd Level: Masterwork weapon, +1 chain shirt (or *bracers of armor +1,* 250 gp), 950 gp

4th Level: Masterwork weapon, +1 chain shirt (or *bracers of armor +1,* 250 gp), *cloak of resistance +1,* 750 gp

5th Level: Masterwork weapon, +1 chain shirt (or *bracers of armor +1,* 250 gp), *ring of protection +1,* 750 gp

6th Level: Masterwork weapon, +2 chain shirt (or *bracers of armor +2,* 250 gp), *cloak of resistance +1,* 50 gp

7th Level: Masterwork weapon, +2 chain shirt (or *bracers of armor +2,* 250 gp), *cloak of resistance +1,* 1,650 gp

8th Level: Masterwork weapon, +2 chain shirt (or *bracers of armor +2,* 250 gp), *cloak of Charisma +2* (or *headband of intellect +2*), 850 gp

9th Level: Masterwork weapon, +2 chain shirt (or *bracers of armor +2,* 250 gp), *cloak of Charisma +2* (or *headband of intellect +2*), *amulet of natural armor +1,* 1,450 gp

10th Level: Masterwork weapon, +3 chain shirt (or *bracers of armor +3,* 250 gp), *cloak of Charisma +2* (or *headband of intellect +2*), *ring of protection +2,* 450 gp

11th Level: Masterwork weapon, +3 mithral shirt (or *bracers of armor +3,* 1,250 gp), *cloak of Charisma +2* (or *headband of intellect +2*), *ring of protection +1, gloves of arrow snaring,* 450 gp

12th Level: Masterwork weapon, +4 mithral shirt (or *bracers of armor +4,* 1,250 gp), *cloak of Charisma +2* (or *headband of intellect +2*), *amulet of natural armor +1, ring of protection +1,* 1,450 gp

13th Level: Masterwork weapon, +4 mithral shirt (or *bracers of armor +4,* 1,250 gp), *cloak of Charisma +2* (or *headband of intellect +2*), *amulet of natural armor +1, ring of protection +2,* 3,450 gp

14th Level: Masterwork weapon, +4 mithral shirt (or *bracers of armor +4,* 1,250 gp), *cloak of Charisma +4* (or *headband of intellect +4*), *amulet of natural armor +1, ring of protection +2,* 1,450 gp

15th Level: Masterwork weapon, +5 mithral shirt (or *bracers of armor +5,* 1,250 gp), *cloak of Charisma +4* (or *headband of intellect +4*), *amulet of natural armor +1, ring of protection +2, gauntlets of Dexterity +2* (or *cloak of resistance +2*), 3,700 gp

16th Level: Masterwork weapon, +5 mithral shirt (or *bracers of armor +5,* 1,250 gp), *cloak of Charisma +6* (or *headband of intellect +6*), *amulet of natural armor +1, ring of protection +2, gauntlets of Dexterity +2* (or *cloak of resistance +2*), 450 gp

17th Level: Masterwork weapon, +5 mithral shirt (or *bracers of armor +5,* 1,250 gp), *cloak of Charisma +6* (or *headband of intellect +6*), *robe of scintillating colors, ring of protection +2,* 3,700 gp

18th Level: *Rod of absorption, bracers of armor +5, cloak of Charisma +6* (or *headband of intellect +6*), *ring of protection +2, gauntlets of Dexterity +2* (or *cloak of resistance +2*), 5,450 gp

19th Level: *Staff of evocation* (or *staff of enchantment*), +7 mithral shirt (or *bracers of armor +7,* 1,250 gp), *cloak of Charisma +6* (or *headband of intellect +6*), *ring of protection +2, gauntlets of Dexterity +2* (or *cloak of resistance +2*), 6,450 gp

20th Level: *Staff of evocation* (or *staff of enchantment*), +7 mithral shirt (or *bracers of armor +7,* 1,250 gp), *cloak of Charisma +6* (or *headband of intellect +6*), *ring of protection +2, boots of teleportation,* 3,450 gp

Cleric, Fighter, Knight, Marshal, or Paladin

1st Level: Masterwork weapon, masterwork banded mail, heavy steel shield, 200 gp

2nd Level: Masterwork weapon, full plate armor, heavy steel shield, 200 gp

3rd Level: Masterwork weapon, full plate armor, heavy steel shield, 700 gp

4th Level: Masterwork weapon, full plate armor, heavy steel shield, *cloak of resistance +1* (or *pearl of power [1st level]*), 500 gp

5th Level: +1 weapon, full plate armor, heavy steel shield, 500 gp

6th Level: +1 weapon, +1 full plate armor, heavy steel shield, 650 gp

7th Level: +1 weapon, +1 full plate armor, +1 heavy steel shield (or *potion of barkskin +3, potion of shield of faith +4*), *cloak of resistance +1* (or *pearl of power [1st level]*), 50 gp

8th Level: +1 weapon, +2 full plate armor, +1 heavy steel shield (or *potion of barkskin +3, potion of shield of faith +4*), 250 gp

9th Level: +1 weapon, +2 full plate armor, +1 heavy steel shield (or *amulet of natural armor +1, potion of barkskin +3, potion of shield of faith +4*), 850 gp

10th Level: +1 weapon, +2 *full plate armor,* +1 *heavy steel shield (or potion of barkskin +3, potion of shield of faith +4), gauntlets of ogre power (or periapt of Wisdom +2),* 850 gp

11th Level: +2 weapon, +2 *full plate armor,* +1 *heavy steel shield (or potion of barkskin +3, potion of shield of faith +4), gauntlets of ogre power (or periapt of Wisdom +2), cloak of resistance +1,* 850 gp

12th Level: +2 weapon, +3 *full plate armor,* +1 *heavy steel shield (or potion of barkskin +3, potion of shield of faith +4), gauntlets of ogre power (or periapt of Wisdom +2), cloak of resistance +1, brooch of shielding,* 350 gp

13th Level: +3 weapon, +3 *full plate armor,* +1 *heavy steel shield (or potion of barkskin +3, potion of shield of faith +4), gauntlets of ogre power (or periapt of Wisdom +2),* 850 gp

14th Level: +3 weapon, +4 *full plate armor,* +2 *heavy steel shield (or amulet of natural armor +1, ring of protection +1,* 200 gp), *gauntlets of ogre power (or periapt of Wisdom +2), cloak of resistance +1,* 850 gp

15th Level: +4 weapon, +4 *full plate armor,* +2 *heavy steel shield (or amulet of natural armor +1, ring of protection +1,* 200 gp), *gauntlets of ogre power (or periapt of Wisdom +2), cloak of resistance +1,* 850 gp

16th Level: +4 weapon, +4 *full plate armor,* +2 *heavy steel shield (or amulet of natural armor +1, ring of protection +1,* 200 gp), *belt of giant strength +4 (or periapt of Wisdom +4), cloak of resistance +2, dust of disappearance,* 350 gp

17th Level: +5 weapon, +4 *full plate armor,* +2 *heavy steel shield (or amulet of natural armor +1, ring of protection +1,* 200 gp), *belt of giant strength +4 (or periapt of Wisdom +4), cloak of resistance +3, dust of disappearance,* 350 gp

18th Level: +5 weapon, +5 *full plate armor,* +3 *heavy steel shield (or amulet of natural armor +1, gloves of Dexterity +2, ring of protection +1,* 1,200 gp), *belt of giant strength +4 (or periapt of Wisdom +4), cloak of resistance +3, dust of disappearance, winged boots,* 350 gp

19th Level: +6 weapon, +6 *full plate armor,* +4 *heavy steel shield (or amulet of natural armor +2, gloves of Dexterity +2, ring of protection +1,* 2,200 gp), *belt of giant strength +4 (or periapt of Wisdom +4), cloak of resistance +3, dust of disappearance, winged boots,* 350 gp

20th Level: +7 weapon, +6 *full plate armor,* +6 *heavy steel shield (or amulet of natural armor +3, gloves of Dexterity +2, ioun stone* (dusty rose), *ring of protection +2,* 1,200 gp), *belt of giant strength +4 (or periapt of Wisdom +4), cloak of resistance +3, dust of disappearance, winged boots,* 4,350 gp

Monk

1st Level: Masterwork weapon, 600 gp

2nd Level: Masterwork weapon, *bracers of armor +1,* 700 gp

3rd Level: Masterwork weapon, *bracers of armor +1, cloak of resistance +1,* 200 gp

4th Level: Masterwork weapon, *bracers of armor +1, cloak of resistance +1, elixir of sneaking,* 750 gp

5th Level: Masterwork weapon, *bracers of armor +1, amulet of natural armor +1, cloak of resistance +1,* 0 gp

6th Level: Masterwork weapon, *bracers of armor +1, amulet of natural armor +1, cloak of resistance +1, salve of slipperiness,* 300 gp

7th Level: Masterwork weapon, *bracers of armor +1, amulet of natural armor +1, brooch of shielding, cloak of resistance +1,* 400 gp

8th Level: Masterwork weapon, *bracers of armor +2, amulet of natural armor +1, brooch of shielding, cloak of resistance +1,* 600 gp

9th Level: Masterwork weapon, *bracers of armor +2, amulet of natural armor +1, brooch of shielding, cloak of resistance +2,* 200 gp

10th Level: *Amulet of mighty fists +1, bracers of armor +2, gauntlets of ogre power, cloak of resistance +1,* 1,000 gp

11th Level: *Amulet of mighty fists +1, bracers of armor +3, gauntlets of ogre power, cloak of resistance +1,* 1,000 gp

12th Level: *Amulet of mighty fists +1, bracers of armor +3, gauntlets of ogre power, cloak of resistance +2, dust of disappearance,* 500 gp

13th Level: *Amulet of mighty fists +1, bracers of armor +4, gauntlets of ogre power, cloak of resistance +3,* 0 gp

14th Level: *Amulet of mighty fists +1, bracers of armor +5, gauntlets of ogre power, cloak of resistance +3,* 1,000 gp

15th Level: *Amulet of mighty fists +1, bracers of armor +5, gauntlets of ogre power, cloak of resistance +3, monk's belt,* 2,000 gp

16th Level: *Amulet of mighty fists +2, bracers of armor +5, gauntlets of ogre power, cloak of resistance +3, monk's belt,* 2,000 gp

17th Level: +4 weapon, *bracers of armor +5, gauntlets of ogre power, cloak of resistance +3, monk's belt, periapt of Wisdom +4,* 700 gp

18th Level: +4 weapon, *bracers of armor +7, gauntlets of ogre power, cloak of resistance +3, monk's belt, periapt of Wisdom +4, ring of jumping, ring of protection +1,* 2,200 gp

19th Level: +4 weapon, *bracers of armor +8, gauntlets of ogre power, cloak of resistance +4, monk's belt, periapt of Wisdom +4, ring of protection +2, winged boots,* 1,000 gp

20th Level: +5 weapon, *bracers of armor +8, gauntlets of ogre power, cloak of resistance +5, monk's belt, periapt of Wisdom +4, ring of protection +4, winged boots,* 0 gp

8. PICK YOUR SPELLS

Choosing spells can be a time-consuming process. This section offers a list of standard, high-utility spells at each spell level, arranged from most to least useful, for each spellcasting class. If you are at a loss for which spells to take at a given level, these lists can help narrow your search.

Limiting the spells you choose to those on the following lists saves both time and effort. If desired, however, you can supplement these lists with specific spells that you prefer.

SUGGESTED BARD SPELLS

0: *Detect magic, read magic, prestidigitation, lullaby, summon instrument, mage hand.*

1st: *Cure light wounds, charm person, identify, disguise self, alarm.*

2nd: *Cure moderate wounds, suggestion, invisibility, eagle's splendor, heroism.*

3rd: *Cure serious wounds, haste, dispel magic, charm monster, displacement.*

4th: *Cure critical wounds, greater invisibility, dominate person, hold monster, dimension door.*

5th: *Mass cure light wounds, greater dispel magic, mass suggestion, persistent image, greater heroism.*

6th: *Mass cure moderate wounds, Otto's irresistible dance, greater shout, project image.*

SUGGESTED CLERIC SPELLS (POSITIVE ENERGY CHANNELERS*)

0: *Detect magic, light, resistance, read magic, detect poison, guidance.*

1st: *Shield of faith, bless, protection from evil, magic weapon, sanctuary, divine favor, command, comprehend languages.*

2nd: *Hold person, bull's strength, spiritual weapon, lesser restoration, inflict moderate wounds, resist energy, align weapon, augury.*

3rd: *Dispel magic, prayer, blindness/deafness, protection from energy, magic circle against evil, invisibility purge, searing light, glyph of warding.*

4th: *Divine power, inflict critical wounds, restoration, dismissal, freedom of movement, greater magic weapon, spell immunity, death ward.*

5th: *Flame strike, true seeing, spell resistance, righteous might, mass inflict light wounds, scrying, plane shift, disrupting weapon.*

6th: *Heal, greater dispel magic, harm, blade barrier, banishment, mass bull's strength, find the path.*

7th: *Greater restoration, holy word, greater scrying, destruction, ethereal jaunt, repulsion.*

8th: *Fire storm, holy aura, antimagic field, mass inflict critical wounds, greater spell immunity.*

9th: *Mass heal, implosion, miracle, true resurrection, etherealness, storm of vengeance.*

*Negative energy channelers should select a *cure* spell as their second spell of each level (for spell levels 1–4) and as their third spell of each level (for levels 5–8).

SUGGESTED DRAGON SHAMAN AURAS

Vigor, Senses, Power, Energy Shield, Toughness, Presence, Resistance

SUGGESTED DRUID SPELLS

0: *Detect magic, light, resistance, cure minor wounds, guidance, know direction.*

1st: *Cure light wounds, shillelagh, produce flame, faerie fire, entangle, charm animal, speak with animals.*

2nd: *Flame blade, heat metal, resist energy, lesser restoration, bull's strength, animal trance, barkskin.*

3rd: *Cure moderate wounds, protection from energy, call lightning, meld into stone, dominate animal, stone shape, spike growth.*

4th: *Cure serious wounds, flame strike, dispel magic, command plants, scrying, freedom of movement.*

5th: *Cure critical wounds, stoneskin, baleful polymorph, wall of fire, call lightning storm, commune with nature, death ward.*

6th: *Mass cure light wounds, fire seeds, greater dispel magic, mass bull's strength, transport via plants, wall of stone.*

7th: *Mass cure moderate wounds, heal, fire storm, true seeing, changestaff, greater scrying.*

8th: *Mass cure serious wounds, finger of death, animal shapes, sunburst, word of recall, whirlwind.*

9th: *Mass cure critical wounds, shapechange, elemental swarm, foresight, storm of vengeance, shambler.*

SUGGESTED DUSKBLADE SPELLS

0: *Ray of frost, touch of fatigue, acid splash, disrupt undead*

1st: *Ray of enfeeblement, shocking grasp, resist energy, swift expeditious retreat, true strike.*

2nd: *Scorching ray, see invisibility, swift invisibility, swift fly, cat's grace.*

3rd: *Ray of exhaustion, crown of protection*, keen edge, protection from energy, vampiric touch.*

4th: *Channeled pyroburst*, dimension door, enervation, fire shield, shout.*

5th: *Chain lightning, waves of fatigue, disintegrate, polar ray, hold monster.*

*New spell (see pages 106 and 108).

SUGGESTED FAVORED SOUL SPELLS

0: *Cure minor wounds, detect magic, light, resistance, read magic, detect poison.*

1st: *Cure light wounds, bless, shield of faith, divine favor, entropic shield, remove fear, comprehend languages.*

2nd: *Cure moderate wounds, spiritual weapon, lesser restoration, align weapon, delay poison, bull's strength.*

3rd: *Dispel magic, searing light, prayer, invisibility purge, daylight, magic circle against evil.*

4th: *Cure critical wounds, divine power, neutralize poison, freedom of movement, tongues, dimensional anchor.*

5th: *Flame strike, true seeing, righteous might, spell resistance, disrupting weapon, wall of stone.*

6th: *Heal, blade barrier, mass cure moderate wounds, greater dispel magic, heroes' feast, harm.*

7th: *Holy word, destruction, greater scrying, summon monster VII, ethereal jaunt, greater restoration.*

8th: *Mass cure critical wounds, holy aura, fire storm, summon monster VIII, antimagic field.*

9th: *Mass heal, implosion, summon monster IX, true resurrection.*

SUGGESTED HEXBLADE SPELLS

1st: *phantom threat*[1]*, expeditious retreat, Tasha's hideous laughter, protection from evil, entropic shield.*

2nd: *invisibility, false life, see invisibility, eagle's splendor, spider climb.*

3rd: *vampiric touch, confusion, protection from energy, hound of doom*[1]*, wind wall.*

4th: *greater invisibility, dimension door, enervation, cursed blade*[1]*, solid fog.*

1 See *Complete Warrior.*

SUGGESTED MARSHAL AURAS[1]

Minor: Master of Tactics, Force of Will, Motivate Dexterity, Motivate Strength, Watchful Eye, Master of Opportunity, Determined Caster.

Major: Motivate Care, Motivate Attack, Hardy Soldiers, Motivate Urgency, Resilient Troops.

1 See *Miniatures Handbook.*

SUGGESTED PALADIN SPELLS

1st: Bless weapon, divine favor, cure light wounds, protection from evil, lesser restoration.

2nd: Bull's strength, eagle's splendor, shield other, resist energy, remove paralysis.

3rd: Dispel magic, greater magic weapon, magic circle against evil, discern lies, daylight.

4th: Holy sword, dispel evil, restoration, break enchantment, death ward.

SUGGESTED RANGER SPELLS

1st: Resist energy, entangle, pass without trace, speak with animals, longstrider.

2nd: Snare, protection from energy, speak with plants, bear's endurance, cure light wounds.

3rd: Darkvision, tree shape, cure moderate wounds, water walk, command plants.

4th: Freedom of movement, tree stride, commune with nature, animal growth, cure serious wounds.

SUGGESTED SORCERER SPELLS

0: Detect magic, read magic, ghost sound, disrupt undead, prestidigitation, acid splash, mage hand, arcane mark, dancing lights.

1st: Magic missile, mage armor, enlarge person, shield, expeditious retreat.

2nd: Scorching ray, invisibility, mirror image, alter self, levitate.

3rd: Fireball, dispel magic, haste, displacement.

4th: Stoneskin, polymorph, greater invisibility, phantasmal killer.

5th: Cone of cold, teleport, Bigby's interposing hand, dominate person.

6th: Acid fog, greater dispel magic, Bigby's forceful hand.

7th: Prismatic spray, limited wish, ethereal jaunt.

8th: Horrid wilting, iron body, prismatic wall.

9th: Meteor swarm, wish, time stop.

SUGGESTED WARLOCK INVOCATIONS[1]

Least: See the unseen, sickening blast, eldritch spear.
Lesser: Eldritch chain, fell flight, beshadowed blast.
Greater: Vitriolic blast, devour magic, eldritch cone.
Dark: Retributive invisibility, eldritch doom, utterdark blast.
1 See Complete Arcane.

SUGGESTED WIZARD SPELLS

0: Detect magic, read magic, disrupt undead, mage hand.

1st: Magic missile, mage armor, charm person, color spray, silent image, disguise self, enlarge person, alarm.

2nd: Scorching ray, invisibility, mirror image, alter self, levitate, spider climb, see invisibility, knock, darkvision.

3rd: Fireball, dispel magic, displacement, haste, fly, suggestion, tongues, water breathing.

4th: Stoneskin, polymorph, greater invisibility, charm monster, lesser globe of invulnerability, scrying, wall of fire, confusion.

5th: Cone of cold, teleport, Bigby's interposing hand, dominate person, hold monster, permanency, persistent image, passwall.

6th: Chain lightning, greater dispel magic, Tenser's transformation, Mordenkainen's lucubration, contingency, true seeing, control water.

7th: Prismatic spray, limited wish, ethereal jaunt, greater teleport, greater scrying, plane shift, mass invisibility, mass hold person.

8th: Horrid wilting, iron body, prismatic wall, polymorph any object, protection from spells, Bigby's clenched fist, mind blank, dimensional lock.

9th: Meteor swarm, wish, time stop, gate, etherealness, shapechange, dominate monster, Bigby's crushing hand.

RANDOM PERSONALITIES

If you want to create a character with a random personality, use the tables below. Roll once on the Random Personality Archetypes table, then roll 1d4 times on the Random Personality Traits table. You can find more information on the personality archetypes and personality traits in Chapter 5 of this book.

RANDOM PERSONALITY ARCHETYPES

d%	Archetype	d%	Archetype
01–04	Agent	53–56	Rebel
05–09	Challenger	57–61	Renegade
10–13	Companion	62–65	Royalty
14–18	Crusader	66–69	Sage
19–22	Daredevil	70–73	Savage
23–27	Explorer	74–78	Seeker
28–31	Innocent	79–82	Simple Soul
32–36	Leader	83–86	Strategist
37–40	Martyr	87–90	Theorist
41–44	Mercenary	91–95	Trickster
45–48	Orphan	96–100	Wanderer
49–52	Prophet		

RANDOM PERSONALITY TRAITS

d%	Trait	d%	Trait
01–02	Ambitious	52–53	Kind
03–04	Angry	54–55	Loyal
05–06	Bold	56	Merciful
07–08	Boastful	57–58	Militant
09–10	Brutal	59–60	Mysterious
11–12	Carefree	61	Naïve
13–14	Calm	62–63	Quiet
15–16	Charming	64–65	Patriotic
17–18	Connected	66–67	Peaceful
19–20	Conservative	68–69	Philosophical
21	Cowardly	70	Phobic
22	Cruel	71–72	Proper
23–24	Dark	73–74	Reformed
25–26	Disciplined	75–76	Religious
27–28	Driven	77–78	Reluctant
29–30	Energetic	79–80	Rude
31–32	Erudite	81–82	Secretive
33–34	Exotic	83–84	Self-absorbed
35–36	Famous	85–86	Self-righteous
37–38	Fatalistic	87	Selfish
39–40	Flamboyant	88–89	Serious
41–42	Friendly	90–91	Skilled
43–44	Foul-mouthed	92–93	Threatening
45–46	Funny	94–95	Tragic
47	Greedy	96–97	Unpredictable
48–49	Hooked	98–99	Vengeful
50–51	Interested	100	Violent

GET YOUR HANDS ON A FIGHT

Encounter a menagerie of monsters ready to invade your **D&D**® game.
Fiend Folio, *Monster Manual II*, and *Monster Manual III* come packed with
hundreds of creatures ready to challenge heroes of any level.

Look for them at your favorite hobby shop or bookstore.

EXPAND YOUR  EXPERIENCE

D&D Introductory Products

D&D® is easy to learn, but can be hard to teach. With the DUNGEONS & DRAGONS® Basic Game, you can quickly bring your friends up to speed and get them ready for more adventure.

⚔ DUNGEONS & DRAGONS Basic Game	❑ 0-7869-3409-3	$24.99	_____
⚔ DUNGEONS & DRAGONS Miniatures Starter Set	❑ 0-7869-3500-6	$19.99	_____

D&D Accessories

Keep your game moving with essential tools that put information at your fingertips. And add excitement to every session with ready-made adventures, maps, and more.

✛ Deluxe Character Sheets	❑ 0-7869-3421-2	$14.95	_____
✛ Deluxe Dungeon Master's Screen	❑ 0-7869-3422-0	$14.95	_____
✛ DUNGEONS & DRAGONS Dice	❑ 0-7869-3513-8	$9.95	_____
✛ Map Folio 3D	❑ 0-7869-3437-9	$9.95	_____
✛ D&D Miniatures Underdark Booster Pack	❑ 0-7869-3522-7	$12.99	_____

D&D Supplements

Add options for developing characters, creating adventures, and building campaigns with books filled with new races, feats, equipment, spells, monsters, magic items, and more.

✛ Lords of Madness: The Book of Aberrations	❑ 0-7869-3657-6	$34.95	_____
✛ Complete Adventurer	❑ 0-7869-2880-8	$29.95	_____
✛ Libris Mortis: The Book of Undead	❑ 0-7869-3433-6	$29.95	_____
✛ Spell Compendium	❑ 0-7869-3702-5	$39.95	_____

D&D Campaign Settings

Explore detailed worlds filled with inspiration, excitement, and adventure. Even if your game is set in a different setting, you'll find maps, monsters, villains, spells, races, and other options that you can use to add depth and detail to your campaign and characters.

✛ EBERRON® Campaign Setting	❑ 0-7869-3274-0	$39.95	_____
✛ FORGOTTEN REALMS® Campaign Setting	❑ 0-7869-1836-5	$39.95	_____

Total: _____

Use this sheet to help friends and family find the products you want and when ordering from your favorite hobby shop or bookstore.

Name: _____ Telephone: _____

Address: _____

City: _____ State: _____ Zip: _____

FIND THE EDGE
YOU NEED TO SUCCEED

Whether you swing steel or sling spells, you want to make sure your character has what it takes to walk out of every encounter with treasure and a tale to tell. Inside *Complete Divine*, *Complete Adventurer*, and *Complete Warrior*, you'll find the stuff of which legends are made.

Look for them at your favorite hobby shop or bookstore.

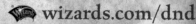 wizards.com/dnd